45,-

Behind State Company Nexus:
One and half century experience of Japanese
economic development in a statistical mirror

Behind State Company Nexus:
One and half century experience of Japanese economic development in a statistical mirror

BY

YOSHIRO MATSUDA
FUMIKO ARITA

ECONOMIC RESEARCH SERIES
NO. 33
THE INSTITUTE OF ECONOMIC RESEARCH
HITOTSUBASHI UNIVERSITY
KUNITACHI TOKYO 186

MARUZEN CO., Ltd.

Tokyo, Japan

Behind State Company Nexus:
One and half century experience of Japanese
economic development in a statistical mirror

by

Yoshiro Matsuda
Fumiko Arita

Published by Maruzen Co., Ltd.
38-3, Hongo 2-chome
Bunkyo-ku
Tokyo 113 Japan

ISBN4-621-04180-0

Distributed in Japan and outside Japan by Maruzen Co., Ltd.
Printed in Japan

Preface

The transformation of agrarian Japan into an industrialized state
has attracted many researchers' attention in the fields of social and
historical sciences. However, most of them have stressed the feudalistic aspects of Japanese society at the start of modernization. One
typical way of thinking is that the state-company nexus, the amalgamation of big merchant families called *zaibatsu* with high government
officials through their vested interests led to the growth of the military-
industrial complex which drove Japan to invasion of other countries.
We will not deny the existence of such a connection in the formative
process during the transition from the Tokugawa regime into the Meiji
government in 1868, when foreign technology was imported to Japan.
However, the role of the *zaibatsu* as promoters of Japanese military
expansion is rather dubious according to recent analysis of history.
The state-company nexus here- defined is a much broader concept implying a close relationship between government and the private sector
through creation of a system for gathering capital for industry by building an institutional entity defined as a company and banking system.
This socio-economic system was further expanded by intervention and
guidance of the government. The connection applied not only to the
legal system but also to creation of demand through the building of
a military capability that was independent of Western materials and
technology. This was considered necessary to prevent Japan from being swallowed up by the imperialistic powers that colonized many of
the Asian countries.

The motive force for modernizing the state from feudalistic Japan
belonged not only to the ruling class of the nation but also to the common people inspired by propagation of the new national educational
system. After the abolition of the feudalistic class structure compris-

ing warriors, farmers, artisans and merchants, all ordinary people were qualified to become soldiers under the conscription system. The introduction of the compulsory education system guaranteed a fairly homogeneous military and labour force.

What we imply by "behind" state-company nexus is the expansion of a factory system comprising individually owned factories in addition to company owned factories. To obtain these facts, in Part 1, we reviewed the history of the statistical survey system created by the new Meiji government and proved the insufficiency of the statistics of those days due to the limitation of computational knowledge and ability. Then, in Part 2, by referring to the supply of such statistical data newly created through our database system for historical statistics, we sketched out the process of industrialization via the development of the factory-company system and the formation of the Japanese Empire through colonization of East Asian countries. Lastly, in Part 3, the basic features of the database system for the historical analysis are explained and then the focus is shifted to the architecture for compiling the micro-data database, especially for compiling longitudinal data. This is closely related to the recent trend of compiling register based statistics as substitute for survey statistics. Due to the limitation of the volume of this monograph series a separate brochure of appendix tables is printed and distributed upon request. The e- mail number of the contact point is cr9e006@srv.cc.hit-u.ac.jp.

The Introduction and Part 1 were written by Yoshiro Matsuda and are based on his experience of building library collection for the Information and Documentation Centre for Japanese Economic Statistics at the Institute of Economic Research, Hitotsubashi University. Part 3 is based on the experiment of compiling the database system whose programme was written by Fumiko Arita through discussion with Matsuda on its architecture. In arriving at the interpretation of the economic development of Japan in Part 2, we relied on both the reconstructed statistical data newly derived from the results of our database for the historical analysis discussed in Part 3, and other statistical data published in the past. Matsuda was principally responsible for the socio-economic interpretation of the data.

The database compilation was supported by various Grants-in Aid for Scientific Research from the Ministry of Education and Culture of Japan. Grant numbers were 383002 (Database compilation based on the census survey system for the period between the two world wars) in 1978–79, 58020015 (Socio-economic analysis of the Great Kanto Earthquake) in 1982–84 and 61830001 (Compilation of the longitudinal database of factories and companies for historical analysis) in 1986–87. The collaborators in the database compilation such as Ms. Kyoko Komaki and others are referred to in the relevant pages in the text. We mention, however, Associate Professor Tsuneharu Ohkubo, ex-research assistant of the Centre, of Suruga-dai University, who helped with the statistical computation and Dr. Miyuki Shimizu of the Statistical Mathematics Institute, who organized the data linkage project during her service as a research assistant at the Centre, and, last but not least, Ms Teruko Yoshizawa who took painstaking care of the computational work for the database construction and tabulation of various statistical tables for our analysis. Refining and typing the manuscript of the entire text and tables and making indexes was done by Ms Setsuko Kanzawa. However, due to an injury to Ms Kanzawa in the last stage of manuscript preparation, typing of most of the tables was transferred to Ms Naoko Tomioka and Tazuko Asami. Proofreading of the English was kindly done by Mr Douglas Dawson, Kia Consultants Co. Editing was done by Messrs Akira Yano and Haruo Aihara of Maruzen Planet Company. Editors of this monograph series were first Professor Yasushi Tsuru and now Professor Yoshiyuki Nishimura. We are especially indebted to them for their help.

This joint work was a result of our past collaborations in almost twenty years stemming from the activities of the Information and Documentation Centre. Thus, we have benefitted from the experience of various persons and from access to archives in collecting statistical data. These persons include Ms Masuyo Takahashi, our documentalist colleague at the centre; late Professor Shozo Maeda of Koshien University, who served for many years at the Economic Research Institute at Kyoto University as a distinguished bibliographer; and the late Associate Professor Yoshiro Ikushima of Kobe University and Professor Shintaro Yakura of Nara Sangyo University, who both served as documentalists at the Documentation Centre for Business Analysis of Research Institute for Economics and Business Administration at Kobe University. Even disregarding the information and documentation science aspects, our work is still a hybrid of computer science and economic historical statistics. Matsuda specially thanks Professor Tairoku Kose, pioneer of computer science in Japan, who suggested the bridge of information science and economic statistics and two maitres, Professor Yuzo Yamada and the late Professor Yuzo Morita; and Professors Mataji Umemura and Toshiyuki Mizoguchi and the late Professor Toshio Furushima, who aroused interests in historical statistics. We, Arita and Matsuda, owe much to the encouragement in our experimental research on the statistical linkage by Professors Takafusa Nakamura and Yoshimasa Kurabayashi of Toyo Eiwa Women's University.

In writing up this English version of the text, the seminal paper was prepared during Matsuda's stay at the Japan Institute of Harvard University enabled by the courtesy of Professor Dweigt Perkins and others in 1981–2 and the final version was designed during his stay at Social Science Information-and Documentation Centre (Social-Wetenschappelijk Informatie-en Documentatiecentrum: SWIDOC) of the Royal Netherlands Academy of Arts and Sciences through the courtesy of Director Arnaud Marks in 1994. Both sabbatical leaves were partially supported by the Grant from Hitotsubashi Foundation.

1996 Spring
Yoshiro Matsuda (Hitotsubashi University)
Fumiko Arita (Toyo Eiwa Women's University)

CONTENTS

Introduction: STATISTICAL SURVEY AND SOCIETY   **1**
1. MEASURE OF STATISTICAL SURVEY'S ACCURACY 3
2. HOW TO INTERPRET SURVEY RESULTS 11
3. PROPOSALS FOR RECONSTRUCTION SURVEY . 12

Part I   **Statistical Survey System**   **15**
1. MAIN FEATURES OF STATISTICAL SURVEY SYS-
   TEM IN JAPAN 17
2. CREATION OF STATISTICAL SURVEY: 1874–85 . . 18
   2.1 Land Map Making and People Registration System 18
   2.2 Trials to Create a Modern Statistical Survey System 19
   2.3 Trials in Creating a Population Census 22
3. FORMATION OF DECENTRALIZED SURVEY SYS-
   TEM: 1885–97 23
   3.1 Ministry of the Interior and its Survey System . . . 23
   3.2 The Agricultural and Trading Correspondence System 24
   3.3 Impetus to Restore the Centralized Survey System 28
4. FORMATION OF COLONIAL GOVERNMENTS
   AND THEIR AFTERMATH: 1890S–1920S 29
   4.1 Population Census Experiments 29
   4.2 The First Population Census in 1920 30
   4.3 Flowering of Social Welfare Statistics 31
   4.4 New Survey on the Company: An institutional entity 33
5. CREATION OF A CENSUS SURVEY SYSTEM 35
   5.1 Towards a Census Survey System 35
   5.2 Evaluation of the Census System Accomplished . . 41
6. COMPLETION OF THE CENTRALIZED CENSUS
   SYSTEM AND ITS COLLAPSE 44
7. THE RATIONING SYSTEM AND THE STATISTICS . 50
8. NEW STATISTICAL SURVEY SYSTEM 50

Part II   Formation of State Company 'Nexus'   61

PROLOGUE: HERITAGE AND REFORM   63

1.   TRANSFORMATION FROM RURAL TO URBAN
     ECONOMY   68

     1.1   Heritage of the Tokugawa Regime   68
     1.2   Data Sources for Description of the Tokugawa Pe-
           riod's Last Days   76
     1.3   What is Rural Society?   77
     1.4   Family Structure   83
     1.5   Level of Production at the end of the Tokugawa
           Period   86

2.   FORMATION OF FACTORY PRODUCTION AND
     COMPANY SYSTEM   92

     2.1   Formation of Factory Production   92
           2.1.1   Factory Production System   92
           2.1.2   Factory Statistics: Technical digression .   92
           2.1.3   Factories in the 1880s and 1890s   96
           2.1.4   Factory Production before the Sino-
                   Japanese War 103
           2.1.5   Factory Production after the Sino-
                   Japanese War 107
     2.2   New System for Organizing Capital: Creation of
           an institutional entity called a company 112
           2.2.1   Company Concept as an Imported Software 112
           2.2.2   Company Statistics: Technical digression   113
           2.2.3   Structure of the Company System before
                   and after the Sino-Japanese War 114
           2.2.4   Company-owned Factories seen in Statistics 122
           2.2.5   Company-owned Factories in 1900 124

3.   GALLOP OFF THE PATH OF INDUSTRIALIZA-
     TION: 1902, 1909 AND 1920 128

     3.1   Expansion of Factories and Companies after the
           Sino-Japanese War: A short sketch 128
     3.2   Transformation of Light Industry to Heavy Indus-
           try: Factories based on various criteria 129
           3.2.1   Factories in 1902, 1909 and 1920 129

3.2.2   Horizontal Expansion and Vertical Expansion 133

3.3 Integration of Banks and Expansion of Companies 141

    3.3.1   Accumulation of Capital 141

    3.3.2   Distribution of Companies all over Japan 143

    3.3.3   Expansion of Companies through Financing by Banks 145

    3.3.4   Longitudinal Data of Companies: 1902–20 145

3.4 Relation between Company-owned Factories and their Owner Company 149

    3.4.1   Our Matching Model and its Results . . . 149

    3.4.2   Features of Factories Defined by the Company's Capital and the Number of Employees 165

    3.4.3   Size Distribution of Enterprises and its Effects on Wage Differentials 170

4. FORMATION OF THE JAPANESE EMPIRE AND ITS COLLAPSE 179

4.1 Exodus of Population to Colonies 179

    4.1.1   Japan Scarcely Escapes becoming a Colony 179

    4.1.2   The Japanese Empire in Population Census 181

    4.1.3   Japanese Race and Other Races in the Japanese Empire 184

4.2 Family Structure of the Japanese Empire 187

4.3 Occupational Structure of the Population 190

    4.3.1   Census Survey System and its Results . . 190

    4.3.2   Emergence of the so-called "Dual Economy" 192

    4.3.3   From the Rural Economy to the Industrialized Society in 1920–40 193

4.4 Natural Disaster: the Great Kanto Earthquake in 1923; human and social disaster; the great depression of 1929 and the wars 195

    4.4.1   The Great Kanto Earthquake and its Effects on the Economy 195

    4.4.2   Human and Social Disasters 201

    4.4.3   Reforming the Japanese Empire for the War 202

4.5 Labour Movement during World War II 205

4.5.1 General Description of the Wartime
Economy during World War II 205
4.5.2 Labour Mobilization in the 1940s 209
4.5.3 Implications of Labour Mobilization in
the 1940s 226
4.5.4 Damage to Human Resources during the
War 230
4.5.5 Damage to Capital Assets 232
EPILOGUE: JAPAN AS A PHOENIX 243
1. THE END OF THE WAR AND THE BEGINNING OF
THE OCCUPATION BY THE ALLIED POWERS . . . 243
2. ORIGINS OF ECONOMIC GROWTH AFTER THE
WAR 244

**Part III   Database System for Quantitative Historical
Economic Analysis   249**
1. INTRODUCTION TO THE DATABASE SYSTEM
FOR HISTORICAL ANALYSIS 251
2. WORKABILITY OF THE DATABASE 252
2.1 Data Sets Contained in the Database 252
2.2 Theoretical Background of Historical Statistics
Compilation 255
2.2.1 Methodological Digression 255
2.2.2 The Most Basic Coverage Problem: Nation, population and its society 258
2.2.3 Evaluation Problem 263
2.3 Usage of Cross Sectional Data 265
2.3.1 Usage of Cross Sectional Data 265
2.3.2 Database based on the Reconstruction
Survey 267
3. CONSTRUCTINGLONGITUDINAL DATABASE
BASED ON REGISTER DATA 269
3.1 Scope of the Database 269
3.2 Elements of the Database 270
3.3 File Structure of Raw Data File 271
4. MICRO DATA MATCHING TECHNIQUES 274
4.1 Linkage between Different Dates 274

4.2 Data Sources of the Database 275
4.3 Supplement of Missing Data: Estimate of capital
    assets 280
4.4 Linkage of Aggregated Data and Census
    Database 284
5. SQUEEZING OUT MICRO DATA INFORMATION
    FROM SUMMARY DATA 285
5.1 Multi-Tabulation and Disclosure Problems 285
5.2 Further Possibilities for Squeezing out Unique
    Records 289
6. COMBINATIONS OF SURVEY RESULTS
    OBTAINED FROM PLURAL SURVEYS 290
6.1 Differences in Coverage and Usages 290
6.2 The Situations after the New Establishment Cen-
    sus Survey 293
7. FURTHER PROSPECTS OF THE DATABASE SYS-
    TEM 293

References 299
Subject Index 315
Name Index 327
    a) Personal Name 327
    b) Place Name 331
    c) Governmental Institution Name 335
    d) Establishment and Enterprise Name 337
    e) Statistical Survey Name 339
Glossary for Japanese Words and Phrases 342

Introduction:
STATISTICAL SURVEY
AND SOCIETY

1. MEASURE OF STATISTICAL SURVEY'S ACCURACY

Most empirical research in the economics field is based on statistical data. This is especially so in the field of econometrics. However, the theoretical framework for evaluating the accuracy of these data is not yet fully schematized because the accuracy of the statistical data is itself a social phenomenon. Thus, the method of evaluating the accuracy of statistical data must take into account both statistical theory and institutional analysis of the statistical survey system. This short introduction aims to present a scheme for evaluating a system of statistical data production by tracing the history of Japanese statistical surveys in the nineteenth and twentieth centuries.

As is well-known, the modern statistical survey system has been established as a device for indirect political control of the people. For example, a population census, a typical modern statistical survey, is designed as a poll tax or military service list, as well as a check list for recruitment, and so forth. Such a statistical system of the modern nation state requires a unified network of administrative agencies which know what they are governing and are qualified to claim the cooperation of the people.

Our basic hypothesis, derived from observations of an industrial society, is that the degree of people's cooperation increases with the degree of industrialization. This is a compound effect of raised literacy rates of people who understand the need to obtain economic statistics, and increasing demand from the business world for material for market demand analysis or vital statistics for realizing goals, and so on. People to be surveyed must share a common national solidarity with the government authorities in so far as they must also be willing to be surveyed. However, this rising degree of cooperation has a saturation point. It will decrease with the formation of a mass society where people lose their desire to unify their society and become very anxious about protecting their privacy. This might be visualized as shown in Fig. 1.

Before evaluating the degree of the cooperativeness of the people, we will classify the statistics into two categories: figures obtained from accounts of daily business or official dossiers, and survey data designed

Figure. 1   Cooperation with the survey

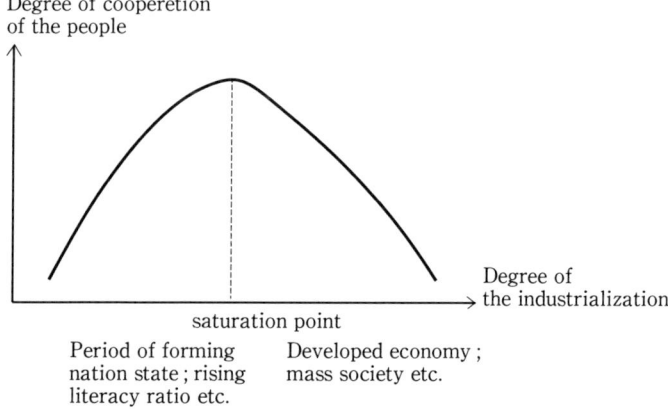

Degree of cooperetion
of the people

Degree of
the industrialization

saturation point

Period of forming   Developed economy ;
nation state ; rising   mass society etc.
literacy ratio etc.

and gathered to obtain specific statistics. The latter type is obtained only where the people are governable under a unified network of administrative agencies, in other words, where administrative agencies are equipped with at least a map indicating the boundaries of their jurisdictions, thus enabling them to identify the people from whom they collect data within the jurisdictional boundaries. Preparation of the map is itself a necessary condition for forming a modern nation state. Any way of identifying a person or institute who answers an inquiry should be defined as an operational concept of a reporting unit. We usually call this an enumeration unit, and we need to differentiate between this and an observation unit because they are entirely different concepts. When the enumeration unit corresponds to the administrative agency, we can get the first type of data by clipping the figures from the dossiers of the officers. These are the most primitive statistics. They must be derived from the unspecified inspection or impression of the government officers and should be distinguished from data based on direct observation of the object to be surveyed. This may belong to the first stage of statistical formation. The first step in producing a metamorphosis of these types of statistics into a result of a modern statistical survey is to build up the semantics of the categories used in the survey inquiry. When a survey is carried out, at least with predetermined survey formats or questionnaires addressed to the local authorities, it is called a Format Survey, or *Hyoshiki-chosa* in Japanese. In this case, it can be expected that the unification of the survey concepts will be fulfilled. The accuracy of the results depends on the propinquity between the administrative agency and the observation unit. The next step in the development of the statistical survey is to shorten this distance. If we want to get more direct access to the observation unit, we should create an operational concept or an institutional fiction which is close to an enumeration unit. For example, not every person can be classified as an enumeration unit. A baby cannot tell his or her name and age. The family head may act as an enumerator of his family members, but a natural concept like family is difficult to identify for operational use because which people are regarded as family members depends on the viewpoint of the respondents. Thus, a concept like "household" needs to be defined to describe one aspect of a family as a well-defined fiction for the enumeration unit of the survey.

It is sometimes said that surveys where the respondents write their accounts themselves is superior to surveys where surveyors interpret the accounts of the respondents. However, this is not a universal theorem, because the accuracy of a survey greatly depends on the competence of the respondents, based on their knowledge of bookkeeping and their level of literacy. Now we will restate the situation using our terminology: the accuracy of the survey may increase with the narrowing discrepancy between the enumeration unit and the observation unit.

By defining the enumeration unit we can say something about the coverage and accuracy of the data. The statistical survey may be classified according to whether the list of an enumeration unit is complete or incomplete. If the list is incomplete, we can say nothing about the accuracy of the survey results. Thus, the first thing we need to consider is the degree of completeness of the list. When the list of an enumeration unit is complete, the next problem is whether it is operationally well-defined or remains as a mere list of administrative units closer to the observation unit. The latter case may correspond to the format survey discussed above. The former case is the birth of the true statistical survey, which may be further subdivided into a census survey, a sort of complete enumeration survey, and a sample survey, which requires partial response from the enumeration units. The selection criteria of

STATISTICAL SURVEY AND SOCIETY

Table. 1 Types of the Survey

Type of survey	Type of formats distributed	Enumeration unit	Survey unit	Phase in history
Mere list-up figures	Unknown	Not specified	Not specified	Traditional
Formats survey	Formats pre-designed	Specified	Not Specified	Formative
Census survey	Questionnaire	Specified	Specified	Modern
Sampling survey				
i) Typical sampling	Questionnaire	Specified	Specified	Formative
ii) Random sampling	Questionnaire	Specified	Specified	Modern

(Note)

1) Phase indicates the period in the history of statistical survey. Phases are: Traditional, Formative and Modern.

2) Typical sampling is also called purposive sampling and selection of samples is based on the subjective judgement about the state of the degree of representativeness of the samples concerned.

the samples to be surveyed are further subdivided into subjective or probabilistic categories. The former are called typical surveys and the latter are called random sampling surveys.

We sum up these types of surveys in Table 1.

In building up a complete census survey system as an ideal model, there may be several ways of constructing the enumeration unit as an operational concept to cover every aspect of the society by various census surveys. We will define three operational concepts which are currently quite commonly adopted in statistical survey systems around the world.

1) Households: where persons share the same building, or at least the same kitchen, and operate under the same budget.

2) Establishments: work places where incorporated organizations

run their businesses.

3) Firms: one or a group of establishments constituting the same accounting unit and/or management unit.

The observational units defined by these three operational concepts sometimes overlap each other. Small shops or work places where one family lives and works with their household members are called self-employed establishments and at the same time self-employed households. Their relations are shown in Fig. 2. The correspondence of the elements defined in these three sets of observation units may be called one-to-one matching or sometimes one-to-many matching. One household may have several household members who will be surveyed as observation units, but the survey unit is still the household as an enumeration unit where its household head represents all the members who answer the inquiry. Another example is the relation between establishments and a firm, or their parent company. One company may run its business with only one establishment and we call it a single establishment enterprise, while another company may operate establishments such as a head office together with factories or shops. We call them plural or multi-establishment enterprises. Thus, the census list of establishments and the census list of companies may overlap at the single establishment companies. The concept of establishment is much broader than that of firms, because it includes governmental offices and non-profit institutions like churches and temples. Using these two censuses which represent all possible economic agencies we can survey various socio-economic factors. Houses and buildings can be surveyed through the persons or institutions who own them. Land and assets can be surveyed via the same lists of holders or users.

Governments that have carried out most statistical surveys wanted to obtain data to assist them in making decisions. What should be surveyed depends on the situation and who needs the statistics. Some may want to know about certain kinds of goods in so far as they were exchanged to be used by others, ignoring in-house consumption. Others may want to know the total amounts produced. Thus, coverage problems stem firstly from the kinds of goods and secondly from the degree of commercialization or non-commercialization. The latter problem closely relates to the level of production of the producers concerned, in another words, to the coverage of the respondents.

Figure. 2   A model of the relationship between enumeration units

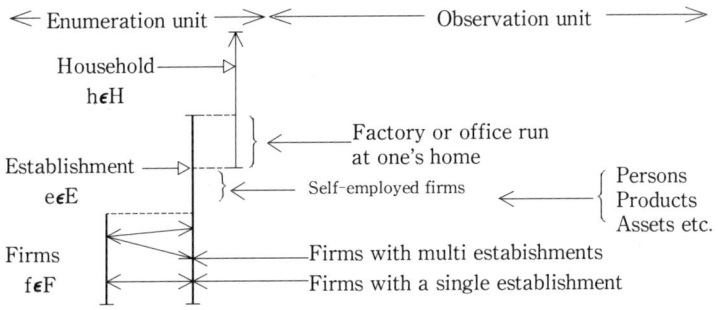

The next problem of coverage is the variation in coverage for different time periods of the same survey. No long-term continuity can be guaranteed, in most cases, especially as to the kinds of survey items and the level of production of the respondents because of changes in social milieu. Thus, coverage problems may stem not only from the scope of the survey design and the contents of the survey items but also from the level of production of the reporting unit or enumeration unit. How it is defined operationally is the most serious problem from the beginning of the statistical survey.

The continuity of the survey is broken every time its scope and the coverage of the enumeration units are changed. If the observation of a rough statistical survey were the same as an observation through a telescope or a microscope, expansion or reduction of its coverage would not affect the accuracy of the observation. However, a statistical survey is a human interaction between the surveyor and the surveyed. People are generally unwilling to make any report and as a consequence, people or reporting units at the borderline of the coverage area are apt to avoid the burden of reporting by claiming that they do not qualify for the enumeration unit. For example, if manufacturing establishments employing more than ten people are requested to make reports, some of them may pretend to be one employing only nine. However, if the survey scope is widened to include those employing more than five, it is more difficult for those employing around nine or ten to avoid reporting or to disguise themselves as employing less than five. Thus, this change in coverage brings out a serious discontinuity of accuracy between the points before and after the change in range.

Up to now, we have not mentioned the difference in response between a census survey and a sample survey. A census is a survey which requires every qualified enumeration unit to answer the questionnaire. A sample survey, however, requires only a certain specified or selected number of enumeration units to answer. Thus, it is more difficult to escape a census survey than a sample survey. However, very detailed follow-up can be done for a sample survey due to the relatively large available budget. Thus, we can expect a much wider range of survey items in a sample survey than in a census survey.

Another problem is duplicate coverage of censuses. In an economic census that focuses on one particular area of business, all economic units, establishments and firms engaged in that area of business should respond. However, this can result in duplication. For example, if an establishment is engaged in both manufacturing and commerce at the same time, that establishment should respond to both industrial censuses. Then if we aggregate the results of the two censuses, that establishment will be counted twice. Even worse, that establishment may escape from both censuses by insisting to both field surveyors that they belong to the other business area. However, such plural industrial censuses will achieve a more exhaustive coverage of the establishments concerned. Thus, the problem is how to organize an overall census system.

If the census system gives a complete picture of a society's make-up, the problem is how to develop a sample survey system using the census as a sampling frame. This is because of the cost and time saving of a sample survey compared with a census survey.

Some words should be added regarding the development of the sampling survey. In most countries, the sampling method was based firstly on the purposive sampling method. Some may call this a typical survey. Then, with the development of probabilistic statistical theory, random sampling methods were introduced in the thirties of this century.

In evaluating the statistical survey system, some concluding remarks are made on the necessity to trace the historical development of the statistical survey system as it is interwoven with the social milieu surrounding it. Statistical surveys require the cooperation of the respondents. In the semi-feudalistic societies where statistical systems were born, respondents often cheated the local officers and the local officers liked to cheat higher officers having more power than them. As in modern states people became more governable, they become more willing to cooperate in surveys. When answering truthfully to surveys is of some benefit to the respondents, the lower income classes in less developed countries will become more cooperative. However, even at this stage of development upper income people are not very cooperative. Industrial development, with the rise of educational standards and participation in politics, will increase the cooperativeness of the people. However, as mentioned before, there must be a saturation point for such willingness and the government will face unwillingness of the people to answer official surveys, especially in the midst of a flood of surveys carried out by private survey companies in developed capitalistic countries where people will not pay enough attention whether it is an official survey or not.

Another side of the coin regarding the people's willingness to cooperate in statistical surveys is the independence of the statistical survey among other governmental policies. Statistical surveys should at least be independent of other administrative activities such as tax collection or conscription. In return, the accuracy of people's reports will be somewhat more reliable. In addition, higher officials and politicians may expect a fairly good mirror of reality in statistics apart from the administrative jurisdictions.

Thus, the problem of accurate measurement has its roots in various aspects of society, so we need to check the statistical results not only against conceptual problems of the figures themselves but at the same time in the context of the historical development of the survey system. Part I describes an example using a Japanese case as a background paper on the historical development of the economy as described in Part II.

2. HOW TO INTERPRET SURVEY RESULTS

In so far as we have discussed summary data of the survey results in a time series, there are some limitations on the discussions of long-term analysis over generations. One way to overcome this difficulty is to construct compiled macro indicators, such as estimates of national accounts, and then to review the estimation procedures and assess the comparability of a time span of these macro indicators. The estimation for compiled data includes extrapolation of the changes in coverage and correction of erroneous survey results detected from other information. The history of estimation procedures of macro indicators comprises a series of revisions, in most cases making the starting points higher than those of the earlier estimates because of new findings of statistical data forgotten in the historical past or the results of new statistical surveys.

An example of the former case is shown in the results of a series of Japanese gross national product revisions from 1874–1935. Most of the estimation improvements stem from findings of new data which had been overlooked in the past. However, some stem from changes in estimation theory. Estimates summarized in a compendium compiled by Yuzo Yamada together with his own estimates are based on the personal approach. However, new estimates were derived from Yamada's estimates by Kazushi Ohkawa and others, using a new method called the commodity flow approach. This comes from the re-evaluation of the reliability of the data in *Fuken-bussan-hyo* obtained in 1874. The propriety of this approach is guaranteed in so far as the coverage of goods produced is large enough compared to that of the personal approach. In most cases, a deep discrepancy occurs in the production statistics at the time of changes to the survey methods. In addition, population statistics classified by occupation and industry have in principle more extensive and exact coverage, but deficiencies in the yearly changes. Thus, the problem of estimation is the choice of bench mark years when comparatively abundant information is available, and the availability of production indicators reflecting yearly changes. On average, fairly good statistics may be available for the number of working people, but the situation is a little bit different for the number of establishments or enterprises. With the development of industrialization, this factor became more important. This is one reason for adopting

11

the commodity flow approach in estimating national income statistics. However, the situation regarding the service sector is different where there is no means of measuring services as a total turnover or number of people engaged in it. Thus, we need to trace the development of statistical survey systems in detail. Further discussion of the problem is left for the analysis in Part II.

The latter example may be found in recent revisions of official figures of national accounts based on the publication of a new input-output table whose compilation requires at least five years. Currently the revisions of the past figures of a system of national accounts in Japan are done systematically every five years after compilation of the input-output tables. Most econometricians tend to construct large econometric models for periods of about ten years, thereby averting the danger of changes due to adjustments for the base years. They implicitly assume that these changes in the functional model parameters will not occur at the same time as changes in parameters reflecting changes in social space. However, historians cannot employ such suppositions, but must rely on a different method.

Some historians in principle favour cross sectional data instead of macro indicators in time series, condemning the application of macro econometric models to a historical context. It is true that there have been many followers of Solowian growth model builders in Japan since the publication of the Klein-Osaka model in 1963 (Klein [1961]). However, none can escape the criticism that Griliches made of growth accounting in the 1970s. Inference based on cross sectional data may be excused from such criticism, but they must rely on verbal explanation of changes in the economic structures of more than two periods described by cross sectional data.

3. PROPOSALS FOR RECONSTRUCTION SURVEY

The most serious defect in relying on the cross sectional approach is the lack of suitable data because of the scarcity of available cross sectional tabulations due to the limited number of publication forms in the past. Thus, historians' efforts have been directed toward gathering individual data from various scattered documents hidden in the dossiers of private families, etc. Thus, the problems remain the same as before the trials of estimating macro indicators, because these fragmented data cannot be used to draw conclusions about overall or national situations. There is no way of inferring something based on ad hoc individual data. With the development of data processing by computer we are freed from this restriction in so far as all individual data of a certain statistical survey remain. For example, lists of enumerators are left as a directory for other uses as a by-product of a statistical survey. If we recompile several lists of this kind into one integrated database, then we can reconstruct a new statistical survey which can be tabulated as we like. We call such a method "reconstruction of a survey" like reconstruction of archeological relics. As an illustration using actual data, we quote our experiment. The Ministry of Agriculture and Trade compiled a directory, probably based on the first comprehensive manufacturing census in 1909. This directory contains not only the names and addresses of manufacturing establishments, but also the numbers of their employees and the horsepower of their engines. It also includes the owners' names. Thus, we can construct a table of owners' names, i.e. the enterprise-establishment bases of the factories. Eventually, we can derive cross-tabulation tables showing the sizes of establishments and enterprises based on the numbers of their employees, and the size and horsepower of their engines. By recombining this directory file with lists of enterprises obtained from other sources, we can, if applicable, further reclassify them according to their capital amounts.

New tabulations sometimes throw a new light on old tables published in the past. A population census, for example in 1930, will supply us with the number of employees in a manufacturing census, and the residuals from the number of employees obtained from the manufacturing census which covers establishments with over five employees will supply us with the possible number of employees working in factories with less than five employees. If we can successfully estimate the number of owners in the manufacturing sector, then the residuals from the population census will provide us with a possible number of manufacturing establishments with less than five employees.

If the list contains the founding date of the establishment, the cohort analysis in the backward direction toward the past will reveal the distribution of such establishments in the past, excluding those vanishing before the survey year. If the number of establishments in past format survey records do not exceed this number, then leakage must have occurred in the format survey.

We are not the pioneers of such compilation techniques and analysis. For example, we found similar trials by manual matching and calculation in the papers of Kazuo Yamaguchi (Yamaguchi & Terashima [1956]) and Toshio Furushima (Furushima [1952], [1967]), but not good followers in the next generations. At the stage of the second generation of mainframe computers we proposed such an analysis based on the database architecture of computer science as a new project in the 1970s, but the results were tentative (Matsuda [1978]).

Part II describes our results, still tentative, of such reconstruction survey projects and discuss what can be derived from these new data. Part III summarizes our database system.

There is a discrepancy between what is known to us now and what was not known to us at the time of the survey. A reconstruction survey will tell us what was not known when the original survey was carried out. However, the directory information which is the main source of a reconstruction survey cannot exceed the information obtained from the original questionnaire. One advantage of researchers in post periods is the knowledge they have about what subsequently changed into a category other than that at the time of the original survey. The classification of industrial codes may be reconstructed according to the schemes of the posterior period.

Another advantage of being in our age is that we can compile longitudinal data sets of more than two periods. In principle, this was also possible for researchers in the past, but practically impossible to match the names of more than ten thousand establishments. Thus, we can pursue the rise and fall of establishments over the generations through their transition matrices.

Part I
STATISTICAL SURVEY
SYSTEM

1. MAIN FEATURES OF STATISTICAL SURVEY SYSTEM IN JAPAN

It has long been the focus of controversy among economists how much of the apparent rapid economic growth of Japan since the Meiji Restoration in 1868 may be attributed to the fictional increase due to the progressive increase in coverage and accuracy of statistical surveys. Many revised estimates seem to reveal an exaggeration of Japanese economic growth. These revisions are in most cases based on new conjecturing processes or estimation techniques, sometimes using newly found statistical reports. However, only a few papers written by specialists on statistical survey systems have paid a lot of attention to a systematic review of past statistical survey systems. These papers, however, rather stress the inaccuracy of the data before the establishment of the census survey in Japan. The precensus period may be called that of *Hyoshiki-chosa*, i.e., format surveys. This method was an elaboration of the traditional survey system called *Kaki-age* surveys, in which figures were extracted from official dossiers. This was seen as the common practice among bureaucrats of the Tokugawa regime. It is commonly said that the starting point of Japanese census surveys can be traced back to the manufacturing census of 1909 and to the population census of 1920. There is no explicit agreement as to the evaluation of the precensus system, or to the period since the census system was completed.

Our hypotheses are as follows:

1) The *Hyoshiki-chosa* survey system is different from the *Kaki-age* survey, which did not use consistent terms and whose semantics were not well-defined. In the *Hyoshiki-chosa* survey system, at least the terms used in the survey were exactly defined and the list of local governments which were responsible for submitting reports to the central government was completed. This *Hyoshiki-chosa* system was developed in about the early 1880s.

2) The formation of a census survey may be traced back to 1894, when manufacturing factories and corporate firms were surveyed by the modern statistical survey method.

3) The statistical system based on the census method reached its peak in 1940, and this may be called a complete census system.

17

After 1940, the reorganization of governments made necessary by World War II led the census system into collapse as a politically neutral system which prohibited to use questionnaires gathered for intelligence information.

These hypotheses may suggest that the exaggeration of economic growth due to the development of the statistical survey system is very probable, especially around the 1890s when the survey system was in transition. Furthermore, in reviewing the development of the statistical survey system, we want to draw the attention of readers to the mutual interaction between the government of Japan proper and those of her colonies. Unlike Western colonial powers, Japan adopted the complete assimilation policy vis-a-vis the colonial people, resulting in the introduction of the same statistical system, and sometimes a more advanced system, before execution in Japan proper. Unfortunately, some of the statistics complied in the colonies before World War II were lost during and after the War. We will discuss this situation in detail in later sections.

2. CREATION OF STATISTICAL SURVEY: 1874–85

2.1 Land Map Making and People Registration System

After the Meiji Restoration, the new government tried to undertake two big surveys. One was aimed at compiling a land map using triangulation on a nationwide scale. This started in 1874 and ended in 1889. This land map compilation was interwoven with a land tax assessment and land proprietorship assignment. It was a necessary precondition to organize local government so that it was directly controlled by the central unified government. The other was the reorganization of the citizens' registration system.

As is well-known, Japan had a quite exhaustive registration system, called *Shumon-ninbetsu*, during the Tokugawa period. Its extension and reorganization was called a creation of *koseki*, which is still actively pursued as the most essential registration system of people today. The Japanese word '*ko*' means a family or a house and '*seki*' means a register. Registration is done under the name of the family head. When the land map was compiled, the proprietorship was registered under the name of the family head. However, this revealed the inaccuracy of the *Shumon-ninbetsu* registration, so it was necessary to carry out a survey for a new registration system. The result of this survey was called *Jinshin-koseki* as it was done in 1872. (*Jinshin* indicates a year in the Chinese almanac system, which has a 120-year cycle.) This survey was supposed to be a sort of statistical survey and the register was to be renewed every three years. However, no more renewal of the whole list as a statistical survey was in fact tried. Instead, inflows (births, marriages, immigration from other territories and so on) and outflows (deaths, marriages, emigration to other territories) from one's *seki* were required to be registered.

It is apparent that this registration system was insufficient as a full population census system. However, it took much time to replace the statistics from the *koseki* with those from the population census.

2.2 Trials to Create a Modern Statistical Survey System

Efforts to the create a modern statistical survey system were made by two different groups. One was led by people who wanted to industrialize the economy. They needed statistical material to develop their policies. These policies were called *kangyo*, or Encouragement to Industrialize the Economy. Their first action, in 1870, was to make a list of regional products. It was far from a statistical survey, but it was soon revised through trial and error. The first statistical report was published in 1875 as *Fuken-bussan-hyo*, Tables of Prefectural Products, of 1873 by the Ministry of the Interior. This ministry took over the function of compiling these figures from the Ministry of Finance, which initiated various statistical surveys such as Import and Export Statistics after 1871. However, before it relinquished this function, the Ministry of Finance published several summary tables of the conditions of the prefectures in 1871.

Following its reorganization based on reports of the Delegation to the United States of America, the Ministry of Finance ran the Bureau of Statistics after August 1871. Another bureau called *Seihyo-ka*, Office of Tableau politique, was, however, launched on by Koji Sugi, Rintaro Katsu's student and former officer of the Tokugawa government, and aimed to compile a Tableau politique based on the population census.

Sugi was one of a few scholars who had an interest in and knowledge about statistics. He learned statistics from the lecture notes of Simmon Vissering, a Dutch statistician and economist, in the 1860s. In 1869 he tested the population census in Shizuoka Prefecture where the Tokugawas retired after the Meiji Restoration. This pilot census was, however, carried out only in Numazu and Hara Towns and its extension to other areas in Shizuoka Prefecture was abandoned by the order of higher officials of the Tokugawas out of fear of interference by the Meiji government. Nevertheless, the results of this survey convinced him of the usefulness of the census system and increased his zeal to fully execute a census. In 1870 the central government called on him to conduct a people's registration survey. However, he insisted on carrying out an entire population census instead of simply a revised version of the *Shumon-ninbetsu* survey under the Tokugawa regime. He wrote petitions to build up a statistical bureau to carry out a population census and to publish a Tableau politique. His petition to organize a Prime Minister's Office of Tableau politique was finally accepted on the 24th of December 1871.

While Sugi organized his office with four staff, the Statistical Bureau of the Ministry of Finance already had almost thirty staff. His efforts were directed to training statisticians at his private school using the book by Max Haushofer, and to replacing the function of Central Statistical Office of the Ministry of Finance with his office, which he had staffed with newly trained statisticians. He issued the first statistical yearbook called *Shinmi-seihyo*, Tableau politique de 1872 (the year *shinmi*) based on the reports of each ministry. When the Ministry of Finance refused to report the figures on the budgets in the requested form, Sugi was compelled to publish the second issue without the budget figures.

The Bureau of Statistics of the Ministry of Finance compiled a more exhaustive statistical yearbook entitled *Tokei-hyo*, Tableau statistique de 1876, based on the figures gathered by the Ministry. It contained about 42 tables. The Bureau further pursued the compilation of statistics through gathering figures directly from prefectural governments, because many surveys which were initiated by the Ministry of Finance, such as the Citizen's Registration System, Tables of Prefectural Products, and so on, were transferred to the Ministry of the Interior. This project was strongly supported by Shigenobu Ohkuma, one of the leading figures of the Meiji government, who realized the importance of statistical information. The Bureau had about sixty members at the end of 1874, while Sugi's office remained unexpanded with only 26 members. It must be noted that the enumeration unit was the local administrative agency and that the figures gathered by them were not traceable to their sources until the enumeration unit became a set of an operationally well-defined observation unit. In most cases the information was collected through listening to or interviewing villagers to gain their impressions. Thus, even though the survey seemed to have been carried out centrally by a certain ministry, the practical procedures were a mere piling up of reports from local administrative bodies. The local administrative bodies were not controlled by the relevant ministry, but by the Prefectural Government who, in most cases, retained the authority to reform the survey formats under their control. Thus, in so far as each ministry wanted to gather accurate information, they were compelled to depend on the Prefectural Governments.

Ohkuma and Sugi disputed heatedly which bureau should act as a national central statistical office having the authority to ask the prefectural governments for statistical information without the prior consent of the ministry responsible for these matters. Without coordination of the central statistical office, the prefectural governments were afflicted by many overlapping questionnaires circulated by many ministries. Ohkuma was eventually defeated and gave up the idea of establishing a unique central statistical office in the Ministry of Finance and restricting each ministry's right to ask for only the statistical information relevant to their particular business.

From a political viewpoint, the defeat of the Ministry of Finance did not mean Sugi's victory. The Prime Minister's Office of Tableau Politique became a unique national statistics office, but it could not control every statistical survey. The Ministry of Finance retained the right to compile complete foreign trade statistics and financial statistics, and the Ministry of the Interior assumed the right to compile production statistics and later seized the power to design the formats of the Prefectural Statistics Yearbook which was originally tried by the Ministry of Finance. Thus, the seed of the decentralized statistical system was sown in 1875.

To ensure consistency, Sugi tried to call conferences with officers from each ministry who were in charge of statistics to schematize the survey formats. The schematization of the survey format at that time was quite important because its operational concept was not yet well-refined. The category semantics became common interests among the statistics officers. The influence of these conferences becomes apparent when we consider the case of the *Fuken-bussan-hyo*. This was shrunk to a more practically manageable scale and revised into the *Nosan-butsu* survey whose items were limited to such main crops as rice and wheat and some industrial crops like soybeans and so on. Similar effects are found in the annual reports or statistical yearbooks published by other ministries. The fruits of his efforts were reaped after his retirement in the form of *Tokei-nenkan* (Statistical Yearbook), a revision of the *Tableau politique* since 1882.

2.3 Trials in Creating a Population Census

Sugi's greatest efforts were devoted to creation of a nationwide population census. His repeated efforts to persuade the authorities of this resulted in the trial at Yamanashi Prefecture, formerly called Kahi-no-kuni under the Tokugawa regime. He organized and delegated a team of experts from the *Seihyo-ka* to execute this *Kahi-no-kuni-ninbetsu-shirabe*. These experts comprised not only officials, but also Sugi's privately educated students.

This survey was tried, together with various original ideas, in 1879–80. They used a questionnaire, *Ie-betsu-hyo*, which was applied to each household. This questionnaire was compiled based on the *koseki*, Family Register, and matched to each household. The household members were defined by their normal status and the information was later transcribed onto a *Tan-mei-hyo*, personal ID card, for data processing. The entire data processing for summary tables required almost two years and the final report was published in 1882. The summary tables contained the age structure, family size and occupational composition of all people over ten years old. This occupational classification scheme was the first trial for crystallizing actual occupations expressed in natural language into operational concepts that are well-defined for classification in Japan.

It should be noted that the *Kahi-no-kuni-ninbetsu-shirabe* was not a mere population census, but also included the housing and establishment censuses which surveyed the housing conditions of each household and the kinds of establishment, such as manufacturing firms, government offices, schools, and temples and shrines. This implies that this pilot census may be called a kind of compound census which really should be termed tableau politique: Sugi's ultimate aim. In the preface of this report, Sugi showed the cost of this survey and estimated the total cost for executing a national census survey.

Soon after finishing the data processing, Sugi extended this statistical survey to a dynamic survey which recorded population changes. However, while executing this dynamic survey in Kahi-no-kuni, Sugi resigned from his post in protest against the sudden cut in size of the regular staff of the Statistics Bureau in response to his plea for the entire reorganization of the ministry system in 1885. Thus, the questionnaires of this dynamic survey were all abandoned before the survey was completed. The ambitious scheme and budget of the national census survey became simply a desk plan and its execution was postponed indefinitely.

Until the end of the nineteenth century, the Japanese statistical system could be called a decentralized survey system, although it retained the name of a central statistical office called the Bureau of Statistics of the Cabinet.

3. FORMATION OF DECENTRALIZED SURVEY SYSTEM: 1885–97

3.1 Ministry of the Interior and its Survey System

With the retardation of the central statistical office, the decentralized survey system became the vogue. Most ministries published their statistical yearbooks for their own functions by compiling figures based on their daily routines. However, few ministries were successful in establishing modern statistical systems. Without modern statistical surveys, the accuracy of the figures collected depended on accessibility to the regional administration units. There were two survey systems which required prefectural governments to submit tables in prefixed formats whose concepts were operationally defined. One was carried out by the Ministry of the Interior, which had the power to control prefectural governments through assigning their governors. This ministry issued a decree to unify the formats of the Prefectural Statistical Yearbooks, which had been published by each prefecture since around the 1870s. Officially, it announced that as this kind of yearbook was not a statistical survey it need not consult or coordinate with the central statistical office. However, these formats were abridged and elaborated versions of those unexecuted formats originally designed by the Statistical Bureau of the Ministry of Finance. Thus, the Ministry of the Interior now gained the position which the Bureau of Ministry of Finance had aimed at. The yearbooks published by the prefectural governments contained almost every statistics obtained, such as geographical conditions, population, education, jurisprudence and police, and industry and trade. Most importantly, this Ministry controlled the People's Registration System, *koseki*, and so the vital statistics and population statistics constituted its most important fields. However, the industry and trade statistics were mostly secondary statistics. On this point, we would draw the reader's attention to the other survey system which had also obtained statistics from the prefectural governments. This was called the Rural Industry and Trade Correspondence system, and was developed by the Ministry of Agriculture and Trade.

The Agricultural and Trading Correspondence System stemmed from the Provisional Rural Correspondence System started in 1877. It was designed to integrate various surveys conducted by the Ministry of Agriculture and Trade, such as the Agricultural Products Survey, the Price Survey and the Wage Survey.

3.2 The Agricultural and Trading Correspondence System

The extension of the Provisional Rural Correspondence System into the Agricultural and Trading Correspondence System via the Rural

Correspondence System involved revising the survey formats and survey techniques. The system started as a pure correspondence of the rural conditions through the eyes of the aged expert farmers in the villages. These expert farmers were at the same time the promoters of modernization of the farming system through better seed dispersion, consolidation of separated fields and so on. The need to obtain an accurate picture of rural conditions in statistical terms required drastic changes to the questionnaire and survey system. The first extensive revision of the formats and the start of the new Agricultural and Trading Correspondence System was in 1883–84. It took two years to compile every format of every questionnaire such as those for Rural and Fishery Matters in 1883, and Industrial Matters, Commercial Matters and Forestry Matters in 1884. The guiding principle in designing the questionnaire formats was not based on statistical theory but on economic theory, ignoring practical survey procedures. For example, the concept of profit was introduced into almost every economic agent, even to the individual farmer. However, farmers' profits were defined cropwise and acreage-wise, and such a definition was practically impossible unless a controlled experiment was executed.

In 1884, the Ministry of Agriculture and Trade called a Conference of Statistical Experts as an extra session of the second Industrialization Promotion Conference. Those experts claimed that full execution of the survey formats proclaimed in 1883–84 was inapplicable. Thus, early in 1886, the survey formats were simplified. The most simplified ones were those of agriculture and forestry. However, those applying to industrialization and Westernization of the economy were followed up through firm surveys and factory surveys, where each establishment was listed as an observation unit. Other units for observation of production figures were not clear or well-defined. Only the enumeration unit was defined, as the county or the village of every prefecture and one or two correspondents were allocated and assigned among the villagers.

The retardation of the survey formats in 1886 was synchronized with Matsukata's deflation policy. The retirement of Masana Maeda, rural reformist from the Ministry of Agriculture and Trade, might have been a factor affecting the retardation. Maeda was keenly interested in developing a rural survey, but not a statistical one, and so his later

Table I.1 Coverage of Joint-Stock Company Survey for 1896 in 1898[1] and our Reconstructed Survey for 1896

Unit: thousand yen

	Number of companies	Capital	Paid-in capital (thousand yen)
(1) Reconstructed file	1,379	254,980	164,103
(2) *Kabushiki Kaisha* Survey	1,383	135,563	133,638
Difference (1)-(2)[2]	−4	110,064	30,464
Rate of discrepancy		43.16%	18.56%
(3) Our Database in Pt. III	4,150	411,995	246,509

(Source)

(1) Matsuda, Arita & Oh'i [1980],

(2) Ministry of Agriculture and Trade, *Kabushiki-kaisha-tokei* (Statistics of the Joint-stock Companies), the 3rd issue. 1989.

(3) Database consists of prefectural annual report for promoting industry, *Kangyo-nempo*, and prefectural statistical yearbook with supplementary information from company directories published by private intelligence information bureaux.

(Notes)

1 The survey covers companies excluding *authorized* banks.

2 Discrepancy is mainly due to the omission of the railway companies mentioned in the original decree but not annotated in the final report. However (2) does not cover various institutes for stock and commodity exchange.

return to the Ministry did not bring about an extension or recovery of the scope of the statistical survey system. However, small revisions towards simplification were followed up after 1886.

The recovery of the survey was realized in 1892 under the direction of Shojiro Goto, the new Minister. The statistics division was again expanded in 1893. The following year Bunso Kure, one of Sugi's statistics students, got his position in the statistical division. Revisions in 1893 included i) the introduction of an individual questionnaire system in a firm survey instead of a listing up method, making the observation unit identical with the enumeration unit, ii) the difference between the extensive survey every five years from the follow-up yearly dynamic survey which was in a simplified form but covered the major flow statistics such as yearly production, etc. and iii), last but not least, the explicit specification of the surveying procedures.

With this revision, this survey system could be classified as a modern statistical survey system. It was the sole survey system of industrial statistics of its day. However, its extension into certain fields was followed by it being cut off from other fields such as domestic and foreign trade, which were entrusted to the Chamber of Commerce in the big industrial cities. In a later phase, this cut off was further extended to other items, for example, in rural situations such as acreages, farmers, tenants and so on. These were entrusted to the *Nihon-nokai*, Japanese Agricultural Cooperatives, in 1902 after the abandonment of the plan for a rural census scheduled in 1901.

A summing up of the 1893 revision of the survey system tells us that the most important feature of the revision was the introduction of the factory and firm census survey system. This implies that the accuracy of the statistics in these fields markedly improved and that the tabulation of the survey results became more flexible with the introduction of cross tabulation instead of the former single tabulation or mere list-up form. It also implies that some part of the increase in the volume of the statistics might be attributed to a statistical illusion due to the changes in the survey method. For example, the most detailed statistics of joint-stock companies of the day were for the *Kabushiki-kaisha-tokei*, Joint-stock companies, for 1894–96 published by the Ministry of Agriculture and Trade based on figures obtained from the registration of joint-stock companies after the creation of the joint-stock company system in 1894. Our reconstruction of the survey revealed that the statistics obtained from daily business of this kind sometimes contained some definitional ambiguity not explicitly mentioned in the report. Table I.1 shows the discrepancy between the *Kabushiki-kaisha-tokei* and our reconstructed figures for 1896.

3.3 Impetus to Restore the Centralized Survey System

Following the *Kahi-no-kuni-ninbetsu-shirabe*, it took more than ten years for government authorities to recognize the importance of a census population survey. The census survey method was introduced into the factory and firm survey in 1893, but this was not an isolated phenomenon. In 1896 and 1897, the upper and lower houses of the diet proposed the execution of a population census and the expansion of the Central Statistical Bureau of the Cabinet. The latter proposal was realized when the responsibility for compiling vital statistics was transferred to the Bureau from the Ministry of the Interior and based on the individual questionnaire method.

The law regarding the population census was proclaimed in 1902 for execution in 1905. However, the Russo-Japanese war of 1904–05 squeezed out every budget surplus not directly interwoven with the war, so its execution was postponed indefinitely. Similar effects of decreased budgets were seen in other branches of statistics. The factory survey, which was introduced in the new agricultural and trading correspondence system in 1894 adopting the questionnaire system showed its survey results in a new report series called *Zenkoku-kojyo-tokei-hyo* covering 1896–1900. For the first issue for 1896 data, data processing took almost three years. However, the processing time decreased to two years for the 1897 data. After that it took three years due to the development of the tabulation technique. However, after the 1900 report published in 1903, no more new issues were published due to decreased budgets.

Although the population census was postponed until 1920, the manufacturing census by the Ministry of Agriculture and Trade started in 1908 as a more extensive and exhaustive census of manufacturing firms than that designed in 1893. This factory census now covered the smaller factories with five to nine employers, which were formerly disregarded.

4. FORMATION OF COLONIAL GOVERN-MENTS AND THEIR AFTERMATH: 1890S–1920S

4.1 Population Census Experiments

In the 1890s there was a great leap toward modernization of the statistical survey system. This great leap can not be separated from other radical changes to the social system that were going on at the same time. The Sino-Japanese War in 1894–95 ended in Japan's victory, which won colonies for Japan such as the Ryoto peninsula, Formosa and other small islands which were annexed, and war indemnity of 20,000 taler. This stimulated various social changes and accelerated modernization and Westernization. Above all, the creation of colonial governments required the refinement of bureaucratic systems. A statistical survey was executed to obtain data about the new territories, which included different ethnic groups and were mostly unsurveyed under the Ching Dynasty. The Taiwan Colonial Government's first task was to survey the territory to produce a land map and to launch a citizen's registration system or *minseki* system, which was analogous to the *koseki* system in Japan proper. This procedure was also applied to other colonial governments such as Korea, Kwantung Leased Territory (Province), South Sakhalin Island and the South Sea Islands (Oceania, Polynesia), which were entrusted to Japan by the League of Nations after World War I.

The most striking characteristic of Japan's colonization of Asian countries compared with that of West European countries, was its complete assimilation policy. Thus, in principle the policies carried out in the colonies aimed to introduce social systems similar to those seen in Japan proper. This also applied to the statistical system. The only difference was that the colonial governments were more centralized, so the statistical system was also centrally controlled. This system made it easier to execute various census surveys in a well coordinated way. Soon after the completion of citizen's registration, the Taiwan Government tried the first population census in 1905 when Japan proper had postponed its already scheduled population census. This pioneering population census, a quarter of a century after the *Kahi-no-kuni-*

Table I.2   The Discrepancy of the Population Figures between People Registration
Survey and the Regional Population Census

Region	People Registration Survey in 1908	Regional Population Census	Difference	Rate of Discrepancy
Tokyo city	2,168,151	1,626,103 in 1908	542,048	33.3%
Kobe city	377,208	340,324 in 1908	36,884	10.8%
Kumamoto city	57,049	54,558 in 1907	2,491	4.5%
Sapporo city	70,075	56,349 in 1909	13,726	24.3%

(Source) Bureau of Statistics [1976] and some corrections by the author.

ninbetsu-shirabe, influenced the 1920 population census in Japan.

During the years from 1905 to 1911, various regional population censuses were executed to investigate the workability of the people's registration system as a proxy of a population census. The results of these regional surveys revealed the inaccuracy of the citizen's registration system in providing population statistics. Table I.2 summarizes the evidence.

These facts attracted many supporters for the statisticians who insisted that a population census should be executed. For example, life insurance companies wanted an actuary based on the exact age structure population statistics. Furthermore, after the two big wars, the Sino-Japanese and the Russo-Japanese Wars, military authorities felt the need for accurate statistics for conscription. All these factors required more accurate statistics on the population structure.

4.2   The First Population Census in 1920

Even in 1915, it was only in Taiwan that the second population census would be carried out. However, soon after World War I, in 1920, Japan executed the first Population Census all over the Japanese Empire except Korea, where the uprising against Japanese rule had broken out in 1919.

In this census, not only the age, sex and marital status, but also the occupational and industrial status of the people were surveyed. Thus, the distribution of working people among various industries and occupations was clarified for the first time. Subsequently, small scale population censuses were executed in 1925 and 1935 all over the Japanese Empire, and large scale ones in 1930 and 1940. The expressions 'small scale' and 'large scale' should be read as 'simplified questionnaire survey' and 'minute questionnaire survey.' The latter asked each person in a household about his/her occupation and the industry where he/she worked. Strictly speaking, the occupational classification scheme used for the 1920 census was not an occupational one in the strict sense, but a kind of industry and occupation mixture classification. What people were asked was the job of the family and not their own personal jobs. If a respondent's work was not the same as the family's work, then he/she was regarded as doing it as a side business in so far as the work was not a regular wage or salary earner's. The conversion of the 1920 data to the 1930 classification schemes which covered occupation and industry was published after the 1930 census report (see Mitsuma [1983], Itoh [1983]).

What this population census makes clear is not only the inaccuracy of the figures of the citizen's registration system, but also the inconsistencies between various census surveys, which tell us the distribution of working people over industries. Thus, it became necessary to integrate the census survey based on the household as an enumeration unit and the census survey based on the establishment as an enumeration unit. This means the creation of a census survey system. This was the next target for statistical survey specialists in the 1920s.

4.3 Flowering of Social Welfare Statistics

The realization of the population census in 1920 gave an impetus to the centralized statistical system. The government eventually executed two big surveys: the household expenditure survey in 1926 and the labour conditions survey in 1924. These two surveys were planned by the Ministry of the Interior in 1922–23, but their execution was transferred to the Bureau of Statistics of the Cabinet. The household expenditure survey was a typical sample survey whose observation units amounted to about 6,500 households and was continued every year after 1931, until 1940. The latter was a kind of three year periodic census survey whose enumeration units were in two stages. In the first stage, manufacturing establishments with more than 50 workers and mining establishments with more than 30 workers were surveyed. In the second stage, each worker in these establishments was required to answer questions regarding wages and working hours and other working conditions.

These surveys that related to social welfare problems were given impetus by the depressions and labour disputes after World War I. The labour disputes required an objective survey of living conditions and labour conditions. Information received from the manufacturing census comprised only aggregated wage bills and numbers of workers, but nothing about differences among occupations within an establishment.

The nationwide household expenditure survey may be traced back to the *Saimin-chosa*, Poor People's Survey, of 1911–12. However, it did not require the daily bookkeeping of the respondents. The survey based on the bookkeeping method for daily expenditure started from the Twenty Workers Family Expenditure Survey designed by Iwasaburo Takano, professor of the Tokyo Imperial University, in 1916. After this, many family expenditure surveys were tried regionally by various institutions and local or municipal governments. Yasujiro Gonda, specialist of the households expenditure survey, once called this period the Household Expenditure Survey Boom. These smaller regional surveys were all absorbed into the nationwide survey, except those applied to the rural families.

The Labour Conditions Survey, *Rodo-tokei-jicchi-chosa*, was the cornerstone of the whole centrally controlled census survey system. Thus, the Bureau of Statistics of the Cabinet tried various ways to overcome the established decentralized survey system.

The Labour Conditions Survey may be called a static survey that describes the patterns of labour conditions in detail. A dynamic survey which described monthly changes in wage rates and so on was conducted by the Ministry of the Interior after 1923. This survey was also transferred to the Bureau of Statistics in 1925. Armed with these statistical surveys, the Bureau of Statistics grew as a unique central statistics organization covering all areas except production statistics and rural affairs statistics, which remained under the jurisdiction of the Ministry of Commerce and Trade and the Ministry of Agriculture, formerly one ministry called the Ministry of Agriculture and Trade.

4.4 New Survey on the Company: An institutional entity

The execution of the first population census in 1920 was a national event for Japan because of the huge budget required to carry it out. Another trend was for new statistical surveys to be integrated based on the establishment of an operational reporting unit. This is found in the new *Rodo-tokei-jicchi-chose* described above. This was legally authorized in 1922 through a new act called the Act for the Execution of Statistical Surveys by Field Surveys. This act clearly prohibited use of questionnaires designed for purposes other than compilation of statistics. Some additional explanation might be necessary to explain the situations created by the decentralized survey system. As explained in the previous sections, the gathering of the majority of industrial statistics had been the responsibility of the Ministry of Agriculture and Trade based on the former Agricultural and Trading Correspondence System. In addition to this correspondence system, two big surveys can be clearly distinguished from other format surveys specified in the decree for the correspondence system. They were for the manufacturing establishment and the company. The expanded questionnaire for the manufacturing establishment was realized in a big manufacturing census designed in 1908 and carried out in 1909. The questionnaire for the company was left untouched for many years since the 1904 revision of the correspondence system. In fact, the 1904 revision itself had been a retardation of the 1900 revision where loss and gain of profits and dividends for share holders and the number of branches were clearly required to be filled in. The accounting systems of companies were not qualified to compile such statistics and these survey items had to be deleted in the 1904 revision. In 1919, the Ministry made a little progress in compiling a more elaborate statistical survey on the company.

The first independent survey report on the situation of the company of 1920 was published in 1922, although the tabulation forms were the same as those in the previous Agricultural and Commercial Statistical Yearbook of the Ministry. They did not supply any information about profits and dividends. After the second issue, the report included some additional items. However, in 1922, the statistical section of the Ministry published a directory called *Taisho-9-nen-kaisha-tsuran*, the directory of the company. In this directory, individual companies' names and addresses were listed, together with various other items of information about the company, such as its establishment date, capital, paid-in capital, cumulated income, loss and profit, dividend rate and amount of issued bonds. The directory bore two dates: the 31st of December, 1919 in the preface and the 1st of January, 1920 on the title page.

By reconstructing the survey based on the database of this directory, we obtain figures comparable to those in the thirty-six issues of the Statistical Yearbook for 1919 and the first issue of Company Statistics of 1920. Detailed discussion on this will be found in Parts II and III. There are some small discrepancies between the two sets of figures, but on the whole the information contained in this directory corresponds to the survey results in the statistical yearbook. However, it was not used, as official company statistics followed. Thus, we have obtained 1919 figures comparable to the 1921 figures and those till these company statistics reports ended in 1944. (In fact, after the division of the Ministry of Agriculture and Trade into two ministries, the Ministry of Agriculture and Forestry and the Ministry of Commerce and Industry on the 31st of March, 1925, an independent act for the company survey was established on the 28th of November, 1925.)

This is a trial to determine the merits of an industrial census system created by the Ministry of Commerce and Industry compared with the census system initiated by the Bureau of Statistics, which will be discussed in the next section. There remains some ambiguity regarding the basic philosophy of the statistical survey created by the statisticians of the Ministry of Commerce and Industry, because they favoured more direct control by the factories and companies through gathering information directly reproduced in the directories. They published two series of directories: one for manufacturing establishments and the other for companies. They were first published without explicit authorization, but later the use of the original questionnaire of the survey for the compilation of the directory was officially acknowledged in 1927 by a special decree.

5. CREATION OF A CENSUS SURVEY SYSTEM

5.1 Towards a Census Survey System

The efforts of the Bureau of Statistics to construct a centralized statistical survey system was supported by the Central Committee on Statistics launched in 1920. The transfer of social welfare statistics from the Ministry of the Interior to the Bureau of Statistics was a result of the activities of this Committee. After this, however, no immediate coordination followed until the participation of the World Agricultural Census in 1930–31. The Bureau of Statistics succeeded in executing the agricultural census as an extension of the decree on the Labour Condition Statistics Survey. The original plan was to cover (i) cultivated land, (ii) production, (iii) farm management and (iv) cattle and poultry. The first category was surveyed in 1929 as farm household base statistics to supply a list of enumerators for the other three survey items. Although no further survey was carried out due to the budget deficit, this was the first attempt to estimate the production conditions of farm households by government statisticians after the shrinkage of the survey scope of the Agricultural and Trading Correspondence System in 1886 and the abandonment of the *Noji-chosa*, Rural Survey, by Masana Maeda in 1890–91.

After the suspension of the Agricultural Census, another rural census was carried out, this time by the Ministry of Agriculture and Forestry in 1938, as *Noka-issei-chosa*, Complete Enumeration Survey of Farm Households. These two surveys revealed the inaccuracy of the statistics gathered by the *Nokai* system. From the Complete Enumeration Survey of Farm Households, we could determine which households specialized in farming and which were doing other business. The Ministry of Agriculture and Forestry continued its census in summer and winter every year after the summer survey of 1941. Their focus shifted to the production statistics needed for food rationing.

What became clear was that the different census systems, such as the population census and the farm census, supplied different figures for the same phenomena without indicating their consistency. For example, in agriculture surveys, the number of households defined by the

STATISTICAL SURVEY SYSTEM

Figure I.1   The Process of Forming National Commercial Census Survey

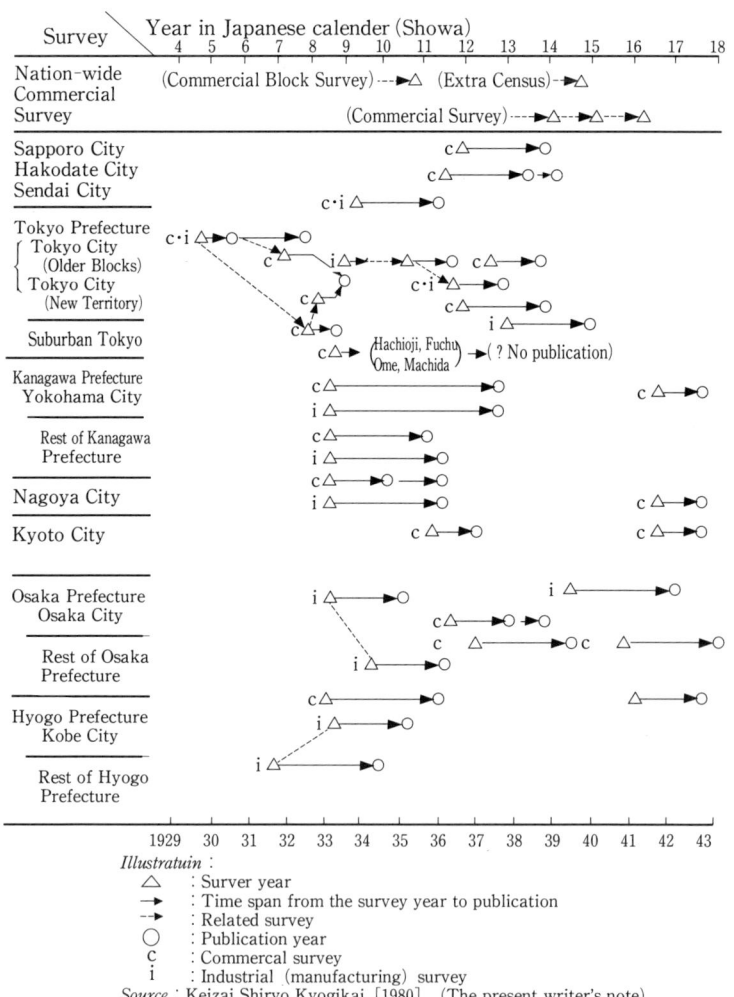

Illustratuin :

- △ : Surver year
- → : Time span from the survey year to publication
- →► : Related survey
- ○ : Publication year
- c : Commercal survey
- i : Industrial (manufacturing) survey

Source : Keizai Shiryo Kyogikai [1980]   (The present writer's note)

household head's occupation differ from the figures defined by those specializing in agriculture. Similar confusion could occur in the case of manufacturing establishments whose scale was smaller than the object of the manufacturing census and closely related to the household shop or firm run by self-employed workers.

Moreover, the industrial statistics compiled by the Ministry of Commerce and Industry lacked commerce statistics entirely. An exhaustive census survey covering all types of establishments was necessary because the surplus labour in the towns resulting from the exodus of people from rural areas during the long depressions, was mainly absorbed into small shops and other service sectors. Pioneering of this kind of establishment census survey was again in the hands of the colonial authorities, as in the case of the population census in Taiwan. This time, Kwantung Province tried the *Gyotai-chosa*, Business Conditions Survey, in 1927, where noncorporate establishments of commerce, manufacturing and other services were surveyed. This census attracted the attention of the Bureau of Statistics experts and they planned an extension of the Labour Condition Statistics Survey as an establishment census in parallel with the population census. The second *Gyotai-chosa* of Kwantung Province was carried out in 1934. However, immediate followers were found in the Commercial Surveys and Manufacturing Surveys done in Metropolitan Prefectures such as Tokyo, Osaka, Kobe, Nagoya, Kyoto and Yokohama, as in the case of the regional population censuses in the 1900s. This time the execution was at the request of the Ministry of Commerce and Industry. These trials in the 1930s are shown in Fig. I.1.

Regional commercial and manufacturing surveys aimed to clarify business conditions such as fixed capital, working capital, turnover, cost and profits. For the big corporate firms, such figures can be found in reports to stock holders, but no such statistics are found for small, privately owned enterprises. In fact, even the statements to the stock holders in most cases contain no detailed accounting on firms' costs or expenditure. The second principal feature of these surveys was that the enumeration unit was firms and not establishments. This means that those firms having more than two establishments reported as one firm. Thus, the distribution of branch factories or shops were surveyed for the first time in Japanese statistics history. (To reveal such a manufacturing structure we have compiled a reconstruction survey for the years 1902, 1909 and 1920. This will be discussed in Part II). There was keen interest among authorities in the size difference of businesses at that time because of increasing cartel formation and the emergence of the stock-holding companies after World War I. In addition, there were many disputes among economists and journalists opposed to anti-monopolistic capitalism.

The unification of various industrial surveys into a well-designed establishment census was a goal in building the census system. However, the long history of the decentralized survey system made it difficult to accomplish. The Bureau of Statistics succeeded in persuading the Ministry of Commerce and Industry to entrust it with carrying out a nationwide commercial census just before overall rationing brought about by wartime conditions. The Extra Census, often called the Goods Census for Distribution, was scheduled to survey every commercial agent, even peddlers, in 1939. The decree on the population census act was applied in carrying out this survey because the literal translation of the population census was Tableau Politique, a wider concept than population census. This census, like the population census, was carried out over the entire Japanese Empire. Survey items were (i) number of employees, capital, turnover and inventories of certain specified goods, and (ii) consumption of goods at service establishments such as hospitals, dormitories and restaurants. The second category items were surveyed by a sampling survey method. Unfortunately, some of the summary tables and questionnaires gathered in Japan proper were unprocessed and lost during World War II, except some parts of tables of a city in metropolitan Tokyo, which published a report entitled 'Survey on the Distribution Agents, Tokyo City, 1941.' However, all the reports published in the colonies are now available thanks to our recent endeavours. A short summary is shown in Table I.3.

The dispute about the jurisdiction of the survey between the Bureau of Statistics and the Ministry of Commerce and Industry, however, was not completely resolved even in 1939. The Bureau of Statistics would have been compromised if its sphere had been restricted to the retail trade. The actual 1939 census covered wholesale traders based on the contention that the amount directly sold to consumers should also be surveyed. The survey was designed to show both retail sales and whole-

Table I.3 Summary of the Extra Census in 1939

	Establishment			Turnover		
	people	%	%	yen	%	%
Sakhalien	8,201	2.2	0.3	138,555,717	1.9	0.2
Korea	246,688	69.1	9.6	4,126,246,784	57.4	7.5
Kwantung	10,228	2.8	0.4	1,439,078,136	20.0	2.6
Taiwan	89,858	25.1	3.5	1,448,811,687	20.1	2.6
The Southern Islands	1,805	0.5	0.0	27,562,320	0.3	0.0
Japan proper	2,195,169		86.0	47,362,488,016		86.8
Total of colonies	356,780	100.0		7,180,254,644	100.0	
Total of Japan Empire	2,551,949		100.0	54,542,742,660		100.0

	Working people			Working people per establishment		
	people	%	%	people	%	%
Sakhalien	23,103	2.5	0.3	2.81	108.9	111.0
Korea	595,115	64.6	9.1	2.41	93.4	95.2
Kwantung	70,207	7.6	1.0	6.86	265.8	271.1
Taiwan	226,850	24.6	3.5	2.52	97.6	99.6
The Southern Islands	5,224	0.5	0.0	2.89	112.0	114.2
Japan proper	5,553,730		85.7	2.52		99.6
Total of colonies	920,500	100.0		2.58	100.0	
Total of Japan Empire	6,474,230		100.0	2.53		100.0

Table I.3 Continued

	Turnover per establishment			Turnover per working people		
	yen	%	%	yen	%	%
Sakhalien	16,894.97	83.9	79.0	5,997.30	79.8	71.1
Korea	16,726.58	83.1	78.2	6,933.51	88.8	82.3
Kwantung	140,699.85*	699.1	658.3	20,497.65*	262.7	243.3
Taiwan	16,123.34	80.1	75.4	6,386.65	81.8	75.8
The Southern Islands	15,269.98	75.8	71.4	5,276.09	67.6	62.6
Japan proper	21,575.87		100.9	8,528.05		101.2
Total of colonies	20,125.16	100.0		7,800.38	100.0	
Total of Japan Empire	21,373.05		100.0	8,424.56		100.0

(Source) Matsuda [1980]
(Note) * Exceptionally high productivity of this area can be explained by
the fact that the bulk of the commercial activities here was transit
trade between the Manchukuo and Japan.

sale sales, but the published tables did not explicitly define this point
for reports covering Japan proper. However, the colonial ones did.
The Ministry of Commerce and Industry retained its right to survey
the wholesale trade and it carried out the *Shogyo-chosa*, Commercial
Survey. However, the coverage has in fact been a wholesale survey since
1939. Although this was done only in Japan proper, resulting figures
show that the distinction between wholesale sales and retail sales is
ambiguous, especially for traders who were half wholesale traders and
half retail traders in 1939. Thus, surveys carried out by the Ministry
of Commerce and Industry after 1939 require careful interpretation of
the coverage of the survey units.

5.2 Evaluation of the Census System Accomplished

The Distribution Census was carried out in 1939, and the regular Population Census was carried out soon after, in 1940. This census surveyed the occupations of household members and the industries in which they worked. The census survey system consisting of the establishment census and the household census makes it possible to compare the distributions of the working population among industries obtained from these two different approaches. In principle, the two figures should be the same except for the double accounting of people who did seasonal work, or who had more than one job. For example, *sake* brewers work only in winter. Thus, they may be registered in *sake* brewing industries if the establishment census happened to take place in winter. Some definitional ambiguity still remains in the industrial classification of establishments. Small factories which produce only to sell directly to consumers may be counted as factories in the production census and as commercial dealers in the distribution census.

Although some leads and lags existed as to the beginning of the census surveys, the census system as a whole spread over the entire Japanese Empire. Fig. I.2 shows the relation between the execution of the census surveys in Japan proper and in her colonies. The basic feature of this survey system was the uniformity of the surveys which covered the Japanese Empire as a whole. However, the survey's consistency, its execution and the publication of its results are another thing. Its execution was reported to have been carried out uniformly, but the processing and publication of its results sometimes suffered from various difficulties in subsequent periods.

Some of the reports published in the colonies had not been sent to Japan proper before the end of the war and even the documents gathered in Tokyo and other places in Japan proper were sometimes lost because of denied access and prohibition of research during the occupation, and those remaining in the former colonies were lost because of denied access by the Soviet army in the North East regions of China and through subsequent political changes. However, we were able to trace almost all surveys, with a few exceptions, executed in Sakhalin and Kwantung Provinces. The Institute of Developing Economies had once tried to compile a union catalogue of governmental publications

STATISTICAL SURVEY SYSTEM

Figure I.2 The Sequence of Nation-wide Surveys in the Whole Japan Empire

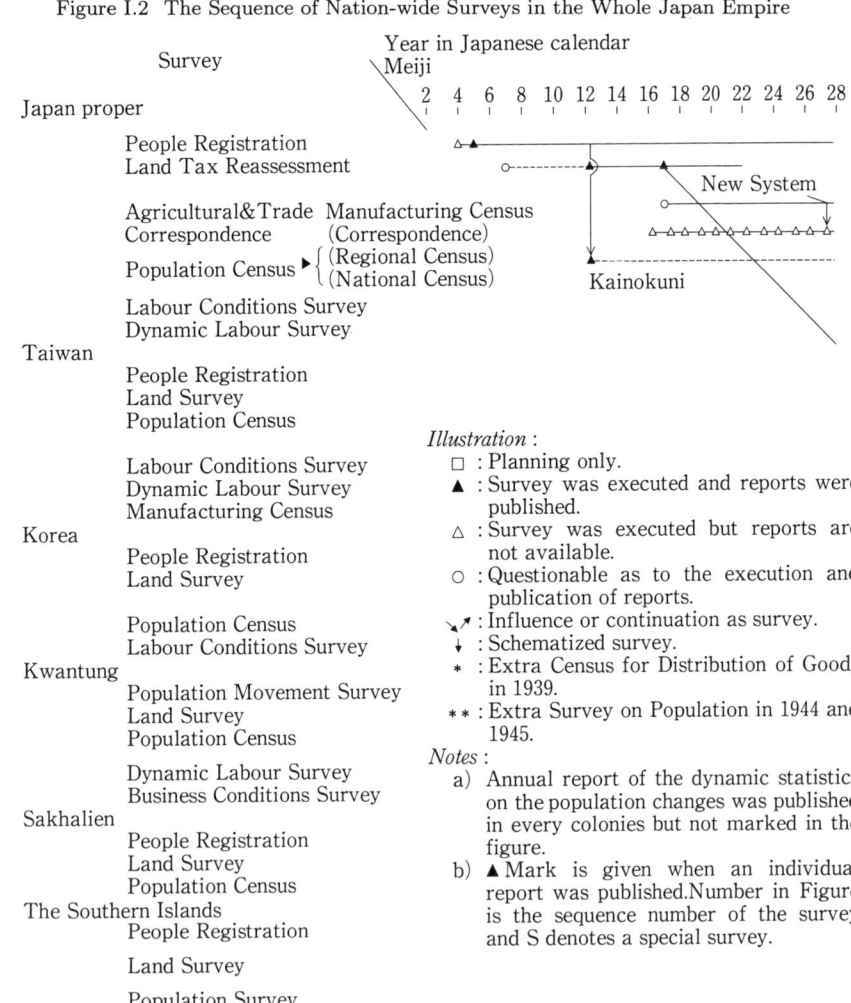

Survey — Year in Japanese calendar

Japan proper

People Registration
Land Tax Reassessment

Agricultural&Trade Manufacturing Census
Correspondence   (Correspondence)
Population Census ▶ { (Regional Census)
                    { (National Census)   Kainokuni
Labour Conditions Survey
Dynamic Labour Survey

Taiwan
People Registration
Land Survey
Population Census

Labour Conditions Survey
Dynamic Labour Survey
Manufacturing Census

Korea
People Registration
Land Survey

Population Census
Labour Conditions Survey

Kwantung
Population Movement Survey
Land Survey
Population Census

Dynamic Labour Survey
Business Conditions Survey

Sakhalien
People Registration
Land Survey
Population Census

The Southern Islands
People Registration

Land Survey

Population Survey

Ching‑tao
Extra Population Census

Illustration :
□ : Planning only.
▲ : Survey was executed and reports were published.
△ : Survey was executed but reports are not available.
○ : Questionable as to the execution and publication of reports.
↘ : Influence or continuation as survey.
↓ : Schematized survey.
* : Extra Census for Distribution of Goods in 1939.
** : Extra Survey on Population in 1944 and 1945.

Notes :
a) Annual report of the dynamic statistics on the population changes was published in every colonies but not marked in the figure.
b) ▲ Mark is given when an individual report was published. Number in Figure is the sequence number of the survey and S denotes a special survey.

Source : Matsuda [1978] & [1980].

42

Figure I.2 Continued

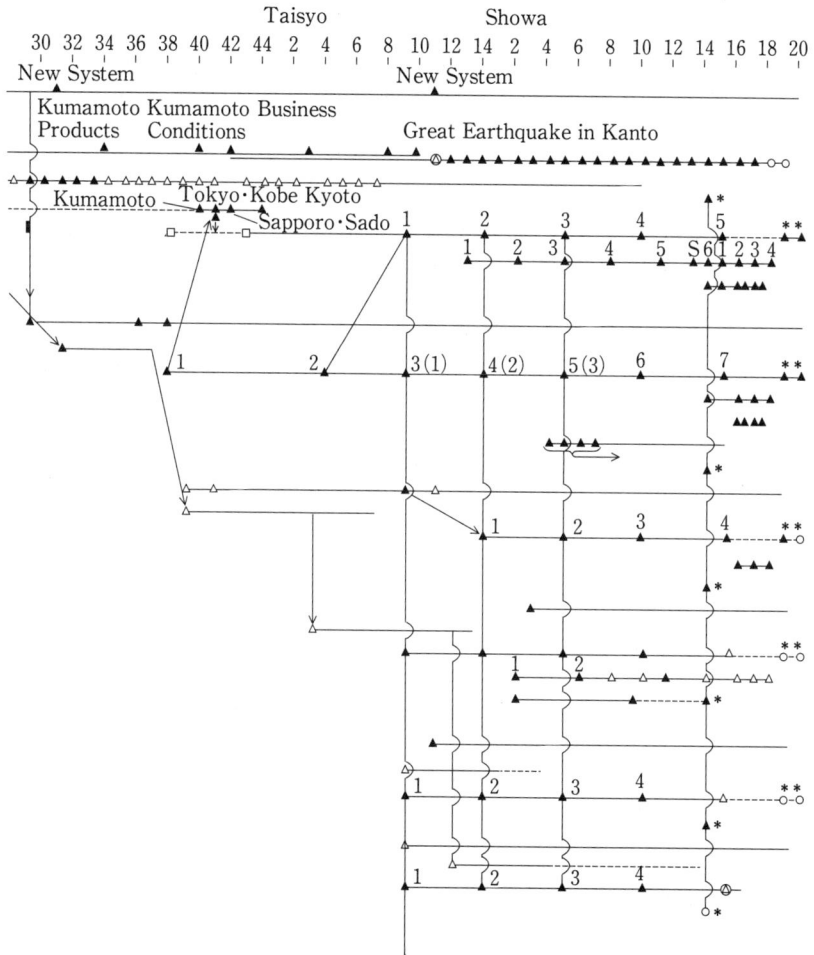

of all Japanese colonies under the direction Sei'ichi Tobata as a responsibility of the former suzerain state (the Institute of Developing Economies, *Azia-Keizai-kenkyujyo* [1973–76], Matsuda [1978])[1]

Note:

1) After that, the Information and Documentation Centre of Japanese Economic Statistics at Hitotsubashi University Institute of Economic Research compiled a bibliographical database for statistical documents and published its results.

6. COMPLETION OF THE CENTRALIZED CENSUS SYSTEM AND ITS COLLAPSE

1939–40 saw the high point in the development of the statistical survey system. In December, 1941 the Sino-Japanese War exploded into the Pacific War with the United States of America, Holland and the United Kingdom. The need for the mobilization of national resources for the war effort brought about radical changes in Japanese society, such as a complete rationing system not only for consumer goods including foods and clothing but also investment goods like machinery and raw materials.

In fact, the economy became what may be called a kind of controlled war-time economy. The shift to the controlled war-time economy had started in 1931 with Japan's build-up in Manchukuo. This was made possible through various laws enacted in 1931 for recovery from the Great Depression, such as the Act for Controlling Important Industries (to enforce a compulsory cartel), the Act for Association of Manufacturing (to reorganize medium and small-scale enterprises), and the Act for Establishing Electricity Enterprises. From 1933 to 1937, various special acts were enacted for controlling the economy, for example, the Act for Establishing the Japan Steel Company in 1933, the Act for Establishing the Petroleum Enterprise, the Act for Controlling Important Fertilizer Industry, the Act for Automobile Production in 1936, and the Alcohol Monopoly 1937. Overall execution of these acts started in 1937.

The year 1937 was quite an epoch making one because of the establishment of the *Kikakuin*, Controlling Agency, which drew up a plan for mobilizing materials for expanding production. The first plan was approved by the cabinet on the 16th of January, 1938. This plan was composed of over 102 items of goods, the maximum number reaching 280 items. The final plan was for the year 1945, but in fact it functioned only until the second quarter of 1944. Fujiwara, the Minister of War Material Production, reported the disastrous situations of the Japanese economy. Thus, the plan was ended in the second quarter of 1945. Various statistics were needed to make this plan. They employed a primitive input-output analysis scheme.

The statistics needed were roughly classified into three categories. The first comprised the production data and the amounts of raw materials required to sustain efficient military production. The plan was roughly classified into production for military use and that for consumer use. The second comprised data on the working population and its mobility between various industries and occupations for war. The third comprised data on the people's consumption rate, and was required to determine their living conditions.

This controlled economy situation again required a decentralized statistical system. Various ministries tried to execute their own statistical survey to get information to assist in their planning. The extension of the distribution census combined with the manufacturing census was never tried by the Bureau of Statistics. The Ministry of Commerce and Industry, later transformed into the Ministry for Military Mobilization of Goods, continued the Manufacturing Census and the Commercial Census, and also started a new dynamic survey of the production of selected items for monthly periods. The Ministry of Welfare began to investigate labour mobility between industries. At the same time, the Bureau of Statistics changed their Labour Condition Survey into a Survey on Engineers and Technicians, but wanted to continue the survey overlapping with the one done by the Ministry of Welfare.

It is said that many duplicate questionnaires were sent to the same factories or firms by different government sections. The production figures sent to the section which had the power to purchase at the official fixed price might be different from the figures sent to the authority which controlled the supply of materials for production. The chaos caused by the lack of coordination among government sections might

Table I.4 Factories Undergoing from Duplicate Surveys during the War Period

(i) Frequency of Regular Reports (in a year (1942))

Name of factory	Type of factory	Daily	Six per month	Three per month	Two per month	Monthly	Six per year	Four per year	Three per year	Two per year	One per year	Total
Ikegai Steel Factory at Kanagawa	A					27		5		2	10	44
Showa Electric Chemical Industry	B					20		2		1	9	32
Nihon Optical at Ohi	C,D		1			36	1	19	2	34	47	140
Diesel Engine Automobile Factory	C					44		7		11	8	70
Tachikawa Aircraft	C				2	23		9		21	33	88
Hitachi Military Goods Factory at Omori	[C]					13		4		25	4	46
Riken Industry at Kumagaya	D					9				4	8	21
Nihon Steel Pipe at Tsurumi	A	2		1	2	31		9		6	38	88
Tokyo Steel Processing	C,D					37			13	42	22	114
Uraga Dockyard	D	1				56		14		1	12	85

(Source) Tomoyasu [1975] p. 192 ff. Tomoyasu was one of the chief statisticians at the Bureau of Statistics during the war-time and preserved several notes about the situations of the statistical surveys at that time. Only these notes quoted in his book remain as an evidence of the witness. Original survey was called "Special survey on the report burden requested to factories."

(Notes) Type of Factory   A: Factory specially designated for promotion of production, B: Factory under the jurisdiction of Ministry Commerce and Manufacturing, C: Factory under the jurisdiction of Army, D: Factory under the jurisdiction of Navy. Factory classified in [ ] is not described in Tomoyasu's quotation.

Table I.4 Continued

(ii) Regular Reports (in a year)

Name of factory	Kinds of reports	Total number of reports	Total number of questionnaires	Cost (yen)	Personnel
Ikegai Steel Factory at Kanagawa	44	1,195	27,000	1,000	14
Showa Electric Chemical Industry	32	389	1,100	40	10
Nihon Optical at Ohi	140	2,156	4,200	300	—
Diesel Engine Automobile Factory	70	940	12,000	2,500	15
Tachikawa Aircraft	88	3,168	65,000	2,400	50
Hitachi Military					12
Goods Factory at Omori	46	636	18,000	624	26
Riken Industry at Kumagaya	21	690	2,070	50	3
Uraga Dockyard	85	2,992	34,500	2,000	19
Nihon Steel Pipe at Tsurumi	88	1,234	4,500	500	—
Tokyo Steel Processing	114	1,815	5,445	800	10

(Source) Tomoyasu [1975] p. 192

be comparable to that caused by the decentralized survey system in the 1870s, but more serious because the rationing system worked upon these statistics (see Table I.4). The worst thing was not that firms lacked the ability to report to so many duplicated questionnaires and the power against such requests, but that the census method which now became common practice among the government statisticians required so much calculation and processing effort, which they could not afford (Tomoyasu [1975]). Furthermore, many questionnaires from households and firms became abandoned or lost through bombing damage during the latter period of the war.

However, the Controlling Agency tried to control the situation. It requested that statistical reports be simplified based on the statistics

STATISTICAL SURVEY SYSTEM

Table I.4 Continued

(iii) Occasional Reports (in a year)

Name of factory	Kinds of reports	Total number of reports	Total number of questionnaires	Cost (*yen*)	Personnel
Ikegai Steel Factory at Kanagawa	37	208	9,000	800	14
Tachikawa Aircraft	965	2,890	45,700	1,800	25
Hitachi Military Goods Factory at Omori	400	1,400	36,000	1,248	
Riken Industry at Kumagaya	64	138	414	10	
Uraga Dockyard	21	204	3,800	300	

(Source) Tomoyasu [1975] p. 193

of a special survey of factories undergoing duplicate surveys during the war period.

One example of a conflict caused by tabulation constraints due to the shortage of computational power occurred when tabulation of some parts of the 1939 extra census for the planning of rationing in the war period was suspended at the request of the army so that the 1940 population census could be tabulated, and was lost forever. In addition, many source tables were lost before they could be published. Letters stating that the local authority had sent the source tables of the 1935 population census of the Southern Islands were kept in the archives of the Statistics Bureau, but no source tables remain. We can trace those of Taiwan to the report published by the Chinese Government in 1953.

The results of the manufacturing census for the years 1943 and after were lost during the heavy bombing in 1944 and 1945. The results of a commercial survey and others suffered a similar fate.[1]

One result of integrating duplicate surveys was the establishment of the Annual Survey of Labour (later called the Census of Labor by Establishments quoted in Memo. Cabinet Bureau of statistics, file 004.06 (8June46)ESS/RS (RS-3)) by the Statistics Bureau of the Cabinet in 1943, based on the Labour Conditions Survey Act. As mentioned above, this Act ran the Labour Conditions Survey for every three years since 1924. However, after the Sixth Labour Conditions Survey in 1939, it was reorganized as the Extra Labour and Technical Engineers Survey in 1940 and then its name was entirely changed to the Technical Engineers Survey, *Roudo-gijitsu-toukei*, in 1941. The Ministry of Welfare ran its own labour survey under the name of the Dynamic Survey of Labour after 1939. However, it was integrated into this new survey. The Statistics Bureau tried to integrate all the other industrial censuses, such as the manufacturing and commercial census surveys, but all other ministries except the Ministry of Welfare rejected the proposal. In 1944, the Technical Engineers Statistical Survey replaced only the Dynamic Survey of Labour.

This reorganization had two purposes; one was to supply data for labour mobilization, especially for the aircraft industry, and the other was to cut out duplicate surveys. The latter aim was only partially fulfilled. The survey was executed three times. The first one was in June, 1944; the second in June, 1945 just two months before the end of the war in 1945 and the third was in June, 1946. The first survey result of the 1944 data was released only a hundred days after the execution of the survey and circulated in copied form in January in 1945. However, some of the tables originally designed to be summarized were not realized and the questionnaires were burnt soon after the end of the war before the occupation. The survey report was published forty years after the survey, in 1986, based on the source table stored in the dossier.

Full evaluation of the statistical work during the war period may be left for further elucidation after we check all documents on the statistical reporting system for that period. The most important of the documents left in the dossiers at the Statistics Bureau had been recompiled as a series of the documents on its centenary (Statistics Bureau [1973–77]. However, some of the documents were said to have been burnt after the war or seized by the occupation army. Some of the documents seized by the occupation armies have since been released to the public by the US government. Unfortunately, the author has not yet had a chance to check this for himself and therefore cannot confirm whether or not these documents can be found in the USA.

Note:
1) As to the data and the controlled-economy system, Yoshio Ando

wrote a comprehensive book on this period because at the end
of the War he was a naval officer who, under the orders of the
Ministry, was engaged in the secret operation to end the War and
so he was in a good position to obtain comprehensive information
about the economic conditions of the day (Ando [1987]). He told
the author that it was his duty as an economic historian to leave
a complete memoir on these topics.

7. THE RATIONING SYSTEM AND THE STATISTICS

Although the government focused mainly on the production of military goods, it still had to take care of the people. Under strict rationing, black markets appeared mainly in urban areas and so dual
market prices, one fixed by the authorities for transactions in rationed
goods, and the free market price (called the Black market price).

There were two special consumer price indexes. One was obtained
by asking housewives to keep records of actual purchase prices. Seki
kept the documents of the survey results for many years and they were
recently published publicly for the first time (Mizoguchi & Nakamura
[1994]). The other index was reconstructed through various hypotheses
such as obtaining purchasing price through household expenditure for
a certain item divided by its volume purchased (Morita [1963]).

The Household Expenditure Survey was partially published in 1941
and this was its last publication during the war period. The 1942
survey source tables were compiled without publication. It is not clear
whether or not the excerpts from the source tables were circulated
among government specialists. It is quite probable that the data were
not used at all for decision making by politicians and bureaucrats at
the time of economic planning.

8. NEW STATISTICAL SURVEY SYSTEM

After the end of World War II in 1945, reconstruction of the statistical survey system was one of the most urgent political issues. The
General Headquarters of the Occupation Army required statistics to

formulate their policies in the guise of indirect occupation. They asked in vain for quick responses from the Japanese government, but soon found out that the census type of survey was preferred by Japanese statisticians to the sampling survey. The General Headquarters of the Occupation Army strongly recommended the adoption of a new survey system that combined sampling surveys with a census survey. For this purpose GHQ, especially the USA, helped Japanese statistical bureaus in various ways. For example, the Statistical Mission, the delegation headed by Stuart A. Rice in 1946, submitted a report entitled 'Modernization of Japanese Statistics' (Ohya [1995] pp. 242–43). The statistical bureaus themselves did their best by recruiting many mathematical statisticians from universities and colleges and designing a blueprint of a new statistical survey system to be presented to the Rice Mission (Asai [1987]).

Among the most drastic changes to the statistical system was the check and balance system incorporated into the decentralized statistical survey system. This was intended to strengthen the Statistical Committee, which was later transformed into the Statistics Council and Bureau of the Statistical Standard of the Administrative Management Agency. Every statistical survey was controlled under this bureau to check for overlap between surveys over jurisdictional boundaries among ministries.

In relation to the survey system, the introduction of an establishment census should be mentioned. This census was expected to act as a sampling frame for sample surveys on an establishment basis. Thus, we have two sampling frames: for households in the population census and for establishments in the establishment census. Most of the sampling surveys, except those of the Ministry of Agriculture and Forestry and the Ministry of Finance, have been designed to use one of these sampling frames. The former executed two big census surveys: one for farmers and the other for fishermen. Sampling surveys by this ministry used these two census results as sampling frames (Tsuchiya [1987]). The latter ministry used the respondents' tax records for the sampling survey.

The Ministry of International Trade and Industry executed two censuses. One was the manufacturing census, executed annually, and the other was the commerce census, first executed every two years and now once every three years. These censuses, which were based on the reports from the establishments, were not well-integrated into the establishment census. However, the ministry adjusted the census survey districts to be the same as the establishment census districts.

These census surveys as a whole were used for sampling frames. Most of the sample surveys were still small scale, but they were executed monthly or yearly to keep up with dynamic changes of situations. One exception was the Housing Survey, which started in 1948 on a comparatively large scale and was executed every five years. With the recovery of the economy, the information needed became complex and so more extensive surveys were needed. Thus, big sample surveys were introduced, with intensive questionnaires and longer intervals between executions than the small scale sampling surveys. The Employment Status Survey first appeared in 1956, followed by the National survey of Family Income and Expenditure in 1964, which covered savings and assets, and the Survey on Time Use and Leisure Activities in 1976. The enumeration units of these surveys were households.

Another group of sampling surveys whose enumeration units were firms was the Survey on Activities and Structure of Medium and Small Scale Enterprises since 1967 and then it was split into Basic Survey on Commercial Activities and Basic Survey on Manufacturing Activities since 1959, retaining its original purpose to survey medium and small scale enterprises.

The introduction of sampling surveys has made it possible to get quicker results than can be obtained under the census survey system. Even the population census adopted a sampling method to get quick and extensive cross-tabulated figures. Firstly, one percent of households were randomly chosen for quick estimates, and then ten percent for extensive tabulations. In addition, we should refer to electronic data processing, which reinforces the rapidity and capability of complex tabulation. For example, Table I.5 shows the date of publication of the population census reports and their volumes. The increase in the volumes of reports has been quite remarkable in recent years and most of them have appeared almost simultaneously.

Two tables might be useful to illustrate the present state of Japanese statistical surveys. Table I.6 shows how many surveys have been conducted by central government. They are classified according

Table I.5 Time-lag of Publication after the Survey
The Population Census from 1950 to 1980

| Published Year | Survey Year: Survey No. =1 | | | | | | | Total |
	1950	1955	1960	1965	1970	1975	1980	
n.d.	3	·	1	·	1	·	·	5
1949	1	·	·	·	·	·	·	1
1951	13	·	·	·	·	·	·	13
1952	21	·	·	·	·	·	·	21
1953	31	·	·	·	·	·	·	31
1954	18	1	·	·	·	·	·	19
1955	1	1	·	·	·	·	·	2
1956	1	18	·	·	·	·	·	19
1957	1	18	·	·	·	·	·	19
1958	·	31	·	·	·	·	·	31
1959	·	13	·	·	·	·	·	13
1960	·	1	1	·	·	·	·	2
1961	·	·	8	·	·	·	·	8
1962	·	·	30	·	·	·	·	30
1963	·	·	32	·	·	·	·	32
1964	·	·	14	·	·	·	·	14
1965	·	·	8	1	·	·	·	9
1966	·	·	·	73	·	·	·	73
1967	·	·	·	80	·	·	·	80
1968	·	·	·	47	·	·	·	47
1969	·	·	·	13	·	·	·	13
1970	·	·	·	5	1	·	·	6
1971	·	·	·	·	49	·	·	49
1972	·	·	·	·	64	·	·	64
1973	·	·	·	·	39	·	·	39
1974	·	·	·	·	8	·	·	8
1975	·	·	·	·	6	1	·	7
1976	·	·	·	·	4	23	·	27
1977	·	·	·	·	·	104	·	104
1978	·	·	·	·	·	77	·	77
1979	·	·	·	·	·	11	·	11
1980	·	·	·	·	·	1	1	2
1981	·	·	·	·	·	·	29	29

Table I.5 Continued

Published Year	Survey Year: Survey No. =1							Total
	1950	1955	1960	1965	1970	1975	1980	Total
1982	·	·	·	·	·	·	107	107
1983	·	·	·	·	·	·	79	79
1984	·	·	·	·	·	1	40	41
1985	·	·	·	·	·	·	6	6
Total	90	83	94	219	172	218	262	1138

(Source) STATIONS database. STATIONS is the abbreviation of Statistical Information System which is compiled by and installed at the Documentation Centre for Japanese Economic Statistics at Hitotsubashi University. The chief compiler has been Professor Setsuo Suoh under the direction of Yoshiro Matsuda in collaboration with other staffs of the centre Ms Fusako Fuse, Satoko Miura, Terumi Taguchi and others.

to their periodicity. However, the point of issue is the recent budget deficit. Table I.7 and Fig. I.3 show the recent trend of expenditure on statistics under national budget constraints. The reorganization of government institutions to reduce the number of the officials employed resulted in the integration of the Bureau of Statistical Standards with the Bureau of Statistics of the Prime Minister's Office into a new Statistics Bureau in 1984. Another repercussion was the change of the periodicity of the survey. For example, the establishment census in 1984 was postponed until 1986. This created additional work for other ministries which had been using that survey as a sampling frame.

Summing up the budget deficit is one of the most serious problems for future surveys in Japan. Thus, in 1985 the Statistics Council formulated an advisory recommendation, called the "Plan for the Statistical Survey System in the Medium and Longer Terms." After ten years the Council revised this plan and made a new recommendation: New Long-term and Medium-term Plan for Statistical Administration in 1995.

Drastic changes have occurred in the socio-economic scene, not only

NEW STATISTICAL SURVEY SYSTEM

Table I.6 Number of Surveys and their Reports Published

Periodicity	Number of surveys	Surveys without reports	Surveys with reports	Total volumes of reports
10 years	2	0	2	4
8	1	0	1	1
6	3	0	3	4
5	43	9	34	100
4	4	1	3	3
3	36	6	30	39
2	11	3	8	9
yearly	243	33	210	256
2 times in a year	20	5	15	19
3 times in a year	5	1	4	4
quarterly	29	3	26	31
1 for 2 months	1	0	1	1
monthly	97	14	83	138
weekly	1	1	0	0
daily	3	0	3	4
others	3	0	3	3
undefined	46	10	36	40
only 3 times	1	1	0	0
Ad hoc	329	111	218	219
Total	878	198	680	873

(Notes)

1. Volumes of the reports are based on the number of volumes disregarding the number of issues of each volume. Thus total 262 issues of the 1980 Population Census Reports are counted as 49 volumes.

2. Figures about ad hoc surveys are sum-up of the past five years until 1983.

(Source) STATIONS Database. Original data file of this part of our database is based on the file complied by the Department of Statistical Standards of Statistics Bureau, 1983 version. This part of STATIONS has been compiled by Associate Professor Tsuneharu Ohkubo when he worked at the centre.

STATISTICAL SURVEY SYSTEM

Table I.7 National Budget and Expenditure for Statistics

Fiscal year	National budget (10 thousand billion yen)	Statistical Expenditure (10 billion yen)
1962	2.43	2.3
1963	2.85	3.0
1964	3.26	3.7
1965	3.66	5.8*
1966	4.31	4.3
1967	4.95	4.6
1968	5.82	5.5
1969	6.74	7.5
1970	7.95	13.2*
1971	9.41	7.5
1972	11.47	9.0
1973	14.28	10.2
1974	17.10	18.8
1975	21.29	24.6*
1976	24.30	12.9
1977	28.51	12.0
1978	34.30	19.3
1979	38.60	24.5
1980	42.59	48.3*
1981	46.79	17.8
1982	49.68	17.8
1983	50.38	20.0
1984	50.63	21.3
1985	52.50	49.3*
1986	54.09	20.4
1987	54.10	16.0
1988	56.70	22.2
1989	60.41	26.1
1990	66.24	62.0*
1991	70.35	24.2
1992	72.22	19.2
1993	72.35	26.1
1994	73.08	36.8
1995	70.99	71.0*

NEW STATISTICAL SURVEY SYSTEM

(Notes)

1. Those marked with * contain the expenditure for the population census. Direct cost of the population census is about 273 yen per person in 1985, i.e. 32,995 mil. yen in total for 1985 population census.

2. Expenditure for statistical survey does not include the cost for personnel of the central governments.

(Source) Statistics Council [1985], [1995]

Figure I.3 Government Budget and Statistical Expenditures

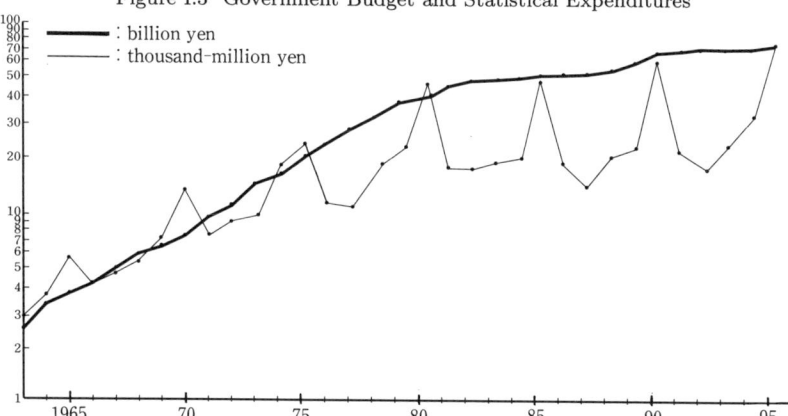

Note : Statistical experditure does not include wagebill of
  the premanent officers at central governments

in Japan but also in surrounding nations, so statistical administration must be updated to take them into account. The proposals to revise and extend the surveys, to install new statistical surveys and to adjust survey cycles in new long- and medium-term plans were quite diversified. Basic constraints faced by the statistical administration are decreases in budget and personnel for the statistical surveys and less willingness by respondents to fully answer questions to protect their privacy and business secrets. However, the requirement for statistical information has increased because of the need to obtain exact data for both public and private policy making. Thus, the target of the Long- and Medium-term Plan is to find a suitable solution to this saddle point problem by imposing the minimum burden on respondents and

57

obtaining the maximum information from the surveys.

To find a good solution, it is necessary to review current survey systems. To slim down the statistical survey system but obtain the maximum information, implies that the survey system must be reconstructed with limited information resources.

Primary needs for new statistical information stem from changes in surrounding socio-economic situations, such as international complexities, aging population structure, diversification of people's values due to higher levels of economic performance and equalization of income and wealth distribution and, last but not least, structural changes in decision making of society from the household's head to individual household members and from establishments to the heads of companies or firms.

The Japanese statistical survey system consists of three major survey units: a) households, b) establishments and c) firms. These survey units are listed by census type surveys, except for firms, which are not covered by any census type survey but by administrative tax records. However, their list has not been open even to other authorities performing statistical surveys. Some parts of the list of big companies used for the corporate surveys by the Ministry of Finance are open to other statistical sections of other ministries.

Points of issue are: a) changes in concepts of households stemming from the collapse of the older compound family dwelling unit system, with increasing numbers of young and old single households living together in the same residence but not sharing the same purse, and b) decreasing self-sufficiency or independence of establishments as accounting units in a firm through computerization of information control of firms and the eventual decline in the importance of establishments as respondents to statistical surveys. The computerization of an entire information system including accounting procedures within firms cannot be restricted to the national domain. This will eventually require a transformation of the survey unit from establishments to firms. These changes should be taken into account in the designing stage of the survey.

One solution is to implant common survey items in different surveys for a micro-statistical linkage for household surveys. Another is to compile an overall business frame, firstly from the reformed establishment census whose name will be changed into an establishment and firm census which is to contain various linkage items, not only between establishments and their headquarters but also between owner companies and those in which they hold a share. These connectors will link domestic and international capital inflow and outflow. The survey records are to be integrated into one comprehensive business frame and its updated information will be gathered from both statistical surveys and administrative record data.

By virtue of this business frame, other industrial censuses and sample surveys will obtain a well-defined sampling and survey frame. In addition, we expect to reveal a firm-establishment complex that will make it easy to carry out a capital stock survey for private firms. This is the last survey item to replace the nationwide wealth survey with an itemwise stock survey. After 1970, Japan did not carry out a nationwide wealth survey and the last Long- and Medium-term Plan recommended that an itemwise survey be carried out instead of a national wealth survey such as a household survey. This kind of survey would cover households' assets including land, housing and consumer durables. In 1994, a land holding survey was realized for both households and firms. However, a survey of tangible assets owned by private firms had not been realized. Judging from economic factors concerning Japan, such as the exodus of investment abroad, it is absolutely essential to evaluate or re-evaluate capital stock according to current acquisition prices to estimate current productivity and the degree of obsolescence of capital stock within a country.

Another purpose of the stock survey is to estimate differences between owned capital stock and borrowed capital stock through lease and rental systems. This also applies to labour such as directly employed workers and delegated workers. The I-O table should contain a tangible stock matrix for compiling nationwide stock figures.

Most of the big sample surveys for households have been reconstructed as five-year surveys to bring them into line with the five-year cycle of the population census. However, establishment or firm survey cycles differ from industry to industry due to recent irregularities in the establishment census, whose cycle was originally three-yearly. However, this original cycle entails a joint execution of population and establishment censuses once in fifteen years. The new plan recommended that a new firm and establishment census be carried out five-yearly, and within this period a detailed mail survey of firm structure to be accompanied by surveys of every establishment of plural establishment firms.

Eventually, other industrial surveys of business areas such as commerce or service industries will be executed five-yearly, including the basic survey of manufacturing and commerce activities and industrial structures. The firm structure survey of the Ministry of International Trade and Industry will be carried out annually instead of three-yearly.

Much has been left for further elucidation, including a) transformation of agricultural statistics due to decrease in weight of national production and b) building up a system of environmental statistics, including information pollutants.

Part II
FORMATION OF STATE
COMPANY 'NEXUS'

PROLOGUE: HERITAGE AND REFORM

There is a big recognition gap between historians who consider events long after they have ended and people who lived through those same events, even when they use the same data. Historians are often privileged with more detailed, newly disclosed information. Time, however, has passed too fast for people today to understand what people have said about events of their day, and so data from the past are often puzzling to present-day people. We should make a greater effort to understand what people of the past meant. This is one reason why, in Part I, we traced the history of the statistical survey system, which told us how statistics were gathered. Another reason was that surveys had their own purpose for contemporary policy making and this influenced their design. Knowing this background illuminates the meaning of the figures. By sharing in this knowledge we can understand the validity of past statistical data. If we correctly interpret the statistics, they will act as a mirror showing why people acted as they did in the past.

In Part II, we trace the development of the Japanese economy through statistics. The statistics we use are mainly those used at the time, and are not reinterpreted data. Instead of estimates or recompiled data, we depend heavily on new data using our own database which we discuss in detail in Part III. The development of the Japanese economy, especially the rapid industrialization after the Meiji Restoration in 1868, has attracted the interest of many historians and economists. In describing this development, economic historians use time series data, firstly original reports of surveys or indexes, and secondly various compiled data after the national accounting system was developed, such as gross national product (GNP), etc.

The compilation of gross national product has itself a long history of estimation projects starting from Kinzo Nakamura's estimates for 1900 published in the same year and Tetsutaro Nakamura's estimates for 1904 published in 1906. There were also some from outside Japan, such as Charles V. Sale's one for 1907 in 1911 and Stamp's one for 1913 in 1919. Finally, there was Hijikata's magnificent one for the years 1900–37 (Hijikata [1933] [1938]) as well as many others including the official estimates by the Bureau of Statistics for 1925 in 1928 and 1930, and 1935 published in 1948 with a revised series for 1887–1935. The reason why these people compiled these data is somewhat different from those of the historians mentioned above. Estimators' principal concerns were how to understand the actual situations of Japan for comparison with other countries. For Japan, the 1930s was a time for establishing her power among the Western powers, and people were quite attentive to these data. As their estimation technique they adopted a so-called personal approach using mainly published figures, the exception being that of the Bureau of Statistics for 1925, 1930 and 1935, because they carried out special estimation surveys.

Then after the end of World War II came the recompilation project of Yuzo Yamada for the years 1875–1948, the results of which were published in 1951 (revised in 1957), and official estimates by the government, predecessor of the Economic Planning Agency of today. They also employed a personal approach. Estimation projects using historical figures had their own importance in their day because the occupying powers needed the figures to assess the level of Japanese productivity to restrict her to subsistence level, fearing a revival of Japan as a world military power. Yamada's estimates stimulated the interest of the research group of the Institute of Economic Research of Hitotsubashi University led by Kazushi Ohkawa, and eventually flowered as the *Long-term Economic Statistics* (LTES) in fifteen volumes. This is quite a big project and is supported not only by many researchers such as Miyohei Shinohara, Mataji Umemura and others, but also by many financial sources in addition to Grants by the Ministry of Education, such as the Asian Foundation and the Rockfeller Foundation from the USA. (See Shinohara (ed.) [1991] as the history of the project in brief.) Their approach is itself quite fresh because they adopt a commodity-flow estimation technique and employ the production figures obtained from *Fuken-bussan-hyo* to estimate the starting point. In return, they should agree with those yearly figures that were smoothed out by moving averaging between bench mark years. The properness of their approach and criteria for selecting source data have been subject to many criticisms. To compile a substitutable series, however, would require so much effort that no-one has dared to try except the group headed by Hideo Aoyama in collaboration with Ippei Sugiura who estimated business cycle indicators.

It took many years for Ohkawa's project to compile the whole series and during this period a new aspect of the historical estimate other than the interest of the occupation army attracted many economic historians' attention. This was the cause and origin of the success of industrialization, which other underdeveloped Asian countries undergoing European invasion in the nineteenth century had failed to attain. This problem leads to the question of what is a broader concept of industrialization as it applies to current problems in the underdeveloped world today, and from this comes the concept of the proto-industrialized economy.

The various past estimates illustrate the history of estimation projects by various authors and organizations and reveal that new estimates have in most cases raised the level of the estimated starting point, and thus lowered the growth rates (see Yamada [1957]). The revised procedures resulted from both the refinement of estimation techniques and findings of new source data that were overlooked in the past. Even Ohkawa's estimation project has produced variants. The latest version is shown in *Patterns of Economic Development*, 1979 (which is quoted in the *Historical Statistics of Japan* as Ohkawa, Yamamoto and Takamatsu estimates, vol. 3, [1988]). The revising procedures were so complex that some basic series used for estimation, such as number factories, differed in ways of estimating each series of figures like production, investment and number of employees, due to the time required to compile the entire series as a joint work of many independent researchers. This also resulted from the limitation of the computational facilities when the project started. It was the time of the *soroban* calculator and the electric calculating machine at best. The revising technique has been changed to extend the estimation from Japan proper to the Japanese Empire. Toshiyuki Mizoguchi organized a project after Umemura and Shigeru Ishikawa, who had tried to estimate the colonial figures. He tried to construct a kind of database system which simultaneously updated other figures influenced by revising a certain value.

We did not revise Ohkawa's estimates by constructing a new time-series database system, but constructed a micro-data database system to overcome the credibility gap of the statistical data in time series, as discussed in Part I. Revising Ohkawa's estimate would be a tremendously big project beyond our capability. In addition, our basic analysis philosophy is to squeeze out all information that can be obtained from past surveys.

Our historical analysis of the statistical survey system shows us that there are roughly four periods with different data credibilities.

(1) The first period is before 1883 when the Rural and Commercial Correspondence system was built. This was the seminal period of statistical survey systems and the figures for this period should be regarded as showing a picture of the last days of the Tokugawa regime, frozen after the Meiji Restoration. (It should be remembered that after the Civil War, called *Boshin-sen'eki*, in 1868 there was a more deadly war, *Seinan-no-eki*, between Satsuma led by General Takamori Saigo, one of the creators of the Meiji Government and retired the cabinet after his defeat at the controversy on the policy for Korea, and the Meiji government in 1877.)

(2) Then came the formative period of the statistical survey system from 1883 to 1908. The industrial statistics were formed, and the population review statistics provided the impetus to carry out a population census. This was the period where the credibility of the data increased year by year. This led to the segregation of factors governing the growth of figures from statistical fiction to socio-economic reality.

(3) The period of the stable statistical survey system was from 1920 to 1940, when the census survey system was accomplished.

(4) The last period was from 1940 to 1947, when the wartime planning system was in operation and many statistical surveys overlapped each other, but were sometimes lost to the bombing before tabulation.

In the following discussion, we will roughly sketch period (1) and the first half of period (2) mainly by reviewing past works. The bench mark years are 1884 and 1892. Then, using our own database, the latter half of period (2) will be analysed and compared with period (3). For periods (3) and (4), we can confidently rely on the official statistical reports. We should just pay enough attention to the transition period between (2) and (3), juxtaposing the figures of different sources by the different survey methods.

For this comparative analysis of these four phases, we set up bench mark years as 1896, 1902, 1908/9, 1920 and 1930. In selecting these bench mark years, we took into consideration the availability of data enabled by improvements to both the statistical survey and the economic situation. It should be noted that between these bench mark years drastic structural changes had occurred because of the Sino-Japanese War in 1894–95, the Russo-Japanese War in 1904–05, and World War I in 1914–18.

By comparing these bench mark years, we trace the path of structural changes seen in Japan's economic development. Among many topics relating to the development of the Japanese economy brought out by industrialization, we will concentrate on topics relating to the formation of the company system as a crucial management system for our economy, especially for the manufacturing industries. The company system is an institutional system that Japan imported from the Western capitalist countries as a modern management system. It took more than three decades to implant this institutional system in her economy. Nevertheless, we should consider two points.

One is that a system similar to the company system in gathering capital to gain profit prevailed in the market system of the Tokugawa regime without getting legal support as an institutional entity. As a result, the Japanese company system has its own peculiarities compared with the Western company system, which also had a long history before institutionalization.

The other is that, although creating this kind of system was first inspired by the opinion leaders of the new Meiji government, many companies had close relations not only with the new government but also with the old powers from the past as patrons for the supply of capital. New governments sold many factories at cheap prices to merchants who had close relations with the new government leaders, and later supplied a lot of money for operating them. Heavy industries from steel making to machinery, including ship building, civil as well as military, were developed with government cooperation. This is a typical example. We call this relation a state company, or nexus for short. This kind of new company, nexus, was seen in the latter periods of our economic development, especially in the formative processes of the colonies as a scout to a new territory, as companies were compulsorily integrated into the wartime controlled economy of the 1930s and in the reconstruction phases from the mid-1940s.

It may be said against this second point that it is a universal phenomenon among late comers to the world market economy, like Germany and Italy, when imperialistic capitalism was dominant. Despite this opposition, this is a real example in the world economy and so we will analyse the hypothesis in more detail.

The next question that will arise is why such an institutional innovation was possible. Our basic assumption is that development of the company system made it possible not only to sustain the high level of manufacturing with new technical innovation, but also to give impetus to development of a new type of venture business which did not exist under the Tokugawa regime. Thus, the achievement of a high level of manufacturing in rural areas before the Meiji Restoration blossomed into the new factory production system early in the 1880s, with capital gathered not only from rural areas but also from merchants in the towns.

Before we tackle the problem of a state company, nexus, we will briefly discuss the heritage of the Tokugawa regime. We will first discuss the governmental system of the *Shogun* and the *han-shu*, head of the clans, and the class structure, and explain how the new system worked with the new ruling classes and sources of capital to invest. Next, we will discuss the population and occupational structure. The analysis of this structure will answer questions about the supply of labour to the new economic system.

1. TRANSFORMATION FROM RURAL TO URBAN ECONOMY

1.1 Heritage of the Tokugawa Regime

We will first establish our starting point by describing what the new Meiji government of Japan inherited from the Tokugawa regime. As is well-known, Japan under the Tokugawa government enjoyed a very peaceful period of more than three hundred years, without wars with other countries or civil wars except regular peasant riots. This was because of her isolation from Europe and other Asian countries. She maintained contact with the outside world through narrow channels at Nagasaki and Hirado, which were open to Korea and the Netherlands from the 17th to the 19th century. (The act for isolation was proclaimed in 1635.) Thus, Japan escaped the massacres and invasions plagued by both Catholics in South America and Protestants in North America. New threats of imperialism by Western countries, Russia, England and France, as well as the United States of America, appeared in the nineteenth century. Before this, the news of the Opium Wars (1839–42, 1856–58) reached the few intellectuals who wrote essays about coming dangers. Nevertheless, the response of the Tokugawa government was slow and stubborn until the threat from the Western powers became critical, that is, when Perry first came to Japan in 1853.

The Tokugawa government could not find a way to overcome this international problem and unwillingly opened the door to the Western powers. This was the start of bloody civil conflicts within Japan over how to open up to the Western powers. The will of the *Ten'no* was said to be to keep Westerners out of Japan as alien invaders. Therefore, the Tokugawa government's policy of compromising with the Western powers was regarded as a betrayal of the *Ten'no*. Faced with the threat of the Western countries' military power, the Tokugawa government did its best to construct military forces to resist invasion. For example, their first trial was to introduce modern ways of making pig iron and steel to make big guns, and its second was to construct a navy by purchasing a gun boat and training seamen. Other hands also tried to bear arms like the navy of Satsuma and the army of Choshu. The factories for producing arms and gun boats were inherited by the Meiji government after the civil war.

We will not dwell on this situation at length. We will simply point out that Yoshinobu Tokugawa, the last *Shogun* of the Tokugawa, surrendered to the new alliance of the Satsuma and Choshu clans who had gained authority from the *Ten'no* on the twelfth of February, 1868. A civil war was fought, however, between clans who sided with Satsuma and Choshu and united under the name of the emperor, and northeastern clans who sided with the Tokugawa Shogun, and the Tokugawa navy headed by Tateaki Enomoto. The Tokugawa navy fought well and the war continued until the Hakodate battle ended on the 18th of May, 1869.

Historians have often argued whether the Tokugawa regime was a mere feudalistic government or a hybrid of capitalism and feudalism called absolutism forming a unified nation state like France under Louis

XIV. To those historians and economists who insisted that the Tokugawa government was a feudalistic one, the Meiji government must have been absolutist with feudalistic elements. Thus, the new government still had the characteristics of absolutism, and it was expected that radical revolution would be necessary to overcome this constitution. Such opinions are expressed in the writings of Eitaro Noro, Moritaro Yamada and others and in the propagation of the Communist Party under the influence of the Comintern in the 1930s.

Those who stressed the absolutism aspect of the late the Tokugawa regime insisted on the necessity for the gradual social reform of the capitalistic government that followed from the Meiji Restoration. Shiso Hattori and Takao Tsuchiya were famous ideologues of this kind. These controversies were closely interwoven with the revolutionary policies on how to modernize and democratize Japan after the end of World War II. However, despite such ideological prejudice concerning the politics of revolution and Marxist economic theories, economic achievement during the Tokugawa regime was surprisingly high. We will not present any comprehensive review of the controversies occurring after the end of the war, because there are already many specialized monographs on this topic. In addition, the radicals have not yet recovered from the collapse of the USSR and the other Socialist countries, and are still at a loss as to how to design future policies. Thus, we are presently free of such ideological biases. The only point we cannot ignore is the effect of the extensive censorship, called press codes, imposed by GHQ during the occupation period. (Etoh [1982] [1989] [1990]). This prohibited expression of any opinion regarding the positive aspects of Japanese governments in the 1930s, because it was feared that such expressions might strengthen Japanese people's militaristic attitude. GHQ's censorship was so effective that no trace of it could be detected by the public. Deleted passages were replaced with suitable words to conceal the secret of such censorship. Disparaging the achievements of the Tokugawa regime would have supplied good supporting evidence for the worst aspects of the Meiji period, which eventually resulted in the oppressive Japanese policies of the 1930s. On the other hand, reading about the higher achievements of the Tokugawa regime made readers quite suspicious about the possibility of the righteousness of Japan's policies against the Western powers and the means of expelling them from Asia in the twentieth century. Apart from the biases of the two groups, we can fairly state the high economic achievements of the Tokugawa regime. (Umemura [1991] pp. 18–22. He pointed out that those writers after the Meiji Restoration had been instinctively standing at the position favouring the achievements of Meiji government.) The left wing opinion leaders had implicitly overlooked the presence of censorship even after the spell of GHQ was removed after the Peace Treatment of 1951.

These high economic achievements made it possible to keep the Tokugawa regime comparatively stable in so far as population growth was kept at a low level: approximately two or three percent per year. Thirty-five to thirty-six million people in only five big islands and some smaller islands scattered through the north and south. These people were governed directly by the Tokugawa government or indirectly by the *han*, clans represented by *daimyo*, the *han-shu*. The period of the *Shoguns*, the heads of the Tokugawa government and the *han-shu*, were succeeded by bloody warfare.

As shown in Fig. II.1, there are areas, called *tenryo*, where the governors of the Tokugawa government were delegated to rule and areas entrusted to be governed by the *daimyo*. The former area covered Kyoto, where the *Ten'no* lived, and Osaka, the most important merchant city, and other import and export towns such as Nagasaki and mining areas such as Sado, Kofu, etc. The latter areas were *hans*.

In June, 1871, just before the *han* system was abolished, there were 261 *han*, three *fu* and forty-five *ken*. The three *fu* were the metropolitan areas of Tokyo, formerly called Edo; Kyoto, the *Ten'no*'s residence; and Osaka. The forty-five *ken*, or provinces, were formerly *tenryo*. This implies that there were as many castle towns as *han* where there were offices for governing the *han* located near houses of *samurai*, the ruling class, and the workshops of merchants and the stores of artisans. In addition to the castle towns, there were many market towns and station towns with hotels or inns located along the main roads connecting the main castle towns. Yamaguchi once listed 93 places as cities and market towns from 20 prefectural statistical yearbooks. Most of them comprised from two or three thousand to ten thousand residences (Yamaguchi [1956], [1957]). Surrounding these towns there were 70,443 *mura*, or village communities, in 1872. Each village comprised about

71

Figure II.1 The Tokugawa regime

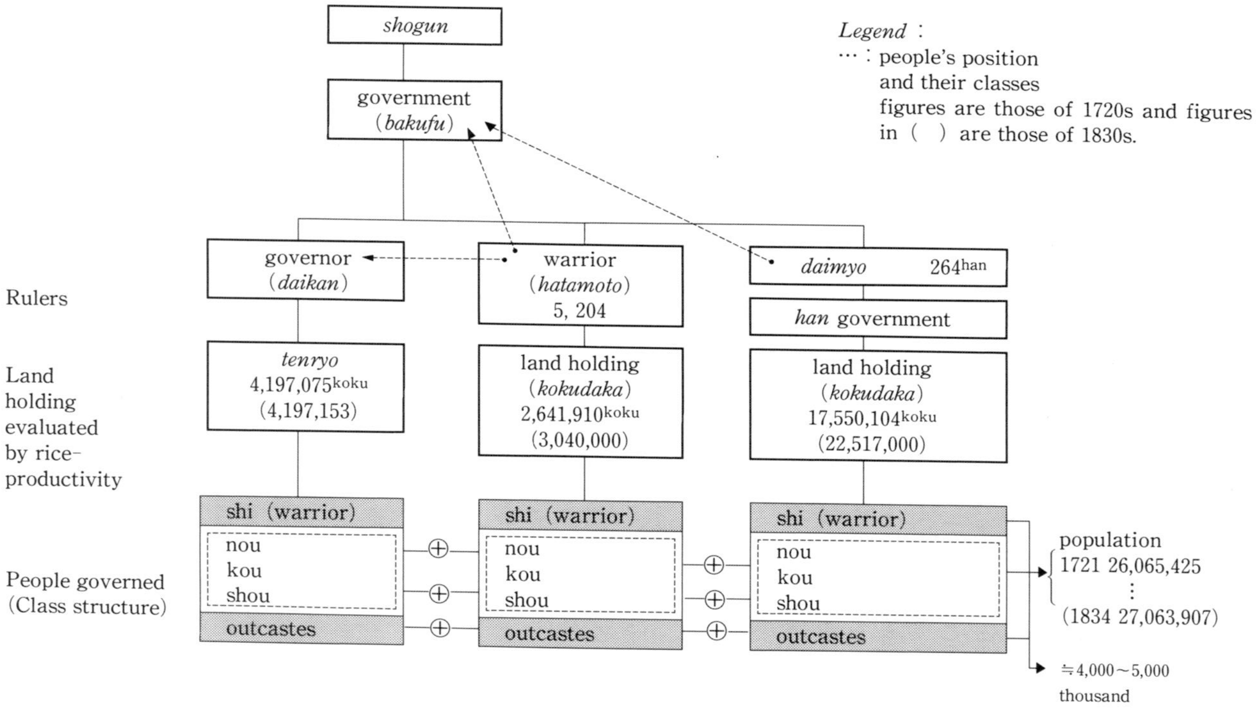

Legend :
... : people's position
and their classes
figures are those of 1720s and figures
in ( ) are those of 1830s.

shogun

government (*bakufu*)

governor (*daikan*)

warrior (*hatamoto*)
5, 204

daimyo   264han

han government

tenryo
4,197,075koku
(4,197,153)

land holding
(*kokudaka*)
2,641,910koku
(3,040,000)

land holding
(*kokudaka*)
17,550,104koku
(22,517,000)

shi (warrior)
nou
kou
shou
outcastes

shi (warrior)
nou
kou
shou
outcastes

shi (warrior)
nou
kou
shou
outcastes

population
1721 26,065,425
...
(1834 27,063,907)
≒4,000~5,000
thousand

Rulers

Land
holding
evaluated
by rice-
productivity

People governed
(Class structure)

72

Table II.1 Population Size of Traditional Castle Towns

(i) Number of Towns Classified by the Size of *Han*s
(1) Expressed by the Rice Products and by
Population of Size of Towns (2)

(2)

(1)	1. less<0.1	2. 0.2	3. 0.3	4. 0.5	5. 1.0	6. <over	total
less<2.0	10	22	22	17	17	4	92
2.1-3.0	1	2	9	17	7	3	39
13.1-5.0	1	2	2	10	13	7	35
5.1-10.0	—	—	2	4	16	23	45
10.1-15.0	—	—	—	—	3	11	14
15<over	—	—	—	—	—	23	23
Total*	12 (4.8)	26 (10.5)	35 (14.1)	48 (19.4)	56 (22.6)	71 (28.6)	248 (100.0)
Relative share to national total of towns	3.0	4.3	9.7	13.9	27.3	55.9	12.1

two hundred households. After the pioneering work by Yamaguchi, Chiharu Kurosaki reviewed the data concerning urban areas based on the various governmental surveys carried out after the Meiji Restoration such as *Nihon-chishi-teiyo*, *Kyobu-seihyo*, *Tofu-meiyu-kokou-hyo* and so on. He also analysed the distribution of cities and towns in 1873–86, describing the characteristics of the castle towns where the Tokugawa government's *tenryo* offices were located, or where the *hanshu*, the head of the *han*, lived. He concluded that many historians had quoted 1,647 towns as urban areas, but that this figure included many villages. The number of communities having more than one thousand inhabitants actually amounted to 2,054 and of these 677 had populations of more than five thousand. Thus, the town dwellers comprised

Table II.1 Contined

(ii) Change of Population
(2)

(3)	1.	2.	3.	4.	5.	6.	total
Increase	1	2	4	8	8	21	44
	(8.3)	(7.7)	(11.4)	(16.7)	(14.3)	(29.6)	(17.7)
Stagnant	4	14	24	29	31	36	138
	(33.3)	(53.8)	(68.6)	(60.4)	(55.4)	(50.7)	(55.6)
Decrease	7	10	7	11	17	14	66
	(58.3)	(38.5)	(20.0)	(22.9)	(30.4)	(19.7)	(26.6)

(Source) Kurosaki [1976]

(Notes) Column means as follows;

(1) Size of *han* (traditional state in Tokugawa regime) measured by rice products (ten thousand *koku*)

(2) Population size (ten thousand people)

(3) Category of population change based on the difference of registered people and resident people in 1844.

* Figure in parenthesis is percentage share.

approximately 27.2% of the total, in so far as towns were defined as areas with more than two hundred families. Purely rural communities comprised 51.8% and those engaged in commerce or manufacturing as well as farming or fishing comprised 22.1%. He analysed 248 castle towns with more than one thousand people. This was the biggest size group, but it comprised only 12.1% of all town dwellers. Numazu and Hara, which are referred to later, had about 6,316 people and 461 residences, which correspond to the group circled in Table II.1. The number of cities and towns must be much bigger and more widely dispersed over Japan than Kazuo Yamaguchi estimated.

To understand the economic conditions of Japan during the Tokugawa regime, we should consider the transportation system. As to the main road, "Tokaido" connecting Edo and Kyoto, the Tokugawa government prohibited construction of any bridges over the rivers for military purpose, just the opposite of what the Romans did. Main roads were not paved and so vehicles ridden or pulled by cattle did not develop. Thus, transportation largely depended on ships on rivers and across the sea surrounding the four main islands. It was forbidden, however, to construct big ships that could sail across the sea to China and South Asian countries such as the Philippines, Thailand, etc. where Japanese towns had flowered once, in the sixteenth and seventeenth centuries before Japan closed her ports to other countries. (Nagamasa Yamada in Thailand was assassinated in 1630.) The closed economic system kept the Tokugawa regime peaceful.

This situation continued through the period when the rest of the world was frantically occupied with construction of cross-continental rail roads and ocean-going steam ships. This is the other side of a coin of the peaceful Tokugawa days.

Officially people were classified by birth into four classes: *shi-nou-kou-shou* i.e., *shi-samurai* (warriors), *nou-noumin* (farmers), *kou* (artisans), and *shou-shounin* (merchants). In addition, there were two outcaste groups. One was a high outcaste group comprising Buddhist and Shinto priests, and the other was a socially lowest group comprising *etta* and *hinin*. As in the world of *Le Rouge et le Noir* by Stendhal, it was possible for a person to attain the position of noir, or priest, if he or she knew letters well, but it was extremely difficult in the long peaceful years. However, in practice the titles of the lower *samurai* class were sold to wealthy merchants or landowners. In addition, the Tokugawa government and many other local *han* employed technicians, engineers and cameralists as temporary *samurai* only for that person's life. One more item should be added about the role of the *samurai*. Their main roles had changed from warriors to bureaucrats, although they were in principle expected to behave as warriors.

The Tokugawa government conducted two important surveys to grasp the nationwide situation. These may constitute a kind of Tableau politique of eighteenth century Europe.

One was the periodic population survey, which started in the days of the Yoshimune *Shogun*. The first, in 1721, recorded about twenty-six million people and the last, the eighteenth, in 1846, counted twenty-seven million. (If the surveys had been done with exact periodicity, the last one should have been the twenty-fifth but it is not clear where it is now, Sekiyama [1958], Umemura [1976].) Thus, approximately five or six million nobles and samurai were excluded from this number, as well as *etta* and *hinin*.

Another is the land productivity assessment called *Kokudaka-shirabe*. Land productivity was expressed by rice production and other areas were converted to the rice production criterion evaluated mostly by market price. In the Kyoho period, 1716–36, the total amount of *kokudaka* was 24 million *koku* of rice. Of this amount, 4 million *koku* (16.67%) were owned by the Tokugawa government, 17.5 million *koku* (72.92%) were owned by the two hundred sixty-four *daimyo* and the rest, 2.5 million *koku* (10.42%), was occupied by small *daimyo* and *hatamoto* warriors who belonged directly to the *Shogun*.

This is a rough sketch of the Tokugawa regime expressed in figures. Many economic historians have struggled to get more information to construct historical statistics of this period. However, we rush to the figures which were obtained just after the Meiji Restoration, assuming that the figures in period 1) discussed above may be regarded as reflecting the structure of the last days of the Tokugawa regime.

1.2   Data Sources for Description of the Tokugawa Period's Last Days

We have three kinds of data sources for the period of formation of the Meiji government, which may reflect the last days of the Tokugawa regime. Firstly, *Hansei-ichiran*, Tableau politique des Hans, which was compiled based on the reports by the last *han-shu* in 1869–70, contains the *kokudaka*, the cultivated land assessed by rice production, taxes, local government running costs, population and the number of families. This was left unprinted for many years and then printed in 1928. Most of the original manuscripts contained the population and the composition of classes, but only thirty-four of them escaped from the fire following the great Kanto Earthquake of 1923. (Among those that escaped burning were records of 16 *han* analysed by Takao Tsuchiya in 1930, Tsuchiya [1930].) It should be noted that *Hansei-ichiran* does not cover the territory of the Tokugawa *Shogun* and the

Ten'no, as they were controlled by the Meiji government and called *fu-ken*.

Secondly, there was a group of surveys initiated by the Meiji government as format surveys. One was a nationwide register of people in 1872. This is assumed to be designed as a statistical survey, but changed into a register. The figures of the subsequent years based on this survey system were published as *Zenkoku-koseki-hyo*, Tableau de population et famille, which contained tables of people roughly classified by age and occupation. Another survey was a nationwide product survey executed in 1873–75, called *Fuken-bussan-hyo*, Tableau du prduit, and later *Fuken-nosan-hyo* because the survey items were shrunk into agricultural products only in 1876–82.

Thirdly, the big project for assessing land tax appeared in 1873, as a reassessment of the land tax act. Then came the execution of the act in 1876. The report of this project was later revived by James Nakamura in the controversy between him and Henry Rosovsky concerning the evaluation of agricultural products for estimating historical GNP by Kazushi Ohkawa and others.

1.3 What is Rural Society?

It is widely believed that Japan in the nineteenth century was an entirely agricultural society. Supporting evidence is that the majority of the population was thought to be farmers, i.e., of the *noumin* class. Tsuchiya estimated that almost eighty percent of the population were farmers.[1] However, the original word implying farmers was *nou*, or *noumin*, meaning people who lived in rural areas, and people called *kou* and *shou* were those who lived in towns, and they were called *machikata*, meaning town dwellers. Thus, *nou* includes both farmers and rural dwellers. In addition, the class classification was based on the occupation of the family, not of individual people. There is some possibility that artisans or merchants were included among farming families in rural areas. The concepts of rural and urban in classifying areas and occupations of the population defined in the *Hansei-ichiran* are therefore not clear.

Tsuchiya only described the class structure of sixteen *han* as 3.99–26.54% warriors, 52.42–89.55% farmers, and 2.55–23.40% town

Table II.2 Class Structure in the *Hansei-ichiran*, tableau politique des *Hans*, of the *Tokugawa Regime* in Fifteen *Hans* and in the New Register Table in 1872

	(i) *Hansei-ichiran*		(ii) New Register	
	Total	Share (%)	Total	Share (%)
Total population	2,813,581	100.00	33,108,438[2]	100.00
Nobles and warriors	102,939	3.66	1,284,833	3.88
Quasi-warriors	158,955	5.65	662,390	2.00
Farmers	2,260,853	80.35	30,837,271	93.14
Artisans & merchants	212,380[1]	7.55		
Shinto priests	13,518	0.48	102,477	0.31
Buddhist priests	20,071	0.71	221,467	0.67
Outcastes	38,726	1.38	—[3]	

(Note)

1) The estimated composition of artisans and merchants was 2.26% and 5.29% each.

2) Inhabitants in Sakhalin were 2,358 as a whole and not included in the total of (ii).

3) Outcastes were not separated in the New Register Table in 1872. The original *jinsin* register contained such information but the registers remained in the local government are not open to the public today even for scientific research.

(Source)

i) The *Hansei-ichiran* was printed in 1929. Original manuscripts were compiled based on the reports of the traditional *hans* reorganized as *ken* in Meiji Restoration excluding three cities, Tokyo (Edo), Kyoto and Osaka and other areas belonged to the Tokugawas. The figures were mainly about 1870-71. However, the printed version contained few *hans* who reported the detailed figures of the urban people, artisans and merchants. Takao Tsuchiya published the data of fifteen *hans* where such figures were obtainable such as Iwaki, Mino, Dewa, Hizen, Iyo, Nagoya, Echigo, Iyo (Uwajima), Higo, Chikuzen, Bungo, Ugo, Tango, Iyo (Matsuyama), and Ise. Tsuchiya was quite cautious to sum up these figures [1930] but we tried it as shown in this Table.

ii) We use manuscripts kept in the National Diet Library.

dwellers, or *chonin*, and did not show any aggregate estimates because *Hansei-ichiran* did not cover the *tenryo* area. However, we have dared to reclassify these fifteen records of *han* shown in Table II.2.[2] One reason for this reclassification is that Tsuchiya included *sotsu* (*ashigaru*) in the *samurai* class with *shi*, although they were excluded from the *samurai* class when the new registration system was created in 1871. Thus, the shares of the warrior class were remarkably decreased. This will illustrate the figures for registered people classified as *kazoku* (nobles), *shizoku* (warriors) and *heimin* (ordinary people), including *shin-heimin* (new ordinary people liberated from outcaste status). We reconsider the pilot census figures of Numazu and Hara surveyed by Sugi as representatives of *tenryo*. Needless to say, these *tenryo* were typical urban areas of the day. Numazu consisted of twenty-three towns (6,316 residences) and three villages (461 residences) and Hara of three towns (2,532 residences).

Although some ambiguity remained concerning the occupational statistics as to whether they indicated the number of households or the number of people, we interpreted the number of occupations without mentioning men or women as household heads. Those explicitly defined men or women were regarded as numbers of workers and we excluded those under fourteen years old and added maids and servants and some sons and daughters. Wives were not counted, but were included as residuals. The proportion of warrior class people was 9.3% including the lower classes *sotsu* and *ji-shi* (*go-shi*), and 3.6% excluding these classes. The proportion of outcasts was only 1.4% and that of priests was 1.1%. The majority, 80.4% were farmers and town people comprised about 7.5%. If the proportions of artisans and merchants of town people were the same in Nakamura *han* in the Iwaki area, artisans comprised 2.3% and merchants 5.3%.[3] Compared with the *kokou-tokei* shown below, people belonging to the lower warrior class seemed to be fewer than those in huge *han* like Satsuma and Choshu. The big *han* and smaller *han* had different occupational structures. The former might include many town people as well as other Tenryos, as shown in Numazu and Hara. We conclude that those people classified as town people included a very small proportion of farmers.

This was the situation just before the abolition of the *han* system in 1871, when a new seventy-three *fuken* system was initiated.

In 1872, the *Jinshin* citizens' registration system was executed and the data of the next year (1873) were released in the *Kokou-tokei* and *Zenkoku-kenbetsu-koseki-hyo* reports. The occupational composition is contained in these reports. The occupational figures were based on working people over fifteen years old and household heads without regarding their age. These groups formed 57.92% of the total population in 1873. The proportion of farmers was 79.2%, and 77.2% in 1873 and in 1874, respectively, that of artisans was 9.5% and 3.6%, and that of merchants was 6.6% and 6.7%. Tsuchiya included government officers, fishermen and workers in the transportation industry as miscellaneous. They constituted 9.1% in 1873 and 9.2% in 1874. The problem is the classification of nearly 80% of the people as farmers. When the warrior class was formed in the seventeenth century (originally the *samurai*, warrior, appeared and became powerful in the worrier's government in the twelfth century in the Kamakura era) and they were mostly farmers. After the abolition of the *han* system and the resulting dissolution of the warrior class as pension earners, many who chose to dwell in rural areas may thus be classified as farmers. Based on the fragmentary data of Aomori prefecture in 1882, formerly Nanbu and Tsugaru *han*, only 0.7% of farmers were of genuine *samurai* class, which might not include the lower *samurai* class called *sotsu* or *ashigaru*. The average percentage of the whole *samurai* class was 2.9%.[4] However, for the lower *samurai* class the story is different. It is said that they came mainly from rural areas. In addition, artisans in the rural area may be included as farmers. Without assuming this hypothesis we cannot explain the existence of the vast number of manufacturers in rural areas. This is revealed through the analysis of factory statistics.

Kazuo Yamaguchi compiled a data set for the occupational distribution of prefectural populations based on nineteen prefectural statistical yearbooks around 1880–82. Roughly speaking, 73.4% were farmers, 3.2% were artisans, 7.6% were merchants and 15.5% were miscellaneous. This still seems to exaggerate the percentage of farmers. The point of issue is that the population here defined implies the working population. Another data set which Yamaguchi compiled is the number of families (households) engaged as merchants. This constitutes about 19.7% of all families. This is more than that of an occupational share of the population. This difference may be attributed to the working

Table II.3 Occupational Structure in 1880–2

(i) Occupational Structure of the population

	Total population	Farmers	Artisans	Merchants	Miscellaneous
02: Aomori	286,827	206,445	4,842	15,830	59,710
03: Iwate	556,115	474,416	12,132	37,734	31,833
04: Miyagi	437,729	358,306	17,771	32,748	28,904
07: Fukushima	647,194	564,038	18,332	40,854	23,970
12: Chiba	718,270	596,925	18,024	45,381	57,940
13: Tokyo	463,986	91,704	60,280	85,375	226,627
18: Fukui	404,437	285,309	19,250	29,182	70,696
19: Yamanashi	264,703	219,017	10,299	14,003	21,384
24: Mie	560,095	429,848	21,924	36,722	71,601
28: Hyogo	868,562	660,811	22,649	56,729	128,373
32: Tottori	247,660	212,064	4,153	23,216	8,063
35: Yamaguchi	897,228	455,284	19,336	59,808	362,800
38: Ehime	1,025,287	733,378	23,886	65,920	202,103
39: Kochi	409,647	261,803	8,498	42,275	97,071
40: Fukuoka	653,451	425,231	35,337	70,711	122,172
42: Nagasaki	875,824	657,066	35,144	94,821	88,793
43: Kumamoto	699,616	578,381	17,855	56,751	46,629
44: Ohita	488,699	439,095	8,756	21,279	19,569
46: Kagoshima	685,756	567,546	9,233	30,288	78,689

(Note) The definition of the population by the occupation was not clear. The age to include to the working population was not explicitly mentioned and it was not certain whether the family members other than family's head were listed or not such as women workers. However, we reproduced what Yamaguchi gathered. Our inference is that the classification schemes used seems to have been much developed than those used in the *koseki-hyo* and the *shokubun-hyo* in 1872 after the *Kahi-no-kuni-ninbetsu-shirabe* in 1879. See Mitsuma [1983].

(Source) Yamaguchi [1956/1963] pp. 39–45. Original data were recorded in the prefectural statistical yearbooks he gathered.

Table II.3 Continued

(ii) Male Workers Ratio of Aomori Prefecture in 1882
Total population on Jan. 1st
in 1884 (estimated by SB)   490,600

Total working population in 1882		Total 286,827	*Shi-zoku* (former warriors) 8,195	*Hei-min* (ordinary people) 278,632
Farmers	total	206,445	1,537	204,908
	male	112,216	817	111,399
	female	94,229	720	93,509
Artisans	total	4,843	184	4,659
	male	4,810	178	4,632
	female	33	6	27
Merchants	total	15,836	706	15,124
	male	15,051	653	14,398
	female	779	53	726
Miscellaneous	total	25,243	295	24,948
	male	18,575	137	18,438
	female	6,668	158	6,510
Intellectuals	total	34,467	5,473	28,994
	male	29,670	4,235	25,435
	female	4,797	1,238	3,559

(Source) Total population estimated by the Statistics Bureau is quoted from the Japan Statistical Association (ed.) [1987] vol. 1. The composition of working population is in Yamaguchi [1963] pp. 50–2.

practice of women and the existence of sons or daughters living together before marriage. Male workers' ratios shown in Table II.3 above comprise 53.7% farmers, 62.5% merchants and 73.6% artisans. The low ratio of male to female farmers reflects the farming practices of the day; it implies that seasonal variations of farming work required the mobilization of every household member during peak times and work away from the fields during off-peak times. The high percentage of rural labourers in addition to tenants in highly productive areas like the Southern districts can be explained by the hypothesis shown above.

1.4 Family Structure

The class structure reflecting occupations in the Tokugawa period is the result of traditional ways of allocating manpower among industries. The adjustment of manpower allocation was quite slow, which naturally built slackening factors into the family structure. Merchant or artisan households in urban areas included many persons who had no kinship with the household members, but worked as clerks, maids or apprentices, or were children these workers, in addition to the household members. In most cases, they did not marry until they were allowed by the household head, the owner of the shop or factory, and continued to live in the shops or work yards. As a result, households tended to be bigger than present-day households, which are mainly nuclear families comprising husband, wife and children. The situation was similar in rural areas. However, households of farmers, except wealthy landowners, did not include non-family members, so there remained many unmarried uncles and/or aunts.

The situation did not significantly change after the abolition of the four classes in 1871, when intermarriage between classes and freedom of employment were realized. Economic factors restricting marriage had not completely disappeared in so far as productivity had not risen.

The average size of families or households in *Hansei-ichiran* was about 4.95. These figures are probably lower than the actual ones because of the exclusion of infants less than one year old and non-family members.

The statistics referred to results from the *Kaki-age-chosa* and so it is very difficult to interpret what these statistics mean. Before closing

Table II.4 Marital Ratio in the Experimental Regional Population Census

(i) Numazu (1869)

Age class	Male population	Male with spouse	Female population	(Age)	Female with spouse*
1–19	1,260	10	1,315	(14–20)	10
20–29	620	193	713	(17–37)	193
30–39	442	317	444	(21–49)	317
40–49	435	338	421	(22–60)	338
50–59	303	245	289	(21–61)	245
60–69	123	83	202	(33–76)	83
70–79	57	26	83	(54–76)	26
80–over	6	3	14	(51–79)	3
Total	3,296	1,215	3,481		1,215

(Note) The figures for the female with spouse (*) correspond to those of male. And the (Age) shows their age distribution. The number of female with spouse is not necessarily the contents of the female population classified by the Age class. The number of male with his spouse must be the same number with the female with spouse because of monogamous practice.

(Source) Tableau politique de Numazu et Hara based on the survey carried out by Koji Sugi in 1869.

this section we will again analyse some pilot censuses: those of Numazu and Hara in 1869 and Kahi-no-kuni in 1879.

The population structure is shown by the age structure of the population often shown in a population pyramid. Unfortunately the marriage ratio by age is only obtainable for males in Numazu and Hara's censuses. Marital ratio figures are summarized in Table II.4.

It is quite striking that only about sixty percent of males over eighteen years old had married. This implies that in urban areas it was still difficult to get married without having a high enough earning capacity. We have data from the pilot census at Kahi a decade later, which tells that the ratio there was about seventy-two percent. Unfortunately we cannot segregate Kofu from the urban area in Kahi-no-kuni. At that time, life expectancy was short and the mortality rate of infants was

Table II.4 Continued

(ii) Hara (1869)

Age class	Male population	Male with spouse	Female population	(Age)	Female with spouse
1–19	542	1	556	(17)	1
20–29	238	79	217	(15–29)	79
30–39	142	96	139	(17–40)	96
40–49	177	134	155	(29–57)	134
50–59	104	71	102	(33–61)	71
60–69	59	33	63	(49–69)	33
70–79	19	8	23	(55–82)	8
80–over	2	1	4	(67)	1
Total	1,273	423	1,259		423

Table II.4 Continued

(iii) Summary of Numazu, Hara (1869) and Kahi (1879)
Marital ratio

Age class	1869 Numazu Male	Numazu Female	Hara Male	Hara Female	1879 Kahi Male	Kahi Female
20–65					73.19	72.80
15–65					63.86	65.15
20 over	59.18	56.09*	57.72	60.11*	72.03	67.64
15 over					63.45	61.31

(Note) Those with * may include those who were under 20 because the age composition of female spouse was not clear.

(Source) Figures for Kahi-no-kuni were based on the survey carried in the Yamanashi Prefecture of today in 1879. (*Kahi-no-kuni-ninbetsu-shirabe*)

Table II.4 Continued

(iv) Summary of various regional censuses around 1900 and national
census in 1920

Region		Around 1900 Marital ratio	1920
Name	Type	Male	
Sapporo	city	36.77	
Tokyo	city	36.68	
Sado	county	44.32	
Kobe	city	41.23	
Tokushima	county	41.54	
Kumamoto	city	35.52	
National			73.91
Urban			64.98
Rural			76.69

high, and these facts were clearly reflected in the population pyramids. The marriage rate of males was affected by both factors. The first increased the ratio because of the low probability of survival of the spouse and the second factor decreased the ratio. To compare these figures with those of later periods, we show various marriage ratios which may be affected by the various factors mentioned above.

The point of issue is whether rural households were large enough to accommodate adult members who had no chance to marry. If there were enough such members, there must have been a surplus labour force to be employed by manufacturers in rural areas.

1.5 Level of Production at the end of the Tokugawa Period

The level of economic production at the dawn of the Tokugawa regime is the most controversial topic among quantitative historians. The *kokudaka-shirabe* data contained in the *Hansei-ichiran* are not very reliable.

The first statistics for whole products were reported in *Fuken-bussan-hyo*, Table of Products of *Fuken*, by the Ministry of the Interior in 1875.

This *Fuken-bussan-hyo* was based on the *hyoshiki-chosa* survey method, but it is very difficult to regard it as a well prepared *Hyoshiki-chosa*. It must be regarded as a sort of *kaki-age-chosa*, a mere compilation of excerpts from various documents in dossiers, except that it was intended to cover all regional prefectures.

Thus, the controversy was concentrated on the reliability of the *Fuken-bussan-hyo* of 1873–75. Reliability was the focus of disputes among government statisticians at that time. The minutes of the discussions at the *seihyo-ka*, section for the Tableau politique headed by Koji Sugi, recorded various appraisals doubting the credibility of the reports of the prefectural governments. The survey was eventually reduced to include only agricultural products in 1876. This continued until 1881 (six years of data), and the *Noshomu-tsushin-kisoku* started in 1883 (the results of this survey were as to 1884). Historians who were interested in the development of statistical institutions had been quite skeptical over the use of the *Fuken-bussan-hyo*. However, economics historians were inclined to trust these figures because the formats survey had some advantages over the writing-up system, whose semantics of the tabulation terms was not well-defined and the coverage of the survey was in most cases vaguely shown. In fact, the *Bussan-hyo* survey was a seminal stage of the format survey and the existence of leakage and insufficient unification of the semantics of terms is undeniable, but the coverage of the survey was national and far more refined than the *Hansei-ichiran*. One well-known example of Sugi's arguments which has often been quoted by skeptical statisticians is that Sugi cynically talked about a nonsense report of Tokyo *fu* concerning the production of *suzumushi*, the bell-ringing insect or homoeogryllus japonicus. However, his reasoning was quite strange for a person who had lived many years in Edo where town people enjoyed *suzumushi* singing in cages in summer. It enjoyed a boom, just like the planting of *asagao* (morning glory). It may be comparable with the tulip speculation of tulipomania in the Netherlands in 1634.

Kazuo Yamaguchi's pioneering work on 1874 data indicated the

Table II.5 Value of Commodity Items in 1874

Commodity items	Product value in million yen	Percentage share among total products
Rice, wheat and cereals	183.9	49.6
Vegetables	12.0	3.3
Farming work materials	30.8	8.3
Cattle and games	7.4	2.0
Forest products	12.1	3.3
Marine products	6.9*	1.9
Fertilizer and cattle feeds	4.2	1.1
Primary industry products	257.3	69.5
Food products incl. beverage	44.5	12.0
Farm products incl. silk, etc.	44.1	11.9
Wood products	4.7	1.3
China and Japan	3.0	0.8
Miscellaneous handicrafts	6.9	1.9
Machinery and vessels	4.8	1.3
Other manufacturing goods	0.7	0.2
Mining and metal processing	4.1	1.1
Manufacturing and mining	113.5**	30.5
Total products	370.8	100.0

(Source) Furushima [1963] p. 20 and then revised in Furushima [1966] p. 74. The basic data are those found in *Fuken-bussan-hyō* of 1874 and were reclassified by Toshio Furushima.

(Note) * *Fuken bussan-hyō* did not contain the products of Hokkaido. Pressed dried herring used as fertilizer amounts to 1.5 million yen in 1874. ** Similar reclassification was done by Yamaguchi (1956), although Furushima excluded the items which were not shown in value terms.

regional differences in commercialization (Yamaguchi [1956], [1963]). Estimating manufacturing products in LTES, Miyohei Shinohara used the values and quantities of 1874 as a starting point for his estimates. He appreciated that, from an international standpoint, the coverage of the survey was extraordinarily extensive.

Then came the work of Toshio Furushima in reviewing the reliability of each product itemwise, and regionally, based mainly on the 1874 data on which Yamaguchi's work was based. This was because of the higher coverage of prefectures than the 1873 data, i.e. the three *fu* and fifty-eight prefectures defined at that time (Furushima [1963]). His conclusion was that the results of introducing Western production techniques and their products were negligible except in production of brick, steam boats and *jinrikisha*, and other small machines. Thus, as a whole the 1873 data reflected the level of production in the last days of the Tokugawa regime (Furushima [1963] pp. 141–43). The composition of products according to his reclassification is shown in Table II.5. Manufactured products, including mining products, amounted to 30.5%, and of this amount food and beverage products belonged to side work in rural areas. Therefore, they must constitute farmers' products and not those of artisans who comprised only 3.7% of all working people (Furushima [1963] pp. 20–27).

A more striking feature of this period is the marked contrast with the regional distribution of manufactured products. We note that the coast along the Japan Sea and on both sides of the Seto Inland Sea were the most flourishing regions, and in addition Kyoto was one of the five most successful manufacturing prefectures along with Osaka, Hyogo, Tokyo and Tochigi.

Furthermore, the populations of these three most productive prefectures were Tokyo 595,905, Osaka 271,992 and Kyoto 238,663. They were mainly supported by the traditional artisan crafts including spinning and weaving. Thus, cotton spinning and weaving should not have been undervalued as a manufacturing industry of the day.

Furushima's supposition of the continuity and equivalence of the production level in *Fuken-bussan-hyo* to that of the Tokugawa regime received strong support from the inspiring work by Shunsaku Nishikawa and Yuya Kimoto, who compared the figures of *Bussan-hyo* of 1874 with comprehensive production figures obtained from *Bocho-hudo-*

Table II.6 Level of Production per capita at Yamaguchi Prefecture 1840–74

		around 1840	1874
(1) Total population		523	840
(2) Products (current price)		100	12,030
(3) Products (1874 price)	(a)	8,500	
			12,000
	(b)	11,050	
(4) Per capita	(a)	16.25	
[=(3)/(1), yen]			14.32
	(b)	21.13	

(Source) Nishikawa [1979]
(Notes) Products evaluated by 1874 price have two variants; (a) based on
   rice-price and (b) adjusted by general price index to rice price in Osaka.

chushin-an in 1842, the Tableau politique of Suhou and Nagato-no-
kuni where Yamaguchi prefecture is currently located (Nishikawa (with
Kimoto) [1979]).[5] They revised both *Bocho-hudo-chusin-an* data and
Fuken-bussan-hyo data by reviewing products itemwise. Their results
are summarized in Table II.6. They show stagnancy or a slight decline
due to the turmoil of the Meiji Restoration. Yamaguchi was the base
of the Choshu clans, who consistently fought against the Tokugawa
government.

Our first concern is how and when this regional distribution
changed. There were at least two strong forces which might have
brought out the regional structural changes of manufacturing from the
late Tokugawa period. One was the impact of foreign trade, which was
formerly restricted to Holland and China. The other was the introduction of the factory production system.

Then the problem became the effects of the rise of the factory system newly introduced after the doors were opened to the Western countries, which was further developed after the Meiji Restoration.

Notes:
1) His reasoning depends on the sixteen *han* data in *Hansei-ichiran*

where farmers were separated from artisans and traders. Farmers amounted to about 80.3% of the population and the percentage of the registered people in 1873 was about 79.21%.

2) *Hansei-ichiran* contained the reports of 281 *han* except the Tenryo area covering the years of 1869–70. As we have mentioned in the text, the subdivision of the population was in most cases *samurai, sotsu,* Shinto and Buddhist priests and others, computable as residuals of the total population. The population seems to be defined as those people more than one year old. Only those *han* Tsuchiya had quoted contained subdivisions of others. Compared with the population figures in 1872 based on the registration data, the population of the amounts to 8.5% of the 1872 figures excluding Sakhalin.

3) Although Nakamura *han* was a smaller one whose total population was 63,629, the subdivision of the town dwellers was clearly mentioned.

4) Since 1873 and then 1875, the lower *samurai* classes were designated as ordinary people. Finally, the class status was reduced into *kazoku,* the nobles; *shizoku,* the warriors; and *heimin,* the ordinary people.

5) *Bocho-hudo-chushin-an* was compiled to cover the area called Choshu where the anti-Tokugawa clans ruled. In 1831, after peasants riots, the Choshu clans began to reform their government system and the policies under Seifu Murata, the chancellor. He submitted a proposal to the head of the clans which was accepted in 1837 and the reform was continued to the 1840s. This tableau politique was a by-product of this reforming process. The fund cumulated through this reform became a source of troops and wars between the Choshu and the Tokugawas in 1864 and 1865.

2. FORMATION OF FACTORY PRODUCTION AND COMPANY SYSTEM

2.1 Formation of Factory Production

2.1.1 Factory Production System

The factory production system was one of the most serious concerns of the Meiji government because it was recognized as a synonym of Western technology at the stage of the *Shokusan-kogyo* Movement. The Meiji government tried to build various kinds of factories, such as iron smelters, shipyards etc; based on the models of the Tokugawa government and various *han*. However, they did not fully understand the difference between traditional workshops and factories. A Traditional workshop is like a handicraft work place in English, l'atlier in French, and Manufakture in German.

When the government gathered statistics on factories in the form of lists of factories in the 1880s, the operational concept for the survey was not well-established (Furushima [1963], Yamaguchi [1956], [1963], Aihara & Samejima [1971], Matsuda [1978], [1981], [1983], Odaka [1995]). The concept of a factory commonly used in the 1880s was a production facility i) using any motive power other than manual labour, such as water, wind, steam or electricity, ii) having a common work yard and iii) employing workers who shared instruments or machinery installed in the work place. Although the conditions of i) are clear, there were many factories which did not use any power machine but shared conditions ii) and iii).

2.1.2 Factory Statistics: Technical digression

There are various statistical figures concerning the number of factories based on the official statistics and those estimated by many scholars.

Here we will explain briefly each series of figures. The points of issue are the definitions and coverage of the factories. Even if we ignore the differences of definitions of factories, there are many series which have different coverages. There were three kinds of series gathered by different statistical authorities and two kinds of estimates. One comprised the estimate obtained by aggregating the individual records and the other comprised the estimate based on the summary figure. One of the series most used by historians is obtained from the Annual Report of the Ministry of Agriculture and Trade (*Noshomu-sho-tokei-hyo*), a handy and unique source of industrial statistics of the day. This series covers factories reported by provincial authorities acceding to the *Noshomu-tsushin-kisoku* for 1884–91, and includes those employing more than ten employees for 1892–1908. It should be noted that the figures for 1884–91, and for 1892–93 were entirely different from those after 1894, for the former covers only those factories operating on more than one thousand yen capital and employing more than 10 employees. (This will be discussed in more detail in later sections.) Then comes a series, which comprises the revised figures of the former published in an independent report in 1899–1904. Of these figures, those of 1996 will be discussed as one of bench mark years. A series of manufacturing censuses had been created in 1909, which covers factories employing more than five employees and was to be carried out five-yearly until 1919, and was then changed to be surveyed every year after 1920. It should be noted that the figures of 1921 cover factories employing less than five employees, but with a power machine. Since 1939, the census was extended to cover every factory regardless of its size and number of employees.

There is another series also favoured by many historians, because it was published in the official statistical year book published by the Prime Minster's Office, whose names were often changed. The definitions of a factory and items surveyed are somewhat different from series of the Ministry of Agriculture and Trade. The basic difference is that they did not contain the number of employees, but the total number of man days of each employee.

There is another kind of series based on a source which did not receive researchers' attention and is regarded as a rather newly found one due to its uniqueness of surveying authority, Ministries of Military Affairs of both army and navy. The reports, *Chohatsu-bukken-shirabe*, may be regarded as a military secret even though many years have passed since their publication, so it was difficult for normal researchers to use them. Then came the days of military documents, when it was prohibited to use them by the occupying army after the end of

World War II. The revival of this series occurred after the 1970s. The definition of a factory is not clearly stated in the survey format, but it is clear that there was no distinction about whether it had power or any special equipment or machinery, or a certain number of employees. It was simply required to consider the building's size. Thus, it must cover manufacturing establishments in the broadest sense compared with other series of figures. We regard this series as comprising census type data without curtailing the smaller factories.

Many economics historians have tried to estimate a reliable series of factories. Their attention first focussed on 1880–1910. The most elaborate and notable estimates were those of Kazuo Yamaguchi and Rokuro Terashima (Yamaguchi and Terashima [1956], and then Yamaguchi [1956]). Their basic idea was that the most basic source reports must be comprised in correspondence from the provincial authorities, and so statistical yearbooks of each prefecture had to be the most reliable reports. Therefore, they collected such yearbooks and recompiled the statistical tables based on the lists of factories in the yearbooks. A similar trial was carried out by Toshio Furushima, whose figures are based on the lists of factories in the Statistical Yearbook of the Bureau of Statistics shown . Their methods were summed up as an aggregation of each individual record of factories. This is a seminal method of ours discussed in Part III, except that they used manual labour due to the limitation of computational facilities of their time. As latecomers, we had the good fortune to be able to use database techniques.

Another group of estimates relies on the summary reports of various statistical agencies and corrects differences in coverage by extrapolation and so on.

Examples are (i) Yamanaka and Odahashi for 1930; (ii) Mataji Umemura and Keiko Akasaka (Akasaka [1988], Shinohara [1972]) for 1896–1920, 1919–42; and Koichi Emi and Hiromitsu Ishi (see Emi [1971]) for 1892–1920.

The former (i) wanted to combine population census figures which were to cover every person working in manufacturing industries without limitation of size of establishments and figures obtained from manufacturing censuses. This was to cover only those establishments employing more than five employees.

The latter trials (ii) were to get a yearly figure for LTES and so they extrapolate the smaller size establishments by various methods. Akasaka used the series of Osaka Province as a correction coefficient for 1926–38 using the comprehensive data of 1939–40. If she adopted Tokutaro Yamanaka and Teijyu Odahashi's method (they applied the method to the 1920 and 1930 census data; see Yamanaka [1933] [1941] [1944]) for 1920, 1930 and 1940, the correction might be more satisfactory. Emi and Ishi assumed that the factories would not decrease in size in a growing economy in a historical perspective, so those years showing a decrease in the number figures were expanded by linear extrapolation. Their reasoning was that for the figures 1892–1900 government authorities said that they could not be sure whether the decrease in number was true or false due to the inaccuracy of the survey procedures (editorial notes for the Annual Statistical Reports of the Ministry of Agriculture and Trade). Their estimation procedures are only supportable in a limited sense and some of the procedures cannot be supported at all. The differences of opinion comes from understanding the survey procedures in the period when the statistical survey system was formed.

The merits of their estimates lie in their conjecture concerning the production of military goods during World War II, because the majority of military goods were contained in a different brochure which was not released to the public. The production of aircraft was not included even in this separate brochure, because it was top secret. Shinohara and Umemura estimated this production in 1930–44.

The controversy concerning the figures' reliability stemmed mainly from the interpretation of the survey system of the Meiji period. Our main concern is about some structural changes reflected in the statistical survey system and not about the yearly changes, so we checked only bench mark years. We will refer on these controversial points only when necessary. The primary method we rely on is to reconstruct the factorywise records using the same research methods as Furushima, Yamaguchi and Terashima. The only difference is our dependence on a computer based database system as we have mentioned before, and so our coverage is expanded as far as our longitudinal data base permits. As to the years before 1902, we made some speculations on the validity of the estimates and summary figures.

It should be noted that the trend of growth of factories is not as striking as was commonly believed. The lines showing the growth of factories suggested by econometric historians today look somewhat as if they exaggerate the actual economic trend. Our discussions rely on the data sets of three periods: a) formation of factory production system from 1884–95, basically shown in estimates from Yamaguchi and Terashima and Furushima, b) expansion of manufacturing after the Sino-Japanese War (1894–95) in 1896–1900 represented in the independent reports of manufacturing survey and c) industrialisation before and after the Russo-Japanese War (1904–05) in 1902–21. The source of data of the last period is our own database shown in Part III.

2.1.3 Factories in the 1880s and 1890s

For the early Meiji period we have only three years of factory production data sets based on different sources. One group is 1882 and 1885, both compiled by Furushima, and the other is 1884 (strictly speaking, based mainly on 1884 but also 1881–87 data) compiled by Yamaguchi and Terashima. The definition of the factory was not clearly stated in the original data sources for the years 1882 and 1884. Furushima prudently stated that the workshops included in the data of the Statistical Yearbook for the figures of 1882 must have excluded those wholesale traders who organized a putting out system which was included in the case of *Meiji-18-nen-kogyo-gaikyo*, general statements of manufacturing in the year 1885, by the factorywise comparison with that of 1885 and those work places where more than two employees were engaged in the production were included, excluding those which were operated by household members outside the peak agrarian or commercial working periods (Furushima [1963], pp. 242–43). He assumed that the definitions of figures were comparable to those of Yamaguchi, although there were 2,033 factories, fifty-two more than Yamaguchi's estimate. (If we exclude mining from Furushima's estimates, the discrepancy is slightly less.) His interpretation of the factories in Yamaguchi's data is that of the 1,981 workshops, half of which had less than ten employees and half of which were without any power, so they should be read as only manufacturers not as modern factories (Furushima [1963] pp. 338–90). However, Yamaguchi made more modest reservations as to the degree of modernization of the work place. He defined a factory as simply a work place where only wage earners worked and had no further implication (Yamaguchi [1963], revised edition of 1956, p. 105).

Another point to be mentioned is the definition of employee. The source of Furushima's estimates of 1882 is the Statistical Yearbook where the total number of employees of each industrial subdivision is included with the number factories. However, the original source of Yamaguchi's estimates is the provincial statistical yearbooks, in which the number of employees was in most cases expressed by the total number of man days worked in a year. Where the number of employees was included, it was converted into man days assuming that each worked 300 days a year (Yamaguchi [1963] pp. 116–17). Samejima once criticized the validity of expressing the number of employees as the total number of man days. Umemura supported this practice due to the wage system by man days resulting in accounts of a total wage bill being expressed as wage rate multiplied by man days. Hiroshi Ohashi once severely criticized Yamaguchi's conjecture as having no empirical background and showed some examples of silk spinning industrial factories whose working days numbered less than 50 because there were two work seasons that occurred during non-busy farming periods (Ohashi [1963] and then in his collected works [1982]). However, the distribution of working days through the year varied among industrial subdivisions. Later in 1900 we got the average number of working days for each industrial subdivision of factories employing more than ten people.

One hundred and six days of tea processing, 157 of sake brewing and 186 of silk spinning mean that they were outside the agrarian calendar, but we cannot explain the 184 of bronze processing by the agrarian calendar. Most other industries' factories operated 280–320 days a year. This seems to correspond to Yamaguchi's conversion coefficient. The procedures for getting an average for the 1900 data were not clearly stated in the report. The industrial classification was expressed by a three-stage tree structure, and the average of the upper level of classification subdivision is just the simple mean of the sum of working days of each lower industrial subdivision divided by the number of lower subdivisions. They did not employ any weighted mean. The procedures for getting the mean of the smallest subdivision were not mentioned at all. However, judging from the above procedures for getting mean values of each industrial subdivision, they simply added each factory's working days and divided it by the number of factories concerned.

If we get a weighted mean of the total manufacturing industry including mining with the total number of employees including apprentices and unskilled workers of each industrial subdivision as a weight, the working days reduce to 267.04, because of the thirty percent weight of the silk spinning industry which operated only 186 days a year and food processing industries which operated 245.90 days a year. Considering the higher percentage of workers in the silk spinning industry in 1884, this strongly supports Ohashi's argument.

Due to the existence of industries with fewer operational days in a year and having a huge number of employees, the weighted average of the total man days in each broader industrial classification is smaller than the simple average shown in the reports. If we calculate the non-weighted average for the entire manufacturing industry as did the report adopted for the broader industrial classification, there are only 296.16 operational days against the 267.04 days of the weighted average. Only the weighted average in four broad industrial classifications showed nearly three hundred days against two industries of less than two hundred and fifty days. If we use the 1900 data for the number of operational days, the conversion of man days figures to the number of employees will shrink to 267 instead of 300 as Yamaguchi and Terashima estimated.

Yamaguchi classified the factories by their location as urban or rural. These definitions were not clearly stated, but he restricted rural areas strictly to rural villages (Table II.7) (Yamaguchi [1963] p. 111).

Basic fact findings stated by Yamaguchi are that 1) there is a vast number of small factories which were difficult to distinguish from mere workshops of artisans, without cooperative systems of parts making in line of working and power machines, 2) such factories for silk and cotton weaving were mainly located in rural areas, although those for manufacturing and dying textiles were located in urban areas. In addition, those for food processing, ceramics, and metals were mainly in rural areas, and those for chemicals, machinery and miscellaneous others were in urban areas. Furthermore, Furushima added other findings, 3) among the urban industries defined by Yamaguchi, including those

Table II.7 Distribution of Factories among Rural and Urban Areas

Industry	Number of factories	Percentage of factories in city and town	Percentage of factories in village
Textile industry			
Silk spinning	961	13.4	86.6
Cotton spinning	18	27.8	72.2
Silken textile	21	85.7	14.3
Cotton textile	30	96.7	3.3
Other	52	76.9	23.1
Food processing			
Rice processing	132	28.8	71.2
Flouring	29	3.4	96.6
Ceramic industry			
China	72	11.1	88.9
Roofing tiles	93	—	100.0
Chemical industry			
Matches	26	76.9	23.1
Paper	21	61.9	38.1
Metal processing			
Metal refining	98	2.0	98.0
Foundry	44	29.5	70.0
Machinery			
Ship building	14	57.1	42.9
Machinery	38	81.6	18.4
Total	1,649	23.0	77.0

(Note)

1. The prefectures covered were totally 43 and the dates of data varied from 1881 to 1887 when data for 1884 were not obtainable due to the lack of prefectural statistical yearbooks.

2. The total factories listed in the prefectural statistical yearbooks were 1,981 but 332 factories whose location would be difficult to classify are excluded.

(Source) Yamaguchi [1956] pp. 93–95. The basic data are gathered from the *Fuken-tōkei-sho* by Kazuo Yamaguchi and Rokurō Terashima.

Table II.8 The Basic Features of the Factories in 1882–92

Year	Coverage	Total	More than 10 employee	Without power	With power	(With water-mills)
1882	all	2,033		1,949	84	
1885	43 prefectures	1,981	1,009	875	1,106	937
1886	all	1,068	932	527	410	n.a.
1892	44 prefectures	2,971	2,163	1,135	1,836	413

(Notes)

1) Coverage of 1882 was restricted to private factories and based on the statistical yearbook, 4th issue. The tabulation was done by Toshio Furushima [1963] pp. 244–45.

2) Coverage of 1885 base (i.e. 1881–87) and 1892 base (i.e. 1889–94) shows number of prefectures where the prefectural statistical yearbooks were published and had remained. Yamaguchi and Terashima tabulated statistics based on the list of factories contained in them. Yamaguchi [1963].

3) Coverage of 1886 was national because of using the data listed in the Statistical Report of Agriculture and Trade, 3rd issue. The tabulation was done by Toshio Furushima.Furushima [1963] pp. 335–39.

4) Yamaguchi's estimation of the employee size of both 1882 and 1892 was based on the hypothesis that the number of employee was total number of days of workers in a year divided by 300 operation days in a year.

producing various goods by traditional industrial techniques, still occupied a large percentage of factories in urban areas but had less than ten employees, and 4) at the same time, various goods which were known as modern Western technological goods found a new market for themselves. 5) Another finding obtained from the Yamaguchi data is that the quite dominant percentage of company owned factories increased rapidly.

Although more than fifteen years had passed since the Meiji Restoration, these findings imply that 1) the heritage of the Tokugawa regime in the manufacturing industries, both rural and urban, cannot be undervalued and 2) the exodus of the labour force from rural areas to urban areas should not be confused with the shift of the labour force from the agricultural sector to the industrial sector, because even rural areas contained a big labour force engaged in manufacturing at the beginning of the Meiji period.

The next point is the increased industrialization due to the modernization since the Meiji Restoration. Of the 2,033 factories in 1882 and/or 1,981 in 1885, only 937 had more than ten employees in 1886 as shown in Table II.8. Furushima remarked that even more than half of those factories having more than ten employees used no power except manual labour. Thus it is difficult to distinguish them from mere manufacturers (Furushima [1963] p. 335–39).

The data sets we have discussed do not include government factories, although they are assumed to include those established by prefectural government, or annexed to government educational institutions. Government factories were established in three ways. The first stemmed from those established by the Tokugawa government and *han*, and included the shipyards at Nagasaki, mining by Saga-*han* and so on. The second were newly installed by the Meiji government, in particular *kaitakushi*, the Hokkaido colonization agency, and others. The third were related to railroad construction. Of these, the printing office, coinage, and the manufacture of military goods were kept under the control of the government, but other factories related to consumer goods and mining were later sold to private people. The act for selling government factories to the private sector was proclaimed in November, 1880. However, it had not yet been realized in 1882, so the figures for government factories and mining indicate the situation at the start point of manufacturing.

The second groups of governmental factories were established by overall industrial encouragement policies based on the introduction of Western technology, inviting foreign engineers and technicians to establish technical schools and research laboratories. This policy was applied not only to manufacturing and mining but also to almost every industry, including agriculture. However, the most striking feature was that it covered light industries like cotton and silk spinning and weaving in order to protect domestic industries and markets where no tariff pro-

Table II.9 Factories owned by the Private Sector in 1882 and those owned by the Government Sector in 1882–83

Industry	Private Sector			Government Sector		
	Number of factories	Number of workers	Value of products (thousand yen)	Number of factories	Number of workers	Value of products (thousand yen)
Textiles	1285	45601	6785	5	827	391
Food and beverage	24	229	78	—	—	—
Ceramics and chemicals	392	6598	1487	7	1399	1561
Machinery	156	3280	820	9	7915	2587
Mining and metal processing	62	2941	991	1	1108	3492
Mis-cellaneous	114	2401	1355	9	9873	1782
Total	2035	61050	11516	31	21122	9816

(Notes) Factories in private sector include those established by villages. Government sector data consist of the figures of 1882. The mining work yards in the Government sector amount to 103 in 9 mines.

(Sources) Toshio Furushima [1963] pp. 240–41 and pp. 250–51. Toshio Furushima [1966] pp. 160–61.

tection existed under the treaties enforced by the gun-boat diplomacy of the Western powers. Most of these modernized governmental factories failed in management and were eventually sold to private industry, but this does not deny the role of government factories in introducing Western technology. (There have been various discussions on these topics; see Hayashi [1986])

Table II.9 shows the situation before government factories were sold to private industry. These factories were established with immense investments in construction and with the help of engineers from Europe and America. If we combine these government factories with private factories around 1882–83, about 61,050 workers were in private sector manufacturing, about 11,730 were in factories and 14,154 were in public sector mining, making a total of 86,934 workers in factory system manufacturing.

The government factories were roughly classified into three groups: 1) light industries such as weaving and production of textiles such as cotton and silk for consumer goods, such as the Tomioka silk weaving factory in Nagano, 2) mining, iron and steel making, and armaments production, and 3) industries producing goods necessary for running the government, like coinage and printing of paper currency.

2.1.4 Factory Production before the Sino-Japanese War

Yamaguchi and Terashima analysed the 1892 data using the same technique as in 1884. Strictly speaking, they used the 1889–94 data to supplement the lack of prefectural statistical yearbooks for 1892. The number of factories had increased by about fifty percent during these eight years. This increase occurred mainly in urban areas. It was found in light industries such as silk spinning and textile industries, rice processing and sake brewing (which had not been included separately in the 1884 data set) earthenware and ceramics. However, we found much more in heavy industries such as machinery and metal processing including ship building where far more employees was engaged.

This implies that building up heavy industries by government investment in the early half of the 1880s must have extended to the private sector by 1892. We will quote one example of the ship building industry. Although the Japanese government had tried to build up naval shipyards in the Tokugawa naval shipyard, they also promoted private ship building. After the Opium Wars, China tried to modernize her army, and especially to build up a strong navy (Rawlinson [1967]). She bought two fully armoured battleships, the Chen Yuan and the Ting Yuan, armed with four 12–inch and two 6-inch Krupp guns on ships of 7,430 tons built in the Vulcan Works at Stettin, Germany. Against this power, the Japanese navy tried to build an equivalent battleship. However, budget constraints of the day did not allow them to build such a big ship and so they asked Emile Bertin

Table II.10 Number of Manufacturing Establishments and Factories

| Prefecture | Chohatsu-bukken-shirabe | | | Kojyo-tokei-hyo |
	1890	1892	1896 a	1896 b
Total	8,325	9,566	13,336	6,455
1 Hokkaido	40	104	214	90
2 Aomori	12	13	20	28*
3 Iwate	88	91	116	73
4 Miyagi	99	107	105	45
5 Akita	87	94	125	41
6 Yamagata	109	128	97	135*
7 Fukushima	166	208	218	100
8 Ibaragi	87	151	253	78
9 Tochigi	38	44	102	64
10 Gumma	59	73	124	105
11 Saitama	74	90	46	29
12 Chiba	474	639	629	77
13 Tokyo	607	657	1,211	321
14 Kanagawa	83	195	250	116
15 Niigata	125	182	266	164
16 Toyama	143	181	244	157
17 Ishikawa	149	120	293	108
18 Fukui	33	47	63	145
19 Yamanashi	317	298	280	201
20 Nagano	801	900	1,111	803
21 Gifu	219	313	452	228
22 Shizuoka	185	237	282	107
23 Aichi	556	659	1,024	584
24 Mie	430	430	482	146
25 Shiga	46	73	198	54
26 Kyoto	258	79	327	339*
27 Osaka	631	666	912	656
28 Hyogo	241	288	704	672
29 Nara	8	10	104	20
30 Wakayama	106	104	173	90
31 Tottori	91	156	123	86

Table II.10 Continued

| Prefecture | Chohatsu-bukken-shirabe | | | Kojyo-tokei-hyo |
	1890	1892	1896 a	1896 b
32 Shimane	109	144	182	139
33 Okayama	312	426	809	325
34 Hiroshima	99	105	251	99
35 Yamaguchi	777	731	323	60
36 Tokushima	223	256	275	75
37 Kagawa	38	51	68	101*
38 Ehime	89	115	152	116
39 Kochi	24	49	53	10
40 Fukuoka	33	31	115	276*
41 Saga	39	37	49	45
42 Nagasaki	82	86	139	83
43 Kumamoto	1	32	52	46
44 Ohita	42	51	47	81*
45 Miyazaki	10	13	27	18
46 Kagoshima	20	73	16	35*
47 Okinawa	65	29	230	n.a.

(Note) Definition of the manufacturing establishment defined in *Chohatsu-bukken-shirabe* was not clearly mentioned in the reports and may be an independent workyard where workers gathered. Definition of the factories in *Kojyo-tokei-hyo* was those having more than ten artisans (employee) and so the coverage of the *Chohatsu-bukken* must be larger than Kojyo-tokei. Those marked with * are larger than the *Chohatsu-bukken*.

to design a 4,277-ton ship armed with only one 12.6-inch gun (Canet) and eleven 4.7-inch guns QF and ordered two from France (one called the Itsukushima at Société des Forges et Chantiers and one called the Matsushima at La Seyne), and built one called the Hashidate after the model ships at Yokosuka DY, the first naval dockyard where various small warships had been built and where private merchant ships were repaired. These were built up just before the war; the Itsukushima and the Matsushima were built in 1888–91 and the Hashidate in 1888–94. After this success, the Japanese navy adopted the policy of building up both naval and private shipyards, such as those at Sasebo, Kure and Kobe. Before that, the Navy ships had been mainly bought or ordered abroad. The Akitsushima, the protected cruiser of 3,100 tons and 19 knots, was built at the same dockyard after the design of Sanaka Sasou, the Japanese naval officer in charge of battleship construction who insisted on shifting from the French style gunboat advocated by Emile Bertin to the British style gunboat. This took more than four years because of the change in the design of arms soon after its completion in 1894, from, for example, replacement of the 6-inch and 4.7-inch guns by the 12-inch Canet on the Hashidate. In fact, the 12.6-inch gun was not operative in the Yalu River battle of the 17th of September, 1894, so the Japanese navy had to fight with the 4.7-inch QF and 6-inch QF on the Fuso, 3,800 tons armoured steel-hull frigate built in Samuda Brothers, Poplar, England as the first armoured ship designed for Japan. However, the Japanese navy defeated the Chinese navy anyway, so the operation of the 12.6-inch gun is another story not related to the current context.

In interpreting the 1892 data in Table II.10, it should be noted that the number of employees was still defined by the total number of man days. The summary figures based on the *Noshomu-tsushin-kisoku*, agricultural and trading correspondence rules, where the factory was defined as having more than ten employees and/or a power machine, yields bigger numbers: 4,635 in 1892 and 5,985 in 1894, including 337 in mining (5,648 excluding mining). The figures obtained from the same survey system but based on a different definition were merely 988 in 1891. Thus, the figures may change depending on the survey system and definitions used. However, there must be much more leakage in Yamaguchi's data set. These figures are to be regarded as indicators of a cross-sectional structure, not as absolute values. There were 9,556 manufacturing yards reported by the *Chohatsu-bukken* that year as shown in Table II.10. This indicates only a 7.5% annual increase from that of 1890 (8,325). We conjecture that the number of factories by *Chohatsu-bukken* is the upper limit for this survey of big buildings, excluding private housing, for the military mobilization. The average size of buildings was 38.8 *tsubo* (128 square meters). The number of silk weaving work yards in 1894 amounted to 336,224, and only 4,367 (1.3%) were factories according to the definition of the *Noshomu-tsushin*.

2.1.5   Factory Production after the Sino-Japanese War

After the end of the Sino-Japanese War, we got a new series of independent reports on the manufacturing survey, called *Zenkoku-kojyo-tokei-hyo*, covering 1896–1900 in Table II.11 as *Kojyo-hyo*. This new series was the result of the new type of survey which used an individual questionnaire for each factory instead of a format survey. This started in 1894, after the trial survey carried out in 1894 where the questionnaire contained many items requiring detailed information. However, this design was too complicated to sum up all the results and it was eventually abandoned without making any final report. In fact, the survey operation which the ministry carried out with this questionnaire was not recorded in any historical memoir of the ministry. We discovered it accidentally in a dossier of archival documents of a local government (Matsuda [1978] pp. 75–80).[1] In this new survey series, they were successful in making four-way cross tabulation based on whether or not power was used, the number of employees (two classes), the prefecture (forty-seven) and the industry classification (68 codes). The number of employees combined with the use of power and the industrial classification formed two classes in 1894–98, and then extended to six classes in 1899–1900. This constituted enormous progress compared with the tables in the Agriculture and Trade Statistical Yearbook, which contained only one-way classification. The items summed up also increased, including the number of workers by age and sex, the average wage rate per day by age and sex since the 1899 report, the number of working hours per day, and the number of working days per year, and in addition the number of apprentices by age and sex and the number of unskilled workers by sex in the 1990 report.

It is often argued that the power revolution in Japanese manufacturing is proved by using number of factories powered or equipped with a steam engine. Ryoshin Minami stressed the importance of power, but evaluated the importance of the water-wheel more like the case of the British industrial revolution brought about by Richard Arkwright's in-

Table II.11 Two Official Series of Number of Factory

| (i) Number of factory | | | | | | |
| | Kojyo-hyo | | | Nou-shoumu-tokei-hyo | | |
	Factory with power	Factory without power	Total	Factory with power	Factory without power	Total
1896	2,967	4,403	7,370	3,037	4,603	7,640
1897	2,971	4,346	7,317	2,910	4,377	7,287
1898	3,002	4,067	7,070	2,964	4,121	7,085
1899	2,763	3,788	6,551	2,305	4,394	6,699
1900	3,381	3,971	7,352	2,388	4,896	7,284

| (ii) Percentage share of factories with power and without power | | | | | | |
			(%)			(%)
1896	40.3	59.7	100.0	39.8	60.2	100.0
1897	40.6	59.4	100.0	39.9	60.1	100.0
1898	42.5	57.5	100.0	41.8	58.2	100.0
1899	42.2	57.8	100.0	34.4	65.6	100.0
1900	46.0	54.0	100.0	32.8	67.2	100.0

| (iii) Growth of number of factories (1896 as 100.0) | | | | | | |
			(%)			(%)
1896	100.0	100.0	100.0	100.0	100.0	100.0
1897	100.1	98.7	99.3	95.8	95.1	95.4
1898	101.2	92.4	95.9	97.6	89.5	92.7
1899	93.1	86.0	88.9	75.9	95.5	87.7
1900	114.0	90.2	99.8	78.6	106.4	95.3

(Source) *Kojyo-hyo*: Tables on Factory, an independent statistical report based on the questionnaire on factory in the Rural and Trade Corresponding System. *Noushoumu-tokei-hyo*: Statistical Table on Agriculture and Trade, based on the Rural and Trade Corresponding System.

vention of the water frame in 1766 and its replacement by the steam engine in around the 1920s (Minami [1976]).[2] Recent research based on the revival of the statistics gathered by the army sheds a new light on the use of the water-wheel.[3] This will again lead to the topic of the definition of the factory discussed above.

The definition of power machines in the first *Noshomu-tsushin-kisoku* applied only to the steam engine and the water-wheel, and since the 1894 formats three kinds of power machine were introduced: those powered by steam, those powered by electricity and those powered by water. The footnote to the Statistical Yearbook for 1894 told us that machines other than those powered by steam and water, i.e.; those using electricity and/or gas, were treated as non-power users. This treatment was altered in the 1895 figures. The independent report series appeared in *Kojyo-hyo*, tables on factory, said nothing on this point concerning the 1896–97 figures. The 1899 report told us that the number of engines possessed by 3,002 (3,003 was a misprint) private factories powered by steam, water, electricity, gas, oil, wind was 3,116, 1,834 (1,883 was a misprint), 84, 31, 17 and 4, respectively. (The average number of engines per factory was 1.70 and the average horsepower per engine was 22.49.) The 1900 report told us that the 4,727 engines belonged to 3,381 private factories and that the division was steam 2,602, water 1,713, electricity 116, oil 107, gas 126, wind 11 and not specified 60. (The average number per factory was 1.40 and the average horsepower per engine was 25.08.) However, there was a discrepancy in the number of factories in the Statistical Year-book between 1898 and 1899 due to the exclusion of the water wheel from the power engine category, as indicated in the footnote. (Minami stressed the irregularity of the figures in 1898 and excluded this data from his argument. This caused him to underestimate the number of power-equipped factories at the starting point of his discussion, Minami [1976] pp. 28–38). However, the treatment in the independent report series was just the opposite and the survey formats in 1904 and after explicitly define the turbine water wheel, the Pelton water wheel and the traditional Japanese water wheel. In addition, electric engines were further subdivided into dynamos and motors. In 1900 the percentage share of total horsepower of the water wheel was 14.13% against 80.19% for the steam engine and 3.87% for the electric engine. The figure for 1899 was quite similar and showed no substantial change of composition. The share of horsepower for the water wheel in 1909 was still 9.20% when we controlled the employee size to be the as same as in 1900.

Based on industrywise analysis, we conclude that the continuity of the rural spinning and weaving industries inherited from the Tokugawa regime was seen in the factory or work place using the water wheel and they were rapidly replaced by motors operated through the electricity network. The transition must be gradual if we consider the vast distribution of water wheels.[4]

The distribution of factories among prefectures indicates the relative importance of the prefectures in manufacturing.

The next topic is the development of government factories. In 1900 there were 27 government factories employing 36,237 employees and equipped with 168 power machines with a total of 6,157 horsepower (excluding four factories with an unknown power machine output). The various machines were installed in many places, for example, 248 at a new Kure dockyard.

Compared with the 1882 figures, most of the factories of light industries such as the Tomioka silk weaving factory were sold out to the private sector. Some of the light industry factories such as those producing woolen fabrics and tinned foods were all for military use.[5] Of the 27 government factories, 16 were for military and naval production. Factories producing guns and rifles and armoured boats required a high-grade steel but most of them were imported as final or semi-final products. Following the bitter experience at the time of the Sino-Japanese War, constructing a high-standard iron and steel industry was an urgent priority to assure a domestic supply unaffected by foreign intervention. Importation of military goods were suspended at Singapore for diplomatic reasons, even though they had already been paid for. The new government iron- and steel-making factory, officially called the "Imperial Japanese Government Steel-Works" began operation in 1901 after many years of struggle. This factory was not the first trial for the Meiji government. It failed to establish a modern iron smelter at Kamaishi. This smelter was designed by L. Bianchie, German, and Takato Ohshima in 1874 and abandoned and sold to the private sector in 1882. Finally, it successfully produced high quality steel in 1886 under the direction of Kageyoshi Noro, Professor of Tokyo Imperial University, and produced 13,000 tons in 1894, which exceeded the amount of national total of iron smelted in the traditional way.

The design of the new iron smelter was also entrusted to German engineers W. F. Luhrman and R. M. Daelen, but eventually modified by the Japanese in the operational stages. It could not supply finished products before or during the Russo-Japanese War in spite of the Japanese government's best efforts (Hayashi [1986] pp. 103–09).

On the other hand, they successfully operated a gun powder factory based on the invention by Masamitsu Shimose in 1899. This factory's name became famous after the Japan Sea Battle in 1905. Many other Japanese inventions were also in practical use at this time, e.g. the Izyuin fuse, the Kimura wireless telegraph, and so on. Military factories along with private ones had accumulated supplies in preparation for the war, which was expected to protest the Russian invasions of Manchuria, the northern part of China and Korea. No-one forgot the interference against Japan by Germany, France and, last but not least, Russia following the Sino-Japanese War in 1985.

In summarizing the achievements of governmental military production, it is necessary to state the naval situation, because the technology of warship construction is the best indicator of technological attainment of the day. It required not only a high level of steel production for both armour and guns, engines, electric wiring, and machine tools, but also skilled labourers to work as assemblers. Just before the Russo-Japanese War the Imperial Japanese Navy consisted of 57 battleships of 2,501,370 tons, 19 frigates of 6,521 tons and 76 torpedo boats of 6,430 tons. Almost ninety percent of them, however, had been produced abroad during the Sino-Japanese War, although most had been made under the orders and design of the Imperial Japanese Navy. As a result of the well-thought out designs, Japanese warships were as a whole well-balanced of 129,715 tons in January 1902 and 234,620 tons in April 1903, against the huge Russian navy of 193,311 tons in January 1902 and 234,620 tons in April 1903. (Figures quoted include only those designed for the open sea and built less than twenty years before: (Fukui [1992] p. 57).

The Imperial Japanese Navy at the time of the Russo-Japanese War consisted of six battleships, all ordered from Britain, of about 12,000–15,000 tons, capable of speeds up to eighteen knots, armed with four 12-inch guns; and six armoured cruisers, four ordered from Britain and two each ordered from France and Germany, of about 10,000 tons capable of speeds up to twenty-one knots, armed with four 8-inch guns. In addition, we should mention the Suma and the Akashi, protected cruisers, called third class cruisers, of about 2,657 tons, capable of speeds up to twenty knots, armed with two 6-inch QFs. Both had been built at the Yokosuka dockyards, for the first time with Japanese materials according to Japanese plans in 1892–96 (the Suma) and in 1894–99 (Jentschura, Jung and Mickel [1977]). They won a high reputation as having fighting tops and the Akashi was distinguished by her higher foremast with a W/T aerial. The Suma was called a bad sea boat because she lacked stability. The Akashi was modified during construction (Jentschura, Jung and Mickel [1977] p. 99).

2.2 New System for Organizing Capital: Creation of an institutional entity called a company

2.2.1 Company Concept as an Imported Software

The initial conditions of modern Japanese industry stemmed to a large extent from the rural areas both regionally and technically. Even exports were predominantly agricultural products such as rice, or semi-processed agricultural goods such as tea and silk. It is often said that after the late 1880s there was an investment boom and that the capitalistic production system became the principal way of organizing industries except in the agricultural sector.

However, what is the capitalistic production system? It is assumed to be a synonym for the company system for gathering capital and organizing employees.

The notion of a company was discovered by Japan early in the 1860s from an investigation tour to the United States by Kozukenosuke Oguri and Yukichi Fukuzawa, to England by Tomoatsu Godai and to France by Sukiun Kurimoto. Many books and pamphlets concerning the company system were published by them and others who had not been abroad, such as Shonan Yokoi (Hori [1975]). The basic idea was to build up a system like a trading section, *bussan-kata* or *kokusan-kata*, of the traditional *han* government who needed to sell and buy various products in a national market mainly organized by merchants at Edo and Osaka. The difference was the method of gathering capital, not from the *han* government but from private citizens. The aim of the company was the same as that of selling goods which were specialties of each *han* or region. However, most of these companies failed to survive due to the lack of capital and because they used unconvertible paper currency issued by the new government called *Dajyo-kan-satsu*.

The names of *tsusho-kaisha*, *kawase-kaisha*, in 1869 were famous as a pioneers of the corporate company (Kan'no [1931], Ueda [1944]). We found similar trials such as the *shoho-kaisho* in Shizuoka by Ei'ichi Shibusawa. We also found a system similar to an unlimited partnership in Mitsui-gumi, Ono-gumi and Shimada-gumi, which had been formed by the wealthy merchant families during the Tokugawa period. Another source of capital was found among the former *han-shu* who had gotten a kind of bond (*kyu-ryoshu-toribun* at the time of *karoku-shobun*) at the time of *hai-han-chiken*, abolishing *han*-system, and then later at the time of issuing *chitsuroku-kosai*, bond to compensate the power of *han-shu* to impose tax, (Furushima [1963] pp. 380–81) proclaimed by *Kinroku-kosai-kofu-jyorei* in 1877.

Bonds and stocks of these companies were gradually sold on the Tokyo and Osaka Stock Exchanges after 1878 (Imuda [1976] pp. (17)–(18)). The names of so and so company (*sha* or *kaisha* in Japanese) were found around 1873.

The introduction of the national banking system in 1873 confirmed the full realization of the corporate company system.[6] However, full authorization of the corporate company system with legal support was not completed until the proclamation of the commercial act in 1890. (This is called the ancient commercial law, which was modeled on German law but incorporated aspects of French law). It was partially executed in 1893 when the legal system of the company was realized and so joint-stock companies, limited partnerships and unlimited partnerships were clearly defined for the first time. Establishing a joint-stock company needed authorization after paying at least one fourth of the nominal capital.

2.2.2 Company Statistics: Technical digression

Unfortunately the statistics of companies were the most incomplete of all statistical surveyed. The statistical year book supplied a table of companies beginning from its second issue published in 1895, which contained figures of June, 1881. From the fourth issue to the seventh issue, the industrial classification scheme varied and only the amount of nominal capital was included. The comparability of data also varied because of the different coverage of prefectures of each issue. From the eighth issue, the classification scheme became stable and the number of share holders was included. Then from the tenth issue the amount of paid-in capital was included. Thus, we were able to get the detailed company figures.

The number of companies varied both with the trade cycle, especially as a result of the deflation brought about by the policies adopted by Masayoshi Matsukata, Minister of Finance, and with the fictional increase or decrease due to the coverage. However, it is difficult to distinguish each effect from the tables in the statistical yearbook. Next came the first boom in 1887, after the so-called Matsukata deflation in 1882–84. The trigger of the boom may be attributed to the introduction of the paper currency convertible system in 1886. (The actual situations can be traced from the statistics gathered by the Ministry of Agriculture and Trade shown partially in line (2) of Table I.1 above. This was the series in the first independent statistical reports of the joint-stock company, but it excluded companies classified as railroad companies and traders organizing stock, silk and rice exchange markets. The revised figures with the correction of coverage are shown in line (1). Our database system indicates possible leakage of companies in various ways and so we show the results in line (3) as kind of reference figures.)

Some remarks about the coverage and definition of the company may be useful to readers. In the eighth issue of the statistical yearbook, the editor's note tells us "an individual enterprise may be included in so far as it uses the word company", and in the 12th issue it further added the clause "capital is higher than 1,000 yen".

2.2.3 Structure of the Company System before and after the Sino-Japanese War

The data sets of 1887 and 1889 show that the company system propagated firstly in banking and secondly but to a smaller degree in the railroad industry. The national banking system started with four banks in 1874, increased to 151 in 1880 and then gradually decreased to 136 in 1886–87 and 134 in 1889–91, and finally vanished in 1898, while the number of private banks and quasi-banks increased rapidly after 1882 (164 and 438, respectively, in 1882, 218 and 741 in 1887, and 155 and 695 in 1889).[6] Kokichi Asakura (Juro Teranishi [1982] p. 41) pointed out that before 1873 there were many quasi-banks which acted as predecessors of national or private banks. (This rapid increase in the number of banks resulted in 45.80% of companies in 1884 being taken over by banks, although this includes quasi-banks.) The money which was produced by the *chitsuroku-kosai* at the time of the *han* system's abolition flooded into these companies (Furushima [1963] pp. 342–46). Next came manufacturing companies, which in number and total amount of capital was a leading group adopting the company system. However, the average amount of capital was not so large compared with that of railroad companies, which had absorbed a huge amount of money from the capital market. The average amount of capital was 233,643 yen for transportation and 31,075 yen for manufacturing, while it was only 8,880 yen for agriculture in 1889.

Imuda pointed out that the number of stock holders varied according to the industrial specification. For example, agriculture had the biggest number of stockholders per company (162.7), then came transportation (92.9), commerce including money lenders (61.1) and lastly manufacturing (27.0). He also analysed the relation between the amount of capital and the number of stockholders in each industry in more detail (Imuda [1976] pp. 24–31).

Then Imuda brilliantly analysed the relation between borrowers from national banks and the security they offered, based on several tables of the day. He concluded that wealthy people established new companies without completely paying up capital, as the law permitted, but submitted the stock as security to borrow money from banks, and then invested the money to establish the new company. This implies that even money lent through the banking system needed to be channeled through personal credibility (Imuda [1976] pp. 20–21, Tables 10.14).

However, we have some reservations about some of Imuda's statements, for example, the high ratio of the paid-in capital especially in cotton spinning, electricity, cement, and shipping industries based on the data of Naosuke Takamura and others (Imuda [1976] pp. 20–22). His statement was quoted by many others. The ratio of paid-in capital to nominal capital had three peaks: low ratios were observed at around 3,500–5,000 yen capital class and 500,000–1,000,000 yen capital class and they varied according to the industrial classification. The difference between these two observations stems from the coverage of the data. Our database covers a much wider range of companies based on both the amount of capital and the industrial classification.

This will illustrate the further results of our database which indicate that the low ratio of paid-in capital to nominal capital was quite common not only in the 1880s but even in the 1900s. In fact it was 64.35% overall in 1882 using our database (Imuda referred to the 1884 figures as 66.8% overall using Statistical Yearbook data, Imuda [1976] p. 42).

Many researchers quoted the analysis done by Imuda, but his basic data was that of the Statistical Yearbook which supplied tables by the industrial classification of 133 codes. By virtue of the list of companies published by the Ministry of Agriculture and Commerce, we were able to construct a database of 1,700 companies in 1889 and then an extended version of 4,150 companies in 1896 after the execution of the Commercial Law in 1893.[8]

The 1889 database includes the amount of nominal capital and paid-in capital and the number of stockholders of each company. Thus, we reclassified them by prefecture and industry.

It should be noted that the ranks of prefectures by the number of companies, nominal capital and paid-in capital differ and the transition of these ranks between 1889 and 1896 is also striking (see Fig. II.2). In 1889 Tokyo, Osaka, Hyogo, Aichi and Hokkaido were the top five in terms of the number of companies, but in terms of total capital the order was Tokyo, Hyogo, Osaka, Hokkaido and Aichi. The average amount of capital was extremely big in Tokyo, Hyogo, Osaka and Hokkaido for they gathered capital from all over Japan. However, in sparsely populated prefectures the average capital was also low and they must have been supported by local people.

The situations were similar for 1896. The top in terms of the number of companies was Osaka, followed by Tokyo, Hyogo, Niigata, Kyoto,

Figure II.2 Companies of Top Eleven Prefectures (Number, capital and paid-in capital)

(i) Number of companies

Rank	1889 Code of prefecture	Number of companies	1896 Code of prefecture	Number of companies	1902 Code of prefecture	Number of companies	1908 Code of prefecture	Number of companies	1920 Code of prefecture	Number of companies
1	13:	378	27:	472	13:	952	13:	1,644	13:	2,963
2	27:	218	13:	310	23:	302	23:	535	27:	1,986
3	28:	81	28:	278	20:	250	20:	430	23:	1,919
4	40:	69	23:	254	27:	241	27:	423	28:	1,780
5	23:	62	15:	223	01:	235	01:	402	01:	1,459
6	01:	59	26:	199	14:	180	14:	401	50:	1,145
7	17:	47*	33:	175	28:	175	28:	384	20:	927
8	22:	47**	22:	167	22:	169	22:	348	14:	870
9	26:	47**	20:	140	15:	167	15:	264	22:	826
10	14:	43**	38:	116	40:	155	09:	235	26:	786
11	19:	43**	41:	105	26:	149	16:	228	34:	580
*						*				
12	33:	40	40:	101	09:	128	34:	159	16:	513
16	15:	30	14:	76	16:	98	40:	155	15:	424
19	38:	27	17:	60	38:	67	26:	151	09:	308
22	41:	25	01:	50	33:	66	50:	141		
30	20:	14	19:	12	41:	34				
Total		1,700		4,150		4,849		8,684		25,494

(Notes)

1) If those companies in the rank under 11th in a certain year appeared in the rank of the top ten in the next year or vice-versa, their rank is annotated with asterisk.(*)

2) If more than two prefectures have the same rank in the top ten, no alteration of reducing rank number having the same rank is done and so the order of arranging the same rank is after the order of prefectural code. Two asterisks (**) are given for these codes of prefectures in the top ten.

Figure II.2 Continued

(ii) Capital of companies (Total nominal capital of each prefecture)

Rank	1889 Code of prefecture	Effective samples	Total of nominal capital	1896 Code of prefecture	Effective samples	Total of nominal capital	1902 Code of prefecture	Effective samples	Total of nominal capital
1	13:	319	88,034,562	13:	286	138,878,109	13:	943	293,759,048
2	28:	78	18,383,725	27:	463	81,202,103	27:	301	73,480,600
3	27:	201	17,698,344	28:	266	36,553,875	40:	150	60,720,854
4	01:	52	13,583,976	40:	95	23,281,091	28:	230	56,297,075
5	26:	43	4,350,000	26:	187	20,708,728	14:	244	35,984,450
6	40:	54	4,063,312	01:	47	19,167,605	24:	80	30,294,500
7	14:	30	2,899,000	23:	238	12,791,430	01:	174	27,816,490
8	23:	56	2,792,500	33:	171	12,680,383	15:	159	22,440,750
9	24:	22	2,480,000	24:	23	10,784,500	26:	144	21,907,045
10	25:	25	2,090,000	29:	52	6,317,750	23:	232	16,387,450
11	15:	27	1,960,500	14:	72	6,088,590	33:	66	9,444,990
*									
15	33:	39	1,477,448	25:	59	3,507,010	29:	20	4,450,500
42	29:	6	230,000	15:	126	3,220,010	50:	19	1,875,000
Total		1,521	183,130,114		3,714	411,995,930		4,645	742,066,133

118

Figure II.2 Continued

	1902		1908				1920	
Rank	Code of prefecture	Rank	Code of prefecture	Effective samples	Total of nominal capital	Code of prefecture	Effective samples	Total of nominal capital
1	13:	1	13:	1,643	708,903,665	13:	2,963	2,906,639,209
2	27:	2	50:	140	251,510,350	50:	1,145	1,729,593,951
3	40:	3	27:	423	140,176,100	27:	1,986	1,322,502,208
4	28:	4	28:	383	85,820,025	28:	1,780	807,372,296
5	14:	5	01:	401	73,354,695	23:	1,918	289,710,548
6	24:	6	14:	396	72,304,980	14:	870	265,041,035
7	01:	7	26:	150	46,786,040	40:	505	212,457,262
8	15:	8	23:	532	46,263,250	26:	786	186,930,942
9	26:	9	15:	261	44,570,005	01:	1,459	159,991,090
10	23:	10	33:	113	21,346,274	33:	569	80,593,685
11	33:	11	40:	154	20,297,630	22:	826	78,250,598
*		*				*		
17	29:	12	24:	106	18,719,600	13		
45	50:	13	22:	345	10,466,638	15:	424	69,460,948
Total				8,632	1,690,457,326		25,491	9,396,628,148

119

Figure II.2 Continued

(iii) Capital of companies (Total paid-in capital of each prefecture)

Rank	1889 Code of prefecture	Effective samples	Total of paid-in capital	1896 Code of prefecture	Effective samples	Total of paid-in capital	1902 Code of prefecture	Effective samples	Total of paid-in capital
1	13:	143	41,385,590	13:	277	84,859,922	13:	376	175,968,381
2	27:	126	9,540,369	27:	446	41,210,376	40:	103	50,184,896
3	28:	20	4,391,131	28:	242	20,118,870	27:	221	48,115,151
4	01:	21	2,577,839	40:	93	19,707,749	28:	169	44,623,959
5	15:	19	1,878,000	01:	46	11,704,470	24:	61	27,878,783
6	26:	22	1,742,264	24:	55	10,547,712	01:	92	20,914,174
7	40:	22	1,535,350	26:	157	8,592,301	26:	102	15,495,332
8	23:	15	1,215,263	23:	231	6,604,237	14:	78	14,772,765
9	25:	13	1,204,900	15:	221	5,198,293	15:	131	12,321,369
10	14:	12	1,090,000	33:	164	4,624,295	23:	167	10,958,364
11	22:	10	1,037,253	14:	70	3,814,039	33:	49	6,469,723
*									
12	33:	6	673,195	25:	33	2,018,985	30 50:	11	1,119,300
15	24:	5	590,260	22:	71	980,346			
Total		529	76,379,240		3,438	246,509,828		2,870	482,098,969

Figure II.2 Continued

1902		1908				1920		
Rank	Code of prefecture	Rank	Code of prefecture	Effective samples	Total of paid-in capital	Code of prefecture	Effective samples	Total of paid-in capital
1	13:	1	13:	421	375,107,658	13:	2,921	1,824,080,598
2	40:	2	50:	81	118,228,975	27:	1,801	820,709,259
3	27:	3	27:	148	82,494,147	50:	900	815,006,931
4	28:	4	01:	130	44,708,450	28:	1,763	486,039,027
5	24:	5	14:	90	36,992,695	14:	861	187,369,219
6	01:	6	28:	210	36,842,532	23:	1,877	180,049,009
7	26:	7	15:	115	26,390,417	40:	505	133,298,047
8	14:	8	26:	68	21,268,940	01:	1,445	97,966,580
9	15:	9	23:	137	19,441,470	26:	468	84,039,267
10	23:	10	40:	96	12,569,551	15:	421	51,448,639
11	33:	11	24:	49	9,684,050	24:	322	45,245,847
*		12	33:	44	6,931,630			
12 30	50:							
* 12								
Total				3,177	862,551,477		24,569	5,479,595,032

Aichi and Okayama. However, Tokyo came first in terms of capital, and then Osaka. In so far as ranking of the prefectures by the cumulated capital from the companies whose capital was known, Tokyo, Osaka, Hyogo, Fukuoka, Kyoto and Hokkaido were the top six. Taking into the consideration paid-in capital, Kyoto came after Tokyo, Osaka, Hyogo, Fukuoka, Hokkaido and Mie. Average capital was highest at Fukuoka then in descending order, Mie, Tokyo, Hokkaido, Osaka, Hyogo and Kyoto. These prefectures were regarded as having big companies.

The transition from 1889 to 1896 shows no remarkable changes in the upper ranking and lower ranking except in Hokkaido where the number of big companies was comparatively stable and lacked small scale companies that utilized local capital. However, in the middle there were many.

The notable point about the composition of companies is the high percentage of those engaged in commerce and transportation compared to those engaged in manufacturing. In particular, money lending companies acting as quasi-banks were found in many prefectures. In addition, the extensive distribution of agricultural companies in almost every prefecture must have had its origin in traditional ways of developing waste land by irrigation to produce new paddy fields, as was found in the later part of the Tokugawa period.

2.2.4 Company-owned Factories seen in Statistics

There are few statistics on the ownership of factories. The formative period of factory statistics left us records about the ownership in a mixed list of companies and factories. Using this data, Yamaguchi and Terashima derived a series of data for 1884 and 1892. Next came the tabulation of 1900 factory statistics, as shown in Table II.12.

However, we have some reservations about the definitions of the company in these figures. Yamaguchi and Terashima's estimates were based on the prefectural statistical yearbooks and they treated those factories which did not fill the capital in the format as n.a. Thus, in 1884 164 factories out of 1,981 belonged to the n.a. group and in 1892 342 out of 2,971 belonged to the n.a. group. Original definitions of the formats specified for the prefectural statistical yearbooks (Decree of the Ministry of the Interior, on the unification of the prefectural statis-

Table II.12 Ownership of Factories in 1900

Industry	Number of factories		Factories owned by companies		Factories owned by individual persons	
	Equipped w/power	No power	Equipped w/power	No power	Equipped w/power	No power
Textile	2392	1763	572	184	1821	1579
Machinery	230	184	75	15	155	169
Chemicals	224	701	124	115	100	586
Foods and beverages	250	585	102	66	148	519
Miscellaneous	170	456	65	73	105	383
Special manufacturing	114	103	36	8	78	95
Subtotal	3381	3971	974	461	2407	3510
Percentage share	45.9	54.1	67.8	32.2	40.6	59.4
	100.0		28.8		71.2	
		100.0		11.6		88.4
Total	7352		1435		5917	
Percentage share	100.0		19.5		80.4	

(Notes) The definition of *kaisha*, company, includes associations and guilds.
The definition of *kōjyō*, factory, is a work yard where more than ten
people work.

(Source) *Meiji 33 nen, Kojyo-hyo* (Table on Factory for 1900).

tical yearbook, 1884) tells nothing about the nature of capital in either
the commercial company list or the factory list. However, *Noshomu-
tsushin-kisoku*, Agricultural and Trading Correspondence Rules, told
us something about the capital. Firstly, in the 1883 formats, the capital in the company list distinguished fixed capital from paid-in capital.
However, in the factory list, those factories that were requested to
fill in the capital had to separate fixed and operational capital. The
former meant land, buildings and machinery and the latter liquidity
for purchasing raw materials and/or paying wages and salaries. Thus,
the concept of capital seems to have meant capital assets as a whole
and is different from the capital in the balance sheet concept used in
the company list. In the 1886 formats, they clearly defined that the
companies in the agricultural and commercial company list should be

those with over 1,000 yen of capital in the case of agriculture and over 5,000 yen of capital in the case of commerce. Furthermore, the factories list required the listing of those companies or unions which owned factories with more than ten employees and/or non-corporate owners' factories with more than ten employees and 1,000 yen of capital. Those companies having factories and engaged in both manufacturing and commerce had to fill in agricultural and commercial company lists or manufacturing company lists according to their principal business. Such restriction in size of capital existed only for the selection rules of factories to be reported and no further definition was required regarding the capital. Since the formats of 1889 introduced the distinction between capital and the paid-in capital, the concept of capital must have changed. However, we have no further evidence concerning the concept of capital. After the 1894 formats, an individual questionnaire for each company was introduced with an individual questionnaire for each factory. The former required the amount of paid-in capital and the latter the owner's name regardless of whether it was an individual or a company. A small amendment to the company questionnaire was introduced in 1896 decree ♯21 on the 9th of September, 1896, where the nominal capital was required to be filled in.

2.2.5 Company-owned Factories in 1900

Thus, the concept of capital in the prefectural statistical yearbooks is not clear and there is no way now of clarifying it. However, we suspect that the values used to derive Yamaguchi and Terashima's 1884 estimates might be total capital assets and not based on the concept of capital in the company system. Because of the monotonous decrease in the number of factories classified by the size of capital in 1884 and of the distribution having double peaks in 1892, the capital value used for their 1892 estimates might be nominal capital.

In the *Kojyo-tokei-hyo* of 1900 there is a table that just tells the total number of factories owned by companies and other associations classified by industry and by with or without power. Associations include the various forms of association such as partnerships, unions or others without any specification. The Ministry of Agriculture and Commerce might have used a description of the owner's name of a factory without matching the questionnaire of the company.

Of 3,381 private factories with power, only 974 were owned by companies (28.8%); of 3,971 private factories without power, only 461 were owned by companies (11.6%). Thus, of a total of 7,352 factories, 1,435 were owned by companies (19.5%). This implies that most of the factories equipped with power were not organized in a company system which mainly governed the production of commodities newly brought out by Western technology. If we compare the number of company-owned factories in the manufacturing survey with the number of the joint-stock companies engaged in manufacturing in our company database, the share of joint-stock-company-owned factories is 28.8% of all company-owned factories in the 1900 manufacturing survey. Our comparison was based on the hypothesis of excluding the possibility of a company having more than two factories. Therefore, the number of company-owned factories must be bigger than the number of companies owning a factory. Needless to say we do not deny the existence of leakage in both data sets. However, this percentage is still quite low and confirms our suspicion that the concept of the company was not yet well-defined in the 1900 survey.

No other series will be obtainable until our database produces estimates based on the directory published by the Ministry of Agriculture and Commerce as a by-product of a manufacturing survey. (The detailed figures of our estimates for 1902, 1909 and 1920 are obtainable in Appendix Tables which will be sent upon request.)

It is quite strange that the statistical section of the Ministry of Agriculture and Trade did not make any tabulation of this kind of ownership of factories after the report of 1900 although they had a special questionnaire for companies which would have supplied enough information to match with a factory questionnaire as we have done in our database system. One possible explanation is that they believed that ownership did not have any substantial effect on the behaviour of factory management because the workers would often change their work places after receiving on-the-job training to pursue higher wage rates, and local factory managers in each establishment were authorized to control employee numbers and wage rates even if they belonged to a certain company.

A more plausible explanation is the time-space and labour- consuming nature of tabulation procedures for the government statisticians in matching two kinds of questionnaires.

Notes:

1) After finding a copy of the report in a small village in Tokushima Prefecture, we found copies of the report from almost all counties in Aichi Prefecture and some counties in Iwate Prefecture.

2) Another point he overlooked is the importance of steam engines used for irrigation in rural areas especially along the coast of the Japan sea like Niigata prefecture.

3) Tomoyuki Sueo first used these military statistics in 1962–68 and later collected his papers in one volume [1980].

4) Naosuke Takamura pointed out this point in his paper (first appearing in 1990 and later in his collected papers in [1995]) where those factories using both water wheel and steam listed in the factory directories should be defined as water wheel only in the case of silk spinning factories. This is because the steam engine for boiling cocoons must have been misinterpreted as a steam engine for power machine based on the National Survey Report on Spinning Factories, *Zenkoku-seishi-kojyo-chosa-hyo*, in 1893 and since, distinguishing these differences of machines. In 1893, factories depending on manual labour had the top share, followed by those depending on water power. Those using steam power comprised only one half of those using water power. In 1896, the number using water power reached the top, but the number using steam still held third position. After 1900, steam reached the top. Takamura further analysed historical documents in Nagano Prefecture and the *Katakura-kumi*, Katakura Company, and proved the importance of the water wheel in the silk spinning industry until the inspection system for quality control of yarn became strict in the United States market in the 1910s. This enforced the replacement of the water wheel, still favoured by the makers of low or middle quality threads, to electric power, which guaranteed constant spindle turning rates (Minami [1976] pp. 142–48,) but Takamura ([1995] pp. 250–51) denied the turning point from the water wheel to the steam engine around the late 1900s and insisted that the water wheel lasted until 1903 in the case of manufacturers along the Tenryu River.

5) The supply of foodstuffs was the main logistical concern to modernize the military system at the time of Meiji Restoration. To build up a naval force the most important works were storage of fresh foodstuffs along with production of gunpowder. A ship's cruising range was determined not only by its fuel capacity but also by its supply of foodstuffs for the crew.

6) The National bank system was organized along the lines of the United States banking system. The Japanese word for 'national' is *kokuritsu*, or 'owned by the nation', but the notion of *kokuritsu-ginko*, national bank in this case, did not imply that the bank was owned by the nation like the national bank system in the United States. The translation of the day should be regarded as incorrect. These national banks were kinds of private banks like those of United States.

7) National banks were allowed to issue bank notes. However, issuing unconvertible currency in the governments' currency made this difficult. Eventually only the *Nippon Ginko*, Japan Bank, was authorized as a sole agent to issue paper currency by the *Nippon Ginko* (Japan Bank) Act in 1882. Detailed statistics and explanatory notes are found in Goto [1970].

8) The former 1,616 company list database consists of joint-stock companies and the latter 4,130 company list database includes companies of other systems such as limited partnerships and unlimited partnerships. As discussed in the Part III, the latter database does not have a complete regional coverage like other base years 1902, 1908 and 1920, but is comparable to them in the sense of definitional coverage of various company system. This is because the latter database has supplementary data sources for getting information other than joint-stock companies, such as prefectural regional statistical yearbooks which lacked consistent data formats.

3. GALLOP OFF THE PATH OF INDUSTRIAL-IZATION: 1902, 1909 AND 1920

3.1 Expansion of Factories and Companies after the Sino-Japanese War: A short sketch

As we have mentioned in a previous chapter, the tight budget constraints during the Russo-Japanese War in 1904–05 compelled the Ministry of Agriculture and Trade to give up the compilation of a survey report of the manufacturing survey after the 1900 issue published in 1903. However, using our database system we have reconstructed some parts of the 1902 survey. This reconstruction will show the situation just before the War. We have also reconstructed tables of the 1909 survey in addition to the official report entitled *Kojyo-tokei-hyo*, manufacturing tables, published in 1911 as a reference for the execution of the factory law proclaimed in 1911. The government had repeatedly tried to realize factory law regulations for the protection of labourers since 1898 against the opposition of capitalists under the umbrella of the chamber of commerce. World War I began in the summer of 1914 and ended in 1918, but the turmoil caused by the Russian Revolution continued till the dispatch of Japanese troops to Siberia in 1918–21. We reconstruct the 1920 survey to synchronize it with the first population census in 1920.

These almost two decades were a time of expansion of the manufacturing industry. We will analyse these three data sets in order to clarify this period of rapid industrialization compared with the days before 1900. As we have discussed in the previous sections, the manufacturing industry had been extensively fed by both the rural sector and traditional techniques in handling raw materials, labour and capital. To determine the source of capital for sustaining the factory system, we need to analyse the company system which absorbs idle money from the private sector.

A statistical survey on companies is the least developed area of Japanese governmental statistics. After 1920, the Ministry of Agriculture and Trade published a new statistical survey called *Kaisha-hyo*, tables on the company, starting from the first issue published in 1922 almost twenty years after the publication of *Kabushiki-kaisha-tokei*, statistical reports of joint-stock companies for 1894–96 in 1894–97. The only source of statistical reports based on the *Noshoumu-tsushin-kisoku* was the Statistical Yearbook of Agriculture and Commerce which was thought to be the final source of the Statistical Yearbook of the Bureau of statistics.

Our database system is based on the directories published by the commercial credit bureaux of Tokyo and Osaka for the years 1902 and 1909 and the directory published by the Ministry of Agriculture and Trade, which must be a reproduction of the questionnaires for the survey requiring the data on just the 31st of December, 1919. We call this the 1920 survey as it shows the starting point as the year 1920, although it corresponds to the survey data one year before the new company statistics on 1920.

Linking the factory directory database with the company directory database we get a new version of factory and company consolidated into one.

Before going further, some remarks about trade cycles during these years might be useful to refresh the memory of readers.

Now, let's see what statistics will tell us.

3.2 Transformation of Light Industry to Heavy Industry: Factories based on various criteria

3.2.1 Factories in 1902, 1909 and 1920

As the summary figures obtained from our database system shows in Table II.13, the growth of the manufacturing sector between 1902 and 1909 was extremely big; the number of factories nearly doubled, both those with power machines and those without. The average number of employees, however, does not show any marked change. The number distribution of employees shows that the increase for factories was brought about mainly by the increase for the class of less than fifty employees, especially in the class for less than thirty. The next point clarified for the first time by our database system is the sharp increase in the number of enterprises which had more than two establishments in 1909. This kind of enterprise was distributed evenly through every employee class.

Table II.13 Summary Figures of Factories

i) Factories more than ten artisants (employee)			
Year	1902	1909	1920
Number of factories	7,597	15,431	24,476
Single factory enterprise	6,727	13,340	20,826
Multiple factory enterprise	870	2,091	3,650
Powerless	4,415	8,784	8,572
Power	3,182	6,647	15,931
Employee per factory	53.88	44.85	59.34

(Note) The coverage for 1909 was adjusted for the factories over ten employee.

However, changes in number for factories were not remarkable from 1909 to 1920. Changes were observed for enterprises having more than two establishments and such changes were concentrated in the classes between fifty and five hundreds employees.

These changes came firstly from changes in the composition of industries. The biggest share by the number of factories was, needless to say, the textile industry. Then, in order, came foods and beverages, chemicals, miscellaneous, machinery and special in 1902. Chemicals and miscellaneous had changed places by 1909. Miscellaneous came after textiles in 1920. The growth rates were highest for foods and beverages (2.74 times those for 1902), then miscellaneous (2.64), machinery (2.55), chemicals (1.86) and lastly textiles (1.85), except specials (1.16). In the next decade, the situation had changed such that machinery came first (2.79 times the 1909 value) then chemicals (1.91), miscellaneous (1.76), textiles (1.37) and lastly food and beverages (1.76). Specials (2.93) occupied a rather exceptional position because they are usually treated as non-manufacturing today such as electricity and gas.

This implies that the focus of manufacturing had been gradually shifting from textiles and foods and beverages to machinery and chemicals. If we include government factories, the focus on machinery became much more pronounced. The total number of workers in naval factories had grown from 26,464 in 1903 to 51,605 in 1920, nearly doubling (1.95 times), but the number in military factories fell from 27,129 to 23,947. Further increases were found in the nationalization of main railway companies and the construction of steel mills.

During the Russo-Japanese War, Japan lost two battleships (the Hatsuse and the Yashima) to mines on the 15th of May, 1904. This was one third of Japan's battleships, so eventually the Imperial navy decided to produce two armoured cruisers at its Kure dockyards. They were to be 13,750 tons each, more than three times bigger than their biggest current vessel, the Hashidate, which the navy had also built. It took about seven years to build the Hashidate, but this time delivery was requested within two years and six months. In fact, the Tsukuba was launched on the 26th of December, 1905 and was completed on the 14th January, 1907 and, the Ikoma was launched on the 9th of April, 1906 and completed on the 24th of March, 1908, after the end of the war. However, the birth of this high speed cruiser of twenty-and-a-half knots, armed with four 12-inch guns, created quite a fanfare in the long race of navy construction. By 1909, three battleships, the Aki, the Ibuki and the Settsu, were under construction at the Kure dockyard and another three, the Satsuma, the Kurama and the Kawachi, were being built at the Yokosuka Naval Dockyard.

Battleships before the Haruna and the Kirishima were top class battleship at the time of their construction, but unfortunately the appearance of the Dreadnought the Second in 1906 made them second class. The Dreadnought the Second was 18,110 tons, armed with ten 12-inch guns, and was capable of 21 knots. With further innovations in the British navy in the shape of the Lion, built at Devon Port Dock Yard from 1909 to 1912, of 26,350 tons and 27 knots armed with eight 13.5 inch guns, Japan decided to order a battleship from Vickers & Sons in 1910 as the first true battleship cruiser designed for the Japanese navy by Sir George Thurston, based on specifications formulated by Baron Motoki Kondo who had designed Japanese-built ships from the

Tsukuba to the Kawachi mentioned above. It was delivered to Japan in 1913 and named the Kongo. It was the first capital ship ordered after the Russo-Japanese War and the last Japanese capital ship built outside Japan. At the time of the contract Japan obtained the right to send technicians to the construction site and to get all the blueprints required to build other battleships in Japan. Using these blueprints the sister battleship, the Hiei was built at Yokosuka Naval Dockyard in 1914. Furthermore, in addition to the construction of battleships at naval dockyards, private ship building companies were also involved in the effort to construct a naval fleet. The Haruna was built by Kobe Kawasaki Shipbuilding Co. in 1912–15 and the Kirishima by Nagasaki Mitsubishi in 1912–15. They were both of 32,200 tons, capable of 27.5 knots and armed with eight 14-inch guns.

The point of issue is that building a battleship is impossible without the development of the related machinery industries necessary for battleship building. This industry requires not only steel but also machine tools and engines. It is like the aircraft or automobile industry today. During the Tsukuba's construction, much of the raw material, steel and armour, as well as many of the machine tools, were imported. However, when construction of the Aki started, the amount of imported steel had dropped to half of the total requirement because of the extension of the Yahata Steel Factory, and by the time the Aki was completed, almost all the steel and armour used were produced domestically (Fukui [1992], vol. 1 pp. 213–44).

Construction of the naval fleet at private shipyards provided a great impetus to the private ship building and steel industries.

The second factor of change was the method of raising capital, especially the corporate enterprise against the individual enterprise system. This was also discovered throughout our database system. Firstly, the dominance of private or individual owners' factories in 1902 continued even to 1909 with an increase of 2.1 times. However, the rate of increase had dropped by 1920. The dominance of the joint-stock company system suddenly accelerated between 1909 and 1920, increasing 4.49 times. Then came the increase in joint partnerships and then limited companies.

This implies that modernization of capital raising through the stock market had made a deep impression on Japanese society by 1920.

3.2.2 Horizontal Expansion and Vertical Expansion

In measuring the size distribution of factories, we use two indexes: the number of employees and the motive power for machinery. As is well-known, there were relatively few big factories, but many smaller ones. It is said that the form of size distribution is log-normal (Ijiri & Simon [1977]). This also applies to our case. However, the coverage of the factories differs according to the survey time. In 1902, the number of employees working in a factory amounted to more than ten per day on average, but in 1909 and 1920 the lower limit became five employees. The directory which we used to compile the database, however, covered only those with more than ten employees. Thus, we get two series; one for more than ten employees and the other for five to nine employees, for 1909 only. Thus, the distribution is truncated at this limit of coverage. Anyhow, the frequency distribution of the number of factories by number of employees and horsepower of its machinery showed a truncated log-normal distribution.

For 1902, the lower end of around ten employees shows somewhat of a decline with a decrease in employee numbers. There must have been many more smaller scale factories and so the distribution must be abruptly truncated. One possible reason for this is evasion by respondents with around ten employees, saying that they had less than ten employees so that they could claim exemption from the survey.

It should be noted that these two size indicators, total number of employees and total horsepower, in one prefecture show different ranking than the forty-six prefectures. For the year 1902, the top five prefectures in order were Aichi, Osaka, Nagano, Tokyo and Hyogo by number of factories; Osaka, Tokyo, Nagano, Aichi and Hyogo by number of employees; and Tokyo, Fukuoka, Osaka, Hyogo and Kanagawa by horsepower. For the year 1909 they were Aichi, Tokyo, Osaka, Hyogo and Kyoto by number of factories; Osaka, Tokyo, Aichi, Hyogo and Nagano by number of employees; and Tokyo, Hyogo, Kanagawa, Osaka and Nagasaki by horsepower. For 1920 they were Osaka, Tokyo, Aichi, Hyogo and Kyoto by number of factories; Osaka, Tokyo, Hyogo, Aichi and Nagano by number of employees; and Tokyo, Osaka, Hyogo, Kanagawa and Hokkaido by horsepower. The differences of orders and the transition of orders result from the composition of the industries

Figure II.3 Factories of Top Ten Prefectures (Number of factories and workers)

(i) Number of Factories of Each Prefectures

	1902		1908		1920	
Rank	Code of Prefectures	Number of Factories	Code of Prefectures	Number of Factories	Code of Prefectures	Number of Factories

a) Total of factories with power and without power

1	23:	663	23:	1,498	27:	2,688
2	20:	566	13:	1,404	13:	2,452
3	27:	507	27:	1,285	23:	2,063
4	21:	333	28:	1,259	28:	1,743
5	13:	314	26:	831	26:	1,075
6	18:	290	18:	711	20:	810
7	28:	273	11:	622	22:	801
8	17:	253	20:	583	18:	721
9	24:	191	17:	520	40:	607
10	33:	180	21:	482	01:	567
*			*		*	
11	26:	174	11 22:	407	15 11:	450
20	11:	99	15 24:	299	20 17:	381
			17 33:	282	21 21:	366
			18 40:	270		
			25 01:	173		

| Total | 7,818 | | 15,418 | | 24,503 | |

and the types of ownership discussed above.

The changes in ranking between three periods for the top ten prefectures are shown in Fig. II.3.

If we look at factories from the urban and rural aspect, regional differences due to the compositions of industry are more clearly seen. We take the measure of urbanization as the administrative jurisdiction of city or county, and then further subdivide them into towns and villages within counties. Factories classified as belonging to the textile indus-

Figure II.3 Continued

(i) Number of Factories of Each Prefectures

	1902		1908		1920	
Rank	Code of Prefectures	Number of Factories	Code of Prefectures	Number of Factories	Code of Prefectures	Number of Factories

b) Factory with power

1	20:	496	23:	738	13:	2,090
2	23:	222	13:	724	27:	1,992
3	21:	221	27:	564	23:	1,478
4	13:	178	20:	537	28:	1,075
5	24:	150	28:	456	20:	776
6	27:	126	21:	276	22:	720
7	22:	110	22:	255	26:	553
8	28:	102	10:	211	01:	480
9	19:	93	26:	184	10:	460
10	14:	89	15:	168	14:	366
*						
11	26:	84	11	24:	164	12	15:	328
15	15:	58	12	19:	156	14	21:	299
30	10:	24	15	01:	119		
			17	14:	107		

| Total | 3,483 | | 6,652 | | 15,854 | |

try are largely located in villages (59%). However, machinery factories are mainly located in cities (63% in cities and only 17.2% in villages). Foods and beverages and chemicals are mainly located in rural areas, but miscellaneous were a mixture of urban and rural. This tendency had not changed even by 1920. This implies that the industrial specification largely determines the location of factories. The dominance of a certain industry in some prefectures like Nagano and Aichi and so on shown in factory distribution is the result of the prosperity of specific industries dating from the late Tokugawa period.

Figure II.3 Continued

(i) Number of Factories of Each Prefectures

	1902		1908		1920	
Rank	Code of Prefectures	Number of Factories	Code of Prefectures	Number of Factories	Code of Prefectures	Number of Factories

c) Factory without power

Rank	Code (1902)	Number (1902)	Code (1908)	Number (1908)	Code (1920)	Number (1920)
1	23:	441	28:	803	27:	696
2	27:	381	23:	760	28:	668
3	18:	259	27:	721	18:	634
4	17:	230	13:	680	23:	585
5	28:	171	26:	647	26:	522
6	16:	147	18:	578	13:	362
7	13:	136	11:	509	46:	339
8	33:	129	17:	446	40:	283
9	10:	117	38:	243	17:	255
10	21:	112	21:	206	33:	219
*				*		*
12	26:	90	11 33:	183	12 11:	203
14	38:	81	12 40:	177	13 38:	196
17	11:	64	16 16:	146	33 21:	67
			21 10:	126		
			28 46:	73		
Total		4,335		8,766		8,649

Next we will analyse the concentration of factories in more detail, using the tabulation assembled by the same ownership. This will show the enterprises or individuals owning one factory and the enterprises or individuals owning plural factories. As discussed in Part III, this assembly procedure depends on both computer matching and manual matching, but it is hardly possible to eliminate all possible error matching and the entire failure of matching because of the shortage of background data. Thus, we have some reservations about the confi-

Figure II.3 Continued

(ii) Number of Workers at Factories					

1902		1908		1920	
Rank	Code of Prefectures	Number of Workers	Code of Prefectures	Number of Workers	Code of Prefectures	Number of Workers

a) Total number of workers in factories with power and without power

Rank	Code of Prefectures	Number of Workers	Code of Prefectures	Number of Workers	Code of Prefectures	Number of Workers
1	27:	58,525	27:	81,129	27:	198,654
2	13:	37,073	13:	74,063	13:	160,413
3	20:	36,645	23:	60,332	28:	139,032
4	23:	31,660	28:	58,124	23:	117,197
5	28:	29,262	20:	52,679	20:	88,255
6	40:	15,068	26:	23,479	14:	61,196
7	33:	13,534	22:	20,082	22:	46,741
8	24:	13,325	11:	19,952	26:	43,940
9	26:	12,401	24:	18,149	10:	41,132
10	21:	12,230	18:	16,355	40:	40,995
*						
14	22:	9,588	12 33:	15,582	12 24:	31,436
16	18:	7,841	13 21:	15,125	16 11:	24,193
19	11:	7,079	14 14:	13,159	17 18:	24,024
			15 40:	13,047		
			16 10:	12,745		
Total		452,649		691,467		1,454,170

dence interval of the matching result.

Our database tells us two ways of expanding the sizes of enterprises in addition to the ordinary way of enlarging the size of one factory, because the possible combination of techniques under the feasible technological boundaries of the day imposes limitations on the expansion of the size of one factory. The first way is by horizontal expansion through having plural factories of the same industry and the other is through vertical expansion by linking various factories under the same

Figure II.3 Continued

(ii) Number of Workers at Factories						

	1902		1908		1920	
Rank	Code of Prefectures	Number of Workers	Code of Prefectures	Number of Workers	Code of Prefectures	Number of Workers

b) Factories with power

Rank	Code	Number	Code	Number	Code	Number
1	27:	43,346——27:		63,039———27:		177,378
2	20:	33,795	13:	61,446———13:		153,054
3	13:	31,911	20:	51,001	28:	120,478
4	23:	18,523——23:		44,490	23:	102,435
5	28:	17,461——28:		35,608	20:	87,251
6	40:	13,373	22:	17,235	14:	58,894
7	24:	11,775	19:	15,261	22:	43,935
8	09:	10,217	24:	15,122	10:	39,198
9	33:	10,180	26:	13,145	26:	34,332
10	26:	10,004	33:	12,212	40:	34,145
*			*		*	
13	22:	8,088	12 14:	11,746	11 24:	28,572
14	19:	7,233	14 10:	9,976	12 33:	24,839
			15 40:	9,268	20 19:	14,047
			18 09:	7,817		
Total		327,250		505,965		1,232,932

owner.

1) Horizontal expansion through plural factories occurred not only as a result of the emergence of joint-stock companies, but also among individuals and associations like quasi-companies. The former case happens in both modern industries like cotton spinning and traditional ones like *sake* brewing. The latter cases were also found in *sake* brewing and in silk spinning.

We found the biggest enterprises of multi-plant expansion in the *zakuri* associations for silk spinning using an improved traditional tech-

Figure II.3 Continued

(ii) Number of Workers at Factories

	1902		1908		1920	
Rank	Code of Prefectures	Number of Workers	Code of Prefectures	Number of Workers	Code of Prefectures	Number of Workers

c) Factories without power

1	27:	15,179	28:	22,516	27:	21,276
2	23:	13,137	27:	18,090	18:	19,666
3	28:	11,801	23:	15,842	28:	18,554
4	17:	6,472	13:	12,617	23:	14,762
5	18:	5,756	18:	11,447	17:	13,453
6	13:	5,162	26:	10,334	46:	12,023
7	16:	5,018	11:	9,366	33:	11,285
8	15:	3,975	17:	8,987	38:	10,468
9	33:	3,354	38:	4,643	26:	9,608
10	20:	2,850	40:	3,779	30:	8,763
*						
15	38:	2,669	15:	3,500	13:	7,359
17	26:	2,397	33:	3,370	40:	6,850
23	40:	1,695	16:	3,246	11:	4,007
24	11:	1,693	20:	1,678		
			46:	1,519		
			30:	1,123		

| Total | 125,399 | | 185,502 | | 221,238 | |

nique like Usui-sha (32 in 1902 and 86 in 1909), Kanraku-sha (6 in 1902 and 68 in 1909), Uzen-sha (23 in 1909), Shimonida-sha (23 in 1909) and so on. They were flocking together in a small area because of the supply of cocoons which had to be gathered and processed within a short time. As a result, they wanted to expand their workshops to nearby villages and run them by mutual friendship and so they did not want to attain the status of legal entities like industrial associations called *sangyo-kumiai*.

Some were organized farmers who believed Sontoku Ninomiya's teaching and such unions were called as *Hou-on-kou*.[1] Kunio Yanagida, bureaucrat of the Ministry of Agriculture and Trade and later known as a distinguished ethnologist, once described and upraised the mutual trustworthiness among the participants, expecting that they would grow into industrial associations protected by law (Yanagida [1906] in his collected works, vol. 16, pp. 140–44, Ohtsuka [1960]).[2]

The next group of multi-plant enterprises was found in sake breweries like Tatsuma-shuzo, which had 43 factories in 1909, and so on. There were few such breweries under the same ownership and there were fewer multi-plant owners in the two periods other than in 1909. This is because they were operated seasonally by only small numbers of employees and so most of the breweries were factories of more than five and less than nine employees. Such a big concentration of factories appeared only in 1909 when this size of factories was covered in the survey. Due to technological limitations, the factories could not be expanded easily, so each enterprise wanted to expand in almost the same place and within the same prefecture. As we mentioned earlier about the data in 1900, *sake* brewing is seasonal, beginning after the new harvest of rice and continuing only one hundred and fifty-seven days a year. The *toji*, specialists in *sake* brewing, came mostly from rural areas in a group after they finished their harvest.

2) Some companies organized factories in vertical lines in order to prepare the parts for their final products or businesses. In most cases they adopted modern Western techniques. For example, a beer brewery company expanded its operation to bottle making and wood bottle container making. Mining companies expanded into electricity generation, brick making, gas production and foundry production. Transportation companies such as railroad companies in most cases owned electric plants and factories for repairing vehicles.

Most multi-plant enterprises were of the horizontal expansion type. We found few examples of vertical expansion. For 1902, enterprises having plural factories and spreading over the five broadest categories of industrial classification were quite rare, amounting to only 23. Of these, only four were joint-stock companies. The biggest and most complex were individual or unlimited or limited partnerships like Sumitomo, Furukawa, Mitsui and Mitsubishi who were engaged in mining. In 1909, the number increased because of the inclusion of smaller factories with more than five and less than nine employees, and the patterns of industrial combination began to vary. However, even in 1920 there were only 69 enterprises which had more than two factories belonging to the six broadest different industrial categories.

Thus, total figures for factories owned by companies show a new size distribution of factories. In so far as factories were expanded by the multiple factory system, they tended to remain within the same prefectural boundary. However, the vertical expansion of factories owned by companies may cause factories to spill over prefecture boundaries, and in addition, horizontal expansion by a company system that may be realized through locating factories near the final consumers or local markets may have the same effect. Thus, we get a distribution for all over Japan or by the location of the owning company, if owned by a company.

Thus, we need to purse the distribution of companies in these three periods.

3.3 Integration of Banks and Expansion of Companies

3.3.1 Accumulation of Capital

First we will analyse companies other than banks. Soon after the Sino-Japanese War, in 1896, the number of joint-stock companies was only 1,201, increasing to 2,662 in 1902. After the Russo-Japanese War, in 1907, there was a severe crisis and this was followed by a depression. However, the number of companies had continued to increase, to 3,212 in 1908–09. Then after World War I, in 1920, it jumped to 11,353. We found analogous increases in both limited and unlimited partnerships. There were 1,582 limited partnership companies in 1902, 3,496 in 1909 and 8,527 in 1920. There were 589 unlimited partnership companies in 1902, 1,933 in 1909 and 4,426 in 1920.

Conversely, the number of banks showed a marked decrease, shrinking from 2,324 in 1902, to 2,171 in 1909 and to 1,958 in 1920. This, however, does not imply a shrinkage of banking activities, because the expansion in banking is not shown in an increase of the numbers of banks, but in the cumulation of capital through merger and amalgamation. For example, soon after the Sino-Japanese War, there was a boom in the setting up of private banks. The total number was 604 in 1893 and 817 in 1895, but the average paid-in capital was only 64 thousand yen because they wanted to install a new bank but did not invest in their own banks to expand and strengthen their capital. To avoid excess competition, the Government declared the Act for Amalgamation of Banks in 1896. This act was absorbed into the Commercial Law proclaimed in 1899 and executed in the same year. However, amalgamation required very trivial and time-consuming procedures, so the government amended the Bank Act in 1920. (This amendment was proclaimed in August, 1920. Goto [1970] p. 55 ff).

Our database chose the beginning of 1920 as one of the base years corresponding to the situation just before this amendment, but still shows a marked decrease in the number of banks and an overall increase in the amount of capital.

We can draw a graph of the distribution of companies by the nominal capital and paid-in capital. We should take into consideration the fact that both nominal capital and paid-in capital are in money value so that they are affected by inflation and/or price changes, unlike the other size indicators defined in real terms such as the number of employees and the horsepower in the case of factories.

The size distribution of nominal capital was almost a one-peak lognormal distribution in 1902 and 1909. However, they look like lognormal but have two peaks in 1920. However, the paid-in capital has only one peak in 1902, 1909 and 1920. The size distributions are similar in 1902 and 1909. However, by 1920 paid-in capital had jumped above the 1909 figure. This implies that the number of companies increased for every capital class, reflecting the existence of newcomers. However, needless to say, the upper tail became longer due to the expansion with time of the amount of capital of big companies.

The size distributions for capital were similar for the same kinds of companies, but most limited and unlimited partnerships were concentrated in the lower capital classes. This does not deny the exceptional cases of enormously big companies in limited or unlimited partnerships, such as Mitsui, Mitsubishi and Sumitomo, which later formed plutocrats called as *zaibatsu*. They rather preferred to remain as family or kinship type partnership organizations in the first stage, but they soon realized the necessity of vertical expansion under the control of modern managers, graduates from commercial colleges and so on instead of recruiting principal managers to marry one of their daughters or using the adopted son system. Aonuma (Aonuma [1965] p. 35) stressed that during the early Meiji period traditional merchants had divided into those who successfully adapted to the new social order and those who failed through competition. However, Man'nari [1965] stressed that in the business world the majority of the business élite (55% in 1880s) were born of the merchant class in the Tokugawa regime, which contradicted Tobata's argument (Tobata [1964], pp. 62–72) regarding the importance of the lower *samurai* class (Man'nari's estimate was 8%, 23%, if all people of *samurai* origin were included. Man'nari [1965] pp. 52–79.) The point of issue is whether the innovative character of "entrepreneurs" by Schumpeter's definition can be found in the merchant class or in the lower *samurai* class. (For recent contributions on these topics, see Hashimoto & Takeda [1992].)

The point at issue is how much money had been provided as paid-in capital at the time of a company's formation and how much was added after that to satisfy legal requirements. We pointed out in the previous section that the ratio of paid-in capital to nominal capital was generally less than 64.35% for joint-stock companies, and this situation did not alter. In 1902 the ratio was still 65%, in 1909 52% and in 1920 61%. The scattered nature of these values shows that both lower capital classes and upper capital classes had a lower percentage of paid-in capital.

3.3.2   Distribution of Companies all over Japan

The years after the Sino-Japanese War were a time of expansion of companies and of gradual changes in methods of capital accumulation. Among the three main cities (called *santo*) in the Tokugawa regime, Kyoto, Osaka and Tokyo, Kyoto had already lost its economic importance even in 1896 as we have discussed in the previous sections. Osaka gradually lost its position as a national commercial centre established in the Tokugawa period. The nominal capital accumulated by companies in Tokyo was almost four times greater than that accumulated by companies in Osaka, and paid-in capital was 3.65 times greater. Average capital per company was 1.27 times greater in terms paid-in capital and 2.15 times in terms of nominal capital. It was reflected in the ratio of paid-in capital to nominal capital as 62% in Tokyo and 65% in Osaka. However, this may be the result of imperfect coverage of the data source. The coverages for limited and unlimited partnership companies in the Western regions including Osaka prefecture in our database were limited to companies with more than ten thousand yen of nominal capital while the Eastern regions had no such exclusion principle. The 1920 figures based on the governmental directory had not gotten such an exclusion principle and so the cumulated nominal capital in Tokyo was 2.19 times greater than that of Osaka and 2.22 times greater in terms of paid-in capital. Thus, the leakage in coverage must have some effect on the regional distribution defined by prefecture. The joint-stock companies, however, had not suffered from such systematic exclusion effects.

The shifts of the positions spanned by the number of companies and the amount of capital gathered prefecturewise from 1889 to 1920 are shown in Fig. II.3. The trends of rapidly expanding prefectures were found mostly in centres of textile industries. Those prefectures which did not accumulate capital in 1902 remained stagnant in 1920.

Features of the regional distribution were the dominance of the shipping lines called *Kitamae-sen*, Northern line, which operated from Hokkaido to Tokyo on the Japan Sea, and stopped over in Osaka, passing through the Seto Inner Channel to Tokyo. It took various cargoes, including rice, to Hokkaido, and brought back red herring as dried food and fertilizer. The next point of note is the prosperity of Aichi and Shizuoka, where the Tokugawas lived.[3] The regional distribution of companies according to their legal types show the dominance of joint-stock companies in Tokyo and Hokkaido and the dominance of limited and unlimited partnerships in Osaka. This regional difference in the method of gathering capital may be the result of differences in the kinds of industries among prefectures. There were many more commercial companies in Osaka than in Tokyo.

3.3.3 Expansion of Companies through Financing by Banks

As quoted in the previous Chapter, Imuda stressed the importance to the growth of companies, of finance through banks. This indirect financing was possible through lending money to merchants or entrepreneurs who organized companies without paying the full amount of nominal capital, but gave stock as a security for money borrowed from banks. If this supposition was still applicable even in the 1900s, then the limit of the financing power of the banks must be the capital of those which had legally limited money to lend. Thus, the total amount of capital of banks in the region would have affected the total capital of companies where localities still existed, even if the banks were allowed to lend money without being restricted by their prefectural boundaries.

The regression analysis using the prefectural cross-sectional data of banks and companies endorses the above reasoning. We have tested as explanatory variables, the number of banks, total nominal capital and total paid-in capital of banks in the prefecture. The better explanatory power lies in the ratio of nominal capital of banks to nominal capital of companies. It varied from 0.9104 of adjusted r-square in 1902, to 0.8330 in 1909 and 0.9506 in 1920.

3.3.4 Longitudinal Data of Companies: 1902–20

By virtue of the longitudinal data created by our database, we linked companies from 1902 to 1920. In principle, companies are expected to remain stable. However, some vanished during these two decades and some new ones appeared. As we will explain in Part III, there are inconsistencies in the database between these three periods. Among companies which appeared in 1902 and did not appear in 1909, some appear again in 1920. These must be leakage from the database of 1909. In addition, some companies appeared in 1909 or in 1920 for the first time, but their dates of establishment recorded in the database were before 1902 or 1909. These must also be leakage. (There is some possibility that their ancestors had different names and we might have overlooked the existence in the linkage procedure or the legal forms of their ancestors if they were not corporate ones.)

If we exclude all those which vanished from the database during

Table II.14 Transition of Companies

(i) Summary table by the pattern of existence, 1902 1908 and 1920

Date of establishment	Existence pattern							
	100	110	101	111	010	011	001	Total
Unknown	171	14	0	0	1,739	0	51	1,975
–1879	6	22	1	49	24	4	134	240
1880–1889	85	92	6	149	7	10	263	612
1890–1899	872	643	24	623	57	66	1,326	3,611
1900–1909	1,026	663	25	377	2,666	1,437	1,343	7,537
1910–1919	0	0	1	0	0	69	20,320	20,390
Total	2,160	1,434	57	1,198	4,493	1,586	23,437	34,419

(Note) Code of existence pattern is shown as: 100=exist in 1902, 10=exist in 1908, 1=exist in 1920. And so
  (1) 111 means that company exist from 1902 to 1920,
  (2) 101 means that imperfection of the survey in 1908,
  (3) other combination of zero shows that no existence before or after, for example, 011 appearing in 1908 and 001 as appearing in 1920, and 100 as varnishing after 1902.

the two base years, we will retain core companies which constitute exact longitudinal data without missing values in these three time periods. Using this core database, a transition matrix classified by the type of company and the amount of capital showed fragility of the smaller companies and of commercial companies in general. On average, joint-stock companies were established much earlier than limited and unlimited partnerships. However, longevity is not always applicable to joint-stock companies, and a limited number of investors does not imply a small amount of capital gathered. This is because some of the limited and unlimited partnerships had their origins in wealthy merchants who kept their company unaffected by outside investors and so they did not dare to make their companies joint stock which were compelled to open their accounts to outside investors. Such an example is found in Mitsui, Sumitomo and Fujita.

Table II.14 shows the number of companies classified by date of

Table II.14 Continued

(ii) Average nominal capital per company

Existence pattern	Establishing year	Number of companies			Average of capital		
		1902	1908	1920	1902	1908	1920
100	Unknown	34	—	—	33,915	—	—
	–1879	6	—	—	26,833		
	1880–1889	84	—	—	1,314,066	—	—
	1890–1899	861	—	—	120,670	—	—
	1900–1909	1,022	—	—	43,916	—	—
	Total	2,007	—	—	129,783	–	—
110	Unknown	4	9	—	21,700	23,700	—
	–1879	20	20	—	153,405	248,032	—
	1880–1889	91	92	—	1,018,463	1,443,596	—
	1890–1899	636	641	—	81,415	114,057	—
	1900–1909	657	663	—	104,100	124,427	—
	Total	1,408	1,425	—	153,415	206,028	—
101	–1879	1	—	1	60,000	—	1,000,000
	1880–1889	6	—	6	21,667	—	144,167
	1890–1899	24	—	24	74,413	—	267,677
	1900–1909	22	—	25	25,727	—	119,900
	1910–1919	0	—	1		—	7,500
	Total	53	—	57	47,960	—	198,145
111	–1879	46	45	49	271,419	816,652	4,187,962
	1880–1889	149	149	149	742,560	1,737,543	5,512,306
	1890–1899	616	619	623	189,328	350,373	1,112,439
	1900–1909	366	371	377	63,629	105,484	292,569
	Total	1,177	1,184	1,198	223,484	465,928	1,527,455
010	Unknown	—	1,734	—	—	52,054	—
	–1879	—	7	—	—	163,929	—
	1880–1889	—	7	—	—	50,371	—
	1890–1899	—	56	—	—	117,517	—
	1900–1909	—	2,665	—	—	236,208	—
	Total	—	4,469	—	—	162,863	—
011	–1879	—	4	4	—	142,500	315,000
	1880–1889	—	10	10	—	293,275	374,570
	1890–1899	—	63	66	—	391,708	753,618
	1900–1909	—	1,435	1,437	—	150,344	372,260
	1910–1919	—	69	69	—	3,392	45,394

Table II.14 Continued

| (ii) Average nominal capital per company | | | | | | |
| Existence pattern | Establishing year | Number of companies | | | Average of capital | | |
		1902	1908	1920	1902	1908	1920
	Total	—	1,581	1,586	—	154,432	373,779
001	Unknown	—	—	51	—	—	623,167
	–1879	—	—	134	—	—	3,787,396
	1880–1889	—	—	263	—	—	903,463
	1890–1899	—	—	1,325	—	—	428,020
	1900–1909	—	—	1,343	—	—	390,234
	1910–1919	—	—	20,318	—	—	249,711
	Total	—	—	23,434	—	—	296,225

establishment and their average nominal capital in each period of our database, i.e., 1902, 1909 and 1920. An upper off-diagonal element shows companies with longer lives. Nominal capital increases with the increase in company life.

Among the companies that existed in 1909, the oldest had accumulated as much as 5.17 times more capital than those established between 1900–09. However, those established during 1880–89 had accumulated 7.08 times as much. As time passed we can see the changes in the amount of capital of those that existed in 1920. These averages were based on the cohort group which excluded those that vanished during 1909–19.

Behind the formation of big companies in the early Meiji period, businessmen having special connections with political leaders got advantages at the sales of the government factories and mines, and they were often called *seisho*, political merchants. However, by the middle of the Meiji period the situation had gradually changed. The generational changes of the managers of the giant family merchants, called *zaibatsu*, such as Mitsubishi, Mitsui and Sumitomo, adopted the company system. What made this possible was the propagation of a new higher educational system for merchants.[4]

3.4 Relation between Company-owned Factories and their Owner Company

3.4.1 Our Matching Model and its Results

The relations between the factory owner and his or her factories are shown in Fig. II.4(i). The owner is defined in a set X where owner (i), i.e. x(i) in a set X, has one or more factories f(i) in a set of factories F. If the owner (i) has two factories, we show them as factories f(i1) and f(i2), while if owner x(j) has only one factory, we show it as f(j.)$=f$(j). We obtain statistics, as discussed in the previous section, as single-factory enterprises (x(j) shown above) and plural-factory enterprises (x(i)). We can confirm whether the owner is x(i) type or x(j)

Figure II.4 Model of relation of ownership

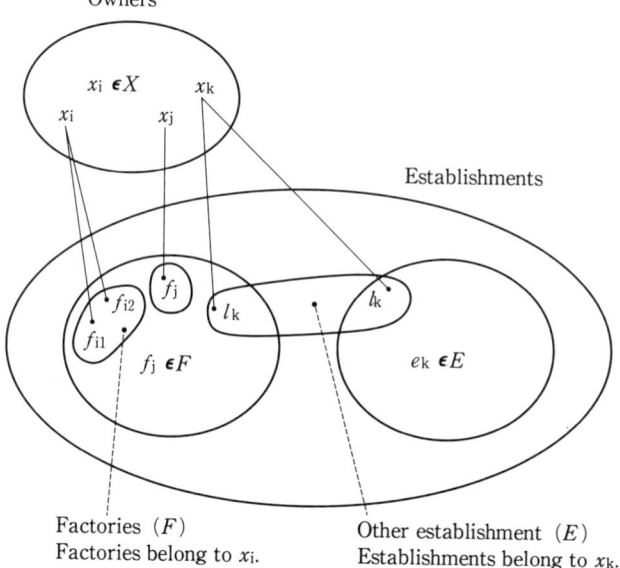

Owners

Establishments

Factories (F)
Factories belong to x_i.

Other establishment (E)
Establishments belong to x_k.

(i)   Relation between owners and their establishments

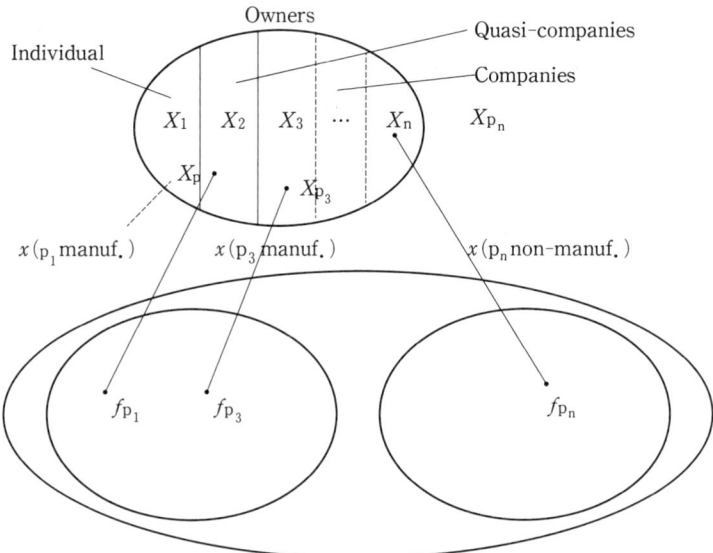

(ii) Relation of owners of establishments and their industry

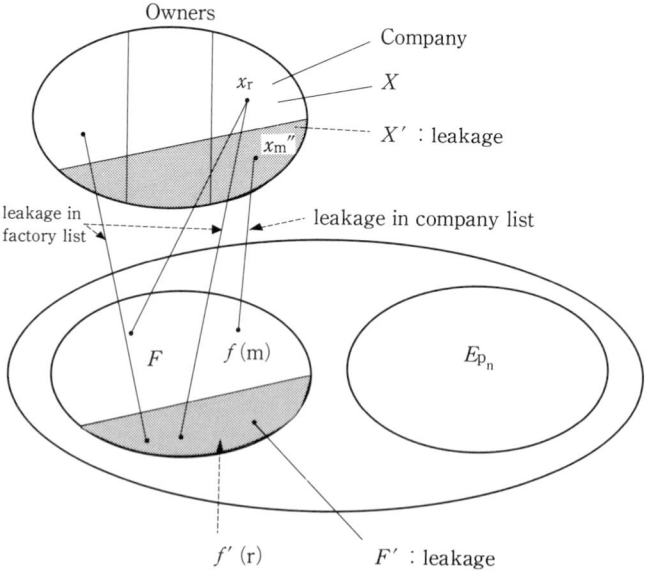

(iii) Difference of coverages of surveys

type from the information about $f(i)$ and $f(j)$. If $x(k)$ has a factory $f(k)$ and another establishment $e(k)$ which belongs to a set E (the other establishment) we do not have information about $e(k)$ because of the absence of a survey of E. Then, owner $x(l)$, having only one establishment $e(l)$ in a set E cannot be identified because of the absence of information on E. Now, we divide a set X into sub sets X_1 to X_n by the legal type of owners from pure individual and quasi-company to joint-stock company as shown Fig. II.4(ii). Then we can classify the company by its industry (q) expressed as $X(p,q)$.

Actual matching with $x(i)$ in a set X to $f(i)$ in a set F will reveal another problem as shown in Fig. II.4(iii). If we trace the owner: $x'(m)$ from the file F, we sometimes encounter no name $x'(m)$ in a set of companies due to the leakage of set X. Conversely, we may find some manufacturing companies $x(i,k)$ that had no factory in a set F, so there must be some leakage in set F. In our database, X' is observable by matching $f(m)$ to $x(m)$ because of the non-existence of the name $x(m)$ in X. However, factory $f'(r)$ of company $x(r)$ sometimes cannot be traced because of the coverage of F excluding subset F', for example, defined as powerless and having less than five employees in 1920, but it is difficult to distinguish whether F' is non-qualified or leakage.

If our classification of an industry as manufacturing is correct, our matching results will show the existence of X' and F'. The results of matching are shown in Table II.15. There are 1,082 members in set X' against 732 in set X in 1902, 1,813 against 1,203 in 1909, and 2,667 against 4,138 in 1920. We controlled the coverage of 1909 to the same size of more than ten employees, but if we include those with more than five and less than nine employees, the numbers are 2,869 against 1,410. Although matched companies increased to 207, unmatched companies increased much more: to 1,560. There must be many smaller companies having smaller factories. If we restrict companies to strictly legal companies, X' becomes much smaller. For example, in the case of joint-stock companies, those in X' decrease to 50 against 490 in 1902 and 67 against 629 in 1909 (77 against 721 in the case of more than five employees) and 531 against 2,730 in 1920. Coverage adjustment of 1902 will tell us that the rate of increase of unmatched companies' names, i.e. leakage of the company directory, increased from 67 to 77 and matched companies' names also increased

Table II.15 Factories Classified by Owners and Matched with Company Directories

(i) Number of factories owned by companies classified by the type of companies 1902

Employee size	K In CD Exist	K In CD Non-exist	K Exist	K Non-exist	M In CD Exist	M In CD Non-exist	M Exist	M Non-exist	S In CD Exist	S In CD Non-exist	S Exist	S Non-exist	C In CD Exist	C In CD Non-exist	C Exist	C Non-exist	Total Exist	Total Non-exist	Grand total
1–9	—	1	1	—					—	1				1			1	3	4
10–29	113	11	21	27					51	77				302			185	417	602
30–49	62	8	12	12					36	64				159			110	243	353
50–99	131	14	18	11					40	54				164			189	243	432
100–499	130	11	14	14					44	25				94			188	144	332
500–999	32	2	4	1					1	1				11			37	15	52
1000–1999	13	2	—	—					2	1				2			15	5	20
2000–2999	2	—	—	—					—	—				—			2	—	2
3000 over	9	—	2	—					1	—				1			12	1	13
Total	492	49	72	65					175	223				734			739	1,071	1,810

(Notes)

1) CD: company directory which contains information about size of capital.

2) Code for type of company: K: Joint-stock company, M: Unlimited partnership company, S: Limited partnership company, C: Quasi-company

3) Employee size was obtained from the data of factories in the factory directory. Our database assembles all the

Table II.15 Continued

	1908 — Type of Company								
	K	M	S	C	n.a.		Total		Grand total
	In CD	In CD	In CD	In CD	In CD		In CD		
Employee size	Exist	Exist	Exist	Exist	Exist	Non-exist	Exist	Non-exist	—
10–29	190	72	155	1	1	966	419	966	1,385
30–49	85	42	55	—	—	313	182	313	495
50–99	130	31	76	—	—	289	237	289	526
100–499	171	44	80	—	—	220	295	220	515
500–999	22	6	10	—	—	16	38	16	54
1000–1999	16	—	3	—	—	7	19	7	26
2000–2999	6	—	—	—	—	1	6	1	7
3000 over	12	—	1	—	—	1	13	1	14
Unknown	—	—	—	—	—	1	—	1	1
Total	632	195	380	1	1	1,814	1,209	1,814	3,023

153

Table II.15 Continued

1908*

Employee size	Type of Company												Grand total
	K		M		S		C		n.a.		Total		
	In CD		In CD		In CD		In CD		In CD		In CD		—
	Exist	Non-exist	Exist	Non-exist	Exist	Non-exist	Exist	Non-exist	Exist	Non-exist	Exist	Non-exist	
1–9	89	11	36	45	71	89	—	871	—	—	196	1,016	1,212
10–29	189	22	72	50	156	140	1	775	1	—	419	987	1,406
30–49	85	11	42	27	55	41	—	243	—	—	182	322	504
50–99	131	12	31	25	76	56	—	205	—	—	238	298	536
100–499	172	16	44	30	80	41	—	137	—	—	296	224	520
500–999	22	1	6	3	10	—	—	11	—	—	38	15	53
1000–1999	16	—	—	—	3	1	—	7	—	—	19	8	27
2000–2999	6	—	—	—	—	—	—	1	—	—	6	1	7
3000 over	12	—	—	—	1	—	—	1	—	—	13	1	14
Unknown	1	—	—	—	—	—	—	1	—	1	1	2	3
Total	723	73	231	180	452	368	1	2,252	1	1	1,408	2,874	4,282

(Note) *: Factory directory used contains factories more than five employee:

Table II.15 Continued

1920

Type of Company

Employee size	K In CD		M In CD		S In CD		C In CD		Total In CD		Grand total
	Exist	Non-exist	Exist	Non-exist	Exist	Non-exist	Exist	Non-exist	Exist	Non-exist	
1–9	3	—	—	—	1	—	1	2	4	2	6
10–29	890	230	261	170	456	254	1	925	1,608	1,579	3,187
30–49	470	102	103	37	153	73	—	218	726	430	1,156
50–99	511	104	95	46	125	56	—	156	731	362	1,093
100–499	653	85	85	28	97	32	—	120	835	265	1,100
500–999	89	9	5	1	11	—	—	14	105	24	129
1000–1999	49	1	5	—	4	—	—	3	58	4	62
2000–2999	19	—	—	—	—	—	—	—	19	—	19
3000 over	36	—	—	—	1	—	—	—	37	—	37
unknown	10	—	2	—	3	—	—	1	15	1	16
Total	2,730	531	556	282	851	415	1	1,439	4,138	2,667	6,805

Table II.15 Continued

(ii) Number of Enterprises in Company Directory matched with factory directory 1902

Capital size (ten thousand yen)	Non-manufacturing Company In FD		Manufacturing Company In FD		Total In FD		Grand total
	Exist	Non-exist	Exist	Non-exist	Exist	Non-exist	—
5 less	20	1,861	321	956	341	2,817	3,159
5–10	4	362	94	169	98	531	629
10–50	5	335	171	137	176	472	648
50–100	2	39	40	13	42	52	94
100–500	5	38	41	9	46	47	93
500 over	6	12	5	—	11	12	23
Unknown	2	109	23	70	25	179	204
Total	44	2,756	695	1,354	739	4,110	4,849

(Note) FD: Factory directory

Table II.15 Continued

Capital size (ten thousand yen)	Non-manufacturing Company In FD		Manufacturing Company In FD		n.a. In FD	Total In FD		Grand total
	Exist	Non-exist	Exist	Non-exist	Exist	Exist	Non-exist	
5 less	83	4,272	524	1,399	—	607	5,671	6,278
5–10	17	553	123	152	—	140	705	845
10–50	47	609	209	134	—	256	743	999
50–100	15	107	51	28	—	66	135	201
100–500	16	101	87	27	—	103	128	231
500 over	7	34	22	7	—	29	41	70
Unknown	3	41	4	12	—	7	53	60
n.a.	—	—	—	—	1	1	—	1
Total	188	5,717	1,020	1,759	1	1,209	7,476	8,685

Table II.15 Contined

1908*

Capital size (ten thousand yen)	Non-manufacturing Company In FD		Manufacturing Company In FD		n.a. In FD	Total In FD		Grand total
	Exist	Non-exist	Exist	Non-exist	Exist	Exist	Non-exist	
5 less	119	4,236	634	1,289	—	753	5,525	6,278
5–10	21	549	143	132	—	164	681	845
10–50	55	601	220	123	—	275	724	999
50–100	16	106	52	27	—	68	133	201
100–500	20	97	88	26	—	108	123	231
500 over	7	34	22	7	—	29	41	70
Unknown	3	41	7	9	—	10	50	60
n.a.	—	—	—	—	1	1	—	1
Total	241	5,664	1,166	1,613	1	1,408	7,277	8,685

Note: *: Factory directory used contains factories more than five employee:

Table II.15 Continued

Capital size (ten thousand yen)	Non-manufacturing Company		Manufacturing Company		Total		Grand total
	In FD		In FD		In FD		
	Exist	Non-exist	Exist	Non-exist	Exist	Non-exist	
							—
							—
5 less	124	8,881	1,261	4,087	1,385	12,968	14,353
5–10	37	1,765	432	655	469	2,420	2,889
10–50	91	2,127	1,056	1,001	1,147	3,128	4,275
50–100	30	477	427	227	457	704	1,161
100–500	68	613	469	207	537	820	1,357
500 over	43	133	99	30	142	163	305
Unknown	—	6	1	2	1	8	9
Total	393	14,002	3,745	6,209	4,138	20,211	24,349

Notes:

1) FD: factory directory used covered factories having more than ten artisans (employee) except the 1908 directory covered factories having more than five artisans. The 1908 matching results are based on the entire 1908 directory and the extracted directory.

2) The definition of manufacturing and non-manufacturing companies depends on the classification adopted in the company directory used.

from 629 to 721. This suggests that there must be some leakage in the company directory. The companies leaked were concentrated in the class with less than nine employees. However, there must have been some companies which operated factories with fewer employees. The size of companies whose factories as a whole employed less than 2,000 employees (Factories $f(j)$ in F of $x(j)$ in X' was on average less than 2,000).

The leakage averaged just below ten percent of the companies founded in X in 1902 and 1909. However, in 1920 it increased to nearly twenty percent. The one year time lag of the factory directory and company directory may be one of the reasons for this increase.

In checking set F', it is difficult to identify the accuracy of encoding of the company as manufacturing. If the encoding of a company in X were not exact, there would be no counterpart in set F'. If the encoding as a manufacturing company is exact, there must be as many factories in F' as there are with no counterpart companies. Only 689 companies found their counterpart factories in set F, against 1,360 in F' in 1902. Where there were more than five employees in 1920, there were 1,154 in F against 1,625 in F'. However, where there were more than ten employees, there were 1,005 against 1,774. This means that the number of companies decreased by 149 in F and increased by 149 in F' due to the change in coverage of the survey. This implies that even manufacturers employing the company system may have factories with less than five employees.

Anyhow we have obtained the company owned factory statistics which tell us the relative capital amounts and numbers of employees of factories owned by companies. The basic feature of this cross tabulation is that even in the smallest capital class, less than fifty thousand *yen*, there were many companies employing more than a thousand employees in 1902 and more than two thousand employees in 1909 and in 1920 (see Table II.16). As mentioned, a company may expand its factory size by making one factory bigger or by juxtaposing similar employee size factories. The expansion of the manufacturing company in the former case is usually accompanied by technological innovations and addition of much bigger machinery. This implies that expansion does not always imply an increase in the number of employees. Thus, it is not always traceable diagonally on two axes of capital and employee

Table II.16 Company having Factories: Enterprises classified by capital size and employee size

| | Number of Enterprise 1902 | | | | | | | | | |
| | Employee size | | | | | | | | | |
Capital size (ten thousand yen)	1-9	10-29	30-49	50-99	100-499	500-999	1000-1999	2000-2999	3000 over	Total
5 less	1	123	65	96	55	1	—	—	—	341
5-10	—	21	19	27	30	1	—	—	—	98
10-50	—	28	18	49	65	10	6	—	—	176
50-100	—	4	3	2	17	12	3	—	1	42
100-500	—	3	—	4	14	10	6	1	8	46
500 over	—	1	—	—	3	3	—	1	3	11
Unknown	—	5	5	11	4	—	—	—	—	25
Total	1	185	110	189	188	37	15	2	12	739

Factory directory used covers those having more than five employee.

Table II.16 Continued

Capital size (ten thousand yen)	1908 Employee size								
	10–29	30–49	50–99	100–499	500–999	1000–1999	2000–2999	3000 over	Total
5 less	275	107	115	99	10	1	—	—	607
5–10	58	17	32	30	2	1	—	—	140
10–50	64	36	64	86	4	2	—	—	256
50–100	7	10	11	29	3	3	3	—	66
100–500	10	9	13	42	12	10	1	6	103
500 over	—	1	2	8	7	2	2	7	29
Unknown	4	2	—	1	—	—	—	—	7
n.a.	1	—	—	—	—	—	—	—	1
Total	419	182	238	295	38	19	6	13	1,209

Table II.16 Continued

1908*

Capital size (ten thousand yen)	Employee size										
	1–9	10–29	30–49	50–99	100–499	500–999	1000–1999	2000–2999	3000 over	Unknown	Total
5 less	144	276	107	115	99	10	1	—	—	1	753
5–10	24	58	17	32	30	2	1	—	—	—	164
10–50	19	64	35	64	87	4	2	—	—	—	275
50–100	1	8	10	11	29	3	3	3	—	—	68
100–500	5	8	10	14	42	12	10	1	6	—	108
500 over	—	—	1	2	8	7	2	2	7	—	29
Unknown	3	4	2	—	1	—	—	—	—	—	10
n.a.	—	1	—	—	—	—	—	—	—	—	1
Total	196	419	182	238	296	38	19	6	13	1	1,408

(Note) *: Factory directory used covers those factories having more than five employee.

163

Table II.16 Continued

1920

Employee size

Capital size (ten thousand yen)	1–9	10–29	30–49	50–99	100–499	500–999	1000–1999	2000–2999	3000 over	Unkown	Total
5 less	1	818	241	182	134	4	1	—	—	4	1,385
5–10	2	239	87	80	57	2	2	—	—	—	469
10–50	—	378	264	246	236	13	4	—	1	5	1,147
50–100	—	96	77	117	147	14	4	—	—	2	457
100–500	1	62	50	93	227	48	37	8	8	3	537
500 over	—	15	7	13	33	24	10	11	28	1	142
Unknown	—	—	—	—	1	—	—	—	—	—	1
Total	4	1,608	726	731	835	105	58	19	37	15	4,138

numbers.

3.4.2 Features of Factories Defined by the Company's Capital and the Number of Employees

It is not always possible to uniquely classify companies having more than two factories in one point of the industrial classification scheme, in so far as we use a classification code for each factory. As mentioned in section 3.2.2, describing factories as multi-factory enterprises and single-factory enterprises may mean that they have more than two industrial classification codes due to the vertical expansion. By virtue of statistics classified by the factory owner, we can cross tabulate employee numbers and capital amounts in so far as the owner is a company. However, further classification by location and industry needs to impose some restriction on the classification criteria such as assigning a location code where the company was registered and an industrial classification code of the company's main business or that of the factory with the largest number of employees among the factories of the company concerned. We have no other information about the level of production or turnover of the company or its factories at present in so far as we depend on our database system with limited available data.

Anyhow, cross tabulation by number of employees and amount of capital will reveal the hidden structure which was unknown to us in so far as we use single tabulation. The problem still lies in what is the true indicator of size of a factory or company. Companies are usually measured by their capital amount, as it is very difficult to obtain figures for turnover, total assets, total added value, etc. Factories are mostly measured by their numbers of employees, not by the size of their tangible assets, which are the most useful indicator reflecting technological aspects of factory size, if we combine it with labour input expressed by number of employees.

Most of the analyses of manufacturing industries presuppose that the size of a factory is expressed only by the number of its employees, because there are insufficient figures regarding its tangible assets. In some cases, the horsepower of its engines is substituted (Minami [1987]). This time we can use the company's capital instead of its tangible assets. Capital is, in most cases, correlated with total assets which certainly include tangible assets. However, as we have just mentioned, this entails the impossibility of further subdivision of capital of a company among its factories, especially those whose industrial classification specifications are different.

As is well-known, some textile factories were operated by huge amounts of manual labour, so they had a comparatively large number of employees. This is closely connected to the formation of a dual structure of the Japanese economy. This often quoted dual structure (Shinohara [1970], Ohkawa [1972]) means that there were two groups of enterprises: one that had easy access to the capital market and to the labour market which supplied a skilled labour force and one that did not. The discrepancy between the two groups was quite deep. The inaccessibility of the latter to a highly skilled labour force meant that the demands of the unskilled labour force were satisfied, but at lower wage rates. The starting period of this dual structure, especially of the labour market, is said to have formed after World War I around the 1930s (Umemura [1955] pp. 256–59, [1961] chap. 9-10, Odaka [1984] pp. 40ff).

The basic source of Umemura's reasoning is the non-existence of wage differentials by number of employees in the manufacturing censuses in 1909 and 1914. However, wage differentials were found in the regional manufacturing and commerce censuses carried out around 1930s where the tabulation of factories or firms classified by their capital appeared for the first time. Yasukichi Yasuba developed another type of reasoning based on the same manufacturing census in 1909 and found wage differentials in textile industries where the dominance of borrowed technology made it possible to offer higher wage rates (Yasuba [1976]). However, wage statistics classified by establishments with large numbers of employees appearing in manufacturing censuses after 1909 cannot escape the problem of whether a factory with a comparatively large number of employees but a small amount of capital cannot be distinguished from a really big factory having both a large amount of capital and a large number of employees. The existence of these kinds of factories having a large number of employees but a small amount of capital is proved through our database for the years 1902, 1909 and 1920 (see the discussion in the section: 3.2.2 above).

Konosuke Odaka analysed the wage records of the ship building industry and the steel industry and concluded that the key factor determining wage rates in the 1910s was not the level of education but the on-the-job-training received by the skilled workers (Odaka [1984]). As Shunsaku Nishikawa commented in his persuasive general economic history (Nishikawa [1985] pp. 251–61.), this fact finding and these topics are closely connected with the turning point controversy when the Japanese economy had departed from the agrarian (see Minami [1970], or its English version [1987]).

Before going further, we will analyse the 1900 wage data of a factory survey. Comprehensive wage data of industrial subdivision were prepared for the first time after the failure of the 1894 manufacturing yard and factory survey. The wage rates of males and females under and over fourteen years of age were tabulated for each industrial subdivision, as an average per worker per day. The average here defined in the formats declared on the 4th of July, 1899 (Decree ♯34) is the mode and not the arithmetical mean. We do not know whether this also applies to wage rates for each industrial subdivision in the survey report. It is confirmed that the average of each upper classification code was a simple arithmetic mean of all lower class wage rates divided by the number of subdivisions concerned. Thus, we should further elaborate within the limited availability of the data.

The wage rates for each industrial subdivision comprise our sole data which are close to the original data. We use them as primary data and regard them as the mode for each industrial subdivision. Using the number of employees as weights, we compute the average wage rates for each industrial subdivision, as shown in Table II.17. The wage rate per day for males over fourteen years of age was thirty-nine *sen*, one *rin* (i.e. 0.391 *yen*), a little bit higher than for daily employed male farmers (0.300 *yen*), and that for females over fourteen years of age was seventeen *sen*, two *rin* (i.e. 0.172 *yen*), comparable to the nineteen *sen* for daily employed female farmers. The wage survey carried out by the Rural and Commercial Correspondence system was only for craftsmen and female workers. We do not have any data for factory workers.

It is evident that substantial wage differentials had already appeared between males and females. The wage differentials for adult employees over fourteen years of age between males and females is 2.27 times larger of male to female as a whole, 2.30 for workers in factories

Table II.17 Wage Differentials in 1900

Industrial sub-division	Male over 14	Female over 14	Male under 14	Female under 14
All	391.03	172.42	126.18	95.02
Weight	3387	717	223	191
Textile	280.99	172.69	121.41	96.88
Machinery	555.47	204.95	168.63	89.41
Chemicals	369.81	168.74	110.07	78.33
Food & beverage	351.16	153.09	117.56	97.08
Miscellaneous	397.17	198.09	127.42	105.06
Special	365.24	173.00	153.00	111.00

(Notes) Weighted average by the size of employee of each subdivision of industrial classification.

with power and 2.21 in factories without power. The wage differentials for non-adult employees under thirteen years of age between male and female is 1.81 times larger of male to female as a whole and 1.36 for workers at factories with power and 1.33 at those without. The wage differentials between male and female is smaller for younger people under thirteen years of age, so the difference between adult and non-adult is bigger for males and smaller for females: 3.09 and 1.81, respectively. These differences are mainly the result of the weights of distribution of workers among industrial subdivisions.

The wage differentials of industrial subdivisions between genders for workers over fourteen years of age show the correlation among the wage rates as adjusted r-square 0.359. In other words, in industrial subdivisions where the wage rates for males are higher, the wage rates for females are also higher. The wage difference between the genders may stem from the difference between the technological structure of the industrial subdivisions. The most important difference is whether certain factories in one industrial subdivision are governed by seasonal changes. As we have seen in section 2.1.3, some of the factories which were operated for less than 250 days a year must be regarded as being governed by the agrarian calendar. That is, they were operated during off-seasons.

The wage rates not only differ among subdivisions of industrial classifications, which may be the result of occupational heterogeneity due to the skill of the labour, but also among the operational days of the factory during the year. Thus, they seemed to closely correlate with the number of working days for each industrial subdivision. Those industries that operate for less than 250 days a year showed remarkably low wage rates. Some of the textile industries such as weaving showed low wage rates, although they belonged to the category of factories that operated nearly three hundred days a year. Similar low wage rates for factories with a large number of operational days per year were found in industries such as match making, traditional Japanese paper making (both classified in the chemical industry) and making of straw products like hats and *tatami* mats (classified as miscellaneous industries).

Thus, we roughly classified industries into two categories: one comprising those of a seasonal nature, mainly in the rural area, with relatively low wage rates; and the other comprising those of a nonseasonal nature, where work is done in factories that operate throughout the year. However, the latter does not guarantee higher wage rates. It is further subdivided into a lower wage rate group and a higher wage rate group. The distinction between traditional and imported technology is not the key factor in determining the wage differentials. We found low wage rates with more operational days per year in industries of imported product makers such as in the match industry, and so on. The machinery industry showed higher wage rates. The unweighted arithmetic mean shown in the report is 53.4 *sen* per day, but the weighted mean amounts to 55.5 *sen* per day: 55.8 with power and 53.2 without power. This implies that the shipping industry and the armaments industry show the highest wage rates (61.4 *sen* and 61.2 *sen*, respectively) and those of mainly traditional machinery factories show a lower wage rate (44.5 *sen* for umbrellas, knives, needles, spades, etc., and 40.0 for bronze) and the employee structure of these factories produces a difference in average wage rates with and without weights of employees. Other high wage rates are found in gas production (58.3 *sen*), leather products (57.0 *sen*) and feather products like brushes (56.5 *sen*).

These higher wage rate groups may be comparable to the figures for the higher wage rates of artisans such as bricklayers (63.0 *sen*), masons

(61.0 *sen*), tailors (59.0 *sen*), ship carpenters and paper hangers (56.0 *sen*), and carpenters and plasterers (54.0 *sen*). These lower wage rates are comparable to those of rural workers. Thus, the labour market may be divided to two groups: urban and rural.

The problem of the difference of skills and the feasibility of paying higher wage rates for managers remains unsolved. As we mentioned above, a large number of employees does not guarantee a big enterprise, and so here we will confirm the existence of wage differentials among different industries. Our fact finding will lead to the conclusion that wage differentials due to differences of industrial subdivision are closely connected with the agrarian character of the industry concerned. Those factories deeply rooted in the rural area can gather cheap labour because of the seasonal nature of the work. Thus, the discussion will be oriented to the problem how to measure of the size of the enterprise.

3.4.3 Size Distribution of Enterprises and its Effects on Wage Differentials

More detailed wage data are obtainable through the realization of the manufacturing census in 1909. The final reports in two volumes published in 1911 show various tables in two-way classification by employee size and industrial subdivision, by prefecture and number of employees, or by prefecture and industrial subdivision. As we have mentioned before, most people using this 1909 manufacturing census deduced that the number of employees did not affect the wage differentials as a whole. However, whether the selection of a size criterion such as number of employees or amount of capital, and patterns of factory ownership really did not affect the wage rate remains an unsolved problem.

Our database using the directory information based on the 1909 survey will tell us that a certain factory located in a certain prefecture can be identified by its employee size and industrial subdivision. Thus, we can link these three two-way classification tables found in the 1909 survey reports into one integrated table. Luckily at that time the government did not adopt the principle of enclosing a single factory cell with other cells to make the individual record unidentifiable.

Eventually, we have squeezed out some individual records of each factory from the summary tables of the 1909 reports combined with our database based on the directory of factories. These disclosed records indicate 645 factories (see Part III for details of squeezing procedures). Incidentally, in addition to these squeezed-out data, we found a copy of the records submitted to the Ministry, which had been preserved in the prefecture archives. Almost all the factories in Aichi Prefecture were available except those in Nagoya City and those in two counties of Gunma Prefecture were available. Thus, the total number of records we can use for the analysis increased to 3,386 factories.

Thus, combined with our factory-company linked database, we obtained factory data such as wage rates, numbers of working days and so on, in so far as they were surveyed in 1909 and tabulated in the reports. The records are summarized in Table II.18.[5] They can be re-classified by amount of capital and number of employees, indicating whether or not the dual structure of the labour market had already appeared by 1909. Another point of issue regarding company owned factory statistics is that factories using modern Western technology started as company owned factories. Traditional technologies, except those like *sake* brewing, which had accumulated a fairly big capital through the Tokugawa period and modernized their management methods, were generally left in the hands of individuals.

Our sample data clearly show that the number of employees was not a unique criterion of factory size, as we have discussed using the factory-company linked database which covered factory data nationwide. A capital size of 500–1,000 thousand *yen* and a number of employees of 500–1,000 may be the transition point between big enterprises and small and medium enterprises. Needless to say the number of employees is crucial and there were many factories with either less capital and more employees, or more capital and fewer employees under this transition point, especially the latter, but only privately owned factories were in the class of more than 1,000 employees.

Of 3,386 factories, 161 belonged to joint-stock companies, 59 to unlimited partnerships and 153 to limited partnerships. In addition, 434 were quasi-companies and 2,556 were private individuals, and constituted more than eighty-eight percent of the total. When we counted only purely privately owned factories, they still constituted seventy-five

Table II.18 Distribution of Factories whose Micro-data Sets are Available (1909)

Capital size (Ten thousand yen)	Size of employee										Unknown	Total
	—	1-9	10-29	30-49	50-99	100-499	500-999	1000-1999	2000-2999	3000 over		
—	376	207	64	43	22	7	2	1	1	—	2,390	3,112
5 less	134	264	110	105	103	7	—	1	1	—	96	820
5–10	29	94	13	32	27	—	1	—	—	—	19	215
10–50	27	125	52	62	86	4	1	—	—	—	19	376
50–100	6	33	12	14	29	6	5	—	—	—	1	106
100–500	11	22	19	33	55	25	12	4	3	—	4	188
500 over	6	16	21	20	38	16	9	5	6	—	6	143
Unknown	3	3	2	—	1	—	—	—	—	—	1	10
Total	592	764	293	309	361	65	30	11	9	—	2,536	4,970

Breakdown by the type of companies and the size of capital:

a) K: Joint-stock companies

Capital	—	1-9	10-29	30-49	50-99	100-499	500-999	1000-1999	2000-2999	3000 over	Unknown	Total
—	—	1	2	2	2	1	1	1	—	—	—	10
5 less	6	8	—	—	—	—	—	—	—	—	—	14
5–10	2	2	1	—	—	—	—	—	—	—	—	5
10–50	2	8	4	3	2	1	—	—	—	—	—	20
50–100	1	2	—	2	4	—	—	—	—	—	—	9
100–500	2	3	1	5	11	6	1	—	—	—	—	29
500 over	—	—	3	2	10	8	—	—	1	1	—	25
Total	14	25	11	14	29	16	2	1	1	1	—	112

b) M: Unlimited partnership companies

Capital	—	1-9	10-29	30-49	50-99	100-499	500-999	1000-1999	2000-2999	3000 over	Unknown	Total
—	4	1	2	2	—	1	1	—	—	—	—	8
5 less	1	—	—	1	—	—	—	—	—	—	—	2
5–10	—	1	—	—	—	—	—	—	—	—	—	1
10–50	—	1	1	—	—	1	—	—	—	—	—	3
Total	5	3	2	2	1	2	—	—	—	—	—	14

Size of employee

Capital size	1-9	10-29	30-49	50-99	100-499	500-999	1000-1999	2000-2999	3000 over	Unknown	Total
c) S: Limited partnership companies											
—	5	8	3	4	—	—	—	—	—	—	20
5 less	3	7	—	2	1	—	—	—	—	—	13
5–10	—	1	—	—	—	—	—	—	—	—	1
10–50	—	—	1	—	—	1	—	—	—	—	2
Total	8	16	4	6	1	1	—	—	—	—	36
d) C: Quasi-companies											
—	26	23	7	5	5	1	—	—	—	—	67
5 less	—	—	1	—	—	—	—	—	—	—	1
Total	26	23	8	5	5	1	—	—	—	—	68
e) Individual owners											
—	337	170	47	32	12	4	2	—	—	2,390	2,994
5 less	124	249	109	102	103	6	—	1	—	96	790
5–10	27	90	12	32	27	—	1	—	—	19	208
10–50	25	116	47	59	82	2	1	—	—	19	351
50–100	5	31	12	12	25	6	5	—	—	1	97
100–500	9	19	18	28	44	19	11	4	3	4	159
500 over	6	16	18	18	28	8	9	4	5	6	118
Unknown	3	3	2	—	1	—	—	—	—	1	10
Total	536	694	265	283	322	45	29	9	8	2,536	4,727
f) Others											
—	3	3	3	3	—	—	—	1	—	—	13
Total	3	3	3	3	—	—	—	1	—	—	13

(Note) Microdata sets are derived from the cross-tabulated tables combined with factory directory and questionnaires reserved in the dossiers of some prefectures.

Table II.19 Average Wage-rates of Workers for 1909

(Unit. *Sen* per day)

(i) Wage-rates of workers over 14 years old

Capital size (ten thousand yen)	Size of employee										
	1-9	10-29	30-49	50-99	100-499	500-999	1000-1999	2000-2999	3000 over	Unknown	Total
a) Male											
—	39	43	44	45	51	55	50	70	—	31	34
5 less	50	49	35	44	—	25	—	55	—	39	41
5-10	55	35	57	—	—	—	—	—	—	43	44
10-50	43	48	53	43	42	39	—	—	—	42	44
50-100	60	36	—	48	47	—	—	—	—	50	46
100-500	51	46	38	43	48	53	50	—	—	41	47
500 over	—	28	47	52	53	48	—	40	38	42	48
Unknown	—	—	—	—	—	—	—	—	—	37	37
Total	39	43	45	45	50	49	50	55	38	32	34
b) Female											
—	11	22	24	31	27	50	27	32	—	15	16
5 less	6	10	17	29	—	20	—	15	—	17	15
5-10	0	9	0	—	—	—	—	—	—	14	12
10-50	13	5	12	22	24	28	—	—	—	11	13
50-100	0	18	—	10	24	—	—	—	—	0	15
100-500	0	7	0	22	25	23	24	25	—	17	19
500 over	—	14	9	9	26	22	—	—	22	21	21
Unknown	—	—	—	—	—	—	—	—	—	0	0
Total	11	20	22	28	26	31	26	24	22	15	16

(ii) Wage-rates of workers under 13 years old

(Unit. Sen per day)

Capital size (ten thousand yen)	Size of employee										
	1–9	10–29	30–49	50–99	100–499	500–999	1000–1999	2000–2999	3000 over	Unknown	Total
a) Male											
—	1	1	2	2	6	4	8	14	—	2	2
5 less	0	0	0	0	—	20	—	7	—	6	4
5–10	0	0	0	—	4	13	—	—	—	1	1
10–50	0	0	8	0	0	—	—	—	—	6	3
50–100	0	0	3	8	4	12	17	—	—	0	2
100–500	0	0	0	3	3	10	—	—	—	4	5
500 over	—	6	0	0	4	9	—	16	24	13	7
Total	1	1	2	2	4	12	11	12	24	2	2
b) Female											
—	0	1	3	3	7	11	9	22	—	3	3
5 less	0	1	0	3	—	17	—	7	—	5	4
5–10	0	3	0	—	—	—	—	—	—	4	3
10–50	0	0	0	0	9	13	—	—	—	3	2
50–100	0	0	0	0	7	—	—	—	—	0	3
100–500	0	0	0	0	3	13	13	—	—	4	4
500 over	0	0	6	6	5	12	—	—	—	14	8
Unknown	—	—	—	—	—	—	—	14	18	0	0
Total	0	3	2	2	6	12	16	14	18	3	3

(Notes)

(1) Average wage-rate per factory is obtained without weighting with the number of employee.

(2) The '—', in capital size indicates those factories whose micro data sets were available but not found in the company directories.

(3) The 'unknown' in capital size indicates those enterprises which were listed in the company directories but without information about capital.

percent of the total, and were mainly in the textile industry (1,376 of 1,725), the chemical industry (416 of 568), miscellaneous (297 of 404) and food and beverages (250 of 378).

As shown in Table II.19, the wage differences for numbers of employees showed no special trend between male and female, but those for amounts of capital showed a distinct trend, but in the reverse direction. Male wage rates increased with capital size and female wage rates decreased. For child workers less than thirteen years of age, wage differentials among boys for number of employees showed no clear trend, but among girls it increased with the number of employees and with the amount of capital. Overall, it seems that child workers were considered as substitutes for adult workers and so boys' wage rates decreased with the amounts of capital. This seems to imply that smaller capital enterprises considered them to be indispensable, sometimes paying them more than half the adults' rate. Female workers, both adults and girls, seemed to be treated as a subordinate labour force, except in textile industries, as reflected in the declining wage rates with the increase in amount of capital.

The factors determining wage differentials must be the difference between rural workers and urban workers related to operational days between industrial subdivisions and the male and female ratio in addition to the adult and apprentice workers' problem in urban and rural areas shown in the 1900 data. However, our sample data in 1909 already showed a similar pattern of dual structure found in Umemura's observations in the 1930 data.

This is a good place to talk about the turning point from a rural society to an industrialized society in Japan. As we saw in Section 1 in relation to Shunsaku Nishikawa's appraisal, in the early Meiji period a market oriented economy was attained through the sale of rice and commercialized agricultural products like textiles and the sprouting of factory oriented manufacturing in the late nineteenth century. Then, when did this turning point occur?

Our tentative hypothesis is that 1) the so-called power revolution of 1920 with the propagation of electricity is not likely to be the cause of the turning point, taking into consideration the importance of water mills, so it must be traced to the much earlier period when the water mills were propagated and 2) the dual structure stemming from the dualistic labour market accompanying the company system as a means of gathering capital and creating a new managerial system must be also traced back to before the 1930s, probably to the 1910s or even earlier. Factories in rural areas must have been transformed before the propagation of electric power.

The limited number of our observations is not sufficient to fully detect the wage differentials among different ownerships of factories and industrial subdivisions. Our statement should be regarded as one possible hypothesis. Further elaboration with more exhaustive data or case studies is needed.

Before ending this section we note that, as we have mentioned in relation to business managers, the propagation of vocational education and technical schools was quite rapid. The dual educational system for liberal education ending at a university and for vocational education ending at a technical college after completing compulsory education created a dual structure labour market in addition to the route through on-the-job training. In 1909, the former courses for liberal education included around 2.6% of those entering elementary school and the latter courses for technical schools included about 4.3%. Among students entering liberal education, some chose business schools or technical schools and later colleges. Even after entering university, many entered engineering courses. For example, among doctoral degree holders (excluding medical doctors), totally 2,046, in 1930 disregarding those who had been dead since 1888, almost 28% of them were granted in applied fields such as engineering, agriculture and forestry. If we include natural science and medicine, this figure increases to 78%. This implies the course Japan was following during this stage of its development (Yasuba [1976]). Now we will turn to the problem of the entire industrial structure of Japan and her empire as a whole.

Notes:

1) In the late Tokugawa period most of the feudal landlords, *han-shu*, tried to raise rural production by employing many rural engineers and cameralists. They believed that farmers' willingness to work must be an important factor in raising productivity and it should be accompanied by an increased the literacy ratio among farmers. Sontoku Ninomiya was one preacher of farmers' morals and ways of farming. His teaching became a kind of reli-

gious sect called *Hou-on-kou*, a money saving association and a network for propagating farming techniques.

2) Kunio Yanagida tried to search for principles to unify the nation where Westernization of the society might have destroyed the national identity. His basic philosophy was that the worship of ancestors in the traditional Japanese manner provided a strong backbone of society. He traced the origin of the Japanese races back to the historical legends of folklore. He was convinced that the origins of the Japanese were in the south Asian islands where rice cultivation had developed.

3) Yoshinobu Tokugawa's surrender to the allied forces of the Satsuma and Choshu han under the name of the Ten'no without making an actual military offensive meant that the chance to deprive the last tycoon of his vested interests was lost. Thus, they were able to invest their money in companies even after the *chitsuroku-shobun*.

4) Aonuma studied the educational background of about five hundred top managers from 1900 to 1950 and about 9,400 in 1962. His conclusion was that in 1900 owner managers comprised more than 60% of the total but by 1928 this had decreased to 2%. (Aonuma [1965] p. 140. Man'nari studied other figures based on 189 managers in the 1880s (early Meiji), 198 in the 1920s (Taisho) and 212 of contemporary as follows, only 17% higher educated in 1880s, 17% out of higher technical schools, 46% out of college and universities in 1920s and 20% out of higher technical school 71% out of college and universities in 1960. (Man'nari [1965] p. 124.)

5) The number of managers and engineers asked in the original questionnaire was not tabulated in all the published reports, so we obtained information only from the data of Gunma and Aichi prefectures. This questionnaire item was not well-answered in these areas.

4. FORMATION OF THE JAPANESE EMPIRE AND ITS COLLAPSE

4.1 Exodus of Population to Colonies

4.1.1 Japan Scarcely Escapes becoming a Colony

It is a miracle in world history that Japan escaped becoming a colony of the Western powers. Many papers have been written on this topic, but we will confine our comments to a few words about India and China, which was called as sleeping lion by Western people, and which they did not dare to conquer. When India surrendered to the power of the East Indian Company, she was under the control of the Mughal Empire, which was itself a colonial power to Indians. The situation of China was similar, because the Sin Dynasty was Manchurian and they were considered oppressors by Han Chinese. The Opium War was started because there were many things that Britain wanted to import from China. However, China was a self-contained country like Japan under the Tokugawa regime and needed nothing from Britain. Therefore, Britain craftily introduced opium to high ranking Chinese officials and wealthy merchants, and then to the common people. This made interregional trade between Britain, India and China possible as China then wanted opium. The Opium Wars broke out in an attempt by China to stop the opium trade, but China was eventually defeated. As a result, Western people began to regard China not as a sleeping lion but as a sleeping cat. There was a famous episode in which the Nei-wu Fu, Imperial Household, spent all the money (four-million tael per year) earmarked for strengthening the Northern navy (the Peiyang fleet) on building an additional Summer Palace now called Yi He Yuan (Rawlinson [1967] pp. 130–31). At the same time (in 1893), the Meiji Emperor spent his money on warships as a means to persuade the diet to approve the budget to build a navy (Fukui [1992], Collected works. v. 1. pp. 68–9). This is one reason why Japan was able to escape becoming subordinated to the Western powers.

The first thing the Meiji government did was to cancel all contracts between the Tokugawa government, including other *han* and Western merchants, to develop a joint-venture company or to give special priv-

ileges to mining (Mining Act proclaimed in 1973, see Nagaoka etc.
[1980] pp. 10–11). They thus restored their right to develop mining
and then canceled the unequal export and import treaty and immu-
nity of criminals treaty. However, this was not realized until the victory
over Russia. Japan cannot blame only the Western powers, however,
because she imposed, first on Korea and then on China, the same
conditions imposed on her by the Western powers. This was the beginning of a sad story of Japan joining the Western imperialistic powers
in building an empire. The first dispute between Japan and China was
the suzerain power over Korea. Japan won the Sino-Japanese War and
assumed sovereignty over the Kwantung peninsular and Taiwan, and
in addition obtained money as reparations amounting to 32,900,980
pounds sterling. France, Germany and Russia intervened in this treaty
and Japan chose to relinquish the Kwantung peninsular for 4,935,147
pounds sterling. After that, Russia got the right of lease over it and
established a naval base with a fortress at Lushun, and eventually extended the trans-Siberia railway to Manchuria. The Russian target
was the Korean markets and they searched for a way to exercise their
power to get suzerain power over Korea. This eventually resulted in
the Russo-Japanese War.

As a result of the Russo-Japanese War, Japan obtained the lease
of the Kwantung peninsular and possession of the Manchuria Railway
Company (like the British East Indian Company) and annexed the
area to the railroad, and recovered the southern half of Sakhalin which
it had relinquished in an exchange treaty for the Chishima Islands in
1875. Needless to say, Sakhalin was discovered by Rinzo Mamiya, a
Japanese adventurer, in 1809 before the Russian invasion of Siberia.
At the time when the Meiji government was being organized, she had
enough power to sustain Sakhalin against Russia. However, in spite of
Japanese diplomatic efforts, she got no reparations in money. Japan
spent a lot of money on the war (1,508,470 thousand *yen*) and eighty-
two percent of it was raised as foreign loans on the New York, London
and Berlin money markets. It was a tremendous burden for Japan after
the war; the total of 8,000,000 million *yen* was almost two times the
national budget in 1905.

Japan had built up a small empire in East Asia and a time of
expansion followed. Japan eventually absorbed Korea in 1910. After

the end of World War I, in 1921, the Southern islands, the former German colonies, were entrusted to Japan by the League of Nations. Chingtao and Chienan, the former German concession but occupied by the Japanese army, were, however, returned to China in 1922.

The legal systems of these colonies were not as we imagine today. Originally, at the time of the Meiji Restoration under the jurisdiction of *Kaitaku-shi*, the Development Agency, Hokkaido, Chishima and Sakhalin were called *gaichi*, or exterior. Sakhalin had been in Russian hands since 1875. That area under the rule of *Kaitaku-shi* had been included in *naichi*, interior, since 1890 and Southern Sakhalin, called Karafuto, after it was returned to Japan, was also included in the interior after 1943. As explained below, under the legal system of the colonial areas, it was important for people to define their race or *minseki*. As to the comprehensive treatment of the whole Japanese Empire, we just quote a recent contribution by Yuzo Yamamoto (Yamamoto [1992]). After many years of socio-economic analysis of the Japanese Empire were revived, some works which started soon after the end of World War II were seen to contain inconsistent treatment concerning Sakhalin and Chishima, probably due to censorship based on the so-called press code of the occupying army in the latter half of the 1940s.

4.1.2　The Japanese Empire in Population Census

The whole picture of the Japanese Empire became clear after the 1920 population census: the first nationwide census. After that, Japan executed the census four times until the collapse of the Empire. However, the big census whose questionnaire contained many more items such as occupation and industries where people worked was executed every ten years and an intermediate census was carried out with a less minute questionnaire in the middle of the ten-year cycle. The composition of the population by race is only obtainable in the large scale census year and the summary figures are shown in Table II.20.

We use the word 'race', but the original expression is *minseki*: registered status of people. This does not exactly match the concept of race, but implies regional origin because a person who registered as *koseki* in Japan proper was called Japanese and his/her register could

Table II.20 Population of the Japan Empire by Race

Regions	Race					
	Japanese			Koean		
Year of survey	1920	1930	1940	1920	1930	1940
Japan Proper						
Male	27,980.989	32,049,065	35,777,983	36,043	297,501	762,578
Female	27,904,003	31,922,960	36,032,039	4,712	121,508	502,471
Korea						
Male	184,200	285,966	374,212	8,695,630	10,398,889	11,839,295
Female	162,296	241,050	333,536	8,195,659	10,039,219	11,708,170
Taiwan						
Male	92,576	124,744	161,834	68	440	1,026
Female	71,690	103,537	150,552	1	458	1,350
Sakhalin						
Male	102,841	160,711	224,474	898	6,328	14,914
Female	42,522	123,487	170,129	36	1,973	4,591
Kwantung						
Male	91,552	121,402	103,535	3,375	9,922	3,769
Female	67,962	103,741	94,753	2,406	8,380	2,615
Southern Islands						
Male	2,872	12,105	44,143	225	151	2,284
Female	531	7,524	32,866	43	47	1,188
Ching-tao						
Male	15,251	—	—	126	—	—
Female	12,630	—	—	46	—	—
Total Male	28,470,283	32,753,993	36,686,081	8,736,365	10,713,231	12,605,584
Total Female	28,261,634	32,502,299	36,813,871	8,202,903	10,171,585	12,214,933
All Total	56,731,915	65,256,292	73,499,952	16,939,268	20,884,815	24,820,517
Regions belonged to Manchuria Railroad Company						
Male	43,566	59,549	—	3,025	8,597	—
Female	33,314	47,678	—	2,180	7,389	—
Manchuko						
Male	—	—	481,027	—	—	789,575
Female	—	—	338,587	—	—	660,809

(Notes)

1) People in Manchuko contained those in regions belonged to Manchuria Railroad Company.

2) Total people in * were 915 male and 582 female.

Table II.20 Continued

Regions	Race								
	Taiwanese			Ainus & others			Micronesia		
Year of survey	1929	1939	1940	1920	1930	1940	1920	1930	1940
Japan Proper									
Male	1,424	3,648	17,584	15	10	545	3	16	153
Female	279	963	4,915	16	12	441	0	2	96
Korea									
Male	0	16	182	0	6	0	0	0	2
Female	0	3	44	0	9	0	0	0	0
Taiwan									
Male	1,785,636	2,192,384	2,776,808	0	0	0	0	0	1
Female	1,684,871	2,121,297	2,733,451	0	0	0	0	0	0
Sakhalin									
Male	0	5	34	984	1,082	191	0	0	0
Female	0	0	1	970	1,082	205	0	0	0
Kwantung									
Male	27	63	334	0	10	0	0	0	0
Female	10	35	216	0	6	0	0	0	0
Southern Islands									
Male	0	1	7	0	5	0	24,877	25,596	26,146
Female	0	0	0	0	2	0	23,628	24,099	24,502
Ching-tao									
Male	3	—	—	0	—	—	0	—	—
Female	1	—	—	0	—	—	0	—	—
Total Male									
	1,783,090	2,196,117	2,794,949	999	1,113	736	24,880	25,612	26,300
Total Female									
	1,685,161	2,122,299	2,738,627	986	1,111	646	23,628	24,109	24,600
Grand Total									
	3,468,251	4.318,416	5,533,576	1,985	2,224	1,382	48,508	49,713	50,900
Regions belonged to Manchuria Railroad Company									
Male	10	34	—	0	1	—	0	0	—
Female	5	12	—	0	0	—	0	0	—
Manchukuo									
Male	—	—	*	—	—	*	—	—	*
Female	—	—	*	—	—	*	—	—	*

(Source) Census Reports

not be removed except by marriage to a person of another *minseki*, or to a person who was registered in Taiwan without abandoning his/her Chinese nationality, or to a person of aboriginal origin, called generally the Takasago races. A female who was born in a colony would be registered as Japanese *koseki* if she married a male of Japanese *koseki*, but a male who was born in a colony would remain *minseki* even if he married a female of Japanese *koseki*. In the first population census in 1920, the Japanese inhabitants of Hokkaido were classified as either ancient aborigines, Ainu, or genuine Japanese and it is not clear how those who had lived in Sakhalin and had compulsorily immigrated to Hokkaido were treated in the register. The Ainus in Sakhalin and Hokkaido and the Gyliaks in Sakhalin and the Chishimas may be ethnologically different races. The legal status of the Ainus in Hokkaido were, however, different from those in Sakhalin because they were called "ancient aborigines" and treated equally from the legal point of view, which may have been different from their de facto treatment by society. They were treated as aborigines in Sakhalin and as ancient aborigines in Hokkaido. The figures for Korea were the registered population, because the first census in Korea was prevented by the turmoil after the uprising on the 1st of March (the third month) called the 3-1 Movement in Japanese.

The figures in "Manchukuo" were based on the extra-population census carried out in 1940. The inhabitants of the Manchurian Railway Company annexed area were counted in Kwantung in 1920–30 and included in Manchukuo in 1940.

4.1.3 Japanese Race and Other Races in the Japanese Empire

In 1920, Japanese people comprised only sixty-nine percent of the total population, 127,631,000, of the Japanese Empire. However, most Japanese people defined as *koseki* (the percentage in Japan proper was about 98.5%) remained in Japan proper. This situation gradually changed in the next two decades.

The percentage of Japanese was seventy-two in 1930 and seventy-four in 1940. However, there is some doubt about this figure because of the uneven accuracy of figures for the colonies.

One reason for the gradual decline in the percentage of Japanese

Table II.21 Results of the Household Survey of Early Twentieth Century Korea

Year	Number of household	Population	Number of people per household
1907	1,384,493	5,793,576	4.18
	2,333,087	9,781,671	4.19
1910	2,742,263	12,935,282	5.29

(Source) Financial Consultant to Korea; *Table of Korean Household* (1908)
Korea: Police Agency; *Minseki-tokei* (People Registration Statistics) (1910)

Table II.22 Population in Taiwan by Census Data

	Whole island	Island excluding mountainous regions	Net increase	People in mountainous regions
1905		3,039,751		
1915		3,479,922	440,171	
1920		3,655,308	175,386	
1925		3,993,408	338,100	
1930	4,592,537	4,503,216	509,808	89,321
1935	5,212,426	5,121,019	617,805	91,407
1940	5,872,084	5,715,674	594,655	156,410*

(Note) *including all non-assimilated aborigines.
(Source) 1905–35: Japan, Governor of Taiwan: Census Reports
    1940: China, Taiwan Province: *Seventh Population Census of Taiwan, 1953*

might be inaccuracies in the population figures for Korea in the early twentieth century as shown in Table II.21 (Matsuda [1978]). A new register system comparable to that of Japan in 1872 was proclaimed in 1909. Korean people were unwilling to accept this register system for fear of heavier taxation. However, the population figures obtained from the register were still much bigger than those estimated from the survey results of 1906 (Kin [1965], Ishi [1972]). It should be noted

Table II.23 Male to Female Ratio in Japan and her Colonies

	1920	1930	1940
Japan proper	99.72	99.60	100.71
Colonies	73.26	82.38	85.63
Passports issued	63.44	71.29	n.a.

that servants were included neither in an independent register nor in the servants' register but in an additional register, *fuseki*, or servants' master's register, and so were included in the household's membership. Later, in 1922, they were excluded from the household's membership. Thus, we got two figures: one for members per household and the other for members per residence. As a consequence, the former (5.3 in 1922) was inevitably smaller than the latter (5.5). Thus, the figures after 1922 may be defined by the homogeneous operational concept, so the 1925 population census figures are regarded as much more reliable.

The census figures for Taiwan in 1920 seem more accurate because of the two additional experiences of population census prior to the first census in Japan proper. Inaccuracy occurred due to the expansion of the governability of the authorities in the mountainous regions where non-assimilated aborigines had lived since the days of the Chinese occupation. Table II.22 shows how the population increase was due to the inclusion of mountainous regions.

Japanese remaining in Japan proper constituted 98.5% of the total in 1920 (as mentioned before), 98.0% in 1930 and 97.7% in 1940. In addition, the Japanese population increased 15.0% in the first ten years and 13.9% in the next ten years. These figures for the Japanese race, excluded those living outside the colonies except Manchukuo.

Japanese living abroad counted by the number of passports issued based on the data of the Ministry of Foreign Affairs numbered 581,431 (355,727 male and 225,704 female) in 1920 and 509,754 (297,587 male and 212,167 female) in 1930. We got only the data for 1938, not 1940, as 1,059,913 (598,490 male and 461,423 female). This constituted only 1.0% of the Japanese people in the Japanese Empire in 1920 and 0.78% in 1930.

Thus, the exodus of Japanese from Japan proper gradually increased. This is proved by the relative decline in the percentage of Japanese people who remained in Japan proper in 1930, as shown in Table II.23. The next problem is the nature of the exodus of Japanese people out of Japan proper. As is easily seen in Table II.23, the female to male ratio among people outside Japan proper was fairly high. The sex ratio is, in principle, lower than one in infancy, but later increases due to the higher mortality of males in infancy. However, the low ratio including adults implies that it was difficult for men to get married outside Japan proper, or that men went abroad due to the difficulty of getting married at home.

The situation was similar for other races who left their homes and went to Japan proper or to other areas. The most striking feature was the movement of Korean people. The compulsory labour movement enforced during the later stage of World War II did not appear in this period.

4.2   Family Structure of the Japanese Empire

The first population census in 1920 shows for the first time the household size by the number of household members in a well-defined operational concept, unlike the previous population figures obtained from the register records.

However, the number of households was based on the de facto principle, i.e. those who were out at the survey time were excluded from the household, unlike censuses after 1947. This made the household size negligibly smaller than that defined by the usual status. This is judging from the number of people contained in quasi-households classified as hotels and inns.

The family size expressed by the definition of the census household size is shown in Table II.24. Here we did not consider differences between races. The ordinary household here defined includes single persons living in a relative's household and/or employed as domestic servants such as maids, cooks, boarded apprentices, etc. Those who boarded in a private boarding house are included as ordinary household members, but those who dared to cook in a boarding house are classified as independent ordinary households even if they live alone.

Table II.24 Household Size by the Population Census, 1920–40 in Japan Proper

Year	Number of households	Number of members	Persons in a ordinary household	Single household
1920	11,122,120	54,336,356	4.89	641,860
1925	11,902,593	58,015,326	4.87	
1930	12,600,276	62,760,821	4.98	694,063
1935	13,383,349	67,249,793	5.02	
1940	14,213,947	70,960,786	4.99	

Table II.25 Composition of Household Members (1920)

	Number (Thousand)			Permillage		
	A Ordinary household members	B Kin members	C Non-Kin members (servants, maids etc.)	A Ordinary household members	B Kin members	C Non-Kin members (servants, maids etc.)
a) Whole Japan proper						
Total	55,849	50,102	5,747	1000.0	897.1	102.9
Male	27,952	24,625	3,327	1000.0	881.0	119.0
Female	27,896	25,477	2,419	1000.0	913.3	86.7
b) Tokyo area						
Total	2,269	1,649	630	1000.0	726.8	273.2
Male	1,245	811	434	1000.0	651.4	348.6
Female	1,034	838	196	1000.0	810.4	189.6
c) Six Metropolitan areas						
Total	5,527	4,214	1,313	1000.0	762.4	237.6
Male	3,008	2,111	897	1000.0	701.8	298.2
Female	2,519	2,103	416	1000.0	834.9	165.1

(Source) Teizo Toda's re-tabulation based on the permillage extracted micro data from population census in 1920.

The size of a household was comparatively big, 4.89 in 1920, and if we exclude single households the size became a little bigger, 5.12, and it increased in a decade to 6.00 in 1930. This implies the existence of a big group of people who could not afford their own household. The ratio of married people was lower than the present average. It was 398 per thousand for males and 403 for females in 1920. Of these, some were in de facto relationships: 66 of 398 males and 64 of 403 females. This means 166 per thousand partnered males and 159 per thousand partnered females. The percentage of married couples excluding de facto couples had decreased since 1898 based on the population survey by the flow concept, called the dynamic survey, as shown in Table II.25. The simple ratio of adults more than twenty years old according to the census was 60% in urban areas and 70% in rural areas.

The splendid work by Teizo Toda referred to in the previous section tells us the differences between families and households which included non-relative members. He systematically extracted one household per thousand, i.e. permillage extraction, and so totally 11,216 households extracted form the results of the population census. Then he excluded 82 quasi-households such as dormitories, hospitals and hotels after exempting special dwelling quarters like ambassadors residences, military barracks and jails.[1] Data on ordinary household members (55,849 in 11,134 households; Class A) were subclassified as those who had some kinship relation or marriage (50,102 [897.1 ‰]; Class B) and non-kinship members like servants and maids (5,747 [102.9 ‰]; Class C). In the permillage data there were 881.0 ‰ and 119.0 ‰ males and 897.1 ‰ and 102.9 ‰ females of classes B and C, respectively.

If we suppose that class C were all unmarried, 483 of 881 males and 493 of 897 females must be children or unmarried young adults in a household, and some might be aged bachelors, widows or divorcees. The non-marriage ratio was 54.8% for males and 55.9% for females for some family people. We further considered that all non-ordinary members in the 20 to 64 age range were included in the unmarried, widowed or divorced category, and excluded those people under nineteen and over sixty-five from the census figures. Thus, the total people of class B (11,709 males) in the Toda samples of 13,594 ordinary households in the 20–64 age range might be divided into 10,269 married people and 1,440 unmarried people. Then 1,885 male non-kinship household members were regarded as all currently unmarried.

Toda supplied further data for Tokyo and the six next biggest cities. Then the share of class C in the total was 348.6 for males and 273.2 for females per thousand people in Tokyo and 298.2 males and 237.6 females in the next six biggest cities. We further extracted only the people among the entire male population from twenty to sixty-four who might have a chance to marry. In this case, the ratio of males in class C in Tokyo increased to 34.7%. This implies that the number of unmarried people and those living away from their own family members might have increased in urban areas in so far as those people were mainly unmarried as the national average indicates.

The biggest proportion of these unmarried working people lived in households whose heads were engaged in commerce and the next biggest in the households of those engaged in manufacturing. This also holds in the 1930 population census.

As the size of households excluding single households increased in the decade from 1920 to 1930, the number of unmarried people also increased continuously from 1920 to 1935. The pressure to marry must have increased, and people must have wanted to go abroad in the hope of making money.

Thus, the problem should be developed toward the analysis of the occupational structure of the entire population.

4.3   Occupational Structure of the Population

4.3.1   Census Survey System and its Results

In the previous sections we have found that even in 1920 there were many factories located in rural areas. They were concentrated in the textile industry, gradually shifting from silk to cotton. However, the rapid expansion of heavy industries gave rise to a growth of factories in urban areas. With the execution of the population census since 1920 and the manufacturing census since 1909 we can analyse the occupational structure of the entire population by official statistics without constructing from either companywise or factorywise data.

The population statistics will supply us with the distribution of people by occupation and industry where they were working during the

Table II.26 Working Population of Japan Proper by Industry (Major Group) (1920,1930,1940,1947)

Year	1920	1930	1940	1947
All industries	27,261,106	29,619,640	32,482,516	33,328,963
Primary industry				
Total	14,672,164	14,710,820	14,392,482	17,811,597
Agriculture	13,948,776	13,955,316	13,557,098	16,622,418
Forestry	189,627	187,068	292,426	479,562
Fisheries	533,761	568,436	542,958	709,617
Secondary industry				
Total	5,597,905	6,002,032	8,442,502	7,401,371
Mining	424,464	315,476	597,755	667,478
Construction	711,983	978,975	981,080	1,294,026
Manufacturing	4,461,458	4,707,581	6,863,667	5,439,867
Tertiary industry				
Total	6,463,586	8,836,206	9,429,391	7,671,782
Electricity, gas, heat supply and water	92,313	122,362	143,418	190,754
Transport and communication	1,046,685	1,169,303	1,372,662	1,518,546
Wholesale and retail trade, eating and drinking places	2,663,157	4,130,747	4,097,839	2,477,492
Financing and insurance	130,534	194,043	274,261	240,003
Real estate			23,868	10,839
Services	1,948,767	2,483,822	2,896,024	2,319,097
Government (Not elsewhere classified)	582,130	735,929	621,319	915,051
Percent distribution (%)				
Total	100.0	100.0	100.0	100.0
Primary industry	53.8	49.7	44.3	53.4
Secondary industry	20.5	20.3	26.0	22.2
Tertiary industry	23.7	29.8	29.0	23.0

three large scale census years (1920, 1930 and 1940) of the five censuses. However, the occupational classification scheme used for the 1920 census basically depended on Jacques Bertillon's draft scheme for classification of occupations proposed at the fourth International Statistical Institute (ISI) in 1893. It was a mixture of industrial classification and occupational classification, but was regarded as the international standard of its day. In 1895, Bertillion proposed a classification scheme for industry at the fifth ISI. Later, the International Conference of Labour Statisticians adopted the system of classification of industries and occupations in 1923. Japan, as a member of the Conference, followed the proposal at the 1930 population census (Mitsuma [1983]) and published the summary figures of 1920 converted by the 1930 scheme as shown in Table II.26.

The essence of the 1920 scheme was still on the continuation of the concept of the business of the family, and so each household was classified by his or her main business and subsidiary business. In addition, Korea did not carry out a 1920 census and Taiwan did not publish the converted 1920 figures by the 1930 classification scheme.

4.3.2　Emergence of the so-called "Dual Economy"

As is well-known, manufacturing censuses starting from 1920 had truncated those factories to those with less than five employees for many years. This was widely accepted as inevitable at that stage of development of the statistical survey system. Instead of carrying out a complete census, statisticians at the Ministry of Agriculture and Trade chose the way of requiring a report of manufacturers of specified important items in the Agricultural and Commercial Correspondence System. However, the execution of a population census shed light on how to estimate the proportion of manufacturers who were operating factories or workshops with less than five employees.

Expansion of the manufacturing industry in the 1900s had occurred in both traditional manufacturing and modernized factory production. This made a sharp contrast between traditional and modernized sectors and so we can see the seminal form of the dual structure. To grasp the share of small scale industries it was necessary to overcome the coverage problem. Tokutaro Yamanaka and Teijyu Odahashi solved this problem by combining the population census result and the manufacturing census for the data of 1930 because the 1930 population census had for the first time a well-defined industrial and occupational classification instead of the occupation and industry mixed classification used in the 1920 census. As a result, the status of manager or owner of a business was separated for the first time. Thus, if the number of factories of specified industrial classifications obtained from the manufacturing census are extracted from the total number of owners of this industrial classification, the residual may correspond to the number of smaller factories which were not covered by the manufacturing census.

4.3.3 From the Rural Economy to the Industrialized Society in 1920–40

The figures obtained from three population censuses have revealed the process of industrialization. Japanese society shifted from rural to industrialized, as was proved by the exodus of labour from rural areas to urban areas and then abroad. As we have discussed, industrialization first spread in the rural areas with silk and cotton spinning. The proportion of factories located in rural areas before 1920 was far larger than the estimates by quantitative economic historians. On this point, the inference by Toshio Furushima was much more persuasive. Then the question is, what happened after 1920?

World War I broke out with the assassination of an Austrian Prince on the 28th of June, 1914 and drew Japan into direct involvement on the 23rd of August. The commitment to the war brought about drastic changes in the manufacturing industry. This time industrialization involved entirely urban areas and caused interregional migration from rural areas to urban areas.

Before the War, the Japanese government had started to modernize the Imperial navy with a plan to construct two escadrilles, battleships and battle cruisers, called *hachi-hachi-kantai*, eight and eight fleets in Japanese. This plan was first designed soon after the Russo-Japanese War, but it was not realized until after World War I, in 1920, when the diet approved the budget. The first one to be constructed was the Nagato of 38,500 tons, armed with eight 16-inch guns, capable of 26.7 knots, and completed in 1920 after three years of construction. Her sister ship was the Mutsu, completed in 1921. Competition to build up a big fleet accelerated industrialization in various fields, not only in urban areas in Japan proper but also in many parts of the Japanese Empire. We should pay attention to the fact that government factories which had been running ahead of private companies gave full support to the building of this big fleet by private companies such as Kawasaki Shipbuilding Company, Mitsubishi Shipbuilding Company and so on, which performed almost half of the total fleet construction in 1909-13.[2]

The percentage of city inhabitants in Japan proper amounted to 18.0% in 1920, 24.0% in 1930 and 37.7% in 1940. The concept of the city was based on the administrative definition. Shigeru Itoh tried to estimate the urban population in a de facto sense. His estimate covering from 1898 to 1920 shows a bigger population compared with that of the administrative jurisdiction, for example, 22.9% in 1920. Urban areas attracted people not only from rural areas but also from abroad. The inflow from the colonial areas was first concentrated in the urban areas and then in mining towns. On the other hand, Japanese people in Japan proper went abroad as we have discussed in the previous section 4.1.3. The exodus from Japan proper was in two streams: one to colonial areas of China, especially to foreign settlements and then to Manchukuo, and the other to the American continents, both North and South.

The exodus to the outside world had excited the feelings of people in many countries where they were afflicted by unemployment due to Japanese immigrants, especially in China and then in North America, for example, in California in 1920. The first dispute concerning the restriction of Japanese immigrants to the United States of America was discussed in 1907, and after that, there had been seven exchanges of memoranda to restrict the flow of immigrants by gentlemen's agreements by 1908.

The nineteen-twenties was a time of turmoil. The power game among countries inspired the expansion of military power and at the same time the search for a reduction in armed forces. The Washington Treaty was approved in 1922. According to this treaty, Japan abandoned its plan for the eight and eight fleet and scrapped the battleship Tosa of 39,330 tons built at Nagasaki Dockyard of the Mitsubishi Shipbuilding Co. , and its sister ship the Kaga, which had been transformed into aircraft carriers like the Akagi. Other battleships such as the Kii, the Owari, numbers eleven, twelve, thirteen, fourteen, fifteen and sixteen, were all abandoned or canceled. Then the competition was shifted to the ten-thousand-ton heavy cruiser.[3] In 1922–26, Japan constructed a compact heavy cruiser called the Furutaka of 7,100 tons, armed with six 8-inch guns, capable of 34.5 knots. This ship was designed by Yuzuru Hiraga, who had designed the light cruiser Yubari, proto-type of the Furutaka, of 2,890 tons, armed with six 5.5-inch guns, capable of 35.5 knots, in 1922–23 and later designed and constructed the Yamato and the Musashi in 1937–42 after the treaty expired in 1936. Their success in constructing excellent fleets of heavy and light cruisers triggered another treaty, called the London Treaty, in 1930 (Pelz [1974]). It should be noted that the Great Kanto Earthquake happened on the 1st of September, 1923. Its effect on the structure of Japanese manufacturing was far more influential than we imagined from the figures. We will not deny that the damage in the Tokyo metropolitan areas was quite large, but the process of recovery attracts our attention. Our tentative hypothesis is that the recovery was a process of replacing older assets and the damage gave the chance to extend to other industrial areas. Thus, the decline of the Osaka area, where light industries had flourished, lost the chance to compulsorily renew its plant, and kept rather obsolete equipment.

4.4 Natural Disaster: the Great Kanto Earthquake in 1923; human and social disaster; the great depression of 1929 and the wars

4.4.1 The Great Kanto Earthquake and its Effects on the Economy

The Great Kanto Earthquake, one of Japan's most terrible natural disasters, killed about 66 thousand people in downtown Tokyo of a total population of 2.27 million, as shown in Fig. II.5. Fortunately, Japan had executed the first population census in 1920, so the Ministry of the Interior did a regional census on the 15th of November, 1923 soon after the earthquake. The figures are summarized in Table II.27(i).

After the earthquake, about 670 thousand people left Tokyo. 360

Figure II.5 Population flow before and after GKE

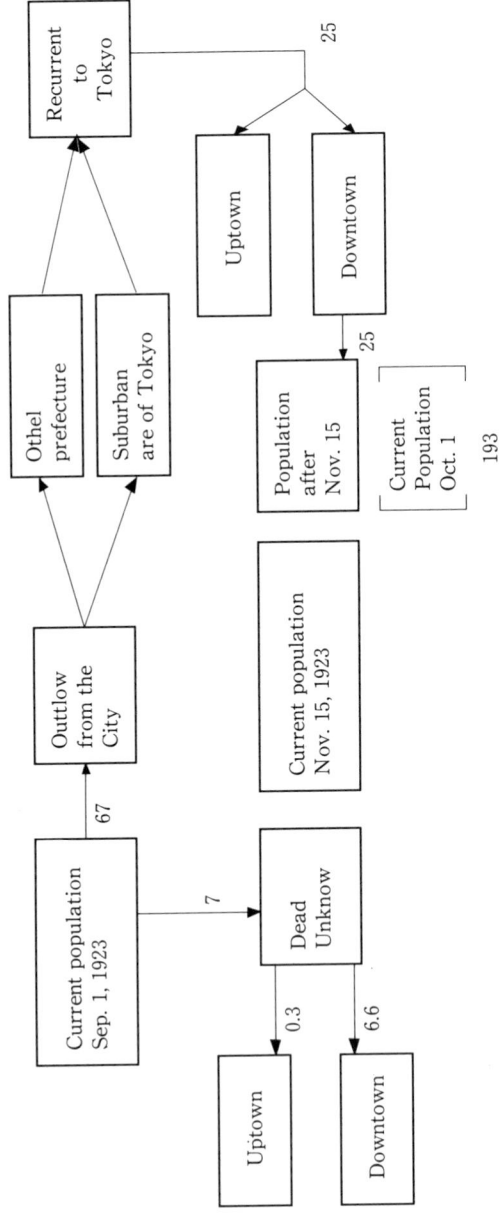

Unit : ten thousand

(Source) Kurabayashi [1983]

Table II.27 Socio-Economic Effects of the Great Kanto Earthquake

(i) Population movement in Tokyo due to the Great Kanto Earthquake

	Estimated population (1st, September, 1924)	Population by the survey (15th, Nov.)	Net migration
Tokyo city area	2,265,000	1,527,277	248,302
Up-town	695,500	747,029	−26,399
Down-town	1,569,800	766,206	246,582
Suburban Tokyo	1,706,700	2,023,468	−82,295
Annex to city	1,422,000	1,733,752	−78,155
Far from city	284,700	289,716	−4,141

(Source) Kurabayashi [1983]

thousand went to other prefectures and then about 170 thousand came back later. 310 thousand went to the outskirts of Tokyo. This eventually transformed the rural area of Tokyo into urban manufacturing or residential areas.

The manufacturing sector was roughly divided into those factories to which the Factory Act applied and those to which it did not apply. The distinction was the number of employees and the rates of damage of each class, as shown in Table II.27(ii). Fifty-six percent of the factories, comprising about forty-one percent of all workers, were located in urban areas and of them eighty-five percent were small factories to which the Factory Act did not apply.

To show the recovery from the damage caused by the earthquake, Fig. II.6(i) shows the number of factories and their real output as a percentage of the base at the end of 1923 under six broad manufacturing categories. Even in 1926, real output and the number of textile factories had not yet recovered to the level of 1923. However, those of foods and beverages had been smoothly restored by 1926. This reflects the nature of a big consumer city. Then came an expansion of chemicals and machinery production in 1926–27. Electricity, gas and metal processing in the special categories of manufacturing soon re-

197

Table II.27 Continued

(ii) Damage to manufacturing in Tokyo due to the Great Kanto Earthquake

	Factories	Percentage share of region	Damage ratio	Before GKE Number of factories	Before GKE Number of workers	Damaged by GKE Number of factories	Damaged by GKE Number of workers	Remainder through GKE Number of factories	Remainder through GKE Number of workers
Total	25,125	100%	43.4%	25,125 (100%)	225,298	10,913 (43.4%)	78,207	14,212 (56.6%)	147,091
a) Factories under Factory Law									
Total				4,079	172,276	1,592	56,432	2,487	115,844
City area	2,013	49.4%	74%						
Suburban area	2,066	50.7%	3%						
Percentage share				(100%)		(39.0%)		(61.0%)	
b) Factories not controlled by Factory Law									
Total				21,046	53,022	9,321	21,775	11,725	31,247
City area	12,188	57.9%	77%						
Suburban area	8,858	42.1%	3%						
Percentage share				(100%)		(44.3%)		(55.7%)	

(Note) GKE: Great Kanto Earthquake.
(Source) Togashi [1983]

Figure II.6 Recovery Process after GKE

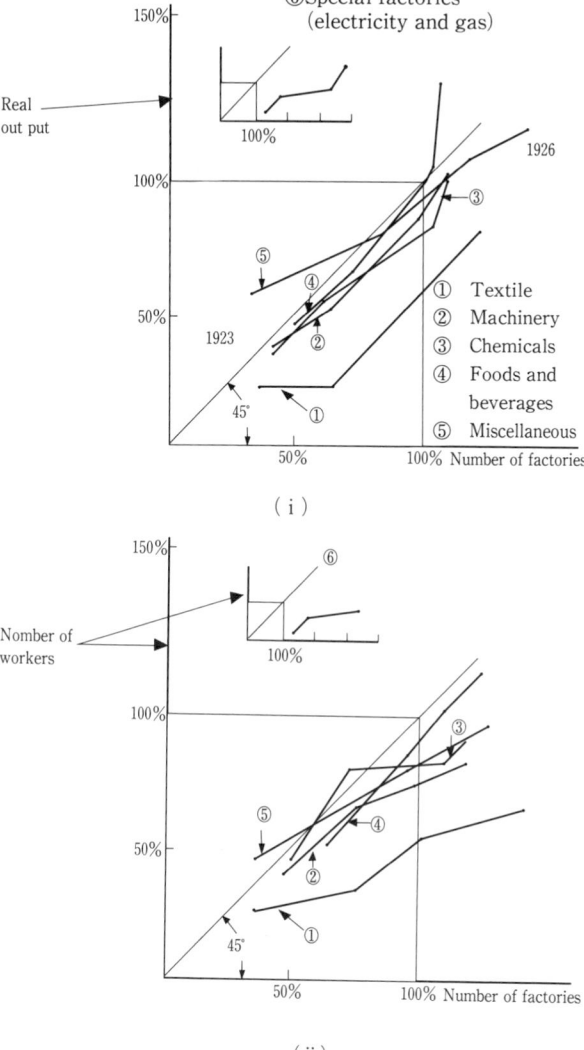

(ⅰ)

(ⅱ)

Figure II.6 Continued

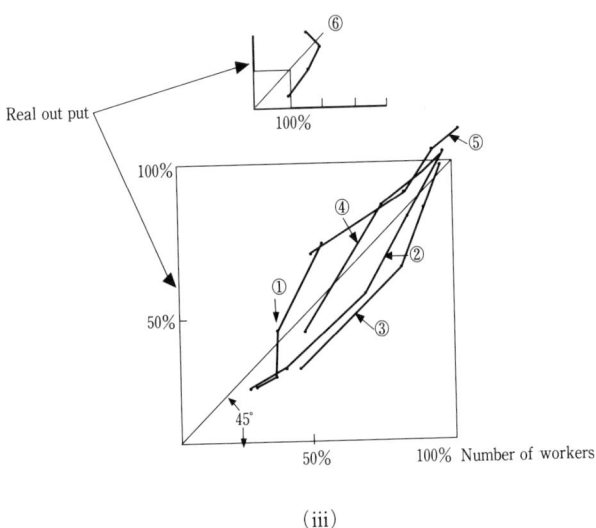

(iii)

(Notes) 1923 (Dec.) as 100.0% and the percentage share from 1924 to 1927.

covered. This was due to the shift of factories from light industries to heavy industries in Tokyo. However, the number of employees did not recover so speedily, as shown in Fig. II.6(ii). The more striking path in Fig. II.6(iii) is the real output by the relatively small number of employees, which required an increase in per capita productivity. The rise of labour productivity as a whole must have resulted from the smooth rise in total productivity brought about by the introduction of new machinery and new technology. This reasoning is based on the balance sheet data of big companies.

Later, manufacturing in the Tokyo area recovered its dominance over that of the Osaka area. Another effect on the government's industrial policy was 1) the principle of dispersing important manufacturing more widely over the Japanese Empire and 2) construction of a social infrastructure, including electric power plants, which had already started in the early twentieth century (Nakamura [1971] pp. 150–3). These principles attracted new entrepreneurs called *shinko-zaibatsu*, a new capitalists group, and they took advantage of the government policies to construct new factories in Korea and other colonies. These companies were called *kokusaku-gaisha*, national policy oriented companies. For example, Mori Konzern launched aluminium manufacturing along with chemical fertilizer manufacturing which depended on electricity. On the other hand traditional capitalist groups such as Mitsubishi, Mitsui, Sumitomo and Yasuda also formed Konzern by creating holding companies, but their main activities were in banking, mining and commerce, and they gradually shifted their weight to manufacturing in the 1930s (Nakamura [1971] pp. 217–221, Hashimoto [1992] in Hashimoto & Takeda [1992]).

4.4.2 Human and Social Disasters

We need to glance briefly at the period before the Great Kanto Earthquake. It was not la belle epoch, but a season of human and social disaster. The skewed income distribution brought out in the wartime boom led to the Rice Riot in 1918 (Nakamura [1971] pp. 127–30, Shiomi [1946]). Soon after the war economy boom during World War I, the economic crisis came in 1920. Needless to say, the depression of 1920–25 was intensified by the Great Kanto Earthquake.

Monetary and financial problems caused by the earthquake were prolonged over the next decade. The crucial period of the Great Depression started in New York with the stock market crash of 1929. This was a time in world history when war and peace were expected at the same time. Many monographs have been published on these topics and so we rush to the final topic of the war economy in the 1930s and 1940s. It is quite difficult to separate wartime and peace time in this period. The Japanese government gradually lost control of the army's military actions, especially in the case of the troops in Kanto-shu, the leased territory in North-eastern China including Port Arthur, or Lüshun, now called Lüta. These actions may be regarded as a counter-revolution against the liberalization movements symbolized by the General Election Act in 1925 which extended the coverage of voters to the election of the lower house of the Diet. Then came floods of assassinations of political leaders, especially in 1932, called five-one-five affair because it happened on the 15th of May, and then in 1936 the one called the two-two-six affair because it occurred on the 26th of February.

Japanese invasions of China were a de facto war starting in September, 1937, but the economy was not yet fully absorbed into war. Recently, many historians have put the starting point of the war period at the 18th of September, 1931, which saw the birth of Manchukuo. The international law problem of the legitimacy of this state is also out of the scope of this small monograph on the economic development and the accuracy of the statistical data.[4]

4.4.3 Reforming the Japanese Empire for the War

World War I was a turning point in the power games among the countries in Europe and North America. It not only symbolized the melting pot of races, but also the dominance of Caucasians over coloured people. In this war, Japan became the first Asian country to enter the power game, and threatened the European and American markets in Asia. At the same time, in a search for independence, nationalism and populism spread, not only among the victims of European and Americans in Asia but also along with the international labour movements over the national boundaries by both communists and anarchists.

During the absence of European and American power in Asia, investment by Japanese cotton spinning companies flooded into China. Fifty three factories were constructed with Chinese capital and thirty three with Japanese capital and only one by British capital during the War. Soon after the War, total investment by Japanese companies rapidly increased and eventually the May 30s strike occurred as an anti-British and anti-Japanese action in 1925 (Nakamura [1971] pp. 276–332, [1983]).

The Chinese market became a crucial diplomatic issue between Japan and America. Both wanted to swallow up the entire market on one's own. This international conflict synchronized with the nationalistic movement to construct a nation state after the Hsinhai Koming (Xinhai Geming), 1911 Revolution, against Ch'ing (Qing) Dynasty, and Sun Wen's Nangching Government proceeded to remove unequal treaties, and especially to establish tariff autonomy. For many years, until 1911, Japan had also suffered from the imposition of the unequal treaty between the United States of America under the gunboat diplomacy represented by Perry in 1851. However, this bitter experience does not motivate Japan to take an initiative on the side of China. Japanese policy to China was just opposite. In 1915 Japan demanded the special position described in the Twenty One Articles Treatment, which stimulated American reaction.

The United States of America took the initiative and firstly accepted China's request for tariff autonomy in 1928, then other countries followed. Japan accepted in 1930. The next issue was the abolition of extraterritoriality. However, this conflicted with the vested interests of Japan in north-eastern China. The difference in the attitudes of the Western powers and Japan to China stemmed from their socio-economic relations and the vested interests of each country. In 1930 Great Britain was running top in investment, but Japan had nearly caught up with her. The former heavily invested in Shanghai but the latter in the North East, especially in Manchuria, with a huge immigration of nearly 283 thousand people. On the other hand the United States of America mainly depended on international trade (Ishii [1987] in Ohishi [1987] vol. 2. pp. 43–47). The intervention to establish a nation state had occurred in various ways such as supporting local military cliques. Then eventually came the appearance of Manchukuo in 1932 and then the absorbed Jehol (Chengteh Province) in 1933. After struggling to stabilize the Yuen of Manchukuo and the Yen of Japan, they were treated equally and this led to the block economy of Japan and Manchukuo in 1935. This created a new international trade structure divided into the Yen currency block and the foreign currency block. The former block was an export surplus and the latter was an import surplus, resulting in a huge deficit of foreign currency in the first half of 1930s (Yamamoto [1992] pp. 126–152, Matsumoto [1992]). Although Japan invested huge amounts of money to construct a base of raw materials including coal and steel for Japan proper, the self sufficiency of the resources of Manchukuo was not enough to sustain such an investment, so she was tempted to invade the northern part of China to build up a China-Manchuria-Japan yen block economy.

The economic policy of Manchukuo was based on the five-year economic plan (1936–41) which may be called a semi-controlled economy
designed by bureaucrats who had been delegated from Japan to organize the Manchukuo government. Their idea of a semi-controlled
economy might have been inspired by the economic planning of the
Soviet Union. However, the plan was eventually abandoned in December, 1941. (After pioneering work by Shigeru Ishikawa [1958], many
papers had been written. See Yamamoto (ed.) [1993]). This was a
proto-type of Japanese war-time economic planning. The Showa Steel
Plant can be regarded as a symbol of such an idea and was settled in
1933 to supply steel for Japan. Various kinds of the highest quality
machinery in the world were imported just before the prohibition of
the export of goods for military use to Japan.

Constructing a Japanese block economy by the most favoured clause
for the trade tariff was an imitation of the treatment of the Sterling
block in 1932. However, her policies to build up a block economy were
betrayed by themselves through military actions against China aimed
at total occupation step by step, and then by her invasion of French
Indochina, the French colonies in Vietnam, on the 25th of June, 1941,
after the formation of the Vichy government in July, 1940. Repeated
American imposed economic sanctions, from the prohibition of export-
ing aircraft and their parts to Japan on 4th of January in 1939 to the
complete shut-down of petroleum exports on the 1st of August, 1941,
twelve times in the short period of only two and a half years. At the
last stage of diplomatic negotiation, America had decoded Japanese
communication by diplomatic secret code, and had therefore already
decided not to accept Japanese concessions. Cordell Hull's note to
Kichisaburo Nomura, Japanese Ambassador, on the 26th of November,
1941, was a de facto ultimatum requiring the collapse of the Japanese
Empire.[5] Japan crossed the Rubicon on the 8th of December by at-
tacking the Pearl harbour naval base, because the Japanese navy had
maintained absolute equality in the Pacific with the allied nations, but
she needed to do something before the accumulated stock of supplies,
especially petroleum, diminished under the prohibition of exports from
the allied nations, later called the united nations (Pelz [1974] p. 220
ff).[6]

The Pacific War was called the Greater East Asia War by Japanese until the prohibition of this term by the occupation army. This naming was to express Japan's intention to emancipate the Asian colonies from Europe and the United States of America. However, this professed intention was in fact realized after the war through the struggles of colonial people. Japan cannot excuse her actions by this magnificent cause. In particular, the slogan of unifying five races in Manchukuo could not hide its brutal invasion of China. The Greater East Asia Coprosperity Sphere, the slogan used to designate the ex-colonies of the allied nations, remained as a synonym for an expanded Japanese Empire against the good intentions of some of the governors and officers delegated from Japan.[7] In the next section, we want to show some aspects of the economy during the war, focusing especially on labour movement.

4.5 Labour Movement during World War II

4.5.1 General Description of the Wartime Economy during World War II

As we have discussed, the most reliable data available were restricted to the census type designed during peace time. After 1936 the economic situation drastically changed, i.e. the wartime economy was instituted. This may be called a kind of planned economy. Although the government tried to suppress publication, research and teaching of Marxian economic thoughts even in higher education, bureaucrats tried to absorb the practical procedures of the planned economy executed by the USSR, the Union of Soviet Socialist Republics, to apply it to the war economy. These younger bureaucrats were called *kakushin-kanryo*, radicals. Some of them hatched their ideas in the semi-controlled economy of Manchukuo.

The war economy had two main features: rationing of both production materials and consumer goods, and job allocation. This required the management system itself to be changed. The merger and amalgamation of enterprises was requested to control production and make it more efficient. The roots of this policy can be traced back to the policy called the rationalization of industry, which was based on the proposals of the commerce and manufacturing councils held on the

13th of December, 1929. Soon after, many proposals were expressed such as the plan for controlling iron and steel production, the act for manufacturing union in 1931 and eventually the act for controlling important manufacturing industries. Thus, many industrywise cartels were formed, especially in the 1930s. However, the war economy was formed in 1937 when the Ministry of Army proposed the first five-year plan for important industries on the 25th of May, 1937 (Hara (ed.) [1995], pp. 1–7). An initial spur may be attributed to the various proposals made by the Japan-Manchukuo economy and finance research group (Yamazaki [1995] in Hara (ed.) [1995] pp. 45–52).

Preparation for the war, especially economic planning for the war economy, was carried out at the Agency for Planning organized in 1937. The history of the Planning Agency is a story of revising the plans for goods mobilization and rationing and labour allocation (Nakamura [1971]).

The actual process of revising economic planning and its effects on the wartime economy have been clarified by the finding of hidden or dispersed documents by economic historians. Many monographs concerning the war economy started with Yoshio Ando's pioneering work in 1987 and continued until the recent contribution edited by Akira Hara (Hara (ed.) [1995]). The most important features concerning the state-company nexus were 1) the compulsory merger of companies and the rationing of raw materials through industrywise company unions or federations of organized companies (Yamazaki [1995] in Hara (ed.) [1955]) and 2) the alliance of parts makers of small and medium companies (Ueda [1995] in Hara (ed.) [1995]).

The Japanese manufacturing industry for military armaments had reached its peak even by world technological standards by the first half of the 1930s, but its development was not even in every field.

As we mentioned in section 4.3.3, the naval fleet grew up absolutely independent of borrowed technology and was regarded as being in the top ranking for every kinds of vessel, for example, the battleships Yamato and Musashi, heavy cruisers of the Furutaka class in 1926, light cruisers of the Mogami class, the aircraft carriers Hosho, the first in the world to be designed from scratch as an aircraft carrier in 1922, and those of the Ryujyo class, and submarines of the *I-go* class. This was realized through competition among private companies and government shipbuilding yards.

Aircraft, which first appeared in warfare in World War I, became firmly established as a new weapon in the 1930s. The Japanese aircraft industry was born of borrowed technology like the battleship building industry but, in this case, it reached an international standard in a short time. An example of technological independence is found in the *koukenki*, the ARI plane, the product of the Aeronautical Institute (*kouku-kenkyujyo*) at Tokyo Imperial University.[8] The Aeronautical Institute was established in 1918. They started to design the *koukenki* in 1932. They were concerned about the vast cruising distances over the Pacific Ocean surrounding the Japan islands. The *koukenki* established a cruising record of 11,651 km in 1932. The navy and army had the same needs and the second test model of the 97 scout plane, named after the Japanese calendar year 2597 for 1937, was lent to the Asahi Newspaper Company, who flew from Tachikawa to London and set the world record for the shortest time of ninety-four hours seventeen minutes in 1937. As a result of such efforts to explore new frontiers to build up an aircraft industry, there appeared many planes of the most advanced standard in the world, such as the Zero naval fighter named after the Japanese calendar year 2600 for 1940, with a range of 2,200 km at 510km/h; the Hayabusa military fighter, the falcon, with a range of 1,760km at 515km/h in 1941; the 97-style military heavy bomber with a range of 2,700km at 478km/h in 1936; the 97-style naval attacker stored in aircraft carriers, and so on.

Military balance in modern war cannot be isolated to the fields of war weapons. The perfect airframe of the Zero fighters was not accompanied by ideal motors. A more serious imbalance was seen in the transportation method from the Mitsubishi Motors Co. to the Kagamigahara naval airport, which was by oxcart due to the bad road conditions. The infrastructure of the 1930s had not been fully developed. The tunnel connecting the mainland with Kyushu island under the Shimonoseki channel was completed in 1942, completing the railroad network from Aomori to Kagoshima through Tokyo, Nagoya, Osaka, Kobe, Hiroshima, Shimonoseki, Moji and Fukuoka. The railroad network on the continent from Fuzan, now called as Pusan in Korea, to Beijing was to be completed in 1948. However, the railroad system in Japan Proper was of narrow gage, 1,067mm, from the beginning and this limited the speed and volume of transportation.[9] The speed of the express Tsubame, the swallow, on the Toukaido-line was a mere 70km/h on average. The international standard, the wide gage of 1,435mm, was adopted in Korea and Manchukuo. On this wide gage, the South Manchuria Railway Co. had already run the express Asia at an average speed of 82.5km/h and a peak speed of 120km/h in 1934. The Japan, Manchukuo and China block economy and then the war in China required a huge amount of transportation within Japan proper in order to carry goods and people, especially troops, to the continent and the railway transportation facilities at the time were not sufficient. To meet the shortfall, the Ministry of Railways planned to build a new wide-gaze line from Tokyo to Shimonoseki in 1947-9. They imagined a line connecting Shimonoseki and Fuzan via a tunnel and eventually reaching Beijing (Maema [1994]). However, with the progress of the war, the idea was eventually abandoned. It was partially realized later as a *shinkansen* line, super-express line, after the war, starting in 1959 and being completed in 1964 (Ikari [1993]). It realized an average speed of 162km/h and a peak speed of 200km/h. Over one hundred years have passed since 1872, when the line connecting Tokyo and Shinbashi was built.

Another imbalance of transportation technology was found in the backwardness of the automobile industry, which shared a common technology with aircraft engines. Likewise, the military tanks used in China were not suitable on the Pacific front because they had been proven to be inferior to the world standard in the defeat of Nomonhan in 1939 by the Soviet army which was equipped with the world's best tanks equivalent to the German ones on the European fronts.

The Japanese economy was insufficient in the long run to meet the wartime demand for military goods in the long run. After the initial accumulation of war weapons was lost she was forced into making piecemeal amendments and could not realize on the production line in which engineers achieved in test production. There are various indexes indicating the level of production during the war, but their bases are rather fragile due to the inaccuracy of statistical surveys and delayed publication of the results which were later lost in the bombing as seen in Part I, section 6. Thus rational revising procedures of economic planning based on adequate and accurate statistics could not be obtainable.

4.5.2 Labour Mobilization in the 1940s

As we mentioned in Part I, the Japanese statistical survey system reached its peak in 1940 when a fifth of the population census was executed. Various statistical surveys were executed all over the Japanese Empire with fairly good accuracy. Unfortunately, not all of them were tabulated and published in due time. Some were published after the end of World War II. The population figures and the labour movement during the war are still a serious concern of historians as the most basic figures.

Takafusa Nakamura and Hirotake Arai estimated the labour movement for the period 1940–47 using the data of national registration for 1940, 1941, 1942, 1943, 1944 and 1945. National registration was designed to check adults who were qualified for mobilization into wartime industries (Nakamura & Arai [1978], Arai [1986](in Nakamura & Hayashi [1986]), [1988] (in Umemura etc. [1988])). With their estimation technique, they first fixed the starting point at 1940, using the population census data, and the terminal at point 1947, using an extra population survey instead of the unrealized 1945 population census, and second they used the 1944 registration data as a passing point for interpolation by a quadratic curve. Thus, industrywise, the numbers of men and women workers were estimated at these three points: 1940, 1944 and 1947.

Their fact findings on the occupational structure after the end of the war in 1944/45 are summarized by four points.

1) The number of workers increased by about 3.26 million, most being people returning from abroad, including army personnel. The biggest group were engaged in agriculture (about 1.15 million) and the rest went into construction, manufacturing and commerce.

2) Women in agriculture seemed to retire from the wartime mobilization.

3) The number of workers in construction and manufacturing increased a lot, except in machinery production.

4) The number of workers in the commercial sector increased by as

much as 1.13 million. Surplus labour was absorbed here.

As the authors said, these estimates depended on too many hypotheses, and the data of 1940 and 1947 were not homogeneous. Interpolation is sometimes quite misleading when applied to such a drastic social change. Our estimates employ an opposite process to that of Nakamura and Arai. We stick to the survey data and the 1940 data are combined with the Dynamic Survey of Labour for the period 1938–43 by the Ministry of Welfare. This survey covered, in principle, every establishment and/or household where someone was employed. We may call this a kind of establishment census. The survey manual, however, did not tell whether the householder here defined was running a certain business or whether it was an ordinary householder simply employing a housemaid or boy. It should be noted that this survey aimed to survey the inflow and outflow of labour in each industry for half a year and at the same time list the initial and terminal stocks of employment with this flow data. Thus, we got figures from the 31st of December, 1940 to the 30th of June, 1943. We do not know whether the survey was continued to the 31st of December, 1943, but in early May, 1943 the Bureau of Statistics of the Cabinet planned to launch a new survey on the working population by integrating various surveys including the Dynamic Survey of Labour by the Ministry of Welfare. The new survey was called the Annual Survey of Workers since 1944 and was combined with the monthly survey which had already started in 1939. The data of the first survey showed one year's movement of labourers since 1st of July, 1943, to 30th of June, 1944, and the stock figures for the end of June in 1944, and the second survey in the following year showed similar figures. The survey itself was continued to 1946 after the end of World War II. This had more extensive coverage of establishments than the Dynamic Survey of Labour because the latter covered only those establishments which employed someone else while the former included all establishments including those that employing and operated by family members only. By comparing the survey results of the two surveys and of Manufacturing and Mining Censuses executed by the Ministry of Trade and Industry, we can reach a fairly reasonable conclusion regarding these survey results, a small volume of which was made public after forty years later in 1986. The data published in 1986, however, covered only part of the survey because

Table II.28 Comparison of 1940 Population Census and 1944 Population Survey with Dynamic Labour Survey and Annual Labour Survey

Industrial classification	Population census 1940	Population survey 1944
Total	32,482,516	28,958,320
1 Agriculture	13,841,576	11,667,177
2 Fishery	542,958	405,686
3 Mining	597,755	778,114
4 Manufacturing	8,132,314	9,131,682
5 Commerce	4,881,538	2,116,141
6 Transportation & communication	1,364,396	1,589,561
7 Government services & others	2,194,893	2,721,893
8 Domestic service	708,945	434,991
9 Miscellaneous	218,141	113,075

the entire source tables of the survey seem to be unnecessary for the general public and the source tables themselves compiled at that time and remained through the war were limited. We can not reconstruct the entire source tables because the original questionnaires gathered did not escape from being burned before the occupation before further processing.

To check the coverage of the Dynamic Survey of Labour, we compare the employment figures of 1940 and the Dynamic Survey of 1943, with the 1944 Population Survey on the 22nd of February. The latter lagged the Dynamic Survey by eight months. It is assumed that the difference might not be so large compared with the figures of 1947 after the war. As shown in Table II.28, the differences in coverage ratios between these two periods are fairly constant. The difference exceeded ten points only in commerce, government officials and professionals, and domestic servants. The latter two may have been greatly influenced by the survey methods of defining enterprises and households to be surveyed, so we may conclude that the coverage ratios were comparatively stable.

Table II.28 Continued

	Dynamic labour survey 1940	%	Dynamic labour survey 1943 & first half	%	Annual labour survey 1944	%
Total	9,551,945	29.40	9,075,202	31.33	15,279,919	45.55
1 Agriculture	229,577	1.36	148,859	1.27	276,720	2.37
2 Fishery	93,908	17.29	66,706	16.44	115,836	28.53
3 Mining	1,140,317	52.42	601,755	77.33	805,512	103.50*
4 Manufacturing	4,845,587	59.58	5,704,320	62.46	10,146,495	111.11*
5 Commerce	1,894,044	38.80	1,175,840	55.56	843,733	39.87
6 Transportation & communication	472,425	34.62	472,591	29.73	1,422,863	89.51
7 Government services & others	595,222	27.11	672,970	24.72	1,387,237	50.96
8 Domestic service	217,743	30.71	178,483	41.03	161,381	37.17
9 Miscellaneous	17,639	28.93	10,800	47.47	18,876	106.24*
10 Labour supply	45,483		42,878		101,266	

(Note) Percentage figures show the cover ratio of the labourers from establishment surveys such as dynamic survey and annual labour survey against the working population obtained from the population surveys covering all households.

Some explanation may be necessary for manufacturing (see Table II.29). We can compare three other source figures; one is from the population census and the second results from the manufacturing census and includes those producing military goods. The latter was published separately from the main reports and covers about 88% of the former. The difference amounts to about 17.4 million, but Mataji Umemura pointed out that the latter did not include the aircraft industry, which he estimated to include about 75,252 employees. Thus, the coverage ratio including aircraft industry became about 89%, which will explain why the difference must be smaller, because the population figures include non-employee workers such as members of individually owned

Table II.29 Manufacturing Census

(i) Number of factories by the size of factory

	1939	1940	1941	1942
Total	717,580	701,795	696,186	648,040
Less than 5 employee	569,827	554,412	550,619	512,802
More than 5 employee	137,767	137,805	136,467	126,892
Factories for military goods	9,986	9,578	9,100	8,346

(Note) Factories for military goods: Published in a separate volume as secret, containing factories both less than 5 employee and more than 5 employee.

factories. Then the problem is the difference between the manufacturing census and the Dynamic Survey. The latter covers about 60% of the manufacturing factories of the former, but 72% of the employees. The average size of factories is 8.15 in the manufacturing census and 13.12 in the Dynamic Survey. This implies that the latter may cover only larger factories. The difference in cover ratios between the manufacturing census and the Dynamic Survey declines by only 6 points for establishments and 4.5 points for employees in 1939–42. In conclusion, for manufacturing we can trace the changes in numbers of labourers through the Dynamic Survey. The third source for comparison was the Annual Survey of Employment in 1944. It showed figures 1.275 times bigger than those the Dynamic Survey after adjusting the coverage. This suggests the under evaluation of the coverage of the Dynamic Survey. Granting this under evaluation, we must take into consideration that the consistency of the movements of labour from 1940 to 1943 in the Dynamic Survey will supply us a fairly reasonable estimate for the labour movement as a whole.

Drastic changes occurred in commerce during wartime due to the regulation of commercial activities, especially those found in the rationing system. Wholesale traders were advised to merge and retail shops were requested to get trading licenses under the rationing system, such as for food grains and clothing.[10] During 1939–40, two population censuses were executed: the 1939 extra distribution census, and

Table II.29 Continued

(ii) Number of workers

Size of factory	Total	1939 Male	Female	Total	1940 Male	Female
a) Number of whole labourers						
Total	6,389,088	4,496,597	1,892,491	6,683,253	4,808,161	1,875,092
Less than 5 employee	1,283,901	916,643	367,258	1,264,332	896,795	367,537
More than 5 employee	4,370,265	2,897,129	1,473,136	4,503,339	3,073,103	1,430,236
Factories for military goods	734,922	682,825	52,097	915,582	838,263	77,319
b) Number of artisan workers						
Total	5,573,688	3,851,813	1,721,875	5,745,530	4,077,582	1,667,948
Less than 5 employee	1,164,634	841,323	323,311	1,143,710	822,273	321,437
More than 5 employee	3,786,247	2,421,725	1,364,522	3,843,220	2,545,161	1,298,059
Factories for military goods	622,807	588,765	34,042	758,600	710,148	48,452

Size of factory	Total	1941 Male	Female	Total	1942 Male	Female
a) Number of whole labourers						
Total	6,897,303	4,934,761	1,962,542	7,157,778	5,246,596	1,911,182
Less than 5 employee	1,281,207	873,834	407,373	1,137,431	759,400	378,031
More than 5 employee	4,524,203	3,083,245	1,440,958	4,756,415	3,351,700	1,404,715
Factories for military goods	1,091,893	977,682	114,211	1,263,932	1,135,496	128,436
b) Number of artisan workers						
Total	5,830,224	4,124,237	1,705,987	4,953,475	3,662,742	1,290,733
Less than 5 employee	1,156,403	799,081	357,322	n.a.	n.a.	n.a.
More than 5 employee	3,786,916	2,509,528	1,277,388	3,924,457	2,709,909	1,214,548
Factories for military goods	886,905	815,628	71,277	1,029,018	952,833	76,185

Table II.29 Continued

(iii) Average number of workers per factory

Size of factory	1939			1940			1941			1942		
	Total	Male	Female	Total	Male	Female	Total	Male	Female	Total	Male	Female
a) Average of whole labourers per factory												
Total	8.90	6.27	2.64	9.52	6.85	2.67	9.91	7.09	2.82	11.05	8.10	2.95
Less than 5 employee	2.25	1.61	0.64	2.28	1.62	0.66	2.33	1.59	0.74	2.22	1.48	0.74
More than 5 employee	31.72	21.03	10.69	32.68	22.30	10.38	33.15	22.59	10.56	37.48	26.41	11.07
Factories for military goods	73.60	68.38	5.22	95.59	87.52	8.07	119.99	107.44	12.55	151.44	136.05	15.39
b) Average of artisan workers per factory												
Total	7.77	5.37	2.40	8.19	5.81	2.38	8.37	5.92	2.45	n.a.	n.a.	n.a.
Less than 5 employee	2.04	1.48	0.57	2.06	1.48	0.58	2.10	1.45	0.65			
More than 5 employee	27.48	17.58	9.90	27.89	18.47	9.42	27.75	18.39	9.36	30.93	21.36	9.57
Factories for military goods	62.37	58.96	3.41	79.20	74.14	5.06	97.46	89.63	7.83	123.29	114.17	9.13

Table II.30 Working Population in Various Census Surveys for Japan Proper

Unit: Person

Manufacturing Census/ Commercial Census (1939/December 31)		Extra Census of 1939 (1939/August 1)		Population Census of 1940 (1940/November 1)	
Establishment more than 5 employee	3,786,247				
Establishment more than 5 employee (A)	1,164,634	Retail shops who produce their merchandise (C)	952,539		
				Manufacturing worker	8,109,998
Sub total	4,950,881				
Wholesale only	223,203	Wholesale	15,677		
Wholesale and retail sale	449,547	Wholesale and retail sale	695,154		
Sub total (B)	672,750	(D)	710,831		
		Retail sale	2,606,751		
		Department store	164,990		
		Peddlar	190,556		
		Grand total	4,625,667	Commercial workers	4,868,229
(A)+(B)	1,837,384	(C)+(D)	1,663,370		
				Agriculture	13,654,726
				Fishery	537,715
				Mining	595,515
				Transportation	1,359,713
				Services	2,185,214
				Domestic	706,453
				Miscellaneous	217,191

Note: Population Census and Extra Census have similar figures on commercial
workers. Thus commercial workers were approximately 4.8 million. However,there might be some overlapping between retail shops who produce their
merchandise(they overlap with small manufactures in Manufacturing Census)
and some of the wholesale traders in Commercial Survey. Thus (A)+(B) may
be comparable to (C)+(D).

the 1940 census. The former was based on the establishment unit and the latter on the household. In addition, the 1939 extra census was executed on the 1st of August, 1939.

The population census figures were about 240 thousand bigger than those of the extra census, because they included whole service industries other than commerce, such as finance and insurance. Fortunately, the census asked the inhabitants living in 1940 about their last job in 1939 (see Table II.30).

The industrial classification of commerce included some of the people working in the service sector such as bankers and clerks. If we suppose that those engaged in commerce and who died in 1940 were all traders, the decrease due to deaths among traders might be 39,156. As the remaining traders numbered 3,284,444, the total decrease in the number of traders was 345,882. This implies that the number of traders constituted 89.4% of the 1939 figures.

However, the Dynamic Survey indicates that the number of establishments decreased to 85.3% and the number of workers to 89.5%, and the movement itself was quite comparable to the movements of population (see Table II.31(i)(ii)). Strictly speaking, the real numbers differ in these series. As we mentioned above, the coverage for commerce in the Dynamic Survey included various service industries other than trading, such as finance, leasing and rental, and amusement. Excluding these and also intermediary trading merchants, the total number of establishments was 295 thousand. A similar coverage of industries in the 1939 extra census showed 378 thousand wholesale and wholesale-retail merchant establishments. Workers in these sectors numbered 1.085 million in the 1939 Dynamic Survey and 1.312 million in 1935 extra census. The former covered about 82.7%, but the distinction between wholesale-retail traders and retail traders was quite dubious, as we can see from the (wholesale) commercial census by the Ministry of Trade and Industry and the extra census. Traders including small retail traders and even peddlers in the 1939 extra census numbered 3.919 million. Thus, the Dynamic Survey covered 27.2% of them.

Changes according to the (wholesale) commercial census by the Ministry of Trade and Industry in 1939 and 1940 amounted to 75.9% in number of establishments and 80.7% in number of workers. Thus, if the decrease for retail traders was similar to that for wholesale traders,

Table II.31 Number of Labourers by Dynamic Survey of Labour and its Accuracy

(i) Number of Establishments Surveyed

Industrial classification	1939	1940	1941 First half	1941 Latter half	1942 First half	1942 Latter half	1943 First half
Total	1,475,291	1,346,773	1,316,314	1,237,016	1,171,936	1,069,468	995,395
Agriculture	173,124	138,330	121,530	115,753	104,894	97,631	86,721
Fishery	14,324	11,717	11,008	10,093	9,562	9,081	8,684
Mining	8,013	7,724	7,552	7,402	7,341	7,338	7,166
Manufacturing	432,883	411,423	416,226	400,629	385,981	347,632	327,798
Commerce	512,152	451,804	435,273	395,714	356,532	303,480	271,481
Transportation & communication	40,608	34,719	29,584	25,764	25,285	24,200	23,617
Public service & others	122,914	108,454	108,849	110,148	110,700	114,255	109,816
Domestic service	164,909	176,645	180,930	166,660	166,673	161,235	155,855
Miscellaneous	3,391	3,742	2,709	2,651	2,831	2,703	2,286
Labour supply	2,973	2,215	2,653	2,202	2,137	1,913	1,971

Table II.31 Continued

(ii) Total Labourers

Industrial classification	1939			1940			1941 First half		
	Total	Male	Female	Total	Male	Female	Total	Male	Female
Total	9,475,932	6,428,710	3,047,222	9,551,945	6,478,195	3,073,750	9,592,782	6,547,879	3,044,903
Agriculture	245,256	165,712	79,544	229,577	150,323	79,254	198,464	133,715	64,749
Fishery	91,400	84,235	7,165	93,908	86,058	7,850	86,805	80,673	6,132
Mining	566,977	498,866	68,111	1,140,317	513,059	627,258	599,518	524,714	74,804
Manufacturing	5,708,249	3,637,658	2,070,591	4,845,587	3,782,737	1,062,850	5,485,897	3,879,062	1,606,835
Commerce	1,544,635	1,179,459	365,176	1,894,044	1,091,410	802,634	1,837,159	1,043,392	793,767
Transportation & communication	438,789	391,606	47,183	472,425	417,553	54,872	486,111	431,055	55,056
Public service & others	607,596	399,581	208,015	595,222	372,671	222,551	616,804	390,985	225,819
Domestic service	191,864	19,992	171,872	217,743	22,619	195,124	217,256	20,416	196,840
Miscellaneous	20,122	14,989	5,133	17,639	13,526	4,113	15,268	12,036	3,232
Labour supply	61,044	36,612	24,432	45,483	28,239	17,244	49,500	31,831	17,669

Industrial classification	1941 Latter half			1942 First half			1942 Latter half			1943 First half		
	Total	Male	Female	Total	Male	Female	Total	Male	Female	Total	Male	Female
Total	9,353,568	6,326,875	3,026,693	9,286,505	6,293,238	2,993,267	9,077,110	6,170,263	2,906,847	9,075,202	6,279,890	2,795,312
Agriculture	194,857	124,864	69,993	173,309	112,632	60,677	165,131	104,877	60,254	148,859	95,522	53,337
Fishery	142,647	136,305	6,342	74,945	69,951	4,994	76,608	71,121	5,487	66,706	61,928	4,778
Mining	541,291	463,514	77,777	624,430	540,250	84,180	612,162	528,487	83,675	601,755	518,393	83,362
Manufacturing	5,460,282	3,854,742	1,605,540	5,517,719	3,911,247	1,606,472	5,549,235	3,949,315	1,599,920	5,704,320	4,164,412	1,539,908
Commerce	1,652,216	886,461	765,755	1,505,428	779,301	726,127	1,296,398	642,794	653,604	1,175,840	571,598	604,242
Transportation & communication	472,970	416,259	56,711	477,759	417,205	60,554	461,683	398,708	62,975	472,591	407,406	65,185
Public service & others	633,173	392,963	240,210	654,726	406,864	247,862	677,369	420,451	256,918	672,970	411,300	261,670
Domestic service	198,409	18,296	180,113	195,384	16,791	178,593	178,745	16,678	162,067	178,483	14,257	164,226
Miscellaneous	13,257	9,791	3,466	14,353	10,830	3,523	12,651	9,520	3,131	10,800	8,128	2,672
Labour supply	44,466	23,680	20,786	48,452	28,167	20,285	47,128	28,312	18,816	42,878	26,946	15,932

Table II.31 Continued

(iii) Estimation Error of Employee Surveyed by the Dynamic Survey

Industrial classification	1939			1940			1941 First half		
	Total establishment	LME	non-LME	Total establishment	LME	non-LME	Total establishment	LME	non-LME
Total	-5.67	5.33	-11.92	-4.62	-2.32	-6.14	-6.96	0.97	-12.36
01: Agriculture	-27.39	659.00	-33.15	-28.79	-37.65	-27.86	-22.82	-41.79	-20.91
02: Fishery	-35.17	-31.18	-35.28	-27.74	-18.43	-27.96	-31.64	-72.12	-30.63
03: Mining	-1.46	-7.12	31.54	-6.27	-10.64	10.56	-0.01	5.67	-17.07
04: Manufacturing	-3.20	7.07	-14.12	-2.46	-1.04	-4.32	-4.83	0.68	-12.08
05: Commerce	-8.28	—	-8.28	-5.48	—	-5.48	-11.38	—	-11.38
06: Transportation & communication	1.20	5.62	-4.21	-6.12	0.40	-14.95	-7.21	0.03	-18.75
07: Public services & others	-11.49	—	-11.49	-3.55	—	-3.55	-6.05	—	-6.05
08: Domestic	-0.93	—	-0.93	-7.96	-16.36	—	-16.36	—	—
09: Miscellaneous	-19.91	—	-19.91	-26.37	—	-26.37	-17.48	—	-17.48
10: Labour supply	-41.43	—	-41.43	-7.65	—	-7.65	-20.84	—	-20.84

Industrial classification	1941 Latter half			1942 First half			1942 Latter half		
	Total establishment	LME	non-LME	Total establishment	LME	non-LME	Total establishment	LME	non-LME
Total	-4.14	0.06	-7.30	-6.74	-1.41	-11.28	-3.78	-0.61	-6.98
01: Agriculture	-22.86	-10.38	-23.69	-22.68	3.78	-24.75	-20.37	-26.63	-19.71
02: Fishery	-27.05	31.41	-27.60	-27.84	21.31	-27.95	-26.26	0.35	-26.56
03: Mining	-0.24	2.38	-9.45	-4.59	-0.22	-20.75	-7.69	-11.48	9.25
04: Manufactring	-2.84	-0.36	-6.59	-5.34	-1.23	-12.18	-2.09	0.83	-8.05
05: Commerce	-7.59	—	-7.59	-10.96	—	-10.96	-6.32	—	-6.32
06: Transportation & communication	-2.62	-0.15	-7.32	-7.04	-5.23	-10.74	-2.01	0.93	-8.42
07: Public services & others	-2.93	—	-2.93	-2.27	—	-2.27	-4.21	—	-4.21
08: Domestic	-4.06	—	-4.06	-10.69	—	-10.69	-0.50	—	-0.50
09: Miscellaneous	7.24	—	7.24	-11.34	—	-11.34	-14.15	—	-14.15
10: Labour supply	-0.98	—	-0.98	-13.03	—	-13.03	-7.86	—	-7.86

(Note) LME: Establishment assigned for labour mobilization. non-LME: Establishment assigned as non-labour

in other words, traders as a whole decreased at the same rate as whole-sale traders, then changes from the extra census in 1939 would have numbered 4,481,860 workers and less than 3,996,000 from the actual population figures of 4,881,538 in 1940. Thus, the number of retail traders would have diminished by less than the conjectured number. As we have mentioned, about 85.3% of establishments and 89.5% of workers decreased in the Dynamic Survey, the population figures of 2,928,321 in 1940 was about 89.4% of the 3,274,203 in 1939. The decrease for retail traders was not yet so severe in 1939–40 compared with that for wholesale traders.

As a whole, the paths of industrywise movements obtained from the Dynamic Survey seem fairly trustworthy, if we take into consideration the adjustments of the absolute levels of each industry to the base year population figures of 1940. Thus, the next criterion was internal consistency within the Dynamic Survey. Fortunately, the Dynamic Survey provided us with two figures for the same phenomenon comprising the ending stock figures for employees and the inflow and outflow figures during the observation periods, first one year and later half a year due to the changes of survey period. Thus, we can estimate the starting stock figures and compare them with the preceding stock figures at the end, and thus estimate the error ratios of the previous end figures to the current starting ones. If the coverage of the survey did not alter, they must coincide. However, some establishments may have been surveyed in the previous survey period but ceased to exist in the next survey period and so the starting stock figures must be smaller than the end stock figures of the previous survey period. For entry of new establishments, the situation was vice-versa. Thus, some part of the error ratio can be explained by changes in the coverage of the survey.

Both the overall and industrywise error ratios for number of employees are shown in Table II.31(iii). Almost all industrywise error ratios were in the 6–7% range. Those over 20% were agriculture and fisheries. This is due to the small fraction in the survey where small changes have a bigger effect on the ratios. The commerce industry was rather exceptional due to the substantial changes made by the adoption of the overall rationing system in the economy. In addition, almost all the ratios were negative. This must be because the mobilization of labour and mergers and amalgamations of enterprises during the wartime controlled economy brought out reporting of establishments that had survived and the last figures must have included employees who worked in closed establishments at the next reporting time.

The most outstanding features of the Dynamic Survey are that we can obtain the total picture of employment inflow and outflow for the entire labour market through netting the inflow and outflow of the labour force, because the questionnaire asked whether inflow was from other establishments or industries or from entirely new entries to the labour market. Thus, we can define the following concepts:

1) new entry to the labour market=sum of past non-employed
2) net inflow or outflow in the labour market
   =sum of those dismissed or dying etc.−sum of those employed
   in other industries
3) social recurrent=(1)−(total employment−total dismissed)
   =(1)−(gross outflow from labour market)

However, we should separate males and females for calculation of the labour movements in order to avoid the miss netting effect of the reverse movements between male and female. The resulting estimates are shown in Table II.32.

Main facts found are as follows:

1) More females than males newly entered the labour market, reflecting the past social customs of Japanese labour market where middle class women had stayed at home as domestic workers, but this increase slowed from its peak in 1941.

2) The social recurrent defined above in equation (3) shows the turnover of the labour force between industries or establishments. Their movements showed complex features. There was a net inflow into the female labour force but no such inflow into the male labour force, except in the latter half of 1941. There was a constant inflow of those who had once worked. We call this phenomenon a social recurrent of the labour force and it was due to the expansion of the war all over the Pacific.

3) Among movements of the labour force between industries, some words should be added about inflow and outflow in the agricultural sector, because this is not well-reflected in the Dynamic Survey. In the 1940 population census, movements from occupations in the previous year were firstly an inflow from non-workers

Table II.32 Net Inflow and Outflow of Labourers in Labour Force by Dynamic Survey of Labour

	1939			1940			1941 First half		
	Male	Female	Total	Male	Female	Total	Male	Female	Total
1: Net decrease	−386,324	120,909	−265,415	−14,783	309,681	294,898	−16,418	288,682	272,264
2: Continued to work	2,521,068	1,090,574	3,611,642	2,932,234	1,246,496	4,178,730	3,376,797	1,366,470	4,743,267
3: New entry (Work experience)	1,844,221	641,280	2,485,501	1,560,205	525,063	2,085,268	1,418,837	492,807	1,911,644
4: New entry (No work experience)	400,617	453,217	853,834	419,781	459,702	879,483	349,651	403,536	753,187
2+3+4−1	5,152,230	2,064,162	7,216,392	4,927,003	1,921,580	6,848,583	5,161,703	1,974,131	7,135,834
Numbers of workers currently employed	6,428,710	3,047,222	9,475,932	6,478,195	3,073,750	9,551,945	6,547,881	3,044,903	9,592,784

(Note)
(code) 1: net decrease=dismiss−new entry with experience
2: continued to work=currently working−(new employment+dismiss)

Table II.32 Continued

1941 Latter half			1942 First half			1942 Latter half			1943 First half		
Male	Female	Total	Male	Female	Total	Male	Female	Total	Male	Female	Total
129,730	305,233	434,963	45,246	282,260	327,506	−26,687	265,546	238,859	−104,721	259,249	154,528
3,139,615	1,274,489	4,414,104	3,659,217	1,463,844	5,123,061	3,892,395	1,614,258	5,506,653	4,036,442	1,601,133	5,637,575
1,328,940	491,444	1,820,384	1,158,515	435,743	1,594,258	1,003,051	334,995	1,338,046	1,061,025	330,371	1,391,396
396,087	460,933	857,020	270,328	374,730	645,058	298,453	352,053	650,506	226,119	274,188	500,307
4,734,912	1,921,633	6,656,545	5,042,814	1,992,057	7,034,871	5,220,586	2,035,760	7,256,346	5,428,307	1,946,443	7,374,750
6,326,875	3,026,703	9,353,578	6,293,238	2,993,267	9,286,505	6,170,263	2,901,847	9,072,110	6,279,890	2,795,312	9,075,202

into agriculture of 927,262, and secondly an inflow from other industries of 203,353, making a total inflow of 1,134,615.

The outflow from agriculture to other industries was 824,258, making a net inflow into agriculture of 310,357.

The next issue is the comparability of the Dynamic Survey of Labour by the Ministry of Welfare and the Annual Survey of Employment by the Bureau of Statistics and how to link these two different series of data at the turning point of 1944 and 1945. As mentioned above, the Bureau of Statistics started a new survey called *nenji-kinrou-tokei-chosa*, Annual Statistical Survey of Employment, which was carried out every June 31st along with the monthly survey. Its purpose was to integrate labour surveys carried out by various ministries since 1944. However, the Dynamic Survey of Labour was not clearly mentioned in the list of surveys to be integrated and the Annual Survey lasted until 1946.

The figures of 1944 show the yearly labour movement, i.e., flow of labour, from the middle of 1943 to the middle of 1944 and the labour used at the survey period, the stock figures at the end of June of 1944. Thus, they are comparable to the seventh survey, the last data of the Dynamic Survey of Labour in the first half of 1943. The time span between two survey periods was the entire year and so we need to make some adjustment for the comparison. The conversion of the 1944 figures in the stock concept on June 30 in 1944 to 1943 figures on July 1st in 1943 can be done by subtracting the inflow and adding the outflow from each establishment within this one year to the figures of 31st of June, 1944. These figures may correspond to those of the Dynamic Survey at the end of August in 1943, but labourers working in establishments vanished from 1943 to 1944, which might have lowered the cover ratio.

The next point to be mentioned is the different coverages of these surveys. The Annual Statistical Survey covered explicitly manufacturing factories (534,699), mines (10,948), transportation and communication facilities (124,364), vessels of more than twenty tons (6,784), and other miscellaneous establishments (353,713) such as commercial shops, agriculture, governmental agencies and households employing servants in 1944. What is needed to explain is that the factories in the Annual Survey did not include head offices of manufacturing and mines which might have been included in the Dynamic Survey as manufacturing factories and mines.

Compared with the total of the establishments surveyed in the Dynamic Survey, 995,401 (839,585 excluding households hiring maids or servants) in 1943, the coverage of the Annual Survey seems somewhat larger. The numbers of establishments and vessels were 1,030,508 (1,023,724 establishment and 6,784 vessels) in 1944 and 318,886 (316,066 establishment and 2,820 vessels) without miscellaneous in 1945[11] and 653,045 (including miscellaneous but excluding vessels) in 1946. One reason for this might be that the Annual Survey included those factories and shops which did not employ non-family members.

The total number of workers excluding engineers and office workers was 9,075,202 (8,896,719 excluding household maids or servants) in 1943 according to the Dynamic Survey, but 12,468,396 (10,860,259 excluding temporary workers) in 1944 according to the Annual Survey data, if we adjusted the coverage of the estimates for 1943 obtained from Annual Survey data in 1944 to be the same as the Dynamic Survey, where total workers might be 15,184,059 (13,575,922 excluding temporary workers) in 1943 according to the estimates deducting the total net inflow from the Annual Survey in 1944. The average number of workers per establishment, i.e., total workers divided by establishment and households was 9.12 (10.59 if excluding maids and servants from the numerator and households from the denominator) according to the Dynamic Survey and 12.06 (10.50 excluding temporary workers) according to the Annual Survey where the original estimates were 14.83 (13.26 excluding temporary workers) from unadjusted coverage figures in 1943. This seems to imply that the average number of workers per establishment in the Dynamic Survey was less than that of the Annual Survey based on the hypothesis that the former must have larger because of the exclusion smaller family workshops. However, industrywise analysis of manufacturing, mining and transportation and communication will supply us with consistent result on this point. The average number of regular workers per establishment between the 1943 Dynamic Survey and the 1944 Annual Survey were 17.40 vs 14.24 in manufacturing and 83.97 vs 57.79 in mines but 20.01 vs 8.98 in transportation and communications. The contradiction in our hypothesis found in the transportation and communications may stem from the treatment of the head offices in these industries.

The discrepancies in the numbers of establishments and workers between the Dynamic Survey and the Annual Survey must be caused partially by the difference of the survey period, nearly one year's time lag, and omission of family workshop in both manufacturing and commerce as discussed in the comparative analysis with manufacturing and commercial censuses, and partially by the lower coverage of reporting units in the Dynamic Survey. Statisticians at the Bureau of Statistics once analysed the results after completing the 1944 Annual Survey and similar conclusions. They tried to adjust the definitional coverage as far as possible in the four major industrial categories. They must have used internal reports that were different than those printed. Both were top secret at the time. Their conclusion was under-reporting of the Dynamic Survey. If we rely on their figures, the average number of workers including engineers and office workers but excluding family members were 19.69 in manufacturing, 84.46 in mines, 41.36 in transportation and communication and 4.29 in miscellaneous according to the Dynamic Survey, 18.13, 71.53, 10.86 and 8.92 according to the Annual Survey. This implies that their under-reporting must have been concentrated around the smaller scale establishments as the sizes of establishments in the Dynamic Survey were larger than those in the Annual Survey. The estimates for 1943 from the 1944 survey data obtained by subtracting net inflow of labour to the establishments shown in Table II.32 above, show that the discrepancies are confined to manual labourers and not engineers and office clerks. This adds further supporting evidence that the leakage of the Dynamic Survey must be from smaller scale establishments where fewer of these kinds of workers were needed.

4.5.3 Implications of Labour Mobilization in the 1940s

We can trace the overall effects of labour mobilization between 1944 and 1945 in specified industries from the Annual Survey. The total number of mobilized workers including temporary workers, university students and school pupils was 12,026 thousand in 1944, and this number shrank to 6,736 thousand in 1945. The highest declines were 49.17% in manufacturing, 34.77% in mining and 10.88% in transportation and

Table II.33 Workers of Main three Industries at the Last Stage of the War

(i) Number of workers

		1943	1944	1945
Manufacturing	Dynamic Survey (March)	6,455,977	7,810,010*	4,221,407*
	Annual Survey (June)	7,248,283	8,770,054	4,743,155
	(including mobilized students)			5,037,326
Mining	Dynamic Survey (March)	605,258	665,042*	440,023*
	Annual Survey (June)	637,777	700,782	463,671
	(including mobilized students)			510,870
Transportation and communication	Dynamic Survey (March)	976,960	976,595*	884,951*
	Annual Survey (June)	1,287,617	1,208,199	1,094,424
	(including mobilized students)			1,187,704
Total of the three industries	Dynamic Survey (March)	8,038,195	9,452,247	5,546,381
	Annual Survey (June)	9,173,677	10,679,035	6,301,250
	(including mobilized students)			6,735,900

Note: *: Estimates: Assuming that the difference of covering ratio of the Dynamic Survey and Annual Labour Survey is the same, the figures of the Annual Survey of Labour of 1944–45 are adjusted for the comparison of the series of Dynamic Survey.

Table II.33 Continued

(ii) Index to the previous year(%)

	1943	1944	1945
Manufacturing	—	120.9	54.0
Mining	—	110.4	66.1
Transportation and communication	—	99.9	90.6
Total of the three industries	—	117.6	58.7

(iii) Index for the 1943 base 1943=100 (%)

	1943	1944	1945
Manufacturing	100.0	120.9	65.3
Mining	100.0	110.4	72.9
Transportation and communication	100.0	99.9	90.5
Total of the three industries	100.0	117.6	68.9

communication. This total overall decline of workers in these three industries of 43.09% in one year did not mean the same production shrinkage rate. As a case study, a factory of the Nakajima Aircraft Company located in Maebashi had about 25 thousand workers and its labour productivity rose from 4.0 persons per aircraft engine in 1939 to 2.86 in 1942, and the loss ratio of products had dropped from 14.0% in 1941 to 7.7% in 1943 (Tojyo [1995] pp. 276–277). However, we can not generalize this particular case up to the 1945 situation. It is more plausible to suppose that total production must have been lower than this because of the shortage of essential materials and various bottle necks in production such as the transfer of factories to the countryside to escape bombing and so on.

The problem still lies in the linkage of the time series data of the Dynamic Survey and the Annual Survey. In so far as we restricted the employment to permanent, engineers and office workers of these three industries, the total number of workers peaked in 1944, based on the application of the rate of under reporting of the Dynamic Survey in 1943 to the estimation of the 1944 and 1945 figures as shown in Table II.33. The adjustment of coverage and exclusion of the temporary workers affected the decline such that the number of workers in 1945 was 59.25% of the 1944 level. As mentioned above, the decline of total employment in these industries without correction was 43.99%. These industries were in a more favoured position in regard to manpower policy. If we suppose the levels of 1943 to be 100.00, they would be 120.48 in 1944 and 65.38 in 1945 in the manufacturing, 109.87 in 1944 and 72.70 in 1945 in mines and 100.00 in 1944 and 90.58 in transportation and communication. As a whole the estimates of these three industries in 1945 shrank sharply, to about 69.00% of the 1943 level or 59.25% of the 1944 level. They were a little bit higher than the data including temporary workers, and so the real production level in general must have been lower than that suggested by our estimates. This supposition will be supported by the analysis of the composition of mobilized labour.

Although the 1945 figures were far below the 1944 ones, they had still included the mobilized students and pupils. The students and pupils mobilized to factories, mines and transportation facilities numbered 735,138 on June 30 in 1945. This was 10.9% of the total workers including non-permanent workers in these three industries. The mobilization of students and pupils had already started in June, 1943 and then it was expanded in March, 1945 when schooling on the campuses for senior classes of elementary and higher grades was stopped for mobilizing of students and pupils. The total number of mobilized students and pupils were 3.43 million boys and 0.47 million girls at the end of the war (Hara [1995] p. 18). Students mobilized in these three industries in 1945, according to the Annual Survey, comprised 18.8% of the total mobilized at the end of the war.

In addition to students, aged people was also mobilized. The age of permanent male manual workers in manufacturing showed two distribution peaks: one at 17–18 and the second from 31–45. The first class comprised 9.8% and the latter 33.6%. Moreover, the age class over sixty-one comprised 2.6%, and over all three industries it comprised 2.4%. If we covered more than age 51, it was over 17.2%. Compared with 1944, they showed marked decrease. It is said that the semi-forced mobilization of aged people only resulted in a high absentee ratio, which caused problems for the manufacturing process of assembly-line system. However, the mobilization of students and pupils was quite effective because of their zeal to win the victory in war and their high discipline. (Tojyo [1995]).

No source tables remain for labour mobility in 1945, but at least the total turnover ratio of employment was high in 1944. More than half of the workers in the previous period were dismissed compared with the new employment. This implies that in the latter period of the war Japan tried to mobilize every possible worker in the country. However, they did not function well due to sabotage of newly mobilized aged people and their in ability to master mechanized production, etc. of modern manufacturing compared with the mobilized students and pupils.[12]

To sum up the manpower policy at that time, higher education at college and university level was almost stopped and all the students were conscripted except those in the fields of science and technology which were regarded as indispensable to the war. Pupils in middle school were driven away to factories or farms. The educational system required to sustain a society nearly collapsed and the schooling system did not function at all. These chaotic policies were extended to the colonial peoples. In Manchukuo the forced mobilization started early in 1941 (Matsumoto [1992] pp. 130–144). and this policy was later extended to Japan Proper. Many Korean and Chinese people were brought by force to Japan Proper from the colonial and occupied areas (Nishinarita [1994] pp. 296–310).

Total mobilization for direct military power was 5,500 thousand for the army and 1,693 thousand for the navy.[13] The negative aspect of the manpower policy at that time was that the government scarcely considered the future of the nation beyond the end of the war. The only positive aspect of that was the unexpected effect of the entire mobilization of manpower which occurred after the war. The army and labour mobilization during the war acted as a training school encouraging people to leave the agricultural sector, where manual labour was still dominant. The on-the-job training the labour force received, even at armaments factories, was also useful for production of civil goods after the war. In addition, the increase in labour productivity with the introduction of various farming machines in the agricultural sector after the war might be traced back to this on-the-job training.

4.5.4 Damage to Human Resources during the War

The total damage to human resources during the war differs a lot depending where the fighting took place. For example, deaths in the Sino- Japanese and the Russo-Japanese wars were restricted to soldiers, except for relatively few who were unwillingly involved in those wars of invasion of China by the Russians and Japanese. Contemporary war has changed its character to total war, and now there is no distinction between the battle line and the home front. Thus, in the latter stage of World War II, far more civilians were killed than soldiers and drafted civilians involved in military operations. Most of the civilian deaths were caused by carpet bombing by incendiaries, which were quite effective in destroying wooden houses, as was proved by the fire at the time of the Great Kanto Earthquake. This is true even if we exclude the massacres of Hiroshima and Nagasaki by atomic bombs.

It must be noted that at the time of the Russo-Japanese War, far fewer soldiers were killed in the battle line than died of beriberi. Medical doctors headed by Rintaro Mori[14] in miliary service stuck to the idée fixe of the bacteria disease of beriberi and thus accelerated the number of deaths. On the other hand, medical doctors headed by Kanehiro Takagi in the naval service adopted the cause of a shortage of certain foodstuffs and thus prevented the propagation of beriberi before Umetaro Suzuki found vitamins in 1911. In World War II, the shortage of logistics was fatal. For example, among the one hundred and forty thousand soldiers sent to New Guinea in July 1943, only ten thousand were alive at the end of the war in August 1945. Those who died in the fighting constituted only three percent of total deaths. The remainder died of starvation or disease. The main reason for the shortage of logistic support was, needless to say, the loss of command of the air after the defeat at the Midway Island naval operation of June 1943, but the inadequate usage of submarines was also a factor. The total tonnage of vessels at the start of the war was about 6.43 million, and this was increased to about ten million with 3.33 million tons of newly built ships and 0.31 million tons of captured ones. About eight million tons were lost during the war. Of these, 56.5% were lost to submarines and 30.8% to aerial bombing. Thus, all the islands Japan occupied were isolated from each other.

Most of the armed forces sent abroad were returned to Japan Proper after disarmament, except those who were captured and forced to work for many years in Siberian prisons by Soviet Russia. Those who escaped starvation were eventually returned to Japan in 1950 (Mark R. Peattie's paper in Hosoya etc. (eds.) [1993] pp. 402–4).

The most extensive research on the damage due to the war was carried out by the Agency for Economic Stabilization, now called as the Agency of Economic Planning, under the direction of Saburo Ohkita in 1947–9. The research reports, except the one entitled "*Hiroshima, Nagasaki ni-okeru genshi-bakudan ni-yoru butteki-higai;fu, jin-teki higai* (Damage for assets by the atomic bombs in Hiroshima and Nagasaki; appendixed with human damages)" were published in five issues including two mimeographed ones.[15]

The total number of people who died according to the report of the Ministry of Welfare was 3.10 million and among them 2.30 were military personnel, 0.50 civilian in Japan Proper excluding Okinawa and 0.30 in outside Japan Proper and Okinawa, which the US Army invaded. Jun Hirota reexamined the figures quoted and estimated that

2.30 million should be read as 2.20, 0.50 as 0.52, and 0.30 as 0.40. However, the figures in the report by the Agency for Economic Stabilization was somewhat lower due to the insufficiency of the data at that time. The report said that the dead totalled 1.85 million and the dead, wounded and missing-assumed-dead totalled 2.53. Of these, 2.53 million were civilians not in the front areas, excluding Okinawa, and in the other colonial areas the numbers were 0.30 and 0.67 including wounded and missing-assumed-dead: the numbers of military personnel wounded and missing were 1.56 and 1.86 million. Ninety-nine percent of the wounded civilian casualties were caused by bombing and the rest mainly by cannonade from the invasion fleet. This amounted to about one percent of the total population in 1944. Today the total dead in the battle of Okinawa is estimated as 94 thousand civilians and 94 thousand military personnel, making total of about 188 thousand. The number of civilian killed on this small island was one third of the dead in Japan proper.

The exact figures of those killed by the atomic bombs are not yet confirmed. The most recent estimates by Minoru Yuzaki and Hiroshi Okazaki are 110 thousand in Hiroshima and around 60 to 70 thousand in Nagasaki on the 1st of November, 1945, but this excluded those who died after that time. The unpublished report of the Agency for Economic Stabilization quoted the figures for Hiroshima Prefecture and Nagasaki city as 78.1 thousand dead and the total number wounded including dead and missing as 129.5 thousand in Hiroshima, and 23.7 thousand dead and the total damaged as 66.6 thousand in Nagasaki. In addition, 176.9 thousand people suffered damage in Hiroshima and 89.7 thousand in Nagasaki. Most of them had been found infected with radioactive contamination. These official figures released soon after the bombing were evaluated as under estimation.

4.5.5 Damage to Capital Assets

It is much more difficult to evaluate the damage to capital assets than the damage to human resources. This is because of inadequate data both about the cumulated capital assets due to the investment rush for producing military weapons during the later stage of the war and deduction of the assets destroyed by US bombing.

The most basic sources often quoted are the survey carried out by the Agency for Economic Stabilization quoted in the previous section 4.5.4. and the one summarized in the United States Strategic Bombing Survey. However, recent researches published after the 1970s have reassessed those figures, but entire reevaluation in the frame work of the national accounts will require a tremendous team effort. Toshiyuki Mizoguchi and Noriyuki Nojima have published revised estimates of flow accounts covering 1940–50 in the area of Japan Proper, excluding colonial areas and the Sakhalin (Mizoguchi & Nojima [1995]). This must be the starting point to estimate the national wealth; stock aspects of the national accounts. Until completion of entirely new estimates in future, we must be satisfied with the figures of the Agency for the Economic Stabilization, because they adopted the methods used for the estimates of the national wealth for 1930 and 1935 by the Bureau of Statistics of the Cabinet. Thus, we can compare them with the past figures. In addition, the Agency surveyed the figures for the production facilities in 1941, the maximum level until the end of 1944, and the level of the 15th of August, 1945, the date of the end of the war. Thus, we can trace the growth during the war.

The shortage of basic data observed is more serious in the colonial areas because the records of investment in capital assets in Japan Proper could be traced fairly accurately, but records in colonial and occupied areas were hardly traceable. For example, steel plants established in Manchukuo had been taken over by the Soviet Union during the Civil Wars in China by the Communist Party and the Nationalist Party. There remains a report submitted to the US occupation army. This was based on reports by the Japanese government and intensive inquiries of Japanese who had been in charge of compiling documents. At the defeat, the Japanese government burnt many top-secret documents. Recently new researches by both Japanese and Chinese have been tried (Matsumoto [1992]). They revealed the importance of the results of extensive investment in these areas.

The estimation of the war damage required an intensive research of the total national wealth. The estimates which we quoted in Table II.34 as those of the Agency of Economic Stabilization had been compiled in order to deal with the reparations problem they were faced with. The method of estimation was to evaluate the bookkeeping value of the assets left after deducting depreciation and then subtract the damaged value. The war damage was estimated in two categories. One was the direct damage by bombing and naval bombardment and the other was indirect damage such that due to insufficient maintenance and updating, dispersal of building and machinery, junking by reformation of enterprises, removal outside Japan Proper, and so on. The first damage category was obtained through the accounting documents for insurance kept by the enterprises. During the estimation procedures, the highest capacity of production in manufacturing was also estimated industry-wise. Thus, the highest production level in 1944 was recorded industry-wise.

The increase of wealth from 1935 to 1945 was all included in the total estimated value of wealth, if it had not been damaged by the war, as 253,130 million yen for non-military wealth excluding woods and forests, roads, fine arts and memorial building such as temples, shrines and castles, and then deducting the total value remaining at the end of the war, as 188,852 million yen for non-military wealth and 6,526 for the military wealth such as airplanes and warships, thus showing the damage due to enemy attack. The value of the total damage, 64,278 for non-military wealth and 40,382 for military wealth, was also estimated. The total value of the damage and the remainder of the military wealth at the end of the war was 40,382 million yen, and the cumulative amount for major military weapons such as air planes and warships in the total military expenditure from 1936 to the 1945 fiscal year was 22,740 million yen. Thus, roughly 10,908 million yen, about half of the expenditure used for the major war weapons, was realized as military assets.

The total value of wealth in 1935 converted to the current price at the end of the war was 186,751 for non-military wealth excluding the value of military wealth. The estimated increase of wealth during the war period was about 66,379 for non-military wealth and about 10,908 for military wealth without being converted to 1945 prices. The total damage to the non-military wealth was about 64,278 and the military wealth was entirely wasted after the war because of the prohibition of possession by the occupation army. The total increase of 77,287 was almost equivalent to the total damage of 75,186. However, the production capacity lost was not so serious, except for military

Table II.34 Damage of National Wealth

(a) Damage of national wealth including that of military use (Unit: million yen, %)

Damage of entire national wealth	Total damage		Direct damage		Indirect damage		Remainder	Grand total
	Value $A=B+C$	Damage ratio (%) A/E	Value B	Damage ratio (%) B/E	Value C	Damage ratio (%) C/E	Value D	Value $E=A+D$
Military assets	40,382	100.0	33,856	83.8	6,526	16.2	(6,526)	40,382
Warships	18,756	100.0	15,086	80.4	3,667	19.6	(3,667)	18,756
Aircraft	21,626	100.0	18,767	86.8	2,859	13.2	(2,859)	21,626
General assets	64,278	25.4	48,649	19.2	15,629	6.2	188,852	253,130
Grand total	104,660	35.6	82,505	28.1	22,155	7.5	188,852	293,512

(Note) Remainder: The national wealth remained at the end of the war (15th of August, 1945).

Table II.34 Continued

(b) Damage of National Wealth by War (composition in detail)

	Direct Damage					Indirect damage				Remainder	Total wealth	Wealth in 1935
	Total of damage (A)	Total (B)	Gov'nt	Public	Private	Total (C)	Scrap	Removal	Un -updated	(1945 Aug.) (D)	E=A+D	F (1945 prices)
Grand total	65,302	49,673	4,819	2,244	42,610	(15,629)	(4,402)	(3,636)	(7,591)	...	...	...
General assets	64,278	48,649	3,800	2,244	42,605	15,629	4,402	3,636	7,591	188,852	353,130	186,751
Construction	22,220	17,016	1,516	1,307	14,193	5,204	—	2,337	2,867	68,215	90,435	76,275
Harbour & canals	132	17	12	3	2	115	—	—	115	1,632	1,764	1,323
Bridges	101	55	55	—	—	46	—	—	46	2,773	2,874	2,288
Machinery	7,994	4,684	221	—	4,463	3,310	1,501	103	1,706	15,352	23,346	8,501
Rail roads	884	104	88	—	16	780	31	5	744	11,618	12,502	10,903
Vehicles	639	364	102	4	258	275	16	—	259	2,274	2,913	2,461
Vessels	7,359	6,564	95	19	6,450	795	—	—	795	1,766	9,125	3,111
Electricities etc.	1,618	898	53	—	845	720	62	—	658	13,313	14,931	8,987

Telecom. & broadcast.	293	243	170	63	10	50	—	—	50	1,683	1,976	1,531
Water supplies	366	271	—	119	152	95	—	—	95	1,814	2,180	1,698
Goods held	17,493	17,446	1,057	575	15,814	47	47	—	—	63,448	80,941	67,065
Furnitures	9,958	9,558	849	566	8,143	—	—	—	—	36,869	46,427	39,354
Productive goods	7,864	7,864	208	9	7,647	—	—	—	—	25,089	32,953	23,541
Coins, gold & silver	71	24	—	—	24	47	47	—	—	1,490	1,561	4,170
Miscellaneous	1,243	987	431	154	402	256	256	—	256	4,964	6,207	2,608
Not classified	3,936	—	—	—	—	3,936	2,745	1,191	—	—	3,936	—
Other wealth	1,024	1,024	1,019	—	5	⋮	⋮	⋮	⋮	⋮	⋮	⋮
Woods in the forest	6	6	1	—	5	⋮	⋮	⋮	⋮	⋮	⋮	⋮
Road	243	243	243	—	—	⋮	⋮	⋮	⋮	⋮	⋮	⋮
Fine arts & relics	775	775	775	—	—	⋮	⋮	⋮	⋮	⋮	⋮	9

(Note) Remainder in D is the current value on 15th of August in 1945 and F is the national wealth in 1935 converted in 1945 prices.

(Source) Nakamura & Miyazaki (eds.) [1995]

237

goods, especially aircraft. Based on the data gathered by the US Mission for the Strategic Bombing, 70.4% of governmental military and naval factories suffered damage, 59.9% as well as the petroleum refining factories and 59.8% of aircraft factories. The rate of damage was measured by the percentage share of the damaged roof against the total space of the factories or the share of the volume of tanks damaged. The damage ratio for the factories for civilian goods was estimated by the Agency for Economic Stabilization in terms of the production capacity of six manufacturing industries of 56 subdivisions. The most seriously damaged industries were petroleum refining and related ones, and electricity production, amounting to about 50%, except hydroelectric power stations. Next was machinery manufacturing, especially for electronic tubes (55.7%) and bicycles (50%). For other subdivisions it was about 20%. For steel production it was about 20%, according to the report of the Union of Steel Production Enterprises. Chemicals overall were damaged seriously but non-ferrous metal industries and textile industries were not so seriously damaged. The production capacity compared with that of 1941 shows a slightly different picture due to 1) decrease in the production capacity through rearrangement of enterprises from the civil area to the military area, especially in textile industries (about 20–40% of 1941 level) and 2) increase in production capacity for machine tools (almost equivalent to the 1941 level).

The total damage was concentrated in buildings, especially residences which amounted to about one third of the total damage. This was the result of the strategy of bombing aiming to destroy the small-scale enterprises concentrated in densely populated areas in towns, because the Americans knew the significance of Japanese small-scale enterprises acting as supporters to big enterprises as parts makers. This implies that war damage and reshaping the composition of manufacturing industries had given the chance to replace old-fashioned equipment without a replacement cost, as in the case of the Great Kanto Earthquake.

The composition of wealth estimated is shown in Table II.35. This wealth became a pre-condition of the revival of Japan after the end of the war, along with the labour force we have just discussed in the previous section.

Table II.35 Estimated Damage of Non-governmental Manufacturing

Estimated Damage

Industry	Buildings	Products	Machinery equipments	Direct damage (total)	Machinery equipments (scrap)
1: Total	1,818(14.5)	6,214(49.5)	4,463(35.9)	12,495(100)	1,256(100)
2: Mining	96	88	—	184(1.5)	—
3: Metal-processing	231	644	761	1,636(13.1)	36(2.9)
4: Machinery	764	3,370	1,736	5,870(47.0)	65(5.2)
5: Chemicals	194	517	617	1,328(10.6)	312(24.8)
6: Ceramics	30	35	71	136(1.1)	—
7: Textiles	159	381	356	896(7.2)	832(66.2)
8: Foods & beverages	70	179	153	402(3.2)	3(0.2)
9: Woods & timbers	28	145	108	281(2.2)	—
10: Gas & electricity	7	24	—	31(0.2)	—
11: Construction	48	49	95	192(1.5)	—
12: Printing	25	83	94	202(1.6)	
13: Others	166	699	472	1,337(10.7)	8(0.6)

Notes:

1) At that time Teizo Toda was a young associate professor of sociology at Tokyo Imperial University, now called Tokyo University, and had just returned from two years' research at Chicago University via Europe and had a chance to analyse the 1920 population census because the execution of this census was a first trial for Japan and the data processing required so many days that the Statistics Bureau used permillage extraction data for the quick summary report which was published in 1924. The copy of questionnaires which Toda used must be this permillage extraction data. Anyhow, he carried out a special tabulation from sociological aspects of the family system. His results were reported in his various articles, which first appeared in 1926. The most comprehensive one is in his monograph entitled *Treatise on the Family*, in Japanese [1926] and later expanded into *Constitution of the Family*, as his doctoral dissertation in 1937.

2) For the technical documents on naval construction, we depend entirely on Fukui's comprehensive research and we find an extensive economic analysis on this problem in Murakami [1985] pp. 199–142. This military-industrial complex had its origin in the protection of ship building in the 1890s (Murakami [1985] pp. 199–203, Hashimoto [1992] pp. 96–100).

3) Yuasa expressed some reservations in his evaluation of the degree of independence of Japanese technological attainments in the military fields in his work [1984] vol. 2, pp. 380–409, esp. p. 397. His conclusion was that the role of huge battleships like the Yamato and Musashi had ended when they were completed. But this was the result of the creation of a new strategy by Japanese navy. There are other opinions that Japan should have advertised its military superiority more strongly as a deterrent by demonstrating its power. In fact the data on the Yamato and Musashi had been kept top secret and so their existence did not act as a deterrent. Intelligence information of allied nations did not detect their real power even after the end of the war until the U. S. Navy Technical Mission to Japan (See, Fukui [1992]. vol. 2, pp. 336–39.). The real turning point of the workability of these military weapons came in the midst of the war. See also another papers by Fukui. Shizuo Fukui,1913–93, served as naval engineering officer for ship building during 1938–44, and then became an assistant to Shigeru Makino, an engineering captain, who summed up the records of the Japanese naval fleet at the Ministry of the Navy after her defeat in 1945. He gathered many documents and photographs of the entire Imperial Japanese Navy and was also a collaborator of Jentschura, Jung and Mickel [1977]. His collected works were published in ten volumes during 1992–4. However, his writings were mainly addressed to the general public and so lacked in technical detail compared with the famous work by Kitaro Matsumoto, entitled *Senkan Yamato: sono shogai no gijyutsu-hokoku* (The battleship Yamato: her entire life from technological aspects) in 1952 after the end of the censorship by the occupation army, and was later reprinted as *Senkan Yamato-Musashi setsukei to kenzo* (Design and building of the battleships, Yamato and Musashi) in 1961.

4) See Yamamoto (ed.) [1993], a comprehensive work on Manchukuo. An overall treatment of the Manchukuo problem in the context of Japanese colonial policy is also found in another Yamamoto monograph [1992]).

5) See the reports at the recent international symposium held in 1991. Hosoya etc. (ed.) [1993]). As we mentioned before, we refrain from discussing the diplomatic historical accounts.

6) It had been hidden from the Japanese why Japan's ultimatum to be delivered at 13:00 was delivered to the United States one hour and twenty minutes behind the designated time, i.e. the critical moment just before the attack on Pearl harbour. President F. D. Roosevelt took full advantage of this fact to convince the American people that the Japanese were shrewd and cowardly. Dr Ichiro Kiyose, lawyer to Hideki Tojyo, accused by the International Military Tribunal for the Far East, clearly said that the authorities of the State Department of the United States had regarded the note of the Japanese Government dated 20th of November, 1941, as the ultimatum and that every affair had been entrusted to military power. Even Roosevelt himself acknowledged the telegram as "This means war." (Etoh [1989]) However, the Ministry of Foreign Affairs did not explain anything to the public. The skeleton in the Japanese cupboard was the mere idleness of the members of Japanese embassy who were deeply absorbed in the play. This is the most scandalous factor that no one can defend. The Japanese Ministry of Foreign Affairs did not make any disclosure until 1994, after the death of Showa ten'no in 1989, who had signed the declaration of war in 1941.

7) Many critics have admitted their sense of guilt to the Asian people, but not to the allied nations' caucasians.

8) Tokyo Imperial University set up a new department for aircraft engineering at the Engineering Faculty in 1918 and its graduates were recruited in many private companies such as Mitsubishi, Aichi, Kawanishi and Nakajima, which were known as producers of various planes that became well known during World War II.

9) Hayashi [1986] briefly discussing the role of railway construction in the modernization of Japan. pp. 131–142.

10) Food stamps were operated in forty-two percent (42%) of cities,

towns and villages in November in 1940, and then a food-grain note system was adopted in six big cities in April, 1941 and so on (Yoji Shimizu [1994] in Ohishi [1994] vol. 3 pp. 338–41). A clothes stamp system started in February, 1942 (Naosuke Takamura [1994] in Ohishi [1994] vol. 3 pp. 220–24.)

11) The figures of 1944 and 1945 did not include those of the small islands near Hokkaido (Chishima), Tokyo and Okinawa, and some of the military factories were excluded due to the delay of the reports.

12) Tojyo stressed in his case study the high absentee rate. This phenomenon was already found in 1941. The sixteen factories of the steel industry showed high absentee rates in 1944 ranging 29.9% at Yodokawa Steel Factory to 10.4% at Amagasaki Steel Factory (Nishinarita [1994] pp. 293–296.)

13) The Ministry of Welfare controlled the repatriation of people from the abroad. Another official source quoted in the Strategic Bombing Research Team says 6,400 thousand for the army and 1,863 thousand for the navy (Hara [1995] p. 15).

14) He was known as Ohgai Mori, the most well-known literary figure as a poet, novelist and critic of the day, and his fame and carrier trained in Germany as a student of Robert Koch dazzled the eyes of the military medical sections.

15) All the reports and unpublished manuscripts were recently made public in one volume with annotations by Toshiyasu Ogawa, who was in charge of compiling statistics on the research and who prepared the reports. Nakamura & Miyazaki (eds.) [1995] in which Miyazaki, the editor wrote a brief introduction, and the damage to resources described below is based mainly on his data. The summary report in English was also prepared as "Overall Report on Damages Caused to Japan by the World War II, Summary," April 7, 1949 in twenty pages. The report entitled "Damage to Assets by the Atomic Bombs in Hiroshima and Nagasaki" was the result of such research, as the occupation army strictly forbade any Japanese from doing so. Saburo Ohkita, who later became Minister of Foreign Affairs and died in 1993, bravely ordered Ogawa to carry out the research and the report was secretly printed in fifty copies by mimeograph. The governors of prefec-

tures were also quite cooperative in the research. The intention of the occupation army regarding the censorship was quite clear as it was called a War Guilt Information Program. It aimed to imprint a sense of war guilt in the Japanese people. The programme was carefully designed especially to hide the massacre by the atomic bombs. See Etoh [1989].

EPILOGUE: JAPAN AS A PHOENIX

1. THE END OF THE WAR AND THE BEGINNING OF THE OCCUPATION BY THE ALLIED POWERS

The War ended on the 15th of August, 1945, when the Japanese Army surrendered to the Allied Powers. Japan lost her colonies and underwent indirect control by the General Head Quarters of the Occupation Army.[1] Occupation was supported by strict press codes suppressing opinions which might express resistance to the occupation. This censorship was quite strict, but any lines or passages suggesting the existence of censorship were entirely hidden in published papers (Etoh[1982], [1989],[1990]).[2] This restricted the framework of thinking even after the end of the occupation because of the widespread implicit belief that the war-time research was carried out in support of militarism. This belief shared a common background as GHQ's imprinting the war-guilt program which had been supported not only by Marxian social scientists but also by liberals who had suffered censorship by the Japanese military police and special police to maintain the régime of the day. In fact, a lot of important research published before and during the war had been completely neglected even by the academic world.

After the late 1980s, the Japanese academic world recovered a sense of balance in research, liberated from the preoccupation with Marxian premises. Before ending this short sketch of Japanese economic development since the Meiji Restoration in Part II, we will summarize the results of the collapse of the Japanese Empire and Japan's subsequent recovery.

Notes:
1) Supreme Commander for the Allied Powers, SCAP, was an official name. The Japanese called it simply GHQ.
2) The author's personal recollection as a pupil of an elementary school is only sealed letters addressed to his parents marked "opened by Mil. Cen. -Civil Mails." However, it was known that even a high school students' newspaper was under the military censorship.

2. ORIGINS OF ECONOMIC GROWTH AFTER THE WAR

The power to carry out a systematic operation was practically ended after the last sailing of the Yamato, the biggest battleship and a symbol of the Imperial Navy, to participate in the battle at Okinawa, escorted by the Yahagi, a light cruiser, followed by nine frigates and without air cover on 7th of April, 1945. This was the funeral march of the Japan Empire. The fuel to go to and return from Okinawa was almost the last supply for a fleet operation. After the sinking of the Yamato, the Nagato, three other battleships and six aircraft carriers remained as targets because of their inability to move due to the shortage of fuel. The number of workable aircraft left to protect against bombing was 2,859 according to the military records of the army and navy, and 15,886 according to production records of the Ministry of Industry and Trade. However, the latter number may include unusable ones rejected by the test and ones missing from the army and navy records. Anyhow, there was insufficient fuel for big operations. Young students drafted from universities and colleges had been lost in *kamikaze* attacks, later called suicide attacks for they were not expected to return. This was the situation just before atomic bomb attacks on Hiroshima and Nagasaki.

After the war, disarmed light frigates were used to withdraw Japanese from outside Japan, including armies. The army and navy was dissolved and the Nagato was used as a target ship with the Sakawa, light cruiser, the Prinz Eugen, German heavy cruiser, and the Nevada, New York and Pennsylvania,US battleships, at Bikini for the atomic bomb experiment by the US army. However, the Nagato, flag ship for Imperial navy for many years at the time of peace, remained afloat for four days and then sank in the night without being seen by anybody, as if she were ashamed to be seen. This was the end of the long story of building modern military power to survive in the days of colonialism of the nineteenth century.

The policies adopted by Japanese Government were first to restore industry and agriculture. Until the end of the war, farmers were cooperative and delivered their products to the government. However, this was changed after the war. The dual markets of the rationing system by fixed price and the black market system by free price were quite popular and hyperinflation resulted. People were afflicted by a vicious circle of price rise and wage rise. To encourage production, vital efforts were made to mine coal. In a country where there was little crude oil, coal was indispensable to maintain transportation such as by railroad and ship to move and to supply fuel to factories which were expected to operate for non-military use.

There is a legend widely circulated not only among Japanese but also in the world, that various social reforms such as land reform, dissolution of the *zaibatsu*, the plutocracy, and so on, had been introduced under the pressure of the occupation army, and that they formed preconditions of rapid economic recovery and subsequent economic growth. But a legend is a legend, not a fact. For example, 1) land reform had been prepared during the war when the labour shortage in rural area was quite apparent and the land reform was partially implemented by the bureaucrats of the Ministry of Agriculture as an Act for Creation of Independent Farmers. It was not executed by sword and gun, but by paying the price for the land purchased. In fact the hyperinflation resulted, so that the money paid to land owners was simply waste paper. The hyperinflation had various effects on the social structure. 2) The dissolution of the *zaibatsu* was strictly operated by the GHQ in order to equalize income and wealth distribution. The common understanding as a result of the US War Guilt Consciousness Program was that the *zaibatsu* was one of the motive forces which drove Japan into the war. We will not discuss the justification of this opinion further, but just point out the importance of the personal decisions of the traditional *zaibatsu* family declining and that most of their

power was entrusted to their managers. The holding companies of traditional *zaibatsu* had been operated in a much more modernized way
than the GHQ believed. Their interests were more in common with
Anglo-Saxon capitalits because their business had been heavily concentrated in commercial activities. The so-called new *zaibatsu* which
had heavily invested in colonial areas and China had different interests from the traditional *zaibatsu*. Anyway, the *zaibatsu* families could
not retain their power after the dissolution, because by the time of
the denomination of the yen currency in 1946 settled down from the
hyperinflation, the convertible maximum amount was very small. The
competition among the companies split over by the dissolution was not
so severe, so they were in most cases re-integrated after the occupation, e.g., Mitsubishi Shoji and Mitsui Bussan. A new way of combining companies formerly belonging to the same *zaibatsu* was liaison
through the lending of money by banks. Kazuyoshi Miyazaki analysed
this relation by compiling his own statistics of the concentration. 3)
Another social reform was of the educational system. Extension of the
years for compulsory education from six years of elementary school to
three years middle school after the elementary school was thought to
have been introduced by the GHQ. However, this also had its roots
in the war time schooling system. Another was the abolition of the
dual educational system, one for professional colleges and the other for
those more liberal-arts oriented, such as imperial universities through
high school. This was the one GHQ wanted to introduce to Japan.

Another legend is that the US army needed Japanese manufacturing
as a logistic support for the Korean war in 1950, and that special pro-
curement brought about the recovery of the manufacturing industry.
This was partially true in so far as it stopped the removal of production facilities as reparation and gave impetus to produce non-consumer
goods such as automobiles produced by Toyota, whose foundation was
laid at this time.

From the stand point of long range observation, the period after
the war as a whole, we find three causes of economic growth.

1) The inheritance of the technology accumulated during the war
was much more important than is usually allowed. For example, both automobile manufacturing and the super express technologies inherited the technology of the aircraft industry (Ikari

[1993], Maema [1994]). The transportation infrastructure had experienced drastic changes caused by motorization and mass transportation by rapid railway system.

2) Learning through the war experience also had a big impact on the management of enterprises. The importance of information and electronic technology related to it was well known after the disclosure of the war time software technology, such as operational research applied to escape from *kamikaze* attacks in the last stage of the war, and the computer technology developed for that. The fatal defeat in the logistic operation of Japanese military power had made a deep impression on those who were engaged in strategic operations and later became engineers and managers after the war. It must be noted that those educated in science and technology had been exempted from conscription and, due to the lack of personnel educated in social sciences including law education, some of them became mangers of private enterprises, bureaucrats and politicians.

3) Last but not least is the equalization of income and wealth distribution accompanied by the flat educational system and increase of those getting a higher education. This produced not only a very even society, but also high mobility between social classes. This stimulated the people's will to work because they expected to move upward between social strata. Eventually it will realize a big market for consumer durables (Matsuda & Terasaki [1980]) and then it will act as a factor in expanding manufacturing industries such as consumer durables.

These three causes have been well combined with government policies. As in the past history of Japan, she would not depend entirely on borrowed technology. On this aspect, Japanese people had been very cooperative with government policies as we had discussed with the formation of state-company nexus in this Part II. The problem lies in the future, when the younger generation acts as differently from the older people who had been educated in the Japan Empire and believed to put public interests as first from their private concerns.

Part III
DATABASE SYSTEM FOR QUANTITATIVE HISTORICAL ECONOMIC ANALYSIS

1. INTRODUCTION TO THE DATABASE SYSTEM FOR HISTORICAL ANALYSIS

The database system is becoming accepted as an analytical tool, even by economic historians who have traditionally been regarded as quite conservative in utilizing machinery as other humanists do. Quantitative economic historians, however, are rather exceptional, and bold enough to manipulate numerical data through computer systems. Recent computer system development called down-sizing from mainframe to work station or personal computer has accelerated this tendency. Next comes the textual database system favoured even by humanists of younger generations. Experience in handling a textual database suggests a new frontier of handling character strings or natural words by computer. Thus, the importance of using intelligence information composed of character strings or natural words like register records is recognized by economic historians, and especially by foreign demographers who have revived church records of births and deaths. The situation is the same in Japan. Akira Hayami has entered a new frontier of demographic analysis on the Tokugawa periods using the *Shumon-ninbetsu-cho* data of demographic analysis on the Tokugawa periods, which may correspond to the church records of demographic analysis on the Tokugawa period. His group has endeavoured to create a new database system using personal data contained in family records held at Buddhist temples.

The database system is gradually invading the library or archive sphere, which historians have depended on as their indispensable assistants. An electronic library as visualized by information specialists is now a key word in the trend toward database utilization. Some of the functions of documentation centres or data banks have been handed over to such new information centres. Before ending this book, we will summarize topics concerning the general characteristics of database construction for historical quantitative economic analysis, and then briefly introduce our database system. Then we will discuss the technical problems which we have encountered in the design of our database system.

2. WORKABILITY OF THE DATABASE

2.1 Data Sets Contained in the Database

To construct a database system, we should first establish what it is to be used for. Here we will discuss the database system for quantitative historical economic analysis, which requires a good indicator of economic development. Measuring economic development is, however, one of the most difficult economics problems to solve. Various kinds of data sets are required to analyse such problems.

We can roughly divide the statistical database system into two types. One is the in-house-use database system and the other is the common-use database. These are further classified into three subtypes according to the data sets they contain.

Firstly, data sets consisting of statistical surveys are the most essential. As to current surveys, such in-house-use databases are often built up by the statistical agency which is commanding the survey. In this case, data processing starts from the sampling frame for inputting questionnaires gathered and the sampling frame, in the case of the sample survey, for the final tabulations for the reports to be published. Thus, the micro data sets play an essential role. Linkage to the next survey must also be included in its scope. However, when surveys were carried out in the past before computerization, such a system in general could not be realized because the original questionnaires rarely existed. In some countries, original questionnaires such as population censuses have been kept up to the present day and their handling is entrusted to historians by virtue of a century clause. This means that the original questionnaires may be open for academic use after a hundred years have passed because there is no longer any need to protect of their contents in so far as identifiers are deleted as they have all passed away in the historical past (Hakim [1979] p. 141 ff).[1] We include the compiling *Shumon-ninbetsu-shirabe* database in this category. However, Japanese population census data after 1920 remain only as summary tables.

Secondly, databases consisting of compiled data are the most common. The data contained are in most cases time series data. This type of database was created for common use by commercial database vendors. They gathered statistical reports or data files released by the statistical agencies and recompiled them for public use. The most well-prepared database of this type comprises time series data sets based on the system of national accounts as a common tool to understand macroscopic economic trends. Among the compiled data set databases, in-house-use databases for agencies which are responsible to a system of national accounts have a special character because of the combination with the entire estimation procedures for a system of national accounts. This type of database appears because of the over-complexity of current national accounting compilation procedures. If a certain value is revised, it will affect various values in the system as a whole, and so even a walking dictionary type person cannot follow up every procedure at once. Application of this type of database construction technique to projects of historical national account estimation has been recently realized. The magnificent project initiated by Kazushi Ohkawa known as the LTES project, i.e. Long-term Economic Statistics (*Choki-keizai-tokei* (in Japanese with short English summary) published by Toyokeizai Shimpo Publishing Co., is also in this category. The seminal predecessor of this project may be found in Yuzo Yamada's estimation of national income known as *Nihon-kokumin-shotoku-suikei-shiryo* (A Comprehensive Survey of National Income Data in Japan) published in 1951. Immediately after its publication Ohkawa organized a research project to recompile the historical national income series (Ohkawa [1957] p. iii). It is fully described in his paper entitled *The Growth Rate of the Japanese Economy since 1878*, as a first issue of this monograph series of the Institute of Economic Research, Hitotsubashi University, in 1957. His first comprehensive report in Japanese was published much earlier, in 1955. Based on these 1955–57 estimates, subsequent revised estimates have been published in other volumes of LTES and in other articles. The first volume of the LTES was published in 1965. More than two decades passed until the publication of the last issue of LTES in 1988. This implies that the LTES was a result of long and sustained efforts. However, the project was a product of the time of artisan crafts of historical statisticians before the computer age. To keep up with the times, we have compiled a database system of LTES for the Information and Documentation Centre of Japanese Economic Statistics at the Institute of Economic Research, Hitotsubashi University. In the beginning, we designed a system for recompiling and updating whole estimation procedures as government agencies, adopting their current estimation of national accounts, but eventually abandoned the idea because there were too many independent estimation procedures in each issue of LTES. Independent revision of estimates results in a lack of consistency, as often mentioned in Part II above, so it will require an entirely new project to construct such a systematic database. What Toshiyuki Mizoguchi did in carrying out estimates for the Japanese Empire depended on his own database system, including his estimation procedures (Umemura & Mizoguchi [1988])[2] Our idea of building an estimation system of national accounts with a computerized database system was partially realized in the estimates of damage caused by the Great Kanto Earthquake, organized by Yoshimasa Kurabayashi in collaboration with Mitsutaka Togashi.

Our LTES database system employs a method of installing all series of data published in every LTES issue in so far as they were regarded as independent sources of data series for their estimation procedures even if they contradicted each other as a final source data for the estimation. Thus, our database adds some supplementary series contained in separate monographs such as *Patterns* and *Kindai-nihon-no-keizai-hatten*, which cover various estimates after the LTES project. After compiling the LTES database system, which was not intended to revise Ohkawa's estimates, we concentrated on constructing the third type of the database system referred to below. The entire recompilation of the Ohkawa project along the lines of Mizoguchi's compilation of the colonial figures should be entrusted to the next generation.

The third type of database consists of register-based statistics. This is a new wave currently pursued by statistical agencies, as discussed in Part I.[3] Our experimental results, described in Part II, should be regarded as an application to historical statistics. Before explaining our database system, we will discuss some topics deeply rooted in the historical statistics involved. When we discuss the development of statistical surveys in Part I and review the figures obtained from such a survey in Part II, we avert complexities by discussing the theoretical problems constituting the background to our discussions. We will briefly summarize such problems.

2.2 Theoretical Background of Historical Statistics Compilation

2.2.1 Methodological Digression

Kazushi Ohkawa persuasively summarized various problems encountered with his estimation procedures using Simon Kuznets's scheme (Ohkawa [1957]). His review is still worth reading, but here we will state the problems in a slightly different way, considering some results which have been clarified since his book was published. He talked about three problems: scope, netness, Ohkawa's terminology after Simon Kuznets's works, (deduction of raw materials to get added values) and valuation. These problems are closely related to the tools for measuring economic development. They have their own history.

The first stage in the history of tools for measuring economic development came with the making of indexes such as price indexes, wage indexes and production indexes. Various indexes for measuring economic changes depend on economic theories which implicitly assume that the composition of the economy is homogeneous, or in another words the agents of economic activities are the same over time, at least before changing the weights of the base year for the cases of Laspyres indexes. This problem led to the functional approach of index number problems and further to discussions on welfare economics revealing the impossibility of forming a social welfare function by aggregating individual welfare functions. Then why is it possible to integrate utility functions of the people in a different time and space as a basic assumption for constructing indexes? This problem remains the same even at the second stage of compiling more systematic and extensive indicators of national income and wealth. Developing an estimation system for national accounts as macro data sets has created a new frontier of econometric model building flowering in the 1930s.

Econometricians tried to escape the problem of assuming some value function for measuring macro indicators through implicitly assuming that economic social space is unchanged or the composition of generations of people is the same. So far as macro econometric analysis using samples of limited time interval is concerned, the problem doesn't look so serious, but in the case of long-term economic historical analysis the problems become more complex and difficult to solve (Fisher [1960]). This is one reason why quantitative economic historians instinctively avert the econometric approach.

The problem lies in the time element and the intertemporal comparison of evaluations by people who are mortal, unlike other economic agents such as firms. Thus, we should construct a social space where the components of economic agents like individuals are gradually changed by replacing old people who die with newcomers such as babies, and then compare the economic activities of these people in different social spaces occurring at different times. How are the economic activities measured and with what measuring standards?

Today even quantitative economic historians have worked within the framework of national accounting statistics (a system of national accounts called SNA) knowing that such a system presupposes various neo-classical economic theories. They always talk timidly on this aspect of the indicators they use. However, J. M. Keynes, who introduced national accounting ideas in his economic theory was clearly aware of this difficulty, and restricted his theory to short-term situations, except in a few chapters concerning long-term expectations in his *General Theory* (Keynes [1936]) and in a short paper, "Some economic consequences of a declining population," published in *Eugenic Review* (Keynes [1937]). In the former, he stressed that the length to the time horizons imagined by different people were quite different due to different aspirations at the time a decision was made. The pessimist hopes for investment returns in the long-term with moderate risk and the optimist hopes for returns in the short-term with high risk. Thus, the economy works with different combinations of expectations, and it entails the existence of the stock market. In the latter short paper, he noted the importance of the population growth rate and how it influences the later discussions on economic growth. We will not discuss such a theoretical problem in detail here, but just point out the importance of the problem to be tackled with long-term compiled economic statistics like macro indicators.

The framework of national accounts does not depend on the constitution of the entire population of the society concerned. It is currently left for another system such as one for socio-demographic statistics, abbreviated as SSDS.

Many database builders tend to construct databases based on a certain system of national accounts or socio-demographic statistics. However, for long-term economic comparison a single system of data sets is not enough for discussion. Another way of constructing databases for historical economic analysis is to use micro data, i.e., individual information of each economic agent in a society. However, this seems like using intelligence information, not statistical information. (On this point, Dunn's analysis for the current information system is quite informative, see Dunn [1974]). However, there is a pitfall for economic historians in neglecting the degree of representativeness of a particular observation or record. It is like a sampling survey without knowing either the sampling procedures or the entire universe or population from which samples were selected.

Our database construction is aimed in a similar direction as we stick to micro data sets. To avoid the trap mentioned above, we have tried to review micro data sets in a framework reflecting the entire structure of the population. Consequently, we are compelled to rely heavily on directory type data sets as a starting point. We reconstruct a statistical survey using these records in the directories (Matsuda [1988]). This is the way recent statistical agencies around the world want to avert non-response or respondents' refusal to be surveyed. This has been deeply rooted in modern society as discussed in the Introduction. Statisticians call statistics obtained this way register record based statistics, to contrast them with traditional survey statistics.

We call our method a survey to reconstruct a past survey, like a reconstruction of an archeological relic, because we use such past survey results as directories compiled after the survey and copies of questionnaires stored in the archives. By virtue of the recent development of computer memories and the workability of processing various types of characters including ideograms like Chinese characters that we Japanese use, we can easily develop a database system such as we have never imagined in the past. The problem is the scarcity of such intelligence information left through the years, and so we need to gather even fragmented data obtained through newspaper clippings as Imuda once tried (Imuda [1976]). He gathered company advertisements that announced balance sheet and income statements for disclosure to the general public concerned with the stock market in around the 1890s.

Based on these data, he tried to summarize company statistics of the day. Furthermore, the results of past surveys will provide us with much more information. If we know something about the survey procedures, the statistical reports will supply us more abundant information than users can normally expect from a statistical report of the day. The topics treated in Part I comprise this kind of information.

2.2.2 The Most Basic Coverage Problem: Nation, population and its society

Without explaining what Japan is and was it is difficult even for Japanese to recognize the coverage of Japan in the database for historical analysis. The concepts of 'domestic' and 'national' used in a system of national accounts seems quite clear for current data, but in the historical perspective these concepts are not so obvious, as we have discussed when discussing colonies and concessions in Part I. The inflow and outflow of people and goods are difficult to survey due to institutional inadequacy, especially in the case of the concession. The Manchurian Railway Company had borrowed an area called a concession annexed to the railroad, but the de facto area treated as concession often expanded and shrank according to the will of Japanese governments. Administrative boundaries even in Japan were sometimes not well-defined, even for the broadest area of prefecture and city, not only at the formation stage of the prefecture system but also in later periods. Before the prefectural system was established, the boundaries of *han* in the Tokugawa period were extremely difficult to define. Sometimes small areas or paddy fields were left in a neighbouring *han* like stepping stones because of the multi-ownership of land under the feudalistic legal system. The traditional coverage of a certain area called a *kuni*, a word designating a nation in today's usage, was used in the past to indicate a jointed ancient province such as Yamato, Musashi or Kahi. This was used in the regional tabulation of the prefectural products in *Bussan-hyo* for it was not affected by changes of ownership and jurisdictional changes at the time of transition. The problem of this conversion is discussed by Umemura and he published a table of the 1890 population linking current prefectural boundaries and those of ancient provinces (Umemura [1983] pp. 3–9 and Table 27). The most important point in making an intertemporal comparison after that period is the expansion of the Tokyo metropolitan area in 1932. There have been several periods of big changes of administrative boundaries. The first came in 1888 when a new town and village system was devised and introduced in 1889.[4] Such legal boundaries are different from what the urban and rural continuum theory supposes.

The economic development theory is apt to assume not only a local community or region as a fixed entity, but also a country or a nation as a clearly separable entity to be discussed, even if one treats historical aspects of a country. However, such an isolated country does not exist according to the assumption of Thünen. If we consider the problem of inhabitants, the problem will become more complex. Every advanced country is faced with inflow and outflow of people, called immigrations and migrations, in addition to changes of borders caused by wars etc.

Apart from these headaching problems, a society consists of people of various generations. In principle, population statistics are expected to be compiled by age, but this is not always obtainable as in the case of the population census. Most economic censuses adopt the number of persons in some certain age groups, sometimes without subdivision by gender. (The age counting system in Asian countries sometimes differs from that in Western countries. For example, those less than one year old are called yearlings and after a new year festival two-year-olds, and so on.)

Thus, demographers favour the graphic presentation of the population pyramids that easily show the structure of the society. In so far as the shape will not change, we can assume a fairly stable society as a whole. Two factors will change the shape: changes in the birth rate and changes in the death rate of each age group. Increase of the former widens the base of population pyramid and the decrease of the latter tends to keep the width constant in so far as no migration and immigration exist. Furthermore, decrease of the death rate of each age group will eventually change the shape of the pyramids making, the top age group wider.

Economists often roughly divide the population into three generational groups such as those from their infancy till just before starting to work, those working and producing the next generation, and lastly those who have retired from daily work. The composition of society depends on these three generational groups. However, the lines dividing them may differ even in the same society at different times due to the development of medical and production-technology. This is a topic favoured by theorists in economic development, but is one of the most headachy problems handling actual data. Kazushi Ohkawa and Mataji Umemura once started their discussion with the concept of the gainfully occupied age group, i.e. those who earned money from their work, and the availability of this kind of data (Ohkawa [1957] pp. 142–49). In some less developed countries, people often start working at a younger age and continue to work until near death. They have a lower life expectancy and no concept of a happy or leisurely retirement. Consequently, for long-term comparison, we are seriously concerned about the age compositions of society and its life expectancy.

The age composition leads to the next problem. The birth rate and the death rate of each age class determines the composition of the next generation. The birth rate closely correlates with the marital status and the breeding situation. This leads to another big topic: the family system, the oldest and most widespread system for breeding the next generation. There are various family systems around the world, such as the nuclear family, the compound family, and so on.

The dominant function of the family system in almost every society and historical phase we are concerned with is to breed children, or to create the next generation. There are a few exceptions in the history, such as the slavery system or Nazism's experiment in selective breeding of mankind, which were not efficiently operated like cattle breeding. Mating and coupling of male and female has been a serious problem in every country whether it is openly discussed or not. The operational concept of the household is far from what sociologists want to obtain, especially in the formative stages of a statistical survey. What Teizo Toda did for the first population census in 1920 was rather exceptional. He got special permission from the statistics bureau to use one permillage sample of household data chosen by systematic sampling and he tabulated them using the sociological concept of the family. Even a recent trial to use deindividualized data sets did not supply us such an informative analysis of family structure. In principle, collaboration between historical sociologists and anthropologists is needed for the historical analysis of economic development.

As we have noted, the division between the working population and the rest leads to the problem of the composition of the working population by occupation and division of labour, even in a world of self sufficient rural societies where division of labour and an exchange system existed from prehistoric times. However, we cannot start the story of economic development from "once upon a time." Among people who are in the productive age group, there were some who were in charge of various occupations related to the production of goods and services. This leads to the problem of standardization of industrial classifications and occupations.

Classifications of industry and occupation have often changed with time and society, especially with technological innovations (Mitsuma [1983]). The semantics of every industrial subdivision differs very much in context. For example, today none would classify match production in the chemical industry, but it was so classified in the formative stages of industrialization. We are accustomed to the current international classification standard of industry and occupation, but the principle which governs the classification procedures are a mixture of various principles. Economists from the time of Colin Clark favoured making a distinction between industries deriving goods from nature, such as agriculture, fishery and mining, and industries producing goods made by humans, such as manufacturing. However, from the standpoint of consumption economics, there are three classifications of goods: food and drink; clothing, housing and related items; and investment goods called associated production for future use, etc. The first is less affected by changes in the society's taste, but the other two greatly depend on the way of living of the society. A modern version for this distinction is the people who are mobilized to guarantee a certain calorie intake to sustain a society.

Thus, a very simple measure of what percentage of the working population are employed in sustaining a society is a good indicator of the level of productivity of a country and its stage of economic development. People often refer to the population engaged in farming. It is, however, very difficult to distinguish farming, forestry and fishery from other kinds of production. Farming and rural society can rarely be separated, except monoculture or plantation agriculture. Forestry work and arts-crafts using wood might be classified as an industry for roundabout production in our present context and so rural villages were sometimes mistaken as being self sufficient societies. In other words, agrarian societies and rural societies are somewhat different. Rural society does not imply the non-existence of a manufacturing industry within the regional community. Thus, the farming occupation sometimes corresponds to the case where the business of the household or family is farming. However, this does not mean that some or all of the household members do not do something besides farming. We should also note that moving from rural areas does not always imply the transition from farming to another business in the urban area, but could be a move from manufacturing in a rural area to manufacturing in an urban area. The opinion is often expressed that the stability of the number of rural households is compatible with the exodus of the rural population to an urban area as a labour force (see the controversy of Minami & Ono [1962], [1971] (Minami [1973] pp. 114–32) and Hatai [1963]). Much of the discussion stems from the confusion between rural households in rural areas and farmers' households (see the author's comment on the problem in Matsuda [1978]).

In addition, in this regard there is one reservation regarding international trade. The substitution of farming in one's native country to farming in others through international trade has often been seen in history with the development of transportation. In the primitive stages of transportation, only valuable and less voluminous foods and drinks were exported, such as pepper, wine and various liquors. Then came the stage of invasion, plunder and deprivation ending with colonization and plantation agriculture. With the end of imperialistic colonization, international trade really flourished.

Unfortunately, the percentage of the working population engaged in manufacturing including mining and construction has no real meaning. The degree of roundaboutness of production and the level of capital accumulation related to the technology of the society may affect this and thus make it difficult to take any definite measure for this purpose.

Another point at issue is the problems of the service sector, including government and military activities. Of these, we can separate those industries that have, in principle, no direct connection with production, such as governments, military forces and religious and artistic activities, which act to promote rules of a society in a broad sense.

We may also add education and research to this last category. The rest of the service sector comprises transportation and communication, which are indispensable in operating decentralized production systems. Banking and insurance may be classified into a kind of communication activity. However, the problem of the service sector will lead to the other headache of money, even if we disregard banking and insurance: determining the prices of services. In this regard, J. I. Gershuny introduced the brilliant concept of formal production and informal production (Gershuny [1983]). He defined formal production as that where the products are intended to be exchanged for money, and informal production as being not observable in the world of money exchange.

2.2.3 Evaluation Problem

Next, we will discuss the old but still important topic, evaluation in terms of money (Ohkawa [1957] pp. 11–15). As is well-known, money is a measure of a transaction and at the same time it is used as a means of hoarding. Thus, the time comparison using money burdens us with another problem. How can we measure values in money terms when estimating economic development in different time periods? Economic development was first measured by various time series statistics for various goods, and then indexes were introduced. We can find elaborate analyses in Tinbergen's pioneering econometric works in the 1930s (Tinbergen [1937], [1939], [1951]). Eventually a system of national accounts was devised, first as a concept of national income by J. M. Keynes as mentioned in earlier section, if we ignore ancient precursors like Lavoissier in eighteenth century France and so on. Systems of national accounts in most cases assume a monetary economy. However, the role of money is quite limited in everyday life where transactions of goods and services as a whole are governed by money and in where money is used has been changing through time. How to evaluate those spheres where money does not function is a big problem. As an example, we will review the role of housewives which is now a target to be included in the systems of national accounts as an imputed value. However, this is not a correct appraisal of the problem. The shift from non-monetary services to monetary services, or in Gershuny's terminology, from informal production to formal production, is the core of the problem.[5] We can divide the functions of housewives into 1) household management, 2) cooking, 3) washing and cleaning, and 4) breeding and raising heirs. Some of these functions have been transferred to servants such as 1) bailers and then lawyers or accountants, 2) cooks, 3) maids, and 4) concubines, nurses, tutors and/or governesses. With increases in wages, these functions have been replaced by machines such as 1) microcomputers and/or wordprocessors, 2) consumer durables such as electric cookers, and 3) other consumer durables such as refrigerators, sewing machines, dish washers, and washing machines. Besides the problems of concubines, raising and nursing work has been mainly transferred to kindergartens and schools. The problem of delivering babies has shifted to the medical field.

Now, let us sum up the situation. Concepts of systems of national accounts should be monetary and other things should be taken into account in so far as they can be translated into money terms. This gives rise to the difficulty of measuring quality of life and making other comparisons in real terms. The price index problems mainly concern how to convert indexes in money terms into real terms. However, as we have pointed out, even the functional approach of index making assumes the homogeneity of persons composing the society concerned. This means that, in measuring economic development, it is necessary to clarify what should be done in the world without money and what should be done in the world with money, and how things shift from the former to the latter and vise versa. The distinction between goods and labour as economic commodities may differ in this context. The next thing is what should be taken into account in comparing living standards, etc., because living standards closely relate to goods consumed without considering whether it is in money terms or not.

What makes the problem more serious is the existence of informal production in the sphere of formal production. Like the work of housewives, formal production includes various types of informal production that sustains the work of production, for example, bookkeeping and distribution of goods. Thus, transportation services or commercial services occupy a big proportion of goods production. If workers engaged in these services form another company or firm as an independent economic agent, whole situations may change. Their work should then be regarded as an independent formal production of services in an economic world. Then comes the labour productivity problem. Informal production and production of services hastens the replacement of these works into the works of machinery, in which it is more easily produced, resulting in an overall cost saving. The case of transportation services is as follows: replacing the manual carrying of commodities by animals such as horses, then by wheeled vehicles, then trains, then automobiles, planes, etc., is all realized by the production of goods. How can we evaluate such an increase in labour productivity by investing in fixed assets and machinery reflecting technological improvements? How to measure such technological progress in monetary terms in different time periods is a central problem of growth accounting and there are still many points unsolved.

2.3 Usage of Cross Sectional Data

2.3.1 Usage of Cross Sectional Data

We have discussed why macro indicators in time series have various limitations for use in discussions on long-term analysis over generations. One way to overcome this difficulty is to review estimation procedures and assess the comparability over a time span of these macro indicators. The history of estimation procedures of macro indicators is a series of revisions, as discussed in Part II. Revision of the starting points often induces new estimates higher than the earlier ones, because of the new findings of past statistical data or the results of new statistical surveys.

Some historians in principle favour cross sectional data instead of macro indicators in time series, confirming the inapplicability of macro econometric models to the historical context (Fisher [1962]). It is true that there have been many followers of Solowian growth model builders in Japan since the publication of the Klein-Osaka model in 1963 (Klein [1961]). However, none can escape the criticism that Griliches made of growth accounting in 1963 (Griliches [1988]). The inference based on the cross sectional data may be excused such criticism. (A more optimistic opinion was once expressed by Kazuhiko Tokoyama in his review of historical macro econometric models on the Japanese economy (Tokoyama [1975]). Because of his sudden death, we cannot receive his appraisal of our speculation. We simply quote his paper while regretting his untimely passing.)

Those who favoured the cross-sectional approach should rely on verbal explanations of the change in the economic structures of more than two periods without having any causal relational models to link them in return. The most serious defects of this approach are the lack of suitable data because of the scarcity of available cross sectional data due to the limitation of publication forms in the past. Thus, the historians' efforts have been directed toward gathering individual data from various scattered documents hidden in the dossiers of private families, etc. Thus, the problems remained the same before the trials of estimating macro indicators, because we cannot say anything about the whole or national situations using these fragmentary data. There remains no guarantee for inferring something based on ad hoc individual data.

Our approach to using a database system to reconstruct a survey will emancipate us from this restriction of using fragmented individual data. If we recompile several list-type data into one integrated database, then we can reconstruct a more powerful body of data that will allow more useful tabulations than we imagined in the past. As an illustration with actual data in Part II, we will not claim the position of the pioneer of such analysis, because we found similar trials early in the 1950s, such as by manual matching and calculation in the papers of Kazuo Yamaguchi (Yamaguchi & Terashima [1956]) and Toshio Furushima (Furushima [1963], [1976]), but they did not have good followers in the next generations because of the tedious and time-consuming nature of the research required by the large amount of manual work. At the second generation of mainframe computers, we proposed such an analysis based on the database architecture of computer science as a new project in the 1970s, with some tentative results (Matsuda [1978], later revised in Matsuda (ed.) [1981], Matsuda, Arita & Oh'i [1980]). After that, many researchers followed a similar line of analysis, such as Kenji Kimura (Kimura [1994] in Kobayashi (ed.) [1994]). In Parts II and III, we try to show our results, although still tentative in nature, of such reconstruction survey projects and what is indicated by these new data.[6]

2.3.2 Database based on the Reconstruction Survey

A reconstruction survey can tell us what was not known at the time the original survey was carried out. However, the directory information that comprises the main source of the reconstruction survey cannot exceed the information of the items filled in on the original questionnaire. One advantage of researchers in post periods is the knowledge of what changed into another category after the time of the original survey. Thus, the classification of industrial codes may be reconstructed according to the schemes of the posterior period.

Another advantage is that longitudinal data of data sets of more than two periods can be compiled. In principle, this was also possible for researchers in the past, but it was practically impossible to match the names of more than ten thousand establishments. Thus, we can pursue the rise and fall of establishments over the generations through the transition matrix of establishments or enterprises.

Notes:

1) After a hundred years, most related persons are in the fourth or fifth generation and have no vested interest in persons in the past. Thus it may be permissible to use the information of the original questionnaires for academic use. However, Japan had no such preservation policy of original questionnaires from the beginning of the population census in 1920. All the questionnaires were burnt after tabulation processing. Recent development of computational technology has made it possible to preserve microdata sets after erasing the indents of the original questionnaires and further trying to preserve image data of all the character strings written by respondents since the 1985 census.

2) Mizoguchi's database system in collaboration with Noriyuki Nojima was described in his discussion papers, but only a rough sketch of the estimation procedure was available in his final monograph.

3) A comprehensive survey is found in Dunn [1974]. For developments after the 1980s, see Kudo [1995], which reviews the system of the Nordic countries. Other documents concerning the US situation after the 1970s are summarized in reports on the Inter Agency Record Linkage Projects.

4) The *fu* and *ken* system introduced in 1871 became stable after 1868. Then a *ku* and *gun* subsystem within *ken* regions was established in 1878.

5) We should restrict our linkage of SNA to the field of money concerns. There are many discussions concerning imputation problems where fictional evaluation in money terms is needed.

6) This must be a good place to mention our collaborators in compiling our register based database. Data file compilation is a very time consuming task requiring minute attention. For the 1908/1909 year data, Ms Hiromi Oh'i was in charge of the team for data selection, input and proofreading, and later Messrs. Masahiro Sato and Kenji Kimura, at the time of their graduate work, were members of the project team. For the 1902 and 1920 year data, Mr. Tsuneharu Ohkubo joined the project team along with Mr. K. Kimura. Later Ms Miyuki Shimizu reviewed the entire data linkage project between 1902, 1908/9 and 1920 by manual checking and completed the factory and enterprise integrated file. Many assistants for the data preparation participated in the project, including Ms Tomoko Yamagishi, Fumiko Konagaya, Fusako Hori, Sanae Hosoi, Terumi Taguchi, Tazuko Asami, Makiko Mori and Etsuko Wakui. Most of the computational work was done by Mr. T. Ohkubo and Ms Teruko Yoshizawa in collaboration with Associate Professor Satoshi Yasuda. Last but not least, we will mention Ms Naoko Tomioka's contribution in up-dating the 1896 company data which was once entrusted to Assistant Professor Masahiro Sato after his graduation from the graduate school. However, his interests shifted to another fields soon after his stay in Oxford in 1991, and this work was entrusted to her in 1994. She worked as an assistant to Assistant Professor Sato for this work in 1986 and completed the painstaking work of compiling the file under Matsuda's direction in a short time.

3. CONSTRUCTING LONGITUDINAL DATABASE BASED ON REGISTER DATA

3.1 Scope of the Database

The ultimate purpose of constructing a register data database is to construct a longitudinal database for quantitative economic historians. The register data database supplies various kinds of tables in quite a plastic way, as a researcher wants to reclassify the original data for his analytical framework. At the same time, he can adjust the classification scheme to another scheme used in different surveys, and so we can make a linkage between various survey results. However, the longitudinal data database will supply us with much more useful information than is available from the independent register data database. The rise and fall of enterprises at one time will affect the composition of the next time period. The causality of such a change will be clarified by juxtaposing one enterprise at a time to the next time period.

For this purpose, we have selected two types of data sources: list type data of an economic entity and aggregate type data contained in a statistical report. The former covers firstly establishments such as factories and shops, and secondly the owners of establishments such as enterprises and firms, both corporate, legal entity and individual. The latter type of data source does not contain information for identifying individual records such as names or other unique identification tags. Databases using various list type data in one integrated database may be called a variant of the micro-data-matching problems which attract statisticians' and computer specialists' attention. Due to the enlargement of the core size of computers and the decrease in their operation time to process mass storage data, this kind of database compilation has now become attainable.

List type databases make it possible to tabulate multi-dimensional tables. Earlier statistical reports lacked minute tables due to lack of computational power. Recent computer development eliminates this restriction.

3.2 Elements of the Database

The database consists of four major types of data files: i) raw data files; ii) dictionary files for linking the codes used in the raw data file with natural words or controlled vocabulary; iii) conversion matrices between different classification schemes; and iv) extrapolation or filling in the missing data processing functions using regression equations, etc. The first type consists of character strings and numbers. The second type, such as (ii) and (iii), is a variant of the information retrieval system specially designed for this database. The third type is regarded as a kind of packaged program software and we have prepared only very limited versions.

Our database has three different sub-files: a) a firm or enterprise list data base containing various attributes of each enterprise; b) an establishment list database, in principle, although our database is limited to factory list data but still contains various attributes of each factory; and c) balance sheets and income statements of firms. For (a) and (b), we have tried to construct a complete enumeration type database, or a census type database. However, for the last file (c), since it is based on business reports distributed to stockholders, it is difficult to construct census type data. Thus, our data file of type (c) comprises a kind of sample survey data. It must be stressed that the sample selection is not random in the sense of statistical theory, but only by chance when the records of a certain company still exist.

Table III.1 shows the coverage of industries selected and the bench mark years chosen. An asterisk indicates cases still under processing. Needless to say, the selection of the dates takes into account the availability of data to construct the database, but more important factors are firstly their ability to show turning points of the economy such as before and after the Sino-Japanese War, the Russo-Japanese War and World War I, and secondly their usefulness in compensating for the lack of official statistical information, such as insufficient cross tabulations and so on.

Table III.1 Coverage of the Database

i) List type data file and micro data sets based on the questionnaires

Date	Firm other than banking firms under Bank Act	Firm/banks under Bank Act	Factory
1882 (M15)	*	*	*
1884 (M17)	*	*	*
1889 (M22)	**	*	*
1895 (M28)	*	*	*
1896 (M29)	**	(*)	(*)
1897 (M30)	*	*	*
1902 (M35)	**	**	**
1909 (M42)	**	**	**
1920 (T09)	**	**	**

* :   Compiled by other authors before computerization
(*): Planned or under examination processing.
** : Completed and reported here.

Table III.1 Continued

ii) Sample data file
Balance sheets and income statements database.

Time span: 1896(M29)–1943(S18)
Coverage: Manufacturing companies totalling 125 in time series and frag-
mented 339 companies in 1896.
(Note)
M=Meiji, T=Taisho and S=Showa

3.3   File Structure of Raw Data File

Raw data files consist of an establishment file (E) and a firm file
(F), and they are integrated into one master file (M).

The elements of the E file are integrated with their owner's name,

Table III.1 Continued

| iii) Summary data file based on the statistical reports | | |
Population census	Manufacturing census	Commercial census
1896	*	
1908	*	
1920 *	*	
1930 *	*	
1939	*	*
1940 *	*	

individual person or corporate body such as a firm. In other words, each firm or individual owner includes all its factories, shops and offices. If there is no such list of member establishments of each firm, then we search for the establishments file by natural word matching (exact matching technique, letter by letter matching of character strings). The integrated M file has a tree structure and the linkage is an identifier code number of establishment. We match the M file with the F file and absorb the necessary elements into the M file. Then the M file can be indexed by the identifier of the F file. M and F are also exactly matched by using character strings.

The data elements of the E file are coded or numerical data such as i) date of establishment; ii) location; iii) industrial classification and products; iv) (employed) workers (men and women, if possible divided by age); v) power (type and amount of horsepower) and other capital assets; and, if possible, vi) volumes or sales of products, wage rates, operational days and hours, etc., and character string data such as i) owner's name and ii) manager's name, and iii) factory's name.

The data elements of the F file comprise coded or numerical data such as i) date of establishment; ii) type of establishment (corporate or individual); iii) location; iv) industrial classification; v) balance sheet and income statement data, or at least capital (paid-in and nominal); and vi) number of stock holders or investors and number of shares, if applicable, and character string data such as i) firm's name. Thus, the resulting M file has the following structure, as shown in Fig. III.1.

Figure III.1 File Structure of Integrated File M

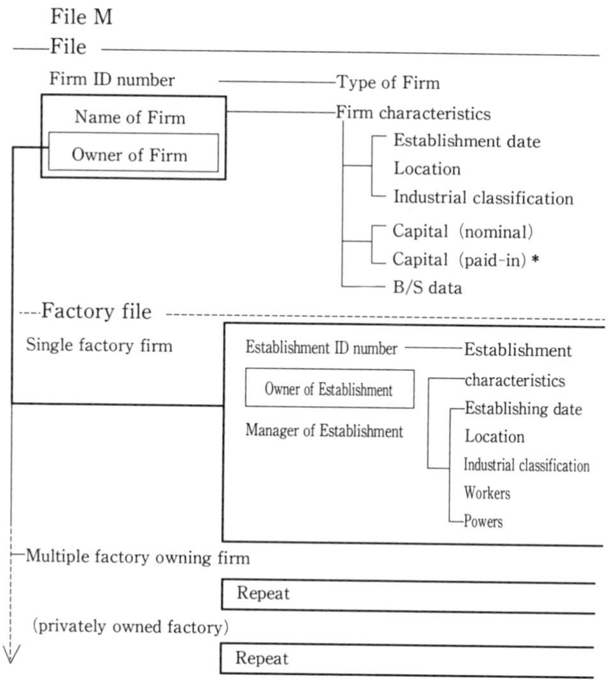

File M

Firm ID number ——————— Type of Firm
Name of Firm ——— Firm characteristics
Owner of Firm
  ⌈ Establishment date
  ⊢ Location
  ⌊ Industrial classification
  ⌈ Capital (nominal)
  ⌊ Capital (paid-in) *
  ⌊ B/S data

Factory file

Single factory firm

Establishment ID number ——— Establishment
Owner of Establishment ——— characteristics
  ⌈ Establishing date
Manager of Establishment ⊢ Location
  ⊢ Industrial classification
  ⊢ Workers
  ⌊ Powers

Multiple factory owning firm

Repeat

(privately owned factory)

Repeat

Unfortunately we have no adequate information about other establishments such as shops and offices.

Firms are now subclassified into i) those without a factory, ii) those with a single factory, and iii) those with multiple factories. Factories are subclassified into i) those that belong to a firm, and ii) those which are privately owned by individuals.

The problem of compiling a consolidated M file is the difficulty of exact matching. The most serious problem is mismatching due to different firms having the same name. The prohibition or registration of a certain name to a specified firm is only applicable within a certain area of the market place. It could be that a firm in one region has the same name as a firm in a different region. The second problem is such technical difficulties as processing Chinese characters having two calligraphies: traditional and the recent abbreviated version. Each calligraphy has its own internal machine code within the system of Chinese letters and the puncher sometimes treats them differently. Another problem occurs when the name of the company is inverted, for example, Standard Oil Company and Oil Company Standard.

Matching experiments of exact match have shown that even if we use a unique identifier such as one used in the SSEL Program, Standard Statistical Establishment List Program, in the United States, we may face a mismatch if we make a mistake in assigning a SSEL number in compiling files. To avoid such mismatch we combine various attributes such as location, date of establishment, etc.[1]

Note:

1) When matching experiments of individual records, various attribute are used, for example, gender, age and place of birth, in addition to the unique identifier like social security number. See, in Bisco [1970].

4. MICRO DATA MATCHING TECHNIQUES

4.1 Linkage between Different Dates

As we stated in Section 3.2 (see Table III.1), the raw data file can be linked between different dates such as 1889–1920. Linked files have a noded graph structure, as illustrated in Fig. III.2.

This graph structure having nodes is the result of vanishing, absorbing or merging, making independent and new entries. This is a kind of transition matrix.

It is sometimes clear that we cannot find a corresponding firm's name in the previous data, although the date of establishment can be traced back. There are two possible explanations for this: leakage of the previous date or a change of the firm's name as a result of a merger.

Figure III.2 Transition Matrix of Different Dates

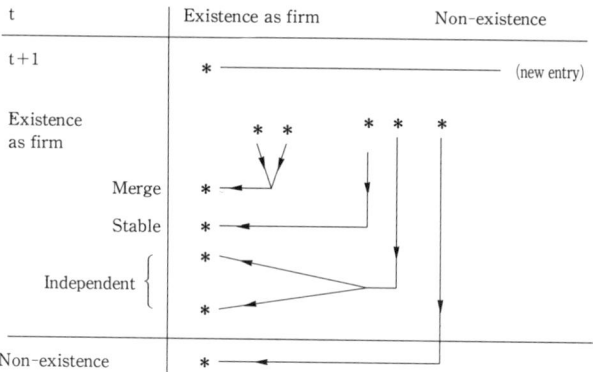

4.2 Data Sources of the Database

It is impossible to rely on a single data source in compiling such a database. Broadly speaking, we have gathered four types of data sources: 1) list data published by governmental agencies, 2) list data published by private institutions such as a commercial inquiry bureaus, 3) statistical reports which contain list data, and 4) statistical reports without list data. The first category of data sources is subdivided into those published by the central government and those published by prefectural governments. The prefectural government publications required very intensive searching in both libraries and archives.

In the Meiji period, even a list data source which was classified as nationwide coverage had to checked against prefectural reports. In addition, sometimes the principles of compilation were not explicitly mentioned. For example, the most well-tabulated joint-stock company statistics, called *Kabushiki-kaisha-tokei*, were published only for the years 1895–97, and comprise a list of joint-stock company names, locations and nominal capital amounts, but contain no explicit statements on coverage. The matching of the list with a Who's Who published by a private commercial inquiry bureau revealed that the *Kabushiki-kaisha-*

tokei was not based on the statistical survey but on a special survey to gather information within the jurisdictional industry of the Ministry of Agriculture and Commerce by a special decree. This means that railway companies other than horse tramway companies are excluded.

Aggregate statistics are used to estimate an individual firm's figures as follows. In the periods under discussion, no serious attention was paid to concealing a single entry figure in cross-tabulated tables. Thus, we can extrapolate the exact amount when the entry is single in multi-tabulated cross-tables and also when we know one or two firms' figures and the total deducted from these figures will show the rest of one firm's figures. Many of the paid-in capital figures of the 1895–97 files are extrapolated in this way.

Following is a list of the major sources we used in compiling our data base.

1) Government Agencies' Publications in List Form

1-1) Data of national coverage.

  1. Bureau of Statistics. *Tokei-nenkan.* (Annual publication but does not contain the necessary information in every year's report.)

  2. Ministry of Agriculture and Commerce. *Noshomu-tokei-hyo.* (Annual publication but the national total figures lack some prefectures' reports at an earlier period of publication. List type data ceased publication after 1891.)

  3. Ministry of Agriculture and Commerce. *Kojyo-tsuran.* (Directory of factories.)

  4. Ministry of Agriculture and Commerce. *Kaisha-tsuran.* (Directory of companies. This was a first and last list of companies compiled by the government. The data contained seems to have been based on questionnaires to companies for 1919 on the first of January, 1920. The figures correspond to the 36th issue of the *Noshomu-tokei-hyo* for the 1919/20 data published in 1921. This *Kaisha-tsuran* listed 26,261 companies, but the 36th issue of the *Noshomu-tokei-hyo* listed 26,280 companies as the first *Kaisha-tokei-hyo*, Company statistics for 1920, referred to the previous year's figures. However, we use this directory as a most comprehensive directory for the year 1920.)

  5. Ministry of Finance. *Ginko-kyoku-nempo.* (Contains figures for

banks under the Bank Act.)

1-2) Data of regional coverage.

1. Prefectural Government. *Fuken-kangyo-nempo*. (Not every prefecture published one each year and not all the books published still exist in libraries and archives. Our bibliographical survey started by Shigeru Yamaki and others can be traced back to the 1960s. The first catalogue contained 656 of 759 issues known to have been published and then the last catalogue which we compiled in 1982 contained 723 (92.0%) of 786 issues which contained manuscripts of issues which were not published. After the catalogue in 1982 we continued our survey and recently found three hitherto unknown unpublished manuscript issues. We roughly estimated that published issues seem to amount to only 46% of the total yearly issues which might have covered forty seven prefectures.)

2. Prefectural Government. *Fuken-tokei-hyo*. (Prefectural statistical yearbooks which had been published from the 1870s and later in a unified form by the Decree of the Ministry of Interior in 1884. This series was regarded as the only reliable prefectural statistical data until the regional tabulation of the statistical agencies of the central governments was well-prepared around the 1910s. As a consequence, Kazuo Yamaguchi and Rokuro Terashima compiled new statistical tables of factories for the 1884 and 1892 base-years (see Part II above). However, our review of the *Fuken-kangyo-nempo* proved that the rural corresponding system which had supplied regional industrial data must be regarded as first hand data and they were reported in the *Fuken-kangyo-nempo* and later abridged in the *Fuken-tokei-sho* series. Thus, we have compiled company data for 1896 based on data obtained from the *Fuken-kangyo-nempo* combined with *Fuken-tokei-sho* data in order to supply leakage in the *Kabushiki-kaisha-tokei*, directory as discussed in Part II.)

3. County (*Gun*) Government. *Gun-tokei-sho*. (Some counties published data but there was no systematic survey of publications.)

4. City (*Shi* or *Ku*) Government. *Shi-tokei-sho*. (Some major cities published one.)

2) Non-government Agencies' Publications in List Form

Commercial inquiry bureaux in the Meiji period did not establish a nationwide network survey.

Osaka was the most advanced commercial town in the Edo period and the Commercial Inquiry Bureau (*Shogyo-koshi-jo*) in Osaka had published *Nihon-zenkoku-shogaisha-yakuinroku* (a who's who of company managers) since 1893 but had listed only major companies. Tokyo Commercial Inquiry Bureau (*Tokyo-koshin-jo*) published *Kaisha-yoran* (List of Companies since 1897) with modest coverage of Tokyo and Yokohama and then with nationwide coverage after 1915. We used these two publications for our database of the base years 1896, 1902 and 1908/9.

1. Commercial Inquiry Bureau (in Osaka). *Nihon-zenkoku-shogaisha-yakuin-roku* (annual publication since 1893).

2. Tokyo Commercial Inquiry Bureau. *Keihin-ginko-kaisha-yoroku.* (Title changes: *Ginko-kaisha-yoroku, Zenkoku-ginko-kaisha-yoroku.*) The coverage of these two directories differs a little bit and there is some duplication of prefectures covered. For the year 1920 we used them to supplement colonial companies which were not covered in *Kaisha-tsuran.* In addition, we used the following:

3. Meihodo. *Shogyo-tokei-kaisha-zenshu.* (1893)

4. Imperial Inquiry Bureau (Tokyo, *Teikoku-koshin-jo*). *Teikoku-ginko-kaisha-yoroku.* (Published since 1912)

3) Statistical Reports

3-1) Statistical reports with nation-wide coverage.

The publications cited above in 1) "Government Agencies Publications in List Form" may contain some statistical tables. In addition, we should mention the following important publications.

1. Ministry of Agriculture and Commerce. *[Meiji] 29-nen, 30-nen zenkoku-kojyo-tokei.* (National factory statistics for 1896/97.)

2. Ministry of Agriculture and Commerce. *[Meiji] 31-nen Zenkoku-kojyo-tokei-hyo.* (National factory statistics for 1898.)

3. Ministry of Agriculture and Commerce. *[Meiji] 32-nen Zenkoku-kojyo-tokei-hyo.* (National factory statistics for 1899.)

4. Ministry of Agriculture and Commerce. *[Meiji] 33-nen Zenkoku-kojyo-tokei-hyo.*(National factory statistics for 1900.) As mentioned in Part II, this publication series was a result of innovation of the tabulation forms, but after publication of Meiji 33 (1900)

figures in 1903, we could not find any publication of this series until the new *Kojyo-tokei-hyo* series appeared in 1909.

5. Ministry of Agriculture and Commerce. *Kojyo-tokei-hyo* (Factory statistics. This was a result of the new statistical survey designed as a census type survey every five years from 1909 to 1919. Between survey years all prefectures were to report by the traditional Corresponding System. After 1920 the survey frequency changed to every year).

6. Ministry of Agriculture and Commerce. *Kabushiki-kaisha-tokei* (Joint-stock company statistics. Figures for 1893 June and 1894 March).

7. Ministry of Agriculture and Commerce. *Dai-2-ji Kabushiki-kaisha-tokei* (The second issue of the Joint-stock company statistics. Figures for 1894 December.)

8. Ministry of Agriculture and Commerce. *Dai-3-ji Kabushiki-kaisha-tokei* (The third issue of the Joint-stock company statistics. Figures for 1895 December).

9. Ministry of Agriculture and Commerce. *Dai-4-ji Kabushiki-kaisha-tokei* (The fourth issue of the Joint-stock company statistics. Figures for 1896 December).

Item numbers 6-9 contain a list of *Kabushiki-kaisha* (joint-stock companies). The series of *Kabushiki-kaisha-tokei* were published simultaneously with the series of *Kojyo-tokei-hyo* on the introduction of a questionnaire survey system for factories and companies, but the *Kabushiki-kaisha-tokei* were not based on this survey but on the special decree of the ministry of Agriculture and Commerce in 1893.

10. Ministry of Agriculture and Commerce. *Kaisha-tokei-hyo, Taisho 9-nen.* (Company statistics for 1920). 1922

11. Matsuda, Arita and Ohkubo . *Taisho-8-nen Kaisha-tokei-hyo* (Company statistics for 1919: Reconstruction tables based on the *Kaisha-tsuran*) in 4 volumes, Tokyo, 1992.

Item 10 covers all kinds of companies in 1920. On this point, this report was different from items 6 to 9, which covered only joint-stock companies. Based on the list data cited in 1-1) as item 4, we reconstructed a statistical report for the year 1919. The figures differ somewhat from the data contained in the 36th issue of the *Noshomu-*

tokei-hyo published in 1921, as mentioned above. It will be listed as item 11). The tables in item 10 are quite limited, but our item 11) is rich in multi-classified tables we referred to as 1920 data in the Part II. However, a more detailed annual report was published after item 10.

3-2) Regional statistical reports

1. Bureau of Statistics *Kahi-no-kuni Genzai-ninbetsu-shirabe.* (Family member survey of Kahi Region. Although they used the traditional survey name, *Ninbetsu-shirabe*, (family member survey), this was an entirely modern population and establishment survey for 1879. It was done in Yamanashi Prefecture whose old name was the Kahi Region, and this was intended as a pilot survey for a nationwide population census.)

2. Kumamoto city. *Meiji-34-nen Kumamoto-shi-seisanhin-tokei-sho* (Survey on the products of Kumamoto city for 1901, first regional census products survey).

3. Kumamoto city. *Kumamoto-shi-shokugyo-tokei* (Occupation survey of the inhabitants of Kumamoto city, figures for 1907, the second population and establishment survey following item 11.)

4.3 Supplement of Missing Data: Estimate of capital assets

After compiling various datasets of the directory data for the same year, we try to identify the same record by matching character strings of company's or owner's name within a subfile consisting of the records having the same location classified by prefectures, cities or counties and the same establishment date. However, the establishment dates were found to contain various erroneous data, partly intentional and partly unintentional, and purely erroneous description. Unintentional cases stemmed from different interpretations of the establishment date, such as the date of legal registration, the date of actual operation or not the establishment date of the company but the birth of its owner company, etc. The natural words of company or factory names included several variants between common names and legal names.

By deleting all duplicate entries we consolidated one integrated file of enterprises (E) and factories (F). Then we summed up the records to produce summary tables of this newly constructed master file (M).

We call this "reconstruction of the survey" and get a new statistical report which contains various cross-sectional tables. When there were old statistical tables or reports we could inspect the consistency of the statistics obtained, as discussed in Part II. By assembling all the establishments or factories under their owner's name we get a new integrated file (M) of owners and their factories, as mentioned above. This shows another method of checking the coverage of the directories, as discussed in detail in Part II where we referred to the leakage of the company's name in the enterprise list which should have contained the owner companies' names obtained from the factory list and vice versa. There is room for error in the latter case, where the manufacturing company's name could not be found in the factory owners' name list because the coverage of the factory was restricted to a certain level, more than ten employees in 1902 and 1920 and more than five employees in 1909.

The resulting integrated file contains various attributes of the records, but some records lack certain attributes because of differences of the source data, so they do not guarantee a uniform supply of attributes of each record. Thus, the problem of imputing a missing value of the attribute occurs.

There are two ways of imputing missing values. One is to impute an attribute in the aggregate data. For example, when lacking paid-in capital which cannot exceed nominal capital, the aggregate of paid-in capital is estimated as a weighted average of the fully-paid capital and under-paid capital. The other is to impute each individual record. Usual imputation techniques employed among various statistical agencies are cold-deck and hot-deck. Recent fashion is to statistical matching technique, a more sophisticated variant of the hot-deck method.

Before going further with the imputation problem some words should be added about compiling a longitudinal file which will show missing records between files of various dates.

Compiling longitudinal files by record linkage leads us to a new method of checking the exhaustiveness of the coverage of the files. If the record in time T is not found in time $T+1$ but is found in time $T+2$, then the record in time $T+1$ must be leakage in the file. Such cross checking requires at least three files of consecutive time periods. When imputing missing records in a longitudinal file we should make some suppositions concerning the state of activity of the enterprise or factory. If the enterprise is big enough, the sleeping of business seldom happens but sleeping of operation often occurs even among big factories in case of severe depression. Thus, imputing the existence of records of an enterprise is comparatively successful but imputing the number of employees in factories is rather difficult.

For example, the longitudinal file of companies for 1902, 1908/9 and 1920 will show the existence of companies between these three base years. It is true that the source data of these three years is different and lacks consistency of coverage. However, the exhaustiveness of the 1902 was supposed to be no better than that of 1908/9, but we found the leakage of companies in 1908/9 to be about 27%. Thus, we can impute the existence of leaked companies in 1908/9, but as to the level of capital of these leaked companies the modest way of imputation is that 1) when the capital in 1902 is equal to that of 1920, it might be assumed to be the same in 1908/9 and 2) when the capital in 1902 is more or less than that of 1920, the modest supposition is that capital should lie between these two boundaries. We should introduce some other hypothesis for imputing the general economic situations of regions and industries concerned. It is more difficult to estimate the number of employees because the number of employees in each factory were on average affected much by business conditions than the amount of capital or the power of motors.

Now we will turn to the problem of imputing the important economic attributes of enterprises: the volume of fixed assets which play a crucial role in measuring the size of an enterprise.

The database is designed to include the balance sheets and income statements as a sample file data. From this sample data file we subtract the figures of capital assets and transfer them to the census M file. However, the coverage of the sample data file is quite limited compared to that of larger and better-known companies. Capital asset data should be extrapolated based on the estimation of the rest of the firms. We used was the regression equation based on the data obtained from the sample data file.

The estimate of the capital assets excluding the unpaid capital is based on the following regression equation. The capital assets are explained by the paid-in capital. The forms of the equation are i) linear, and ii) log-linear. The coefficient of the log-linear version corresponds

Table III.2 Total Capital Assets Estimated for 1896

Industrial classification	Number of (Joint-Stock Company)	Nominal capital	Paid-in capital	Assets of the companies whose assets were known	Estimated assets (log-linear)	Estimated assets (linear)	Number of companies used for estimation
a) Joint-stock companies established:							
Total	1,201	255,463,241	164,326,533	290,153,694	326,311,150	454,404,656	317
1 Exchange market	144	24,735,544	9,848,336	36,743,548	39,746,399	40,107,152	83
2 Commerce	312	17,495,173	8,176,832	14,571,344	29,113,046	49,991,538	42
3 Transportation	126	121,381,910	88,986,282	143,528,350	129,967,234	194,348,024	45
4 Manufacturing	413	67,221,850	41,163,489	69,321,551	95,156,544	132,937,136	119
5 Mining	110	15,980,370	11,132,770	18,377,611	24,416,285	29,183,986	13
6 Agriculture & fishery	68	1,515,094	815,141	360,210	0	0	0
7 Electricity & gas production	28	7,133,300	4,203,684	7,251,080	7,911,641	7,836,820	15
b) Joint-stock companies to be established							
Total	178	27,400,100	2,217,660	7,663,039	62,214,254	65,651,736	22
1 Exchange market	9	3,325,000	0	0	0	0	0
2 Commerce	52	3,265,100	92,500	360,556	9,765,467	10,916,054	4
3 Transportation	19	2,430,500	645,000	1,542,425	0	0	0
4 Manufacturing	87	17,268,500	1,330,160	5,359,840	52,448,787	54,735,682	18
5 Mining	8	1,045,000	150,000	400,219	0	0	0
6 Agriculture & fishery	2	36,000	0	0	0	0	0
7 Electricity & gas production	1	30,000	0	0	0	0	0

(Notes)

1) Total assets include both tangible and intangible assets in the balance sheet open to the stock holders.

2) Estimation is applied only for the joint-stock companies because of the availability of the balance sheet data.

3) Estimation technique is using the regression equation based on information about the companies whose balance sheet data are available. the equation is linear and non-linear using variable of paid in capital as an explanatory variable.

to the elasticity of paid-in capital to capital assets. The estimation is ordinarily the least squares method.

There were 339 companies used, classified by industrial classification schemes. The equations are applied industrywise. The classification schemes are i) that used in the *Kabushiki-kaisha-tokei* of the Ministry of Agriculture and commerce (57 industries under the broad category of commerce, industry and agriculture), ii) that of industries in (i) after the current industrial classification scheme, as analogous as possible (21 industries under 7 broad categories).

Some industries in scheme (i) lack enough samples to make an estimate and even the aggregated scheme of (ii) has enough samples for agriculture and fishery. The seven broad classification schemes of (ii) are applicable. Some ambiguity remains as to the homogeneous character of the aggregation.

The results of the estimation of capital assets by extrapolation for firms for which there is no data are summarized in Table III.2.

4.4 Linkage of Aggregated Data and Census Database

The 1909 Manufacturing Census Survey explored the output figures of a questionnaire put to individual factories for the first time. The survey list published later is our main data source for compiling the F data file for 1909. However, this list shows that many factories which produced several items belonged to an entirely different industry. Thus, aggregated statistics classified by industry, such as wage bills, workers and power of motors cannot correspond to the output figures classified in a certain classification scheme.

To link these two different classification schemes in a tree structure, we can compile a conversion matrix between product classifications based on the individual list data of the factory. The compilation procedures are the aggregation of the smallest units of industrial classification which share common factories and leveling-up in a tree structure by amalgamating the lower-level in a tree structure of classification. This is a rough approximation between two classification schemes because some classification items may overlap each other even among higher level or broader classification categories and unique aggregation was not possible.

5. SQUEEZING OUT MICRO DATA INFORMATION FROM SUMMARY DATA

5.1 Multi-Tabulation and Disclosure Problems

To obtain summary data from the survey results, we fix the tabulation formats in n ways and aggregate each summary item from the questionnaires that has fallen into each cell of n-way classification schemes. This n-way classification is called a source table[1] from which we further subtract two n-1-way classification to make it easier to look at. The easiest classification is a two-way classification scheme and so we have at least $_nC_2$ two way classification schemes.

Today we avoid showing a unique entity in one cell in order to protect the privacy of individuals or business secrets in the case of a census type of survey. We need not be bothered with the sampling survey because of the impossibility of identifying a person or corporation with an actual entity. There are two ways to conceal the figures concerned. One is to merge at least two cells, thus gathering three entities in one cell. If there are two entities per cell, we may infer the other by subtracting the data of one from the summary figures, or vice versa. The other way is to just put an x mark for the single entry cell without showing the figures. However, in this case other cells which contain more than one observation are also concealed to avoid inference by subtracting cells other than x from the total (US, Department of Commerce, Office of Federal Statistical Policy and Standards [1980]).

Until the 1940s there were no such strict tabulation rules in Japan, although the protection of the privacy of individuals or business secrets in the questionnaires gathered by the government authorities was clearly defined in each survey act (Matsuda [1978]). Thus, we can observe a single entry in one cell in a certain summary table without further processing to conceal figures for confidentiality. Thus, by gathering single entry cells in various summary tables we can obtain individual records of the survey results in so far as we can identify each single entry cell with the respondents in order to avoid duplicate identification. This is the first procedure for squeezing out an indi-

Table III.3 Squeezing out Micro-data Sets through Combination of Cross-tables without Concealing Single Entry

i) Number of cells in the summary tables

	Prefecture × industry × employee size	Prefecture × industry ×	Industry × employee size	Prefecture × employee size
Summary table	n.a.	available	available	available
All cells	33,229	4,747	707	329
No sample cells	29,044	2,762	202	51
Cells with samples	4,185	1,985	487	278
Cell with 1 sample	1,744	553	95	34
with 2 samples	661	288	46	11
Residuals	1,780	1,150	383	256
Max samples in a cell	659	1,003	2,152	2,391
Average samples in a cell	7.8	16.2	61.6	107.3

vidual record. The second procedure is as follows: if there are some cells containing two records, one of which is identified through the first procedure, then the sum of these two records may be partitioned into two records, one of which was not known in the first procedure. Then we can proceed to the third procedure to detect another record based on the second procedure and so on until no further squeezing out is possible.

The 1909 Manufacturing Census data was the case for which we achieved success in squeezing out single entry records from the tabulated summaries. Based on our factory-list database, we reproduce the facsimile classification tables of the summary tables having 4,747 cells by prefecture and industry, 707 cells by industry and number of employees and 329 cells by prefecture and number of employees in the census reports from the source table of 33,229 cells having identification names of the factories in each cell. By comparing facsimile tables with the census report database, we constructed squeezed out records for each single entry for factories. Of 33,229 cells, only 1,744 have samples and rest of the 21,485 cells has no samples. Of 32,291 factories 1,704

Table III.3 Continued

ii) Distribution of Factories whose Micro-data Sets are Available

Capital size (Ten thousand yen)	Size of employee									Total
	1–9	10–29	30–49	50–99	100–499	500–999	1000–1999	2000–2999	3000 over	
5 less	10	15	1	3	—	1	—	—	—	30
5–10	2	4	1	—	—	—	—	—	—	7
10–50	2	9	5	3	4	2	—	—	—	25
50–100	1	2	—	2	4	—	—	—	—	9
100–500	2	3	1	5	11	6	1	—	—	29
500 over	—	—	3	2	10	8	—	1	1	25
Total	17	33	11	15	29	17	1	1	1	125

Breakdown by the type of companies and the size of capital:

a) K: Joint-stock companies

Capital size (Ten thousand yen)	Size of employee									Total
	1–9	10–29	30–49	50–99	100–499	500–999	1000–1999	2000–2999	3000 over	
5 less	6	8	—	—	—	—	—	—	—	14
5–10	2	2	1	—	—	—	—	—	—	5
10–50	2	8	4	3	2	1	—	—	—	20
50–100	1	2	—	2	4	—	—	—	—	9
100–500	2	3	1	5	11	6	1	—	—	29
500 over	—	—	3	2	10	8	—	1	1	25
Total	13	23	9	12	27	15	1	1	1	102

Table III.3 Continued

	1	2	3	4	5	6	7	8	9	Total
b) M: Unlimited partnership companies										
5 less	1	—	—	1	—	—	—	—	—	2
5–10	—	1	—	—	—	—	—	—	—	1
10–50	—	1	—	—	1	1	—	—	—	3
Total	1	2	—	1	1	1	—	—	—	6
c) S: Limited partnership companies										
5 less	3	7	—	2	—	1	—	—	—	13
5–10	—	1	—	—	—	—	—	—	—	1
10–50	—	—	1	—	1	—	—	—	—	2
Total	3	8	1	2	1	1	—	—	—	16
d) C: Quasi-companies										
5 less	—	—	1	—	—	—	—	—	—	1
Total	—	—	1	—	—	—	—	—	—	1
Breakdown by the Industry:										
Textile dying	2	6	1	3	10	10	1	1	1	35
Machinery	3	7	1	3	3	2	—	—	—	19
Chemicals	4	7	5	5	9	3	—	—	—	33
Food & beverages	4	4	1	5	1	—	—	—	—	15
Miscellaneous	—	1	2	—	1	1	—	—	—	5
Special factories	4	8	2	3	1	—	—	—	—	18

(Note) Microdata sets are derived from the cross-tabulated tables combined with factory directory. The total number of factories in ii) may be smaller than the sum of a single entry and dual entries referred in the table i) because of the difficulty of exact identification in the factory directory.

are identified by this procedure. In the census reports, only three kinds of two way classification tables are found. As shown in Table III.3, the total of single entry cells include 553 in prefecture vs industry table, 95 in industry vs number of employees table and 11 in prefecture vs number of employees table. Of these, only 603 are identified in three way classified source tables because some samples are duplicated in them. After identifying single-entry cells, we search for two entry cells where one of the entries has been identified by the first procedure. Thus, subtracting the single entry attribute from the two entry cells will reveal a residual which is the single entry. Thus, iterative subtraction will show a further single entry as a residual. After eight iterative procedures, 645 cells or samples, as a whole, are identified as a unique sample.

The problem is that such single entry cells are rather marginal in the original distribution and they may be regarded as outliers. For example, single entry cells are mostly distributed in the biggest employee number by both prefecturewise and industrywise tables. However, in Tokyo, Osaka and Kobe, where big factories are concentrated, not all biggest employee number cells doubly classified by industry and employee size revealed unique samples.

Fortunately, in addition to the census reports, we found two provincial records of the original questionnaires reserved in the archives of the prefectural governments such as Aichi and Gunma Prefectures. They were not complete sets of all the responding factories, but big enough to supply other than marginal information. The factories disclosed amount to 3,386. Using these datasets, we further tried to combine with enterprise data and we eventually derived the relation of the wage rates with numbers of employees and amounts of capital. The results are used to prove the formation of the dual structure in industrialisation process of the Japanese economy in Part II.

5.2 Further Possibilities for Squeezing out Unique Records

Even though there was no limitation on the disclosure of single entries in a summary table, such a squeezing out procedure is not always applicable. The manufacturing census report for 1896 referred to as item 1 in section 3-1) listed above did not conceal the unique entry but almost no attributes are tabulated in the same form. Only juxtaposing attributes in line without cross tabulation such as numbers of factories by kinds of motor power (water or wind wheel, steam engine and electric power) classified by the number of employees followed by wage rates classified by the number of employees without distinguishing whether they had motor power or not. The cross tabulations are quite limited in number so it is difficult to derive a unique record.

In a later stage of development of the survey, the number of classification criteria was so limited that the number of cells in the summary tables was not big enough to detect a unique record. After 1920 the year 1930 seems to be qualified enough for such process of squeezing a unique record in the summary tables from the side of the manufacturing census. However, the directory information in the factory list lacks the number of employees. Thus, we should turn over the core of our database system from the register based statistics compilation system to the traditional survey reports system.

Note:

1) The concept of source table was formed in the formative stage of compiling summary tables when data processing was carried out with a calculator and or a counting machine before the computer age.

6. COMBINATIONS OF SURVEY RESULTS OBTAINED FROM PLURAL SURVEYS

6.1 Differences in Coverage and Usages

Broadly speaking there are two kinds of surveys classified by the reporting or enumeration units: one addressed to households and the other to establishments. When the majority of enterprises was organized as a single establishment, it was unnoticed impossible to distinguish between an enterprise and an establishment. The best-known are population censuses for the former and manufacturing censuses for the latter. Both may supply us with two sets of figures for expressing the same facts. For example, the number of workers in each industry is obtained by counting the occupations of household members and the number of workers in factories. If the coverage of the manufacturing census is exhaustive, the number of workers in the manufacturing sector in the population census must be definitionally equal [in so far as the respondents to the manufacturing census, managers or owners, and the respondents of the population census shared a common notion about the definition of the industry as to the factories and workers,] except for seasonal differences for workers due to differences of survey date, i.e., the last day of the year for the manufacturing census and the first of November for the population census. In addition, there are various factors that bring out differences in the data. One is double accounting due to the existence of persons who work at more than two work places as part time workers. Another more serious factor lies in the encoding of industrial classifications by the individual respondents and the establishments where they are working.

Thus, we can infer the credibility of both sets of data by comparing those which might correspond in so far as we ignore the differences in definition and coverage. However, such an elementwise comparison of these two data sets will bring us much richer information than the single use of the two censuses. The population census provides us with the occupational and industrywise workers figures. In the occupational classification scheme there exist elements of status classification such as employers, owner-operator workers, employees and unpaid family workers. The actual classification schemes of occupations are a mixture of occupational classifications and the status classifications (see the discussion in Mitsuma [1983]). Using these figures, economic historians have been discussing the size of small enterprises run by owner-operator workers with unpaid family workers (Nakamura [1971] pp. 188–92). This is closely related to the dual structure problem of the Japanese economy. Unfortunately the actual classification scheme used defined such business owners in the same way as owners and managers of big companies, making it very difficult to exclude all such employed managers and non-owner-operator businessmen. As mentioned in the Part II, Yamanaka and Odahashi tried to overcome this difficulty by combining two kinds of survey such as the manufacturing census and the population census. Because the manufacturing census covered only factories of more than five employees, they inferred the difference in the number of owners and managers in the manufacturing industries and in the number of factories as owner-operator businessmen in the manufacturing sectors. There may be overestimates of the number of owner-operator businessmen due to the process of excluding managers in big establishments.

We have two surveys concerning the labour conditions of industries. One is the census type, such as in the manufacturing census and the commercial census, and the other is called the *Rodo-tokei-jicchi-chosa*, labour conditions survey, covering much larger establishments of more than thirty employees (coverage of the industry and the number of employees has varied according to the survey year). There is another series of managers in the summary tables. If we utilize them as matching factors, the estimates of the number of owner-operator businesses will improve, showing that past estimates exaggerated the weights of the smaller businesses.

We tried similar experiments for the 1930 censuses by using our database. The results are referred to in Part II. The number of workers covered by the manufacturing census amounts to 32.0% of those surveyed in the population census. In other words, only 3.63% of all the manufacturing workplaces were covered by the factories surveyed by the manufacturing census. The factories operated by the owner without employing any other person except their family member seems to share 60.98% of the estimated total number of factories and those with less than five workers seem to comprise 35.38%. The merit of using the database is the possibility of trial and error procedures of matching two industrial classification schemes by aggregating or disaggregating certain codes of classification schemes till the number of managers or owners of the factories with less than five employee will converge into a reasonable range of number of establishments, i.e. no negative numbers of establishments will appear at the residuals of the number of factories with less than five employee in each industrial classification code.

As for the figures of the 1940 census, the wholesale traders were surveyed by the commercial census and so we obtained smaller scale commercial establishments excluding retail traders. However, close examination of the commercial census for the wholesale traders in 1939 with the extra census for the commercial establishments in 1939 reveal only the possible upper bound of the nuder of smaller establishments for the 1940 population census figures. After the coverage of the manufacturing census was extended to all establishments in 1939, the difference between the two censuses became smaller (Matsuda [1978],[1991]).

6.2 The Situations after the New Establishment Census Survey

In 1939 the extra census surveyed commercial establishments and we can compare the workers in the fields of commerce and manufacturing with those obtained by the 1940 population census. After that, the Statistics Bureau tried to establish an overall establishment census to get adequate wage and employment statistics. However, fully realization of this kind of census should wait for the establishment census of 1947. After two surveys in subsequent years, the survey was carried out once in three years. Thus, we had a chance to cross check the working population at an establishment base with the one obtained from the population census at a household base once in fifteen years in 1960 and 1975, but after that the cycle of the establishment census was changed to once in five years and we lost this cross checking system (Matsuda [1991]).

Similar combinations or cross checking of plural surveys can be realized in a well designed database system, for example, the volumes of manufacturing goods obtained through the dynamic survey of manufacturing and the manufacturing census (Koshihara [1986]). With the development of computational technology, the summary tables which may be included in the database system look like requiring no further elaboration like the statistics of single establishment enterprises, and multi-establishment enterprises as in the tables which we have compiled for the years 1902, 1909 and 1920 are now obtainable from the official reports of the establishment census for 1948 to 1975 and 1981. However, cross combination of manufacturing census and commercial census will bring out much richer information (Matsuda [1991]).

7. FURTHER PROSPECTS OF THE DATABASE SYSTEM FOR HISTORICAL ANALYSIS

Our database system covers only a limited time span during the course of the historical development of the Japanese economy since the Meiji Restoration in the 1860s. Before closing this Part, we will review the possibility of further extension of the database system. Our database system consists of three sections such as 1) micro datasets in a longitudinal data form, 2) integrated summary tables combined with various surveys and 3) estimates using micro datasets and summary tables of statistical reports.

1) Micro datasets have been compiled for the base years and the annual and/or bi-annual data which are based on list data and other balance sheet data. The ultimate form of the micro datasets is a longitudinal file and the records are linked to each other as enterprises and their owning establishments and the ultimate owner of the enterprise by the capital investors. It requires various information about the records included to be liked to each other. Thus, the compiled dates are rather limited.

For example, the enterprise and factory linked database covered only such base years as 1902, 1908/9 and 1920. However, the company list database can be traced back to 1889 and 1896 and it is possible to extend the enterprise and factory linked database to 1884 when the Corresponding System started. Although the number of factories and companies is not as large as in later base years, it will require tremendous manual labour to edit the raw data, because the quality of raw data worsened in so far as we traced back to earlier periods of statistical survey.

On the other hand, an extension of the base years to later periods requires larger amounts of records to be processed with less information in each record. The factory lists of 1930 and 1940, which can be used for the extension of 1920, contain only the main kind of business, the name and location of each factory without having the number of employees and the power of motors etc. which are obtainable in the lists which we used for the compilation of the datasets of 1902, 1909 and 1920. Some regional directories which information like that of Tokyo, Osaka and Hyogo are available but systematic collection of such directories is quite difficult. Company list directories and source books with much more information compiled by private publishers are available, but their coverage is limited to larger companies whose stocks were traded on the stock markets. Thus, from the viewpoint of cost-benefit, compilation of the micro datasets covering these periods is not recommended. After World War II the situation has changed due to the execution of the Establishment Census Survey which covers establishments of all industries with their directories.

The necessity for extension of the micro datasets is more serious for the earlier periods where the tabulation of the survey was primitive compared with our current standard. We can produce various statistical tables which are not available from official survey reports using the micro dataset database. However, as shown in Part II, what we can substitute to basic summary tables of official survey reports are, to a large extent, limited to information printed in a data source.

The fruits of the extension to the formative stage of the statistical survey in Japan is the increase in the accuracy of the survey results for the reconstruction survey where we can supplement leaked data with a combination of other sources, which we have tried for the company list of 1896. This will lead to the next problem of checking the quality of the official statistical reports.

2) The quality of official statistical reports has increased survey after survey. In addition, the number of surveys has also increased with time, and the possibility of coupling survey results has also increased. On this point much can be done in future along with our trials discussed in the previous section. The most promising one is a combination of the list data with summary tables in order to correct errors and leakage of the survey results.

For example, leakage or aversion of the survey respondents can be implemented by compiling longitudinal datasets. Based on our experience (Arita [1989]), by combining the 1909 factory lists those of with 1902 we can detect the probable aversion of respondents of factories with less than ten employees as follows.

The extension of the coverage of factories with more than five employees in 1909 caused confusion among the respondents because the coverage had been kept to those with more than ten employees since the beginning of the survey in 1884. The first survey cycle was once in five years for the new factory survey which was required to report factories with more than five employee and the rest of the four years was to follow the traditional more than ten employee size. Thus, the growth rate of the number of factories dropped sharply off in the year 1910. The growth rate from the next survey year of 1914/1915 did not drop so sharply. This must be the result of the aversion of the managers of factories with around ten employees in the next survey year and the degree of aversion must have decreased.

This was proved by the compilation of the longitudinal data sets. Of the factories which were established before 1902 and still existed in 1909, 6,444 did not answer the survey in 1902. There are two possible reasons for this. One is a mere growth of the employee numbers that were smaller in 1902 and need not answer statistical questionnaires and the other is a change of factory managers' cooperativeness with the survey because the marginal factories whose numbers of employees was around ten wanted to avert the answer saying that their factories had less than ten employees. However, the change of the lower limit of the size of employee has been changed up to five employee and so those factories with around ten employees could not escape the survey.

The size distribution of the leaked factories was not even. In the subset of the factories established before 1902 and lasting to 1909, only 2,385 (33.3%) of 7,152 were leaked in the 1902 list file and those with more than 20 employees but 3,759 (55.2%) of 6,807 with between 10 and 19 employee were leaked. If the rate of leakage in the range between 10 and 19 employees was the same as that for more than 20 employees, the leaked factories should remain at about 1,224. This implies that more than 2,535 factories, 39.3% of the totally leaked ones in 1902, should be attributed to the intentional aversion to the increase of coverage. Needless to say, the stability of the business operation of the smaller factories must have been compared with those of larger factories and the number of factories which should have vanished before 1909 must have been larger in the range between 10 and 19 than in the range of over 20 employees. The level of willingness to cooporate with the survey must have been higher for smaller factories.

3) The last but most important work lies in the compilation of the multi purpose database system consisting of micro data sets supplemented with the leaked data by estimates and derived aggregates from the micro data sets. As we have mentioned, what can be constructed by this method such as longitudinal datasets will shed a new light what cannot be obtained by the traditional summary tables in the past survey. However, they are quite limited in their information contents. Thus, we should still stick to the summary tables in the past surveys.

For this purpose, to compile a database system which is "to record the original data as accurately as possible" (Morita's Preface to Japan Statistical Association [1987]) must be a cornerstone of the further development, because without such a database system the sophisticated system for the system of national accounts and its satellite accounts is unrealizable as we have discussed in Part II.

Our past trials shown in this Part III are restricted mainly to the first and second categories and partly to the third category. In principle, we refrain from constructing an entire estimation system of national accounts or satellite accounts because of the limitation of our resources for such a big project as we referred to in Part II. However, we are convinced that we have laid the foundation for future trials by adventurers in coming generations.

Our message in this tentative conclusion is that the experience of compiling a database system for historical analysis will shed light on those who are struggling to find a way in the formative stage of statistical systems for their societies in this computerized world. The topics we have discussed have similar features to those in developing countries, and survey execution and these data processing methods can be applied to them with improving degrees of reliability. For this purpose we are trying to open our system on an on-line network system in the near future in the coming twenty-first century, if circumstances will allow.

REFERENCES

Aihara, Shigeru and Samejima, Tatsuyuki (eds.) [1971], *Tokei Nihon Keizai* (Japanese Economy in Statistics: History of Japanese statistics and the development of Japanese economy) (in Japanese), (Keizaigaku Zenshu 28).

Akasaka, Keiko [1988], "Sangyo-betsu koyo no suikei, iv. Seizou-gyo (2): Taisho 8–Showa 17, 2. Suikei (Estimates of employment of each industry. iv. Manufacturing (2): 1918-42), 2. Estimates)" in Umemura etc. [1988]

Ando, Yoshio [1987], *Taiheiyo-senso no keizai-shi-teki-kenkyu: Nihon-shihon-shugi no tenkai-katei* (Economic historical analysis of the Pacific War: development of Japanese capitalism). Tokyo, Tokyo-daigaku-shuppankai.

Aonuma, Yoshimatsu [1965], *Nihon no keiei-sou* (Managers' social class in Japan). Tokyo, Nihon keizai-shinbun-sha. (Nikkei shinsho, 12)

Arai, Hirotaka [1986], "Taihei-yo-sensou-ki ni okeru sangyo-betsu-yugyo-jinkou no suii (Changes of working population of each industry during the Pacific War)," in Nakamura & Hayashi [1986].

— [1988], "Taihei-yo-sensou yugyo-jinkou no suikei (Estimates of working population of each industry during the Pacific War)," in Umemura etc. [1988]

Arita, Fumiko [1989], "Ijiten-kan no kojyo-meibo o riyo-shite longitudinal-data-file o hensei-suru giho-nitsuite (A technique for compiling longitudinal data files using data from different time periods: analysis based on Chinese character string data file of factory listings from the Meiji Period)," [*Toyo-eiwa Jyogakuin-Daigaku*] *Jinbun-shakaikagaku-ronshu*. no. 1.

Asai, Akira [1987], "Problems of Survey Techniques in Japanese Official Statistics," *Bulletin of the International Statistical Institute, Proceedings of the 46th Session in Tokyo.* 52-(4).

REFERENCES

Association for Documentation in Economics [1979-1980], *Nihon-keizai-tokei-shiryo sougou-mokuroku* (Union catalogue of economic statistics of Japan). 3 vols. in 6 issues. Tokyo, Douhou-sha.

Azia keizai kenkyujyo, see Institute of Developing Economies.

Bisco, Ralph L. (ed.) [1970], *Data Base, Computers, and the Social Sciences*. New York, John Wiley.

Bulmer, Martin (ed.) [1979], *Censuses, Surveys and Privacy*. London, Macmillan.

Bureau of Statistics, Japan, see Statistics Bureau, Japan.

Curry, Jane Leftwich and Dassin, Joan [1982], *Press Control around the World*. New York, Praeger Publishing Co.

Dunn, E. S. [1974], *Social Information Processing and Statistical System—Change and Reform*. New York, Wiley-Interscience Publication

Emi, Koichi [1963], *Government Fiscal Activity and Economic Growth in Japan 1868-1960*. Tokyo, Kinokuniya. (*Economic Research Series* No. 6)

— [1971], *Shihon-keisei* (Capital formation) (in collaboration with Hiromitsu Ishi) Tokyo, Toyo Keizai shimposha. (LTES vol. 4.)

Etoh, Jun [1982], "The Censorship Operation in Occupied Japan," in Curry & Dassin [1982] (More expanded monograph was published by the same author as Etoh [1990].)

— [1989], *1946nen-kempou; sono kousoku sonota* (The constitution in 1946; its constrains and other essays). Tokyo, Bungei-shunjyu-sha. (Recompiled volume of two collected essays published in 1980 and 1981.)

— [1990], *Tozasareta-gengo-kukan; senryo-gun no ken'etsu to sengo-nippon* (Closed world of speaking; Censorship operations by the Occupation Army and the post-War Japan). Tokyo, Bungeishunjyu-sha.

Fisher, Franklin M. [1960], "On the analysis of history and the interdependence of the social sciences," *Philosophy of Science*, vol. 27.

— [1962], *A Priori Information and Time Series Analysis*. Amsterdam, North Holland.

Fukui, Shizuo [1992–4], *Fukui shizuo chosaku-shu* (Collected works of Shizuo Fukui). 6 vols have been published in 10 vols. Tokyo, Kojinsha. vol. 1. *Japanese battleships.* I. vol. 2. *ditto.* II. vol. 3. *World aircraft carriers.* vol. 4. *Japanese cruisers.* vol. 5. *Japanese light cruisers.* vol. 6. *World battleships.* vol. 7. *Japanese aircraft carriers.* vol. 8. *World cruisers.* vol. 9. *World submarines.* vol. 10. *Japanese auxiliary vessels.*

Fukushima, Masao [1967], *Nihon shihonshugi to "ie" seido* (Capitalistic development and the family system in Japan). Tokyo, Tokyo-daigaku-shuppankai.

Furushima, Toshio [1963], *Shihonsei-seisan no hatten to jinushi-sei.* (Development of capitalistic production and the land owners). Tokyo, Ochanomizu-shobo.

— [1976], *Sangyo-shi* (History of manufacturing industries). Vol. III. Tokyo, Yamakawa-shuppansha. (Taikei-nihonshi-sosho (Systematic exposition of Japanese history)).

— and Ando, Yoshio [1975], *Ryutsu-shi* (History of distribution and transportation). Vol. II. Tokyo, Yamakawa-shuppansha. (Taikei-nihonshi-sosho (Systematic exposition of Japanese history)).

Gershuny, J. I. [1983], *Social Innovation and the Division of Labour.* Oxford, Oxford University Press.

Goto, Akira and Suzuki, K. [1989], "R and D capital,rate of return on R and D investment and spill over of R and D in Japanese manufacturing industries," *The Review of Economics and Statistics.* 71-(4).

Goto, Shin'ichi [1970], *Nihon no kin'yu-tokei* (Statistics on monetary phenomena). Tokyo, Toyo-keizai shimposha.

Griliches, Ziville [1988], *Technology, Education, and Productivity: early papers with notes to subsequent literature.* New York, Basil Blackwell.

Hakim, C. [1979], "Census Confidentiality in Britain," in Blumer (ed.) [1979].

Hara, Akira (ed.) [1995], *Nihon no senji-keizai: keikaku to shijyo.* (Japanese war economy: planning and market). Tokyo, Tokyo daigaku-shuppan-kai.

Hashimoto, Jyuro and Takeda, Haruhito [1992], *Nihon keizai no hatten to kigyo-shudan.* (Development of Japanese economy and company groups: research project with joint-auspice of Information Centre of Industry at Hosei University). Tokyo, Tokyo daigaku-shuppan-kai.

Hatai, Yoshitaka [1963], "Noka jinko-ido to keiki-hendo: Minami, Ono, Namiki ronso nitsuite (Trade cycle and population migration from rural area: on the controversy between Minami-Ono and Namiki," *Kikan Riron Keizaigaku* (The Economic Studies Quarterly). 14-(1).

Hayashi, Takeshi [1986], *Gijutsu to shakai: Nihon no keiken.* (Technology and society: Japanese experience. Japanese version of the United Nations Project entitled *Japanese experience* in English). Tokyo, United Nations University.

Hayashi, Shuji and Nakamura, Takafusa [1986], *Nihon keizai to keizai-tokei* (Japanese economy and economic statistics). Tokyo, Tokyo daigaku-shuppan-kai.

Hijikata, Seibi [1933], *Kokumin-shotoku no kousei.* (Composition of national income). Tokyo, Nippon-hyoron-sha.

— [1938], "Wagakuni saikin no kokuminshotoku (National income of recent Japan)," *Keizaigaku-ronshu* (Economic Review), 8-(7).

Hori, Tsuneo [1975], *Meiji keizai-shiso-shi.* (History of economic thoughts of Japan in Meiji period). Tokyo, Meiji-bunken.

Hosoya, Chihiro, Hosoya Nagayo, Irie Akira, Hatano Sumio (ed.) [1993], *Taiheiyo-senso* (The Pacific War). Tokyo, Tokyo daigaku-shuppan-kai.

Hosoya, Shinji [1974–80], *Meiji-zenki nihon keizai-tokei-kaidai-shoshi: Fukoku-kyohei-hen* (Annotated Bibliography of the Statistical Documents of Early Meiji Period: The days for enrichment of the country and strengthening military power) 3 vols in 5 issues. Tokyo, Documentation Centre for Japanese Economic Statistics at Institute of Economic Research, Hitotsubashi University. (Tokei-shiryo-series)

Ijiri, Yuji and Herbert A. Simon [1977], *Skew Distribution and the Size of Business Firms*, Amsterdam, New York and Oxford. North

REFERENCES

Holland Publishing. (Studies in Mathematical and Managerial Economics, 24)

Ikari, Yoshiro [1993], *Chou-kosoku ni idomu; shinkansen-kaihatsu ni kaketa otokotachi* (Challenging to Super Express: men devoted to realise the new super express line). Tokyo, Bugei-shunjyu-sha.

Imuda, Toshimitsu [1976], *Meiji-ki Kabushiki-kaisha bunseki-jyosetsu.* (Introduction to the analysis of Joint-stock companies in Meiji era, his collected papers I) Tokyo, Hosei-daigaku shuppankai.

— [1976 a], *Meiji-ki kinyu-kozo-bunseki jyosetsu.* (Introduction to the analysis of financial structure in Meiji era, his collected papers, II). Tokyo, Hosei-daigaku shuppan-kai.

Institute of Developing Economies [1973–81], *Kyu-shokuminchi-kankei-kikan-kankoubutsu-sougou-mokuroku* (Union Catalogue of the Publications by the Former Colonial Institutions of Japan Empire). in 5 vols. Tokyo, Azia-keizai kenkyujyo (Institute of Developing Economies).

Ishi, Yoshikuni [1972], *Kankoku no jinko-joka no bunseki.* (Analysis of population growth in Korea). Tokyo, Keiso-shobo.

Ishi'i, Kanji [1987], "Kokusai-kankei (International relations [during the Great Depression Period])" in Oh'ishi [1987] vol. 2.

Ishikawa, Shigeru [1967], *Economic Development in Asian Perspective,* Tokyo, Kinokuniya (Economic Research Series No. 8)

Itoh, Shigeru [1983], "Meiji=Taisho-ki no kengyo=fukugyo-toukei (Statistics of Subsidiary Jobs in Meiji-taisho Era)," in Umemura etc. [1983]

— [1985] "Toshi-jinko (Urban population)," in Umemura etc. [1985]

Japan Statistical Association (ed.) [1987–88], *Historical statistics of Japan,* in five volumes. (Japanese title: *Nihon-choki-tokei-soran,* with English and Japanese annotations.) Editorial supervision by Japan, Management and Coordination Agency, Statistics Bureau. Tokyo,Japan Statistical Association. (Cumulative and recompiled version of Statistical Yearbook started in 1882 covering 1868–1985 and expected to continue to the 1986 issue of the Statistical Yearbook.)

Jentschura, Hansgeorg, Dieter Jung and Peter Mickel [1977], *Warships of the Imperial Japanese Navy; 1869–1945*. Translated from *Die Japanischen Kriegsschiffe 1869–1945* (1970) by David Brown and Antony Preston. Revised ed. of 1970. London, Arms and Armour.

Kan'no, Wataro [1931], *Nihon Kaisha-kigyo hassei-shi no kenkyu*, (Origin of Company System in Japan). Tokyo, Iwanami-shoten.

Keizai-Shiryo Kyogikai see Association for Documentation in Economics

Keynes, J.M. [1936], *The General Theory of Employment, Interest and Money*. London, Macmillan.

— [1937], "Some Economic Consequences of a Declining Population" *Eugenic Review*.

— [1939], "Professor Tinbergen's method: review of Tinbergen, Statistical testing of Business cycles, I," *Economic Journal*, pp. 558–578. Tinbergen's reply [1940]. *Economic Journal*, p. 141 ff with Keynes' comment, pp. 154–156.

Kimura, Kenji [1994], "Kaisha-rei no jisshi to kaisha-setsuritsu-shutai (Execution of Company Act in Chosen and Entrepreneurs in Establishing Companies)," in Kobayashi [1994]

Kin, Tetsu [1965], *Kankoku no jinko to keizai. (Population and economy of Korea)* Tokyo, Iwanami-shoten.

Klein, L.R. [1961], "A model of Japanese economic growth, 1878–1937," *Econometrica*, 29-(3).

Kobayashi, Hideo [1994], *Shokumin-chi he no kigyo-shin-shutsu Chosen- kaisha-rei no bunseki* (Expansion of Companies into Colonial Areas: Analysis of Company Act in Chosen). Tokyo, Kashiwa-shobo.

Koshihara, Hisao [1986] "kogyo-tokei to seisan-dotai-tokei no kairi: chosa no gosa (Difference of the survey results between manufacturing census and dynamic survey of manufacturing: measurement error of the survey" in Hayashi and Nakamura (eds.) [1986]

Kudo, Hiroyasu [1995], "Register-base no tokei (Statistics based on the register system)" in *Feasibility Study of Compiling Global Statistics, Report of the Grant-in Aid Research*, ed. by Yoshiro Matsuda with

REFERENCES

Kudo's other papers published on register based statistics systems.
Kurabayashi, Yoshimasa [1983], "Kanto-daishinsai no SSDS (A System of Socio-Demographic Statistics for the Great Kanto Earthquake)." *Keizai-kenkyu* (Economic Review) 34-(2)
Kurosaki, Chiharu [1976], "Meiji-zenki no Nippon no toshi (Cities in eary Meiji)," in *Suryo-keizaishi-ronshu*, 2 (Proceedings of the Conference of Quantitative Economic History).
Maema, Takanori [1994], *Dangan-retsusha: maboroshi no Tokyo-hattsu Peking-yuki cho-tokkyu* (Raiload like a bullet: a super express running from Tokyo to Beijing in a phantom). Tokyo, Jitsugyo-no-nippon-sha.
Man'nari, Hiroshi [1965], *Bizinesu eriito–nihon ni okeru keieisha no jyoken*, (Business élite: qualification for the managers in Japan). Tokyo, Chuou-kouron-sha. (Chukou-shinsho, 71)
Matsuda, Yoshiro [1978], *Data no Riron* (Treatise on Data). Tokyo, Iwanami Shoten. (Hitotsubashi Daigaku Keizai Kenkyu sosho, 30).
— [1980], Kyu-shokuminchi niokeru showa 14 nen Rinjikokuseichosa Sairon (Rejoinder: On the Extra Census of 1939 executed in Japanese Colonies), (Institute of Economic Research Hitotsubashi University, Discussion Paper Series, 31).
— [1981], "Formation of the Census System in Japan: 1871–1945: Development of the Statistical System in Japan Proper and her Colonies." *Hitotsubashi Journal of Economics* 21-(2).
— [1983], "Kanto-daishinsai ga oyoboshita shakai-keizaiteki-eikyo (Socio-economic effects of the Great Kanto Earthquake)." *Gekkan-shobo* (Monthly Firemen) 5-(11).
— [1987], "Historical development of Japanese statistics." *Bulletin of the International Statistical Institute, Proceedings of the 46th session in Tokyo*. 52-(4).
— [1988], "Manufacturing and Corporate Firm System in Meiji Japan," in Uno and Shishido (eds.) [1988]
— [1989], "Longitudinal Data File Compilation for Historical Analysis," *Historical Social Research*, 14-(3).
— [1991], *Kigyo-kozo no tokei-teki sokutei-hoho* (Treatise on the mea-

surement of patterns of enterprises). Tokyo, Iwanami-shoten. (Hitotsubashi Daigaku Keizai Kenkyu Sosho, 40).

—, Arita, Fumiko and Oh'i, Hiromi [1980], *Meiji Chuki no Kabushiki-
kaisha no Kozo* (Patterns of Corporate Firms in Meiji Period; 1896),
(*Tokei Shiryo Series*, 16).

—, and Terasaki, Yasuhiro [1980], "Economic Development and the
Distribution of Conumer Durables Ownership: Japan and Taiwan,
1945–75," *The Philippine Economic Journal*, 19-(2).

— (ed.) [1981], *Meiji chu-ko-ki kigyo=kojyo-togo database hensei-
giho*, (Compilation technique for company and factory consolidated
database.) Tokyo, Hitotusbashi University, (Tokei-shiryo series,
20).

Matsumoto, Toshiro [1992], *Shinryaku to kaihatsu: Nihon-shihon-shugi
to chugoku-shokuminchika* (Invasion and development: Japanese
capitalism and the colonialisation of China). Tokyo, Ochanomizu-
shobo.

Matsumura, Satoshi [1992], *Senkan-ki nihon sanshi-gyo-shi kenkyu:
katakura seishi o chushin ni*, (Research on the silk industry between
two World Wars, especially with the collaboration of Katakura silk
spinning company).

Mills, Edwin S. and Song, Byung-nak [1979], *Urbanization and Urban
Problems*. Cambridge, Harvard University Press (Studies in the
Modernization of The Republic of Korea: 1945–1975)

Minami, Ryoshin [1973], *The Turning Point in Economic Development*.
Tokyo, Kinokuniya, (Economic Research Series No. 14).

— [1987], *Power Revolution in the Industrialization of Japan: 1885–
1940*. Tokyo, Kinokuniya. (Economic Research Series No. 24)

— and Ono, Akira [1962], "Noka-jinko ido to keiki hendo tono kankei
nitsuite no oboegaki (Memoire on the relation between migration
of rural people and the trade cycle)," *Kikan Riron Keizaigaku* (The
Economic Studies Quarterly), 12-(3).

Mitsuma, Nobukuni [1983], *Keizai-tokei-bunrui-ron: shokugyo/sangyo
bunrui no keisei*. (On the economic classification system: formation
of the occupation and industrial classification). Tokyo, Yuhikaku.

REFERENCES

Miyamoto, Mataro and Abe, Takeshi (eds.) [1995], *keiei-kakushin to kogyo-ka* (Managerial innovation and industrialisation). Tokyo, Iwanami-shoten. (*Nihon keieishi*, 2).

—, —, Udakawa, Masaru, Sawai, Minoru and Kitsukawa, Takeo [1995] *Nihon keieishi: Nihon-gata kigyo-keiei no hatten –Edo kara Heisei he.* (History of Japanese Management: specialty of Japanese company management from Edo period to Heisei, now) . Tokyo, Yuhikaku.

Mizoguchi, Toshiyuki [1995], *Reforms of Statistical System under Socio-economic Changes: overview of statistical data in Japan.* Tokyo, Maruzen Co. Ltd.

— and Nojima, Noriyuki [1993], "1940–1955 nen ni okeru kokumin-keizai-keisan no ginmi(Review of the estimates of Japanese national accounts in 1940-55)," *Nihon tokei-gakkai-shi* (Journal of the Japan Statistical Society), 23-(1).

— and Umemura, Mataji (eds.) [1988], *Kyu-nihon-shokuminchi keizai-tokei; suikei to bunseki* (Basic Economic Statistics of Former Japanese Colonies, 1896–1938: Estimates and findings). Tokyo, Toyo-keizai-shimposha.

Morita, Yuzo [1944], *Jinko-zoka no bunseki* (Analysis of the increase of the population). Tokyo, Nihon-hyoron-sha.

— (ed.) [1963], *Bukka* (Price level). Tokyo, Shunjyu-sha.

Murakami, Katsuhiko [1985], "Shihon-chikuseki (1): jyuko-gyo. (Capital Accumulation (1): heavy industries," in Ohishi (ed.) [185] vol. 1.

Nakamura, Takafusa [1971], *Senzenki nihon-keizai-seicho no bunseki* (Analysis of the Japanese economy before the World War II). Tokyo, Iwanami-shoten.

— [1983], *Senji-nippon no kahoku-keizai-shihai* (Japanese economic control over North China). Tokyo, Yamakawa Publishing Co.

— and Arai [1978], "Taiheiyo-senso-ki ni okeru yugyo-jinko no suikei: 1940–1947" (Working population during the Pacific War: 1940–1947). *Tokyo Daigaku kyoyo-bu shakai-kagaku-kyo*, 27.

— and Miyazaki, Masayasu (eds.) [1995], *Shiryo: Taiheiyo-senso-*

REFERENCES

higai-chosa-hokoku (Historical Documents: Survey report of the damages brought out by the Pacific Ocean War). Tokyo. Tokyo-daigaku-shuppan- kai. (Ten reports and manuscripts were contained in this reprint with annotations by the editors.)

— and Mizoguchi, Toshiyuki [1994], *Dai-niji-taisen-ka seikatsushizai-yami-bukka shukei-hyo*. (Summary tables of the black market prices of consumers' goods during the World War II). Tokyo, Hitotsubashi Univ. (Tokei-shiryo-shiriizu, 44.)

Nishikawa, Shunsaku [1979], "Choshu-Yamaguchi Ken no Sangyo-hatten (Industrial Development in Yamaguchi Prefecture)" in *Suryo Keizaishi Ronshu*, 2 (Proceedings of the Conference on Quantitative Economic History).

— [1966], *Chiiki-kan rodo-ido to rodo-shijyo: showa senzenki-seni-rodosha no chiikikan-ido* (Interregional labour mobility and labour market: labourers in textile industries in 1920–35). Tokyo, Yuhikaku.

Nishinarita, Yutaka [1994], "Roudou-ryoku-doin to roudou-kaikaku (Labour mobilization and Labour Reform)" in Ohishi (ed.) [1994] vol. 3.

Nojiri, Shigeo [1937], *Nomin-ri-son no jissho-teki kenkyu* (Empirical research of the farmers' exodus from rural villages). Tokyo, Iwanami-shoten.

Odaka, Konosuke [1984], *Roudou-shijyo-bunseki* (Analysis of labour market). Tokyo, Iwanami-shoten.

— [1995], "Kojyo-seido no teichaku to romu-kanri." (Formation of factory system and employment management). in Mataro Miyamoto and Takeshi Abe [1995].

Ohashi, Hiroshi [1963], *Meiji-tokei no ichi-kosatsu.* (On Japanese statistics in Meiji period), in *Chiho-sangyo no hatten to jinushi-sei.* (Regional industry and the landowners: his collected works), Tokyo, Rinsen-shoten [1982]

Ohishi, Kaichiro [1985,1987,1984], *Nihon-teikokushugishi* (Japanese imperialism). Tokyo, Tokyo-daigaku-shuppankai. in 3 vols.

Ohkawa, Kazushi [1957], *The Growth rate of the Japanese Economy*

REFERENCES

since 1878. Tokyo, Kinokuniya-shoten.

— [1972], *Differential Structure and Agriculture, Essays on Dualistic Growth*, Tokyo, Kinokuniya (*Economic Research Series* No. 13)

— and Minami, Ryoshin [1975], *Kindai-nihon no keizai-hatten: "Choki-keizai tokei" ni yoru bunseki* (Economic Development of Modern Japan: Analysis based on "Long-term Economic Statistics"). Tokyo, Toyokeizai-shimposha.

—, Shinohara, Miyohei, and Umemura, Mataji (eds.) [1965–88], *Choki-keizai-tokei: suikei to bunseki* (Estimates of Long-term Economic Statistics of Japan since 1868). 14 vols. (Abbreviated as LTES),Tokyo, Toyokeizai-shimposha.

— and Shinohara, Miyohei with Larry Meissner [1979], *Patterns of Japanese Economic Development, a quantitative appraisal*, New Haven and London, Yale Univ. Press.

Ohya, Yusetsu [1995], *Tokei-jyoho-ron* (On statistical information). Fukuoka, Kyushu daigaku-shuppankai.

Otsuka, Katsuo [1960], *Nihon-kindai-seishi-gyo no seiritsu: Nagano-ken Okaya seishigyo-shi-kenkyu* (Formation of modern silk spinning industry in Japan: case study of Okaya district in Nagano prefecture). Tokyo, Ochanomizu-shobo.

Patrick, Hugh (ed.) [1976], *Japanese Industrialization and its Social Consequences*, Berkley and Los Angels, Univ. California Press.

Pelz, Stephen E. [1974], *Race to Pearl Harbor: The failure of the second London Naval Conference of World War II*. Cambridge (Mass.) and London, Harvard Univ. Press.

Rawlinson, John L. [1967], *China's Struggle for Naval Development: 1839–1895*. Cambridge (Mass.), Harvard Univ. Press.

Sale, Charles V. [1911], "Some Statistics of Japan," *JRSS*, Apr. 1911, 74-4 pp. 467–534.

Sekiyama, Naotaro [1958], *Nihon no jinkou* (Population of Japan). Tokyo, Shibun-dou.

Shimizu, Yoji [1994], "Shokuryo-seisan to nouchi-kaikaku (Food Production and the Land Reform)" in Ohishi (ed.) [1994] vol. 2.

REFERENCES

Shinohara, Miyohei [1962], *Growth and Cycles in the Japanese Economy*, Tokyo, Kinokuniya (*Economic Research Series* No. 5)

— [1970], *Structural Changes in Japan's Economic Development*, Tokyo, Kinokuniya (*Economic Research Series* No. 11)

— (ed.) [1991], *Nihon-keizai no dynamism: "Choki-keizai-tokei" to watashi* (The Dynamism of Japanese Economy: we and *"The Longterm Economic Statistics"*).

— [1972], Ko-ko-gyo (Mining and Manufacturing). Tokyo, Toyo-keizai Shimposha (LTES, vol. 10).

Shiomi, Saburo [1946], *Kokumin-shotoku no bunpai* (Distribution of National Income) in collaboration with Mori Otto, Takeda Shotaro and Masuda Yukio. Tokyo, Yuhikaku.

Sorifu Tokeikyoku, see Statistics Bureau.

Stamp, J. [1919], "Wealth and Income of the Chief Powers," *JRSS*, pp. 488–89.

Statistics Bureau [1973–77], *Sorifu-Tokeikyoku hyakunenshi-shiryo-shusei* (Collected Documents of the Statistics Bureau in the Past Hundred Years). 3 vols. in 7 issues.

Statistics Council [1985], *Medium-and Long-term Plans for Government Statistical Activities*. Tokyo, National Federation of Statistical Associations in Japan.

— [1995], *New Strategies for Government Statistical Services for the Coming Decade*. Tokyo, Management and Coordination Agency.

Sueo, Tomoyuki [1980], *Suiryoku-kaihatsu=riryo no rekishi-chiri* (Development and utilisation of water-power in historical geography.) Tokyo, Taimei-do.

Takahashi, Chotaro [1959], *Dynamic Changes of Income and its Distribution in Japan*. Tokyo, Kinokuniya (*Economic Research Series* No. 3)

Takamura, Naosuke [1985], "Shihon-chikuseki(1): Kei-kogyo (Capital accumulation (1), Light industries) in Ohishi (ed.) [1985] vol. 1.

— [1987], "Shihon-chikuseki (2): Kei-kogyo (Capital accumulation (2) Light industries) in Ohishi (ed.) [1987] vol. 2.

— [1994], "Minjyu-sangyo (Industries for Non-military Demands," in Ohishi (ed.) [1994] vol. 2.

— [1995], *Saihakken: Meijiki no keizai.* (Reconsideration of the economy in Meiji period.) Tokyo, Hanawa-shoten.

— (ed.) [1988], *Nichiro-senso-go no nihon-keizai.* (Japanese economy after the Russo-Japanese War). Tokyo, Hanawa-shobo.

— (ed.) [1992], *Kigyo-bokko: Nihon-shihonshugi no keisei.* (Flowering of companies: Formation of Japanese capitalism). Tokyo, Mineruba-shobo.

Teranishi, Juro [1982], *Nihon no keizai-hatten to kin'yu* (Economic Development of Japan and her Monetary System). Tokyo, Iwanami-shoten.

Tinbergen, J. [1937], *An Econometric Approach to Business Cycle Problems.* Paris, Hermann & Cie. (Actualités scientifiques et industrielles, 525:Impresses Economiques II.)

— [1939], *Business Cycles in the United States of America. 1919–1932.* Geneva, League of Nations. (Statistical testing of business cycle theories. Vol. II.)

— [1951], *Business Cycles in the United Kingdom 1870–1914.* Amsterdam North-Holland Pub. Co. (Verhandelingen der Koninklijke Nederlandse Akademie van Wetenschappen. afd. Litterkunde. Nieuwe reeks deel LVII, no. 4.)

Tobata, Sei'ichi [1964], *Nihon shihonshugi no keisei-sha: samazama no keizai-shutai* (Constructors of Japanese capitalism: various economic agents). Tokyo, Iwanami-shoten. (*Iwanami Shinsho*, 513).

Toda, Teizo, [1926], *Kazoku no kenkyu* (Treatise on the Family). Tokyo, Koubundou-shobo.

— [1934], *Kazoku to kon'in* (Family and marriage). Tokyo, Chubunkan. (Reprinted in his collected papers, vol. 3.)

— [1937], *Kazoku-kosei* (Constitution of the family). Tokyo, Koubundo-shobo.

Togashi, Mitsutaka[1982], "Kanto-daishinsai niyoru higaigaku no suikei (Estimates of the damages caused by the Great Kanto Earthquake)"

(Socio-economic Research Unit on Natural Disaster, Discussion Paper Series.)

Tojyo, Yukihiko [1992], "Shoki-seitetsu-gyo to syokko-shakai," (Early period of forming modern steel industry and the artisan society.) in Takamura (ed.) [1992]

— [1995], "Roumu-douin (Labour Mobilization)" in Hara (ed.) [1995]

Tokeikyoku, see Statistics Bureau

Tokoyama, Kazuhiko [1975], "Choki-moderu no tembo to hyoka (Review of Long-term Econometric Models of Japanese Economy)" in Ohkawa & Minami [1975]

Tokei-kyo-kai see Japan Statistical Association.

Tomoyasu, Ryoich [1975], *Tokei Chosa Soron* (Principles of Statistical Survey). Tokyo, Dai-ichi-houki-shuppan.

Tsuchiya, Keizo [1987], "The Development of Japan's Agricultural Statistics and its Problems," *Journal of the Japan Statistical Society, Special issue on Japanese Statistics.*

Tsuchiya, Takao [1930], "Meiji-shonen no jinko-kosei ni kansuru ichi kosatsu (One Aspect of the Composition of the Population in early Meiji Period)." *Shakai-keizai-shigaku* (Journal of the Socio-economic History Research) 1-(1).

Tsuru, Shigeto [1958], *Essays on Japanese Economy.* Tokyo, Kinokuniya (*Economic Research Series* No. 2)

— [1968], *Essays on Economic Development.* Tokyo, Kinokuniya Bookstore Co., Ltd. (*Economic Research Series* No. 9)

— and Ohkawa, Kazushi (eds.) [1955], *Nihon-keizai-no-bunseki* (Analysis of Japanese economy), in two vols. Tokyo, Keiso-shobo.

Tsurumi, E. Patricia [1977], *Japanese Colonial Education in Taiwan, 1895-1945,* Cambridge (Mass.), Harvard University Press.

Ueda, Hiroshi [1995], "Senji-keizai-ka no shita-uke kyoryoku-kogyo-seisaku no keisei (Formation of subcontract system in manufacturing in war-period)" in Hara (ed.) [1995].

Ueda, Teijiro [1943], *Jinko-mondai* (Population Problems), Tokyo, Nihon-hyoron-sha. (Ueda Teijiro zenshu (Collected works of Ueda Teijiro), vol. 6.)

— [1944], *Kabushiki-kaisha-ron* (On the Joint-stock Companies), (1st edition in 1913 and revised edition in 1921). Tokyo, Nihon-hyoronsha. (Ueda Teijiro zenshu (Collected works of Ueda Teijiro), vol. 2.)

Umemura, Mataji [1955], "Chingin-kakusa to Rou-dou-shijo," in Tsuru and Ohkawa (eds.) [1955] vol. 2.

— [1961], *Chingin, koyo, nogyo* (Wage, employment and agriculture). Tokyo, Taimeido

— etc. [1983], *Chiiki-Keizai-tokei* (Regional Economic Statistics). Tokyo, Toyo-keizai-shimposha. (LTES. vol. 14).

— etc. [1988], *Roudou-ryoku* (Labour Force). Tokyo, Toyoukeizaishimposha. (LTES vol. 2)

— [1991] "Kindai-seicho no shoki-jyoken: Kinsei and kindai. (The initial conditions of modern economic growth: *kinsei* (before invasion of Western culture but after the medieval time in Japanese economy) and modern or after invasion of Western culture.)" in Shinohara (ed.) [1991]

Uno, Kimio and Shishido, Shuntaro (eds.) [1988], *Statistical Data Bank Systems.* Amsterdam, North Holland Publishing Co.

US, Department of Commerce, Office of Federal Statistical Policy and Standards [1980], *Report on Exact and Statistical Matching Techniques.* (Subcommittee on Matching Techniques of the Federal Committee on Statistical Methodology.) Washington D.C. (Statistical Policy Working Paper. 5.)

Uyeda (i.e. Ueda), Teijiro and Associates [1938], *The Small Industries of Japan; their growth and development.* London, Oxford University Press.

Yamada, Yuzo [1957], *Nihon Kokumin-shotoku-suikei-shiryo.* (Compendium of national income statistics of Japan) Revised version of 1951.

Yamaguchi, Kazuo [1956], *Meiji-zenki-keizai no bunseki.* (Analysis of the Early Meiji period). Tokyo, Tokyo-daigaku-shuppankai.

— [1963], op. cit. revised version.

— and Ishii, Kanji [1986], *Kindai-nippon no syohin-ryutsu.* (Commodity distribution in modern Japan.) Tokyo, Tokyo-daigaku-shuppan-kai.

Yamamoto, Yuzo [1992], *Nihon-shokuminchi-keizaishi-kenkyu* (On Japanese colonial economy in historical perspectives). Nagoya, Nagoya University Press.

— (ed.) [1993] *"Manshu-koku" no kenkyu* (On "Manchukuo"). Kyoto, Institute for Humanities at Kyoto University.

Yamanaka, Tokutaro [1933], *Nihon-shakai-keizai no kenkyu* (Socioeconomic studies on Japan). Tokyo, Moriyama-shoten.

— [1941], "Nihon-kogyo niokeru reisaisei (Skewed distribution cumulated at small scale of Japanese manufacturing)." *Shakai-seisaku-jiho* (Journal of social politics). 248 and 249 issues.

— [1944], *Nihon-sangyo-kozou no kenkyu* (Research on Japanese Industrial Structure). Tokyo, Yuhikaku.

Yamazaki, Shiro [1995], "Senji-kogyo-doin-taisei (Labour mobilization in war period)" in Hara (ed.) [1995]

Yanagida, Kunio [1906], "Houtokusha to shinyou-kumiai" reprinted in his collected works. vol. 16.

Yasuba, Yasukichi [1963/65], "Senzen no Nihon niokeru kogyo tokei no shimpyosei nitsuite (On the accuracy of manufacturing statistics in the pre-war period)," *Osaka Daigaku Keizaigaku* (Osaka University Economic Papers), 17-(2,3).

— [1976], "The Evolution of Dualistic Wage Structure," in Hugh Patrick (ed.)

Yasuoka, Shigeaki and Amano, Masatoshi [1995], *Kinseiteki keiei no tenkai* (Development of modern management). Tokyo, Iwanami-shoten. (Nihon keieishi (History of Japanese management), 1).

Yuasa, Mitsutomo [1980], *Nihon no kagakugijutsu 100 nen-shi.* (A century of Japanese development in science and technology.) Tokyo, Chuou-koron-sha. in 2 vols. (Shizen so-sho)

SUBJECT INDEX

A

absolutism 69
accuracy of encoding 160
accuracy of statistical data 3
accuracy of statistical survey 3, 17, 297
accuracy of the observation 8
Act for Amalgamation of Banks 142
Act for Association of Manufacturing 44
Act for Automobile Production 44
Act for Controlling Important Fertilizer Industry 44
Act for Creation of Independent Farmers 245
Act for Establishing Electricity Enterprise 44
Act for Establishing the Japan Steel Company 44
Act for Establishing the Petroleum Enterprise 44
Act for Execution of Statistical Surveys by Field Surveys 33
administrative boundaries 258
administrative unit 5
age composition 260
aged people mobilized (see also labour mobilization) 229
Agricultural and Trading Correspondence System 24
aircraft
Hayabusa military fighter 207
koukenki (ARI plane) 207
97 scout plane 207
zero naval fighter 207
aircraft carrier
Akagi 195
Hosho 206
Kaga 194
Ryujyo 206
aircraft industry 207, 212
armoured battleship
Chen Yuan (China) 103
Ting Yuan (China) 103
armoured cruiser
Akitsushima 106
Hashidate 105f, 131
Itukushima 105
Matsushima 105f
assassinations of political leaders 202
Five-one-five Affair 202
Two-two-six Affair 202
atomic bombs
experiments of atomic bombs at the Bikini 244
massacres of Hiroshima and Nagasaki by atomic bombs 230f
damage to capital assets by atomic bombs 242

B

Bank Act 142

battleship
  Akagi (changed to aircraft carrier
    by Washington Treaty)   195
  Aki   131f
  Haruna   131f
  Hatsuse   131
  Hiei   132
  Ibuki   131
  Ikoma   131
  Kaga (changed to aircraft carrier
    by Washington Treaty)   195
  Kawachi   131f
  Kii   195
  Kirishima   131f
  Kongo   132
  Kurama   131
  Musashi   195, 206, 240
  Mutsu   194
  Nagato   195, 244f
  Nevada (USA)   244
  New York (USA)   244
  number eleven to sixteen (aban-
    doned or canceled by Washington
    Treaty)   195
  Owari   195
  Pennsylvania (USA)   244
  Satsuma   131
  Settsu   131
  Tosa   194
  Tsukuba   131f
  two escadrilles (hachi-hachi kan-
    tai)   193
  Yamato   195, 206, 240f, 244
  Yashima   131
beriberi   230
black market   245

block economy (see also currency
  block)   204
  Japan, Manchukuo and China
    block economy   208
borrowed technology (see also technology)   166, 206, 207, 247
boundary
  administrative boundary   258
  jurisdictional boundary   4
budget   28, 33
  national budget   56ff
building battleship   132
business cycle   64

C

calculator
  soroban calculator   65
capital
  fixed capital   37, 123
  paid-in capital
              116, 124, 142, 144, 281f
  nominal capital
                116, 142, 144, 275
  operational capital   123
  working capital   37
capital raising   132
cartel   38, 44, 206
category
  semantics of the category   4
censorship by GHQ   70f, 181, 243f
census survey (see survey)   5f, 17
census [survey] system   6, 35, 41
Chamber of Commerce   27
China and South Asian Countries 75
Civil War   66
  Boshin-sen'eki   66 (see war)

(China)   233 (see war)
Seinan-no-eki   66 (see war)
class
    artisan class   75
    farmer class   75, 77, 79f
    lower warrior (*samurai*) class
                                  79f, 143
    merchant class   75, 143
    ordinary people (*heimin*) class 79
    outcaste class   75, 79
    ruling class   71
    town dweller (*chomin*) class
                                     77, 79
    warrior (*samurai*) class 71, 75, 79
classification
    of industry   41, 97, 261, 292
    of occupation   23, 261, 291
    schemes   23, 31, 269, 284f, 292
classification criteria   290
clothes stamps   242
cohort analysis   13
cohort data (see longitudinal data,
    see also data)
colony of the Western powers   179
commerce   227
commercial census   292
commercial credit bureau   129
commercial inquiry bureau (see com-
    mercial credit bureau)
                                275, 278
Commercial Law   113, 116
    Ancient Commercial Law   116
companies
    big companies   148
    fragility of the smaller companies
                                       146
    leakage of companies   145, 160

longevity of companies   146
private companies   195
regional distribution of compa-
    nies   144
company   7, 33, 58, 112
    corporate company   113
    commercial company   124
    holding company   201
    joint-stock company
        27, 113, 127, 132, 140, 144
    limited partnership company
                                       141
    manufacturing company   124
    pioneers of the corporate com-
        pany   113
    unlimited partnership company
                                       141
company directory database   129
company statistics
                     33ff, 113, 258, 276
company system   67, 114
compiled data (see data) 11, 63, 252
    (recompiled data 63)
complete enumeration survey (see
    survey)   5
compulsory education (see also edu-
    cational system)   177
compulsory labour movement   187
computational power   48
concentration of factories   136
concept
    operational concept   4f
controlled economy   44, 49, 67
cooperative   10
counter-revolution   201
coverage   11, 17, 210, 211,
                      221, 224, 271, 290

adjustment of coverage   228
imperfect coverage of the date
source   144
coverage of Japan   258
cross section data (see also data)
                         13, 145, 265f
cruiser, heavy cruiser
    Furutaka   195, 206
    Prinz Eugen (Germany)   244
cruiser, light cruiser
    Mogami   206
    Sakawa   244
    Yahagi   244
    Yubari   195
cruiser, protected
    Akashi   112
    Suma   112
currency block
    Yen currency block   203

D

daimyo   71, 76
damage (see war damage)
damage to capital assets   232
damage to human resources   230
data
    missing data   280
    compiled data   11, 63, 252
    cohort data   13
    cross section data   12, 145, 265f
    time series data   65, 228
database
    commercial database vendor 252
    common-use database system 252
    in-house-use database system
                                252f

textual database   251
database system for historical analy-
    sis   251
decentralized survey system (see sur-
    vey system)   23, 38, 45, 47
definition of factory   92
definition of employee   97
definition of power machines   109
deindividualized data sets   260
demographic analysis   251
disarmament   231
    London Treaty   195
    Washington Treaty   194
disaster
    natural disaster   195
    human and social disasters 201
distribution
    income and wealth distribution
                           245, 247
    size distribution of capital 142
distribution of companies   143
domestic servants   187, 211
dual economy   192
dual educational system (see also ed-
    ucational system)   177
dual structure   166, 176

E

economic growth
    exaggeration of economic growth
                                 18
educational system
    compulsory educational system
                           177, 246
    dual educational system   177
    Ωat educational system   247

level of education   167
on-the-job-training   educational
system   125, 167, 177, 230
employment
total turnover ratio of employment   229
engineers   178
enterprise   129
medium scale enterprise   44, 52
merger and amalgamation of enterprise   205, 221
multi-establishment enterprise
                                7, 292
multi-factory enterprise   130, 165
multi-plant enterprise   140
single establishment enterprise
                                7, 292
single-factory enterprise   130, 165
size distribution of enterprises
                                  170
small-scale enterprise   44, 52
entrepreneur   143
enumeration unit   4, 9, 25
erroneous data   280
establishment (see enterprise)
              6, 58, 129, 210, 225
establishment census   293
exodus
from Japan proper   194
of Japanese   187
of the labour force   101
of the rural population   262
expansion
horizontal expansion   137
vertical expansion   137
expenditure
military expenditure   237

statistical expenditure   56ff
export
rice   112
silk   112
tea   112
Express Tsubame   208

F

factory
company-owned factory
                          125, 141, 153
concentration of factories   136
equipment of factory   94
government factory   110
individual-owned factory   123
joint-stock-company-owned factory   125
operational days of the factory
                              169
power of factory   94
factory directory database   129
Factory Act   197
factory production   96, 103
factory production system   92
factory-company linked database
                             171, 294
factory-list database   286
family (see also household)   19
compound family   58
nuclear family   83
family member   292
family size   187
family structure   83
family system   260
family workshop   226
farmers   77

female to male ratio 187
feudalistic legal system (see also law system) 258
financing
    indirect financing 145
financing by banks 145
firm 7, 59
Five-one-five Affair 202
Five Year Economic Plan (Manchukuo) 204
food stamps 241
formal production (see also production) 263f
format survey 5, 17, 33
French law 113
frigate 244

Hayabusa military fighter (see also aircraft) 207
Hsinhai Koming (see Revolution) 202
homoeogryllus japonicus 87
horizontal expansion (see also expansion) 137
household 5f, 210
    non-kinship household member 189
    single household 58, 189
household head 58, 83
household members 189
household size 187, 189
housemaid (see domestic servants) 210
housewives 264

G

German law 113
government factories 101, 110
governmental military production 111
Great Depression 44, 201
Great Kanto Earthquake 76, 195, 230, 238, 254
Greater East Asia War (see Pacific War) 205
Greater East Asia Co-prosperity Sphere 205
growth
    economic growth 17
gun-boat diplomacy 102

H

han-shu 68, 71, 73, 76, 113, 177

I

Imperial Japanese Navy 111
imperialistic capitalism 68
importation of military goods 110
imported technology (see technology) 169
in-house-use database 253
income and wealth distribution 245, 247
individual enterprise system 132
industrial classification (see classification) 41, 97, 217, 261, 292
industrialization 3, 11, 25, 193
    rapid industrialization 128
industrialized society 193
industry
    heavy industry 129
    light industry 129
inΩation

hyperinΩation 245
informal production 263ff
information
  intelligence information 251
information control 58
infrastructure 207
input-output analysis 45, 59
interference by France, Germany and
  Russia 111, 180
intervention by France, Germany and
  Russia 111, 180

J

Japan Sea Battle 111
Japanese water wheel (see also water
  wheel) 109
joint-stock company (see also company)
  27, 113, 127, 132, 140

K

kaki-age-chosa 83
kamikaze attacks 247
kinship (see non-kinship household
  member) 83, 143, 189
Konzern 201
Korean war 248
koukenki, the ARI plane 207
Kwantung Leased Territory 29
Kyoho period (1716–36) 76

L

labour force 222
  skilled labour force 166

unskilled labour force 166
labour market 166, 176, 222
labour mobilization 49, 209, 226
  compulsory labour mobilization
    187
  of aged people 229
  of students and pupils 226, 228
land owners 245
land reform 245
late Tokugawa period (see Tokugawa
  period) 122, 135
law system
  feudal law system 258
  French law 113
  German law 113
leakage 160, 226, 274
  in coverage 144
legitimacy of the state 202
level of education 167
linkage
  micro-statistical linkage 59
list of an enumeration unit 5
literacy rate 3, 177
log-normal distribution 133
  truncated log-normal
    distribution 133
logistic operation 247
logistics
  shortage of logistics 231
London Treaty (1930) 195
longitudinal data 145f
longitudinal data base 95, 269
longitudinal data sets 14, 267, 295f
LTES project, i.e. Long-term Economic Statistics 253

M

maid (see domestic servants)
79, 83, 187, 189, 225, 264
managers   178
  higher educational system for
    managers   147, 148
  modern managers   143
manpower policy   229
manual labour   101
manufacturing   225
  traditional manufacturing   192
manufacturing census   13, 33
marital ratio   84
Marxian economic thoughts   205
Marxist economic theories   70
Matsukata deΩation   114
Meiji government   20, 66f, 69f, 71,
      76, 77, 92, 101, 110, 179, 180
Meiji Restoration
    17f, 20, 63, 66, 68, 70f, 73, 76,
      90, 100f, 127, 181, 243, 294
merchants
  political merchants   148
Metropolitan Prefectures   37
micro data matching techniques   274
micro datasets 252, 257, 267, 294–96
micro-statistical linkage (see linkage)
                                      58
Midway Islands Naval Operation 231
migration   259
    interregional migration   193
mining   225
missing data   280
mobilization of national resources 44
modern industry   112
modern managers   143
modernized factory production   192

N

nation state   3, 69
national banking system   113
nationalism   202
nationality   184
naval battle (see Japan Sea Battle,
    Midway Island Naval Operation,
    Yalu River Battle)
naval construction   240
naval Ωeet   206
Nazism   260
New Long-term and Medium-term
    Plan for Statistical Administra-
    tion   54
non-kinship household member   189
non-marriage ratio   189
non-ordinary household member   189
nuclear family (see family)   83
number of employees   97

O

observation unit   4f
Occupation Army   205
occupational classification (see clas-
    sification)   23, 291
occupational statistics   79
occupational structure   209
on-the-job-training
              125, 167, 177, 230
operational concept   7, 187, 260
Opium Wars   69, 103, 179
outcaste status   79
owner-operator businessmen   291

P

Pacific War 44, 205
panel data see longitudinal data
Pearl harbour naval base 204, 241
Pelton water wheel (see water wheel) 109
people
  cooperativeness of the people 3, 10
  literacy rates of people 3
  political control of the people 3
People's Registration System 24
Plan for the Statistical Survey System in the Medium and Longest Terms 54
planned economy 205
plutocracy (see zaibatsu, Konzern) 142, 245
political control of the people 3
political merchants (see merchants) 148
population census 3, 13, 22, 28, 66, 252, 260, 267, 292
  regional population census 30
population pyramid 84, 259
populism 202
power game among countries 194
power machine 109
press code of occupation army (see censorship by GHQ) 181, 243
price
  black market price 50
  free market price 50
prisons by Soviet Russia 231
production
  factory production 103
  formal production 263f
  informal production 263f

protected cruiser
  Akashi 112
  Suma 112
Provisional Rural Correspondence System 24

Q

questionnaire 9, 14, 25, 27, 33, 252
questionnaire format 25

R

race 181
rail-road network 207
railway construction 241
railway transportation facilities 208
rationing system (see clothes stamps, food stamps) 47, 50, 205, 245
reconstruction survey see survey
reforms
  social reforms 245
register data 269
registration system 18
respondent
  willingness by respondents 58
Revolution 203
  (see also Meiji Restoration)
  Hsinhai Koming (Xinhai Geming) 202
  Russian Revolution 128
Rice Riot 201
ruling class (see class) 71
rural economy 193
rural society 262
Russian Revolution 128
Russo-Japanese War

28, 30, 67, 96, 111, 128, 131,
141, 180, 193, 230, 270

S

sake brewing   140
semi-controlled economy   204
services
    monetary services   263
    non-monetary services   263
Seto Inland Sea   89
Shogun   68f, 71, 75f
silk weaving yard   107
Sino-Japanese War   29, 30, 44, 67,
        96, 107, 110, 142, 230, 270
size distribution   142, 296
size
    indicator of size of a factory or
    company
                                                    165
    size of enterprise   137
    size of factory by number of em-
    ployees   165
    size of factory by tangible assets
                                                    165
social infrastructures   200
social recurrent   222
social reform   74, 245
sociological concept   260
soroban calculator (see calculator)
source table   48, 50
South Sakhalin   29
South Sea Islands   29
speculation of tulipomania   87
starvation   231
state-company nexus   67, 206, 247
statistical data

accuracy of the statistical data 3
statistical matching technique   281
statistical survey
    modern statistical survey   19
statistical survey system   3, 209
statistical fiction   66
statistics
    register-based statistics   254
    aggregate statistics   276
students and pupils mobilized to fac-
    tories, mines and transportation
    facilities   228
submarine
    I-go   206
suicide attack see *kamikaze* attack
summary data   11
summary tables   22, 38, 285f, 289
survey
    census survey   5
    complete enumeration survey   5
    format survey   5, 33
    reconstruction survey   13f, 95,
        145, 149, 257, 267, 281, 295
    sampling survey   9, 52, 257
    statistical survey   5
survey cycle   60, 295
survey system
    centralized survey system   28
    decentralized survey system
                                        23, 38, 45, 47

T

Tableau politique   20, 87, 90
tabulation constraints (see computa-
    tional power)   48
technology

borrowed technology
166, 206f, 247
imported technology   169
traditional technology   176
transportation technology   208
Western technology   125, 140
technology of warship construction
111
Ten'no   69
time series data   65, 228
Tokugawa government
20, 69f, 80, 179
Tokugawa naval shipyard   103
Tokugawa period   86, 122, 251, 258
late Tokugawa period   122, 135
Tokugawa regime   66ff, 70, 74, 76,
83, 86, 89, 100, 110, 143, 179
total number of man days worked in
a year   97
traditional technology   171
transportation   225
Twenty One Articles Treatment 203
Two Escadrilles (hachi-hachi-kantai)
193
Two-two-six Affair   202

U

under-reporting   228
university student and school pupil
226
unmarried working people   190

V

vertical expansion   137

W

wage differentials   170, 176
wage differentials between males and
females   167
wage differentials by number of employees   166
wage differentials for non-adult employees   168
wage differentials of industrial subdivisions   168
wage rates   167f, 176
war
Civil War   66, 233
Greater East Asia War   205
Korean War   248
Opium Wars   69, 103, 179
Pacific War   44, 205
Russo-Japanese War
28, 30, 67, 96, 111, 128, 131,
141, 180, 193, 230, 270
Sino-Japanese War   29, 30, 44,
67, 96, 107, 110, 142, 230, 270
World War I   29, 30, 32, 67, 128,
141, 181, 193, 202, 270
World War II 38, 50, 64, 70, 94f,
181, 187, 230f, 242, 295
war damage   230, 233, 237
War Guilt Consciousness [Informa-
tion] Program   243, 245
wartime controlled economy   67
wartime economy   205f
Washington Treaty (1922)   195
water wheel   109, 126
Japanese water wheel   109
Pelton water wheel   109
way of organizing industries 112

wealth
  military wealth   237
  non-military wealth   237
Western colonial powers   18
Western technology   125
wholesale traders   213, 292
working population   210, 261
World War I   29, 30, 32, 67, 128,
            141, 181, 193, 202, 270
World War II   38, 50, 64, 70, 94f,
            181, 187, 230f, 242, 295

X

Xinhai Geming (see Revolution)

Y

Yalu River battle   106

Z

zaibatsu   143, 148, 245f
Zero naval fighter (see also aircraft)
                                    207

NAME INDEX

a) Personal Name Index

A

Aihara, Shigeru	92
Akasaka, Keiko	94f
Ando, Yoshio	49f
Aonuma, Yoshimatsu	143, 178
Aoyama, Hideo	64
Arai, Hirotake	209f
Arita, Fumiko	266, 295
Arkwright, Richard	107
Asai, Akira	51
Asakura, Kokichi	115

B

Bertillon, Jacques	192
Bertin, Emile	103, 116
Bianchie, L.	110
Bisco, Ralph L.	274

C

Clark, Colin	261

D

Daelen, R. M.	111
Dunn, E.S.	257, 267

E

Emi, Koichi	94
Enomoto, Tateaki	69
Etoh, Jun	70, 241, 243

F

Fisher, Franklin M.	256, 265
Fujiwara, Ginjiro	45
Fukui, Shizuo	111, 132, 179, 240
Furushima, Toshio	14, 88f, 92, 94, 96, 98, 100ff, 113, 115, 266
Fukuzawa, Yukichi	112

G

Gershuny, J.I.	263
Godai, Tomoatsu	112
Gonda, Yasujiro	32
Goto, Shin'ichi	127, 142
Goto, Shojiro	26
Griliches, Zvi	12, 265

H

Hakim, C.	252
Hara, Akira	206, 229
Hashimoto, Juro	143, 240
Hatai, Yoshitaka	262
Hattori, Shiso	70
Haushofer, Max	20
Hayami, Akira	251

Hayashi, Shuji 209
Hayashi, Takeshi 102, 111
Hijikata, Seibi 63
Hiraga, Yuzuru 195
Hirota, Jun 231
Hori, Tsuneo 112
Hosoya, Chihiro 231, 241
Hull, Cordell 204

I

Ijiri, Yuji 133
Ikari, Yoshio 208, 246
Imuda, Toshimitsu
113, 115f, 145, 257
Ishi, Hiromitsu 94
Ishi, Yoshikuni 185
Ishii, Kanji 185, 203
Ishikawa, Shigeru 204
Itoh, Shigeru 31, 194

J

Jentschura, Hansgeorg 112, 240
Jung, Dieter 112, 240

K

Kan'no, Wataro 113
Katsu, Rintaro (Katsu Kaishu) 20
Keynes, John Meynard 256, 263
Kimoto, Yuya 90
Kimura, Kenji 266, 268
Kin, Tetsu 185
Kiyose, Ichiro 241
Klein, Lawrence R. 12, 265
Kobayashi, Hideo 266

Koch, Robert 242
Kondo, Baron Motoki 131
Koshihara, Hisao 293
Kudo, Hiroyasu 267
Kurabayashi, Yoshimasa 196f, 254
Kure, Bunso 26
Kurimoto, Sukiun 112
Kurosaki, Chiharu 73f
Kuznets, Simon 255

L

Lavoissier, Antoine Laurent 263
Luhrman, W.F. 111

M

Maeda, Masana 25, 35
Maema, Takanori 208, 247
Makino, Shigeru 240
Mamiya, Rinzo 180
Man'nari, Hiroshi 143, 178
Matsuda, Yoshiro
14, 42, 44, 54, 92, 107, 185,
247, 257, 262, 266, 285, 293
Matsukata, Masayoshi 25, 114
Matsumoto, Kitaro 240
Matsumoto, Toshiro 203, 230, 233
Mickel, Peter 112, 240
Minami, Ryoshin
107f, 126, 165f, 167, 262
Mitsuma, Nobukuni
31, 192, 261, 291
Miyazaki, Masayasu 242
Miyazaki, Kazuyoshi 246
Mizoguchi, Toshiyuki
50, 65, 233, 254, 267

Mori Ougai, see Mori, Rintaro 242
Mori, Rintaro 230
Morita, Yuzo 50, 297
Murakami, Katsuhiko 240
Murata, Seifu 91

N

Nakamura, James 77
Nakamura, Kinzo 63
Nakamura, Takafusa
50, 201f, 206, 209f, 242, 291
Nakamura, Tetsutaro 63
Ninomiya, Sontoku 177
Nishikawa, Shunsaku 90f, 167, 176
Nishinarita, Yutaka 230, 242
Nojima, Noriyuki 233, 267
Nomura, Kichisaburo 204
Noro, Eitaro 70
Noro, Kageyoshi 110

O

Odahashi, Teijyu 94f, 192,
Odaka, Konosuke 92, 166f,
Ogawa, Toshiyasu 242
Oguri, Kozukenosuke 112
Ohashi, Hiroshi 97
Ohishi, Kaichiro 203, 242
Ohkawa, Kazushi 11, 64ff, 77, 166,
253, 255, 260, 263
Ohkita, Saburo 242
Ohkubo, Tsuneharu 55, 268
Ohkuma, Shigenobu 21
Ohshima, Takato 110
Ohya, Yusetsu 51
Ohtsuka, Katsuo 140

Okazaki, Hiroshi 232
Ono, Akira 262

P

Peattie, Mark R. 231
Pelz, Stephen 195, 204
Perry, Mattlew Calbraith 203

R

Rawlinson, John 179
Rice, Stuart A. 51
Roosevelt, F. D. 240
Rosovesky, Henry 77

S

Saigo, Takamori 66
Sale, Charles V. 63
Samejima, Tatsuyuki 92
Sanaka Sasou 106
Schumpeter, Joseph 143
Seki, Seiichi 50
Sekiyama, Naotaro 76
Shibusawa, Ei'ichi 113
Shimizu, Yoji 242
Shimose, Masamitsu 111
Shinohara, Miyohei 64, 89, 94f, 166
Shiomi, Saburo 201
Simon, Herbert A. 133
Solow, Robert Merton 12, 265
Stamp, J. 63
Sueo, Tomoyuki 126
Sugi, Koji 20–23, 26, 84ff, 87
Sugiura, Ippei 64
Suoh, Setsuo 54

Suzuki, Umetaro 231

T

Takagi, Kanehiro 231
Takamatsu, Nobukiyo 65
Takamura, Naosuke 126, 242
Takano, Iwasaburo 32
Takeda, Haruhito 143, 201
Teranishi, Juro 115
Terasaki, Yasuhiro 247
Terashima, Rokuro 14, 94, 266, 277
Thünen, Johann Heinrich 259
Thurston, George 131
Tinbergen, Jan 263
Tobata, Sei'ichi 44, 143
Toda, Teizo 188f, 239f, 260
Togashi, Mitsutaka 198, 254
Tojyo, Hideki 241
Tojyo, Yukihiko 228
Tokoyama, Kazuhiko 265
Tokugawa, Yoshinobu 178
Tokugawa, Yoshimune 75
Tomoyasu, Ryoichi 46ff
Tsuchiya, Keizo 51
Tsuchiya, Takao 70, 76f, 78,

U

Ueda, Hiroshi 206
Ueda, Teijiro, see Uyeda, Teijiro 113
Umemura, Mataji 64, 76, 94f, 166,
    176, 209, 212, 254, 258, 260
Uyeda, Teijiro, see Ueda, Teijiro

V

Vissering, Simmon 20

Y

Yamada, Nagamasa 75
Yamada, Moritaro 70
Yamada, Yuzo 11, 64, 65, 253
Yamaguchi, Kazuo 14, 73f, 81f, 87f,
    90, 92, 94, 96f, 98f, 266, 277
Yamaki, Shigeru 277
Yamamoto, Yuzo 65, 181, 203f, 241
Yamanaka, Tokutaro 94f, 192
Yamazaki, Shiro 206
Yanagida, Kunio 140, 178
Yasuba, Yasukichi 166, 178
Yokoi, Shonan 112
Yuasa, Mitsumoto 240
Yuzaki, Minoru 232

b) Place Name Index

A

Aichi   104f, 116, 122, 133, 135, 144,
        171, 178, 289
Akita   104
Aomori   80f, 81f, 104, 207
Arthur Port (see Lüshun)   201

B

Beijing   207
Berlin   180
Bikini Islands   244
Britain see England
Bungo   78

C

California   194
Chengteh   202
Chienan   181
Chikuzen   78
Chiba   81, 104
China   75, 91, 179, 180, 194, 202f,
              206, 208, 230, 246
Chingtao   181
Chishima   181, 184, 242
Choshu   69, 90f, 178

D

Devon Port   131
Dewa   78

E

Echigo   78
Edo (see Tokyo)   71, 74, 113, 278
Ehime   81, 105
England (Britain)   (see United
Kingdom)   69, 106, 111, 179

F

Formosa see Taiwan
France   69, 111, 180
Fukui   81, 104
Fukuoka   81, 105, 122, 133, 207
Fukushima   81, 104
Fuzan (see Pusan)   207f

G

Germany 68, 103, 111, 180, 208, 242
Gifu   104
Gunma   104, 171, 178, 289

H

Hakodate   69
Hara   20, 84f
Higo   78
Hirado   68
Hiroshima   105, 207, 232, 242, 244
Hizen   78
Hokkaido   101, 104, 116, 122, 133,
                144, 181, 184, 242

Holland see Netheerlands

Hyogo
81, 89, 104, 116, 122, 133, 294

I

Ise   78
Ibaragi   104
India   179
Ishikawa   104
Italy   68
Iwaki   78f
Iwate   81, 104
Iyo   78

J

Japan proper   18, 29, 39ff, 184,
                        186f, 194, 207, 230f
Japan Sea   89

K

Kagamigahara   207
Kagawa   105
Kagoshima   81, 105, 207
Kahi   22f, 28f, 84f, 258, 280
Kamaishi   110
Kanagawa   104, 133
Kanto-shu (see Kwantung Leased
    Territory)   201
Karafuto see Sakhalin
Kobe   30, 37, 86, 106, 132, 207, 289
Kochi   81, 105
Kofu   84
Korea   29, 39f, 66, 68, 111,
                        180, 184f, 207f, 246

Kumamoto   30, 81, 86, 105, 280
Kure   106, 131
Kwangtung   184
Kwangtung Leased Territory
                        29, 37, 39f 182, 184
Kwangtung peninsular   180
Kwangtong Province   37
Kyoto   37, 71, 74, 89, 104, 122, 143
Kyushu Island   207

L

London   180, 207
Lushun (Lüshun or Lushen, now
    called Lüta) (see Arther Port)
                                        180, 201

M

Maebashi   228
Manchukuo   44, 184, 186, 202–06,
                                        208, 230
Matsuyama   78
Midway Islands   231
Mie   81, 104, 122
Mino   78
Miyagi   81, 104
Miyazaki   105
Moji   207
Musashi   258

N

Nagano   104, 126, 133, 135
Nagasaki   68, 81, 105, 132, 194,
                                232, 242, 244
Nagato   89

Nagoya 37, 78, 171, 207
Nakamura 79
Nanbu 80
Nara 104
Netherlands 44, 68, 87, 90
New Guinea 231
New York 180, 201
Niigata 104, 122
Nomonhan 208
Numazu 20, 84ff

O

Oceania see Southern Islands
Ohita 81, 105
Okayama 105, 122
Okinawa 105, 231f, 244
Osaka 37, 71, 89, 104, 113, 116, 122, 129, 133, 143f, 195, 200, 207, 242, 289, 294

P

Pearl Harbour 204, 241
Peking see Beijing
Phillipines 75
Polynesia see South Sea Islands
Poplar 106
Pusan 207

R

Russia 69, 180, 230
Ryoto peninsula 29

S

Sado 86
Saga 105
Saitama 104
Sakhalin (see also South Sakhalin) 91, 180f, 184
Sapporo 30, 86
Sasebo 106
Satsuma 69, 178
Seto Inland Sea 89
Shanghai 202
Shiga 104
Shimane 105
Shimonoseki 207
Shinbashi 208
Shizuoka 20, 104
Siberia 128
Singapore 110
South Sakhalin 29, 39f
South Sea Islands see Southern Islands
Southern Islands 29, 39f, 48, 181
Stettin 103
Suhou 89

T

Tachikawa 207
Taiwan 29, 39f, 48, 180, 185
Tango 78
Tenryu River 126
Thailand 75
Tochigi 89, 104
Tokaido 74
Tokushima 86, 105
Tokyo (see Edo) 30, 37, 71, 81, 86f, 89, 104, 113, 116, 122, 129, 133, 143f, 190, 195f, 200, 207f,

242, 259, 278, 289, 294

Tottori	81, 104
Toyama	104
Tsugaru	80

U

Ugo	78
United Kingdom (see England)	44
United States of America	44, 69,
	126f, 194, 202, 206, 241
Uwajima	78

V

Vietnam	204

W

Wakayama	104

Y

Yamagata	104
Yamaguchi	81, 90, 105
Yamanashi	22, 81, 104, 280
Yamato	258
Yokohama	37
Yokosuka	132f

c) Governmental Institution Name

A

Administrative Management Agency
53
Agency for Economic Stabilization
234–6, 240,
Agency for Economic Planning see
Economic Planning Agency
Aeronautical Institute at Tokyo Im-
perial University   211

B

Bureau of the Statistical Standard
53, 56
Bureau of Statistics (see Statistics
Bureau)   21, 33f, 37, 40, 47, 56,
67, 214, 227, 236, 241, 278, 282

C

Central Committee on Statistics 37
Central Statistical Bureau   30
Controlling Agency   46, 49

E

Economic Planning Agency 68, 234

G

General Headquarters of the Occupation Army (GHQ)

52f, 74, 245, 247f

H

Hokkaido Colonization Agency 105
Hitotsubashi University 46, 68, 255

I

Imperial   Japanese   Government
Steel-Works   114
International   Statistical   Institute
(ISI)   196

L

League of Nations   31, 186

M

Ministries of Military Affairs   97
Ministry for Military Mobilization of
Goods   47
Ministry of Agriculture   34f, 247
Ministry of Agriculture and Com-
merce see Ministry of Agriculture
and Trade
Ministry of Agriculture and Forestry
36f, 53
Ministry of Agriculture and Trade
13, 26f, 29f, 35, 97, 120,
129, 132, 144, 196, 278, 280f
Ministry of Commerce and Industry

34, 36, 39f, 42, 214, 218, 246
Ministry of Finance
    21ff, 24, 26, 53, 60, 278
Ministry of Foreign Affairs
                    190, 243f
Ministry of International Trade and
    Industry   53, 61
Ministry of the Interior
    21, 23, 26, 30, 33, 34, 91, 279
Ministry of the Navy   240
Ministry of Trade and Industry see
    Ministry of Commerce and Indus-
    try
Ministry of War Material Production
                            47
Ministry of Welfare 47, 50, 214, 227
Mughal Empire   179

                O

Office of Tableau politique   22f

                S

Statistical Committee   53
Statistics Bureau   25, 50f, 56
Statistics Council   53, 56
Supreme Commander for the Al-
    lied Powers (SCAP) see Gen-
    eral Headquarters of Occupation
    Armies

                T

Taiwan Colonial Government   31
Tokyo Imperial University
                    34, 114, 241

                U

United States of America   46, 53
    Department of Commerce, Office
    of Federal Statistical Policy and
    Standards   287

                V

Vichy Government (France)   208

d) Establishment and Enterprise Name

A

Aichi Aircraft Company 241
Amagasaki Steel Factory 242
Asahi Newspaper Company 207

D

Devon Port Dock Yard, England 131
Diesel Engine Automobile Factory
46ff

F

Fujita (family) 146
Furukawa (family) 141

H

Hitachi Military Goods Factory,
Omori 46ff

I

Ikegai Steel Factory, Kanagawa, 46ff
Imperial Japanese Government
Steel-Works (governmental) 110
International Statistical Institute
(ISI) 192

J

Japan Bank see Nippon Ginko

K

Kanraku-sha 139
Katakura-kumi
(Katakura Company) 126
Kawanishi Aircraft Company 241
Kawasaki Shipbuilding Company,
Kobe 132, 194
Kawase-kaisha (Banking company)
113
Kure Naval Dock Yard 110, 131

M

Mitsubishi (Iwasaki family)
141f, 148
Mitsubishi Konzern 201
Mitsubishi Motors Company
207, 241
Mitsubishi Shipbuilding Company
194
Mitsubishi Shoji [trading company]
246
Mitsui (family) 141f, 146, 148
Mitsui Bussan [trading company]
246
Mitsui Konzern 201
Mitsui-gumi 113
Mori Konzern 201

N

Nagasaki Mitsubishi Shipyard (see

Mitsubishi Shipbuilding Company) 194
Nagasaki Shipyard (Tokugawa Government) 101, 103
Nakajima Aircraft Company 228, 241
Nippon Ginko 127
Nippon Optical Co., Ohi 46ff
Nippon Steel Pipe Co., Tsurumi 46ff

O

Ono-gumi 113
Osaka Stock Exchange 113

R

Riken Industry, Kumagai 46ff

S

Samuda Brothers, Poplar, England 106
Société des Forges et Chantiers, La Seyne, France 105
South Manchuria Railway Company 208, 258
Shimada-gumi 113
Shimonida-sha 139
Shoho-kaisho, Shizuoka 113
Showa Steel Plant
Sumitomo (family) 140f, 146, 148
Sumitomo Konzern 201

T

Tachikawa Aircraft Company 46ff

Tatsuma-shuzo (sake breweries) 140
Tokyo Steel Processing Co. 46ff
Tokyo Stock Exchange 113
Tomioka Silk Weaving Factory 103
Toyokeizai Shimpo Publishing Co.
Tsusho-kaisha (International Trade Company) 113

U

Usui-sha 139
Uzen-sha 139
Uraga Dockyard 46ff

V

Vickers & Sons, Barrow, England 131
Vulcan Works, Stettin, Germany 103

Y

Yahata Steel Factory (governmental) 132
Yasuda (family)
Yasuda Konzern 201
Yodokawa Steel Factory 242
Yokosuka Naval Dock Yard 105, 112, 131, 132

NAME INDEX

e) Statistical Survey Name

A

Agricultural and Trading Correspondence (Rules) System
24ff, 106, 123, 129, 167, 192
Annual Survey of Labour
48, 210–230

B

Basic Survey on Commercial Activities 52
Basic Survey on Manufacturing Activities 52
Business Conditions Survey 37

C

Census of Labour (see Annual Survey of Labour) 48
Census of Commerce see Commercial Census
Commercial Census (see Extra Census in 1939) 45, 292
Commercial Survey (Major cities and prefectures) 36f
Company [Statistical] Survey 279
Complete Enumeration Survey of Farm Households 35

D

Distribution Census see Extra Census in 1939
Dynamic Survey of Labour
49, 210–230

E

Employment State Survey 52
Establishment Census
51, 60, 293, 295
Extra Census in 1939 (see Goods Census for Distribution)

G

General Statements of Manufacturing in 1885 (Predecessor of Manufacturing Census) 96
Goods Census for Distribution
38, 41, 217

H

Household Expenditure Survey 50
Housing Survey 52

J

Joint-stock Company Survey
26f, 128f, 275f, 279, 284

L

Labour Conditions Survey 32f, 48

M

Manchukuo   Population Census see
Population Census
Manufacturing Census   28, 33, 93,
107, 124, 128, 284, 288, 291
Manufacturing Survey (Major cities
and prefectures)   36f

N

National Survey of Family Income
and Expenditure   52

O

Occupation Survey of the Inhabitants in Kumamoto City (1907)
280

P

People's Registration System of
Japan (see Tableau de population
et famille)   24, 84
People's Registration System of Ko-
rea   185
Poor People's Survey   32
Population Census   13, 24ff, 28–30,
41, 86, 181ff, 291f
regional population census
30, 86
Kahi (regional)   22–23
Manchukuo   184, 186
Numazu and Hara (regional) 83f
Taiwan   29, 185

Provisional   Rural   Correspondence
System   24

R

Rural Survey (1890–91)   35

S

Survey on Activities and Structure of
Medium and Small Scale Enter-
prises   52
Survey on the Assets Potentially Us-
able for War Supply
93, 104–6
Survey on Damage for Assets and
People by the Atomic Bombs in
Hiroshima and Nagasaki   231f
Survey on the Distribution Agents in
Tokyo (1941)   38
Survey on the Products of Ku-
mamoto City (1901)   280
Survey on Time Use and Leisure Ac-
tivities   52
Survey on the War Damage by the
Pacific War   231–8, 242

T

Tableau de poplation et famille   77
Tableau du produit see Tables of Pre-
fectural Products
Tableau politique (1872)   20
Tableau politique of Kahi-no-kuni
(see population census)   22–23
Tableau   politique   of   Suhou   and
Nagato-no-kuni   89–91

Tables of Prefectural Products (later
Prefectural Agricultural Products)   19, 22, 64, 77, 87
Technical Engineers Statistical Survey   49

U

United States Strategic Bombing
Survey   232, 242

GLOSSARY FOR JAPANESE WORD AND PHRASES

A

asagao = a kind of flower called a morning glory in English or ipomoea sp.
87
ashigaru = the lowest class of the *samurai*, sometimes excluded from the
orthodox *samurai*. 79f

B

Bocho-fudo-chushin-an = Tableau politique of Suhou and Nagato where Yamaguchi prefecture is currently located. 89–91
Boshin-sen'eki = a civil war in 1868. 66
Bussan-hyo = Tables for prefectural products. 87, 89, 90, 258
bussan-kata or kokusan-kata = a trading section system in traditional *han*
governments to sell their specialties in the *han* for a national market
which had been mainly controlled by merchants at Edo and Osaka. 112
bussan = products of the certain area
kata = section of the government of the day
kokusan = genuine products of the area

C

Chitsuroku-kosai = bond to compensate the power of the *han-shu*, former
rulers, to impose taxes at the time of abolishing *han* system. 113, 115
Chitsuroku-shobun or karoku shobun = reform to abolish feudalistic rights
of the ruling class. 178
Chohatsu-bukken-shirabe = Survey on the Assets Potentially Usable for War
Supply. Meiji government tried a nation wide survey in order to assess
facilities and animals in the private sector to mobilize for war logistic
supply such as big factories water mills, agricultural products etc.
104–06

bukken = materials etc.

GLOSSARY FOR JAPANESE WORD AND PHRASES

chohatsu = commandeer goods and personnel for logistic purpose
shirabe = survey
chonin = town dwellers other than samuari class.   77

D

daimyo = ruler of *han*.   71, 76
dajyo-kan-satsu = paper currency issued by new government symbolized by
the *dajyokan*.   113

E

etta and hinin = outcaste which were regarded as socially lower groups whose
rights were severely restricted in their residence place and occupation in
the Tokugawa days and liberated in 1871 after the Meiji Restoration and
included in the ordinary people class. See *shi-nou-kou-shou*.   75, 79

F

fu = metropolitan areas such as Tokyo, formerly called Edo, Kyoto and
Osaka.   71, 87, 89, 268
fuken system = new local government system consisting of *fu* and *ken*.
77, 79, 87
Fuken-bussan-hyo = Tables of prefectural products.
11, 19, 22, 64, 77, 87f, 89f
fuken-kangyo-nempo = prefectural statistical yearbooks containing the reports obtained from the Agriculture and Trade Corresponding System.
277
Fuken-nosan-hyo = Tables of agricultural products.   77
fuken-tokei-sho or hyo = prefectural statistical yearbooks whose tabulation
formats had been controlled by the Ministry of Interior since 1884.
81, 99, 277
fuseki = additional register for servants in traditional Korea register system.
It was appended to the record of his or her master's register.   186
fu = additional or supplementary
seki = register

G

gaichi = exterior such as Taiwan, Korea etc., sometimes Hokkaido, Chishima, Sakhalin were contained. This word is used in contrast to *"naichi"* (interior). 181

ginko = bank. 127

Ginko-kaisha-yoroku = directory of banks and companies. 278

Ginko-kyoku-nempo = Yearbook published by the Ministry of Finance to contain figures on banks under the Bank Act. 276

go-shi = farmers whose ancestors were in samurai class and so got privileges like lower samurai class people. 79

gun = subsystem of local government like a county within *ken*, mostly rural areas. 268

gun-tokei-sho = county statistical yearbook. No exhaustive survey on their publications in the past had not been done and so no bibliography exists. 277

Gyotai-chosa = business conditions survey, non-corporate establishment of commerce, manufacturing and other services were also surveyed. Forerunner of the establishment census. 37

H

hachi-hachi-kantai = eight and eight Ωeets, or two escadrilles of battle ships and battle cruisers. Imperial Navy 's plan to strengthen their power but eventually abandoned after the Washington Treaty in 1922. 193

hachi = eight

kantai = Ωeet

hai-han-chiken = a policy to abolish traditional *han* and reorganize them in *ken*, prefecture, system at the time of the Meiji Restoration. 113

han = clans represented by *daimyo* in the Tokugawa regime.
71, 73, 75, 76f, 79f, 90f, 91, 102, 112f, 115, 178f, 258

han-shu = head of the *han, daimyo*. 68, 71, 73, 76, 113, 177

Hansei-ichiran = Tableau politique des *Hans*, which was compiled based on the reports by the last *han-shu* in 1869–70, containing the *kokudaka*, taxes, local government running costs, population and the number of families. The coverage was area governed by the daimyos excluding those areas governed by the Tokugawas and so all Tenryos were excluded. The manuscripts were not printed when the survey was finished and only the excerpts were published later.   76, 78, 83, 86f, 90f, 91

hansei = how the hans were governed.

ichiran = summary in a table form.

hatamoto = warriors who belonged directly to the *Shogun*.   76

heimin = ordinary people class after the Meiji Restoration. The class structure was *kazoku*, the nobles, *shizoku*, former *samurai* class, and *heimin* including the former outcastes.   75, 79, 91

hinin see etta and hinin.

Hou-on-kou = a kind of a religions sect of Sontoku Ninomiya's teaching, farmers' morals and ways of farming, money saving association and a network for propagating farming techniques. Also organized farmers who believed Sontoku Ninomiya's teaching and joined such unions, *kou*.

140, 178

hyoshiki-chosa = a sort of *kaki-age-chosa*, format survey, used in the pre-census periods, and then used for the governments register record statistics.   5, 17, 87

I

Ie-betsu-hyo = a questionnaire which is applied to each family(*ie*) or house-hold. Firstly this was used in the *Kahi-no-kuni-ninbetsu-shirabe*.   22

J

ji-shi (go-shi) = lower warrior class, see *ashigaru*.   79

jinrikisha = a rickshaw.   89

jinshin = to indicate a year in the Chinese almanac system, *kanshi*, cycling 120 years.   19, 79

Jinshin koseki = a new register based on the register system and called as it was compiled at the year *Jinshin*, i.e. 1872.   17, 79

K

kabushiki-kaisha =joint-stock company.

Kabushiki-kaisha-tokei = statistics of joint-stock companies or a statistical report of joint-stock companies for 1894–96 in 1894–97.

27, 124, 275, 277–80

Kahi-no-kuni = ancient name of the region, where the Tokugawa Government controlled directly as one of the *tenryos*, now Yamanashi prefecture.

22f, 84

Kahi-no-kuni-[genzai]-ninbetsu-shirabe = an experimental population census which included the housing and establishment, i.e. the housing conditions of each household and the kinds of establishment such as manufacturing firms, government offices, schools and temples and shrines.

22f, 28–30, 280

kaisha or sha = institution employing company system. 113

Kaisha-hyo = a new statistical survey published by the Ministry of Agriculture and Commerce which covered all kinds of companies. 128

Kaisha-tokei-hyo = a report for the company statistics first issued as 1920 issue but which was referred to the previous year's figures of economic activities at the end of the year. 276, 279

Kaisha-tsuran = directory of companies. 276, 278f

Kaisha-yoran = list of companies since 1897. 278

Kaitaku-shi = Development Agency to explore the Hokkaido and other colonial areas such as Sakhalin and Chishima. 101, 181

kaki-age = clipping up the relevant figures to elaborate the traditional survey system in the Tokugawa regime. 17, 83, 87

kakushin-kanryo = radicals, younger bureaucrats who had tried to absorb the practical procedures of the planned economy executed by the USSR, Marxian economic thoughts. 205

kakushin =radicals.

kanryo = bureaucrats.

kangyo = a policy to let people want to industrialize the economy. 19

kangyo nempo see *fuken-kangyo-nempo.*

karoku-shobun see *chitsuroku-shobun.* 113

kawase-kaisha = a seminal form of a company introduced at the beginning of the Meiji Restoration. 113

kazoku = nobles newly created after the Meiji Restoration. They consisted of the ancient nobles, former *daimyo*s and those who had risen after the Restoration. (see also *heimin*) 79, 91

ken = provinces, prefecture. See *fuken* system. 71, 278

kikakuin = Controlling Agency which drew up a plan for mobilizing materials for expanding production during the World War II. 44

Kinroku-kosai-kofu-jyorei = Act to issue bond for the former rulers. See *chitsuroku-shobun.* 113

Kitamae-sen = the dominant shipping lines starting Osaka across the Japan Sea to Hokkaido, Northern line. 144

kojyo or seizojyo = factory or work yard for artifacts where artisans gathered. Kojyo-tokei-hyo = Report for the manufacturing census.

124, 128, 278–280

Kojyo-tsuran = directory of factories obtained from the factory's report to the *Kojyo-tokei-hyo.* 276

Kokou-tokei = family register statistics. 79f

kokou = family or household. 19

koku = a unit of volume, especially for crops, 1 *koku* = 180 litre. 72, 76

kokudaka = productivity of a certain area expressed by the rice production by volumes or its equivalent for other products. 76

Kokudaka-shirabe = the land productivity assessment by *kokudaka.*

76, 86

kokuritsu-ginko = a banking system introduced to imitate the national bank system in USA. 127

kokuritsu = national or owned by the state except the case of the *kokuritsu-ginko,* national banks.

kokusaku-gaisha = national policy oriented companies in 1930s, e.g. Mori Konzern etc. 201

kokusan-kata see *bussan-kata.*

kokusei-chosa = population census. Original meaning is the survey for the Tableau politique or *seihyo.* Thus the act for the population census was entitled as the act of Tableau politique in order to include all industrial censuses after the population census. 30

kokusei = the strength of the nation.

koseki = Family Register, *ko* means a family or a house and *seki* means a register. See *Jin-shin koseki.* 19f, 22, 24, 29, 181, 184

kou = artisans. See *shi-nou-kou-sho.* 75, 77

Koukenki = the ARI plane. The product of the Aeronautical Institute. 207

Kouku-kenkyujyo = the Aeronautical Institute at Tokyo Imperial University. 207

ku = ward, district, section. subsystem of local government within *ken* before the *shi,* city, system was introduced. 268, 277

Kumamoto-shi-seisanhin-tokei-sho = Survey on the products of Kumamoto city for 1901. 280

Kumamoto-shi-shokugyo-tokei = Occupation Survey of the Inhabitants of Kumamoto City, figures for 1907. 280

kuni = the traditional calling of a nation, in fact, a certain area where a certain governor was appointed by the *ten'no* in the past but nominal assignment in the days of the Tokugawa and the area name was only to indicate a jointed ancient province such as Yamato, Musashi or Kahi. 228

Kyobu-seihyo = Tables as the results of the *Chohatsu-bukken* Survey. 73

kyu-ryoshu-toribun = a kind of bond given to *daimyo* at the time of *hai-han-chiken*. 113

M

machikata = town dwellers except *samurai* class such as *kou* and *shou*. 77

Meiji-18-nen-kogyo-gaikyo = general statements of manufacturing in the year 1885, the predecessor of the *kojyo-tokei-hyo*. 96

Meiji-29,30,31,32,33-nen zenkoku-kojyo-tokei-hyo = National factory statistics for 1896, 1897, 1898, 1899, 1900 based on the new reporting system using an individual questionnaire for each factory. See *kojyo-hyo*. 278

minseki = a citizen's registration system in colonial areas which was analogous to the *koseki* system in Japan proper. 29,181,184

mura = village communities. 71

N

naichi = interior, Japan proper. See *gaichi*. 181

Nenji-kinrou-tokei-chosa = Annual Statistical Survey of Employment. 224

Nihon-nokai = Japanese Agricultural Cooperatives. 27

Nihon-Zenkoku-Shogaisha-Yakuinroku = a who's who of company managers. 278

ninbetsu-shirabe see *shumon-ninbetsu-shirabe*.

Noji-chosa = Rural Survey, to estimate the production condition of farm household. 35

Noka-issei-chosa = Complete Enumeration Survey of Farm Households to provide data for the World Agricultural Census. 35

nokai = Agricultural Cooperative, unit of the National Agricultural Cooperatives. 35

nou = farmers. See *shi-nou-kou-shou.* 75, 77

noumin = farmers. 79, 77

nousan-butsu = main crops as rice and wheat and some industrial crops like soybeans. 22

Noushomu-[sho]-tokei-hyo = report of the Ministry of Agriculture and Commerce, a handy and unique source of industrial statistics of the day. This corresponds to the summary of the *fuken-kangyo-nempo* but the national total figures lack some prefectures' reports at an earlier period of publication. 93, 261, 279f

Noushomu-tsushin-kisoku = Rules for the agricultural and trade corresponding system. 87, 93, 106, 109, 123, 129

noushoumu-tsushin = agricultural and trade corresponding system in order to gather information from grass roots designed by the Ministry of Agriculture and Trade. 107

kisoku = rules, lower than act in a legal system.

R

rin = a unit of Japanese money, 1 *sen* = 10 *rin.* 167

Roudo-gijutsu-tokei = Technical Engineers Survey, formerly called *Roudo-tokei- jicchi-chosa.* 49

Roudo-tokei-jicchi-chosa = Labour Condition's Survey. 32f, 292

S

Saimin-chosa = Poor People's Survey. 32

sake = Japanese alcoholic drink. 41, 97, 103, 134, 140, 170

samurai = the ruling class, *shi.* See *shi-nou-kou-shou.* 71, 75, 78–80, 91, 143

sangyo-kumiai = industrial associations. 140

santo = three main cities in the Tokugawa regime, Kyoto, Osaka, Tokyo.143

Seihyo-ka = Office for the Tableau politique headed by Koji Sugi, predecessor of the Statistics Bureau of the Cabinet. 20, 22, 87

seihyo = Tableau politique.

Seinan-no-eki = a civil war between the Meiji Government and the Satsuma led by the former general Takamori Saigo, one of the creators of the Meiji government and retired the cabinet after his defeat at the controversy on the foreign policy for Korea at the Cabinet meeting of the Meiji government in 1877. (Professor Toshihiko Mouri expressed a new interpretation of the cause of the controversy. Saigo did not insist on sending troops to Korea but delegating a mission headed by him for negotiation with Korea. However, Toshimichi Ohkubo's maneuver resulted in Saigo's resign from the cabinet.) 66

seisho = political merchants, businessmen having special connections with political leaders got advantages at the sales of the government factories and mines. 148

sen = a unit of Japanese money, 1 *yen* = 100 *sen*. 167, 170

sha or kaisha = a company. 113

shi = city, autonomous local district in a *ken*. 277

Shi-tokei-sho = statistical yearbooks of cities. Some of the major cities regularly published their own statistical yearbook. 277

shi = *samurai*, warriors. See *shi-nou-kou-shou*. 79

shi-nou-kou-shou = *samurai* (warriors), *noumin* (farmers), *kou* (artisans), *shounin* (merchants). Class system in the Tokugawa regime. See *etta* and *hinin*. 79, 81

shin-heimin = new ordinary people liberated from outcaste status. 79

shinkansen = rapid super express running on a new tokaido line of wide gaze since 1964. 208

shinko-zaibatsu = new entrepreneurs, a new capitalists group. They took advantage of the government policies to construct new factories in Korea and other colonies. 205

Shinmi-seihyo = Tableau politique de 1872, the first statistical yearbook, for the year *Shinmi* (i.e. 1871). 20

shizoku = warriors. See *shi*. 79, 91

Shogun = head of the clans, and the class structure. *Shogun* in Edo period was the Tokugawas. 68f, 71, 75f, 76

Shogyo-chosa = commercial census survey by the Ministry of Commerce and Industry who wanted to retain his right to survey the wholesale trade against the Extra Census in 1939 by the Statistics Bureau. 40

Shogyo-koushi-jo = the Commercial Inquiry Bureau. 278

Shoho-kaisho = the corporate company in Shizuoka by Ei'ichi Shibusawa. 113

Shokusan-kogyo see *kangyo*. 92

GLOSSARY FOR JAPANESE WORD AND PHRASES

shou = merchants. See *shi-nou-kou-shou.*   75, 77

shumon-ninbetsu = a quite exhaustive registration system based on the sects of the temples or shrines where ancestors' graves lay like church yards in Christian parish.   18–20

Shumon-ninbetsu-cho = data of birth and death related to the *shumon-ninbetsu* system in the Tokugawa period.   251

Shumon-ninbetsu-shirabe = survey for the *shumon-ninbetsu.*   252

soroban = traditional calculator.   65

sotsu (ashigaru) = lower *samurai* class with *shi*, although they are excluded from the *samurai* class when the new registration system was created in 1871.   79, 80, 91

suzumushi = bell-ringing insect or homoeogryllus japonicus.   87

T

Tanmei-hyo = personal ID card, for data processing for *the Kahi-no-kuni ninbetsu-shirabe.*   22

tatami = traditional Japanese straw mat.   169

Teikoku-koshin-jo = Imperial Inquiry Bureau.   278

Ten'no = emperor.   69, 71, 76, 178, 241

tenryo = areas where the governors of the Tokugawa government were delegated to rule an area excluded from the area governed by the *daimyo.*   71, 73, 79, 91

Tofu-meiyu-kokou-hyo = Tables of the population classified by the towns and rural areas.   73

toji = specialists in *sake* brewing who, mostly worked as seasonal workers from rural area in winter.   140

tokei-hyo = a statistical yearbook.   20

Tokei-nenkan = a statistical yearbook which was traced back to a revision of the Tableau politique since 1882.   22, 276

Tokyo-koshin-jo = Tokyo Commercial Inquiry Bureau.   278

tsubo = a unit of area, 1 *tsubo* = 3.3 square metres.   107

Tsusho-kaisha = a name of the company in 1869 which is famous as a pioneer of the corporate company.   113

Y

yen = a unit of Japanese money after the Meiji Restoration, 1 *yen* = 100 *sen*.
See *sen* and *rin*. The relation is as follows:
1 *yen* = 100 *sen*
1 *sen* = 10 *rin*.
114, 115f, 124, 142, 144, 160, 167, 170, 180, 203f, 237, 246

Z

zaibatsu = enormously big companies in limited or unlimited partnerships, such as Mitsui, Mitsubishi and Sumitomo which later formed plutocrats.
143, 148, 245f

zakuri = associations for silk spinning using an improved traditional technique. 138

Zenkoku-kenbetsu-koseki-hyo = Tableau de population et famile classified by the prefectures. 80

Zenkoku-kojyo-tokei-hyo = Statistical Tables for the Factory Survey which was introduced in the new Agricultural and Trade Corresponding System in 1894 adopting the questionnaire survey system. This grew up to the manufacturing census. 28, 107

Zenkoku-koseki-hyo = Tableau de population et famille, which contained tables number of people roughly classified by age and occupation. 77

Zenkoku-seishi-kojyo-chosa-hyo = the National Survey Report on Spinning Factories. 126

KET

AoeT
BoMoM

nLU 1/12 KS

Behind State Company Nexus
Appendix Tables

compiled by Yoshiro Matsuda and Fumiko Arita

Contents:

Table 1. Prefectural Area Codes

Table 2. Company Statistics: 1889, 1896, 1902, 1908 and 1920

Table 3. Factory Statistics: 1902, 1908 and 1920

Table 4. Size of Enterprises by Capital and Employee: 1902, 1908 and 1920

Table 5. Composition of Households Members by the Kinship Relation (1920)

Table 1 Prefectual Area Codes

Code	Prefecture	
01	Hokkaido	[Sapporo**]
02	Aomori	
03	Iwate	
04	Miyagi	
05	Akita	
06	Yamagata	
07	Fukushima	
08	Ibaragi	
09	Tochigi	
10	Gumma	
11	Saitama	
12	Chiba	
13	Tokyo	
14	Kanagawa	
15	Niigata	[Sado island (county)***]
16	Toyama	
17	Ishikawa	
18	Fukui	
19	Yamanashi	[Kahi-no-kuni*]
20	Nagano	
21	Gifu	
22	Shizuoka	[Numazu**. Hara***]
23	Aichi	[Nagoya*]
24	Mie	
25	Shiga	
26	Kyoto	
27	Ohsaka	
28	Hyogo	[Kobe**]
29	Nara	
30	Wakayama	
31	Tottori	
32	Shimane	
33	Okayama	
34	Hiroshima	
35	Yamaguchi	
36	Tokushima	
37	Kagawa	
38	Aichi	
39	Kochi	
40	Fukuoka	
41	Saga	
42	Nagasaki	
43	Kumamoto	
44	Ohita	
45	Miyazaki	
46	Kagoshima	
47	Okinawa	
50	Ex-colonies which are not coded in JIS.	

Notes for Prefectural Area Codes:
Prefectural area code system is as follows. This system is the same as Japan Industrial Standard (JIS) and the Statistical Standard of Area Code since 1968. The name of places in the blankets [ ] with asterisk is referred in the tables in the text. The asterisk * indicates the historical area name like Musashi and Yamato, ** does city and *** town or county.
Those cities which have same name as the prefecture are excluded in the lists in the blankets but their area are in principle smaller than the prefecture. Even Tokyo, capital city, has city area and suburban area

Table 2 Company Statistics: 1889, 1896, 1902, 1908 and 1920

(i) Number of companies (Prefectures ordered by the rank of the number of companies)

1889		1896		1902		1908		1920	
Code of prefecture	Number of companies	Code of prefecture	Number of companies	Code of prefecture	Number of companies	Code of prefecture	Number of companies	Code of prefecture	Number of companies
13:	378	27:	472	13:	952	13:	1,644	13:	2,963
27:	218	13:	310	27:	302	23:	535	27:	1,986
28:	81	28:	278	14:	250	20:	430	23:	1,919
40:	69	23:	254	28:	241	27:	423	28:	1,780
23:	62	15:	223	23:	235	01:	402	01:	1,459
01:	59	26:	199	01:	180	14:	401	50:	1,145
17:	47	33:	175	22:	175	28:	384	20:	927
22:	47	22:	167	15:	169	22:	348	14:	870
26:	47	20:	140	20:	167	15:	264	22:	826
14:	43	38:	116	40:	155	09:	235	26:	786
19:	43	41:	105	26:	149	16:	228	34:	580
33:	40	40:	101	09:	128	08:	171	33:	569
16:	33	34:	95	10:	103	10:	171	16:	513
10:	32	07:	80	16:	98	17:	163	40:	505
43:	31	10:	80	11:	91	07:	161	17:	499
15:	30	16:	77	24:	86	34:	159	21:	458
05:	29	14:	76	34:	79	21:	157	15:	424
25:	27	32:	74	37:	67	40:	155	38:	399
38:	27	18:	66	38:	67	26:	151	07:	383
09:	25	25:	63	33:	66	50:	141	05:	367
24:	25	37:	62	17:	65	11:	129	10:	363
41:	25	17:	60	21:	65	33:	114	04:	327
12:	22	21:	57	08:	62	05:	113	24:	322
42:	22	24:	56	04:	61	06:	111	09:	308
07:	19	30:	56	12:	57	19:	111	39:	278
08:	16	44:	56	06:	56	24:	106	03:	276
11:	16	29:	55	25:	55	37:	99	30:	268
18:	16	01:	50	18:	51	12:	94	11:	263
21:	16	39:	50	07:	48	18:	87	06:	256
20:	14	43:	49	19:	46	04:	84	18:	243
32:	14	42:	44	30:	45	25:	82	37:	235
35:	14	02:	39	35:	44	38:	79	12:	233
04:	12	35:	39	39:	42	02:	76	31:	230
44:	12	12:	36	44:	41	35:	70	25:	226
34:	11	08:	32	42:	35	30:	60	42:	226
30:	10	05:	30	05:	34	32:	58	08:	213
39:	10	06:	30	32:	34	03:	57	19:	199
02:	8	11:	27	41:	34	42:	57	44:	199
36:	8	45:	27	43:	34	41:	54	32:	195
31:	7	04:	26	02:	29	43:	50	35:	194
37:	7	31:	25	36:	27	36:	49	43:	183
45:	7	09:	22	29:	25	39:	47	02:	180
46:	7	46:	22	45:	23	46:	37	41:	175
29:	6	03:	19	46:	21	44:	36	36:	158
06:	5	36:	18	50:	20	29:	30	46:	138
03:	3	19:	12	03:	16	31:	28	29:	113
				31:	11	45:	26	45:	87
				47:	8	47:	17	47:	48

Table 2 Continued

(ii) Capital of companies (Total nominal capital of each prefecture)

Code of prefecture	1889 Effective samples	Total of nominal capital	Code of prefecture	1896 Effective samples	Total of nominal capital	Code of prefecture	1902 Effective samples	Total of nominal capital
13:	319	88,034,562	13:	286	138,878,109	13:	943	293,759,048
28:	78	18,383,725	27:	463	81,202,103	27:	301	73,480,600
27:	201	17,698,344	28:	266	36,553,875	40:	150	60,720,854
01:	52	13,583,976	40:	95	23,281,091	28:	230	56,297,075
26:	43	4,350,000	26:	187	20,708,728	14:	244	35,984,450
40:	54	4,063,312	01:	47	19,167,605	24:	80	30,294,500
14:	30	2,899,000	23:	238	12,791,430	01:	174	27,816,490
23:	56	2,792,500	33:	171	12,680,383	15:	159	22,440,750
24:	22	2,480,000	24:	23	10,784,500	26:	144	21,907,045
25:	25	2,090,000	29:	52	6,317,750	23:	232	16,387,450
15:	27	1,960,500	14:	72	6,088,590	33:	66	9,444,990
42:	21	1,771,783	25:	59	3,507,010	12:	52	6,604,250
22:	42	1,683,800	38:	115	3,343,001	20:	152	4,956,108
10:	31	1,595,110	15:	126	3,220,010	25:	55	4,757,600
33:	39	1,477,448	34:	95	3,013,740	30:	41	4,560,500
12:	22	1,422,094	30:	54	2,347,516	22:	162	4,516,660
05:	23	1,376,487	16:	69	2,269,725	29:	20	4,450,500
07:	19	1,342,273	22:	157	2,260,815	18:	45	3,901,250
09:	24	1,207,000	43:	47	1,971,135	09:	126	3,794,467
19:	40	1,046,985	12:	35	1,890,754	37:	60	3,524,100
17:	47	974,275	39:	49	1,878,208	34:	74	3,504,150
38:	26	959,706	37:	24	1,613,170	04:	57	3,498,525
20:	6	839,600	09:	22	1,606,675	16:	87	3,458,860
34:	11	802,829	17:	56	1,462,580	17:	63	3,447,069
16:	31	711,000	07:	79	1,404,761	38:	61	3,156,456
43:	30	695,516	20:	123	1,156,485	35:	40	2,956,750
32:	14	650,149	35:	38	1,142,245	07:	44	2,740,820
35:	12	631,875	44:	54	1,102,589	10:	101	2,616,627
21:	14	617,100	41:	90	958,695	36:	27	2,375,750
11:	13	598,500	10:	73	943,628	06:	53	2,302,890
41:	23	547,030	18:	63	784,825	42:	33	2,209,100
44:	12	474,500	21:	47	757,950	39:	39	1,986,275
46:	3	446,000	04:	26	671,278	46:	17	1,927,340
08:	15	366,474	32:	65	631,642	50:	19	1,875,000
06:	5	330,875	06:	29	598,432	11:	89	1,818,829
30:	9	317,327	05:	25	488,168	43:	34	1,730,160
18:	16	310,350	02:	35	426,665	19:	44	1,511,460
39:	10	267,000	08:	32	366,695	21:	60	1,509,050
04:	11	246,123	36:	18	339,280	41:	34	1,491,600
37:	7	243,500	42:	19	326,092	05:	33	1,401,769
36:	8	240,500	11:	26	264,102	08:	56	1,217,080
29:	6	230,000	46:	20	258,025	44:	37	902,455
02:	8	156,126	19:	8	184,020	02:	25	821,035
45:	7	97,860	45:	27	180,861	32:	29	747,927
31:	6	80,000	31:	7	138,490	45:	19	405,020
03:	3	37,000	03:	2	32,500	03:	15	371,250
						47:	8	283,200
						31:	11	201,000

Table 2 Continued

	1908			1920	
Code of prefecture	Effective samples	Total of nominal capital	Code of prefecture	Effective samples	Total of nominal capital
13:	1,643	708,903,665	13:	2,963	2,906,639,209
50:	140	251,510,350	50:	1,145	1,729,593,951
27:	423	140,176,100	27:	1,986	1,322,502,208
28:	383	85,820,025	28:	1,780	807,372,296
01:	401	73,354,695	23:	1,918	289,710,548
14:	396	72,304,980	14:	870	265,041,035
26:	150	46,786,040	40:	505	212,457,262
23:	532	46,263,250	26:	786	186,930,942
15:	261	44,570,005	01:	1,459	159,991,090
33:	113	21,346,274	33:	569	80,593,685
40:	154	20,297,630	22:	826	78,250,598
24:	106	18,719,600	34:	580	75,210,065
22:	345	10,466,638	15:	424	69,460,948
35:	69	7,995,850	24:	322	66,578,562
09:	235	7,797,375	38:	399	65,163,840
08:	171	7,618,450	30:	268	64,924,650
20:	425	7,562,067	35:	194	64,366,700
16:	227	7,464,753	42:	226	60,924,246
34:	159	6,924,900	07:	383	57,178,465
07:	161	6,905,480	36:	158	52,657,530
30:	60	6,050,500	16:	513	52,614,472
38:	78	6,034,956	10:	363	52,239,845
17:	157	5,906,340	17:	499	49,534,557
12:	94	5,489,190	04:	327	44,325,734
37:	97	5,410,200	39:	277	43,663,907
10:	170	5,304,588	41:	175	41,418,971
39:	47	4,890,640	46:	138	38,544,510
46:	37	4,846,840	20:	927	37,402,953
05:	113	4,634,665	43:	182	36,600,215
43:	50	4,457,265	21:	458	34,002,613
06:	111	4,311,100	37:	235	29,067,610
11:	129	3,851,609	09:	308	28,238,867
21:	156	3,611,020	44:	199	28,094,750
42:	56	3,596,400	11:	263	28,072,988
04:	84	3,569,871	18:	243	26,895,025
25:	81	3,395,259	12:	233	25,910,158
41:	54	3,274,796	05:	367	24,407,700
19:	109	2,775,100	25:	226	24,243,015
18:	84	2,463,900	03:	276	20,702,654
02:	75	1,988,270	06:	256	19,154,632
36:	48	1,918,600	02:	180	19,093,197
03:	55	1,801,550	32:	195	15,493,766
32:	57	1,662,070	31:	230	13,292,320
47:	17	1,616,200	08:	213	12,649,218
44:	36	1,537,470	29:	113	12,578,750
29:	29	1,292,000	19:	199	9,652,570
45:	26	994,800	45:	87	8,886,771
31:	28	984,000	47:	48	4,298,550

Table 2 Continued

(iii) Capital of companies (Total paid-in capital of each prefecture)

	1889			1896			1902	
Code of prefecture	Effective samples	Total of paid-in capital	Code of prefecture	Effective samples	Total of paid-in capital	Code of prefecture	Effective samples	Total of paid-in capital
13:	143	41,385,590	13:	277	84,859,922	13:	376	175,968,381
27:	126	9,540,369	27:	446	41,210,376	40:	103	50,184,896
28:	20	4,391,131	28:	242	20,118,870	27:	221	48,115,151
01:	21	2,577,839	40:	93	19,707,749	28:	169	44,623,959
15:	19	1,878,000	01:	46	11,704,470	24:	61	27,878,783
26:	22	1,742,264	24:	55	10,547,712	01:	92	20,914,174
40:	22	1,535,350	26:	157	8,592,301	26:	102	15,495,332
23:	15	1,215,263	23:	231	6,604,237	14:	78	14,772,765
25:	13	1,204,900	15:	221	5,198,293	15:	131	12,321,369
14:	12	1,090,000	33:	164	4,624,295	23:	167	10,958,364
22:	10	1,037,253	14:	70	3,814,039	33:	49	6,469,723
33:	6	673,195	29:	52	3,103,565	12:	32	4,462,275
42:	4	651,836	38:	106	2,710,869	29:	15	4,018,994
20:	4	627,100	25:	33	2,018,985	30:	33	3,713,760
24:	5	590,260	37:	60	1,826,794	25:	44	3,425,045
09:	8	529,254	34:	92	1,708,814	37:	50	2,685,220
12:	4	467,500	12:	35	1,693,660	22:	115	2,505,858
05:	5	446,116	30:	53	1,403,327	16:	75	2,496,090
07:	5	426,341	16:	70	1,336,092	38:	54	2,411,576
19:	8	404,448	07:	79	1,128,778	35:	28	2,072,775
11:	4	400,000	09:	22	1,090,600	20:	115	2,045,343
38:	8	365,060	22:	71	980,346	17:	48	2,003,772
34:	5	348,270	43:	43	965,747	46:	13	1,718,840
21:	3	335,656	20:	133	919,465	09:	44	1,701,752
46:	1	327,100	39:	18	841,690	36:	21	1,505,781
44:	4	315,000	35:	36	827,377	34:	50	1,494,730
10:	5	293,000	42:	39	661,257	18:	41	1,445,340
35:	3	269,780	41:	23	560,185	10:	43	1,271,275
32:	5	241,088	44:	53	544,226	06:	40	1,178,534
30:	2	190,827	21:	46	501,180	50:	11	1,119,300
41:	2	150,000	10:	28	493,869	04:	41	1,104,941
37:	1	130,000	05:	29	455,199	41:	21	1,090,010
08:	3	122,000	06:	25	392,032	42:	24	1,026,730
06:	2	108,000	04:	11	389,045	43:	21	821,438
04:	2	100,000	02:	35	377,645	19:	29	794,610
36:	1	80,000	31:	24	327,945	05:	18	745,669
17:	3	79,450	17:	14	315,167	44:	32	740,755
39:	2	55,000	08:	32	295,986	21:	47	731,975
43:	1	55,000	18:	20	255,000	39:	31	727,592
02:	0	—	46:	20	250,425	07:	29	725,554
03:	0	—	11:	26	247,402	11:	36	563,541
16:	0	—	36:	14	244,742	02:	22	518,185
18:	0	—	32:	44	240,894	32:	24	472,127
29:	0	—	45:	27	165,381	08:	32	448,440
31:	0	—	03:	18	152,375	45:	16	214,473
45:	0	—	19:	5	101,500	47:	8	183,950
						03:	12	170,125
						31:	6	39,700

Table 2 Continued

(iii) Capital of companies (Total paid-in capital of each prefecture)

	1908			1920	
Code of prefecture	Effective samples	Total of paid-in capital	Code of prefecture	Effective samples	Total of paid-in capital
13:	421	375,107,658	13:	2,921	1,824,080,598
50:	81	118,228,975	27:	1,801	820,709,259
27:	148	82,494,147	50:	900	815,006,931
01:	130	44,708,450	28:	1,763	486,039,027
14:	90	36,992,695	14:	861	187,369,219
28:	210	36,842,532	23:	1,877	180,049,009
15:	115	26,390,417	40:	505	133,298,047
26:	68	21,268,940	01:	1,445	97,966,580
23:	137	19,441,470	26:	468	84,039,267
40:	96	12,569,551	15:	421	51,448,639
24:	49	9,684,050	24:	322	45,245,847
33:	44	6,931,630	33:	569	43,839,938
08:	29	5,571,080	22:	826	41,076,817
22:	154	4,323,281	35:	190	40,744,665
30:	34	3,943,175	34:	579	38,974,495
35:	44	3,657,540	30:	268	38,970,800
09:	60	3,348,512	10:	363	31,633,884
16:	117	3,270,995	16:	508	30,777,757
37:	64	2,942,975	36:	158	29,405,830
20:	120	2,926,812	07:	375	27,864,913
38:	43	2,861,166	41:	175	27,641,457
10:	57	2,707,958	42:	223	25,792,201
46:	20	2,587,390	17:	499	25,306,801
07:	49	2,409,000	20:	926	24,260,027
17:	73	2,312,812	38:	398	21,690,088
34:	88	2,239,415	39:	270	20,597,613
11:	35	2,158,595	46:	137	19,490,085
25:	37	2,145,580	21:	458	19,483,395
39:	20	1,911,590	43:	182	19,085,724
43:	21	1,842,235	04:	327	18,733,329
21:	50	1,761,152	12:	233	17,986,028
06:	51	1,621,207	05:	367	16,667,331
05:	29	1,514,990	44:	198	16,554,277
41:	21	1,355,775	09:	306	15,699,914
04:	35	1,324,363	18:	243	15,276,175
19:	52	1,272,375	11:	263	15,094,732
44:	27	1,249,285	37:	235	15,089,704
12:	24	1,113,150	25:	222	14,642,827
42:	29	1,089,085	06:	256	12,803,881
03:	18	978,683	03:	272	10,953,984
02:	33	969,730	31:	227	9,840,574
18:	44	920,523	32:	195	9,064,227
32:	34	687,690	02:	180	8,718,504
29:	14	679,560	29:	112	8,576,954
36:	17	666,478	08:	212	8,299,759
47:	16	636,700	19:	198	7,050,810
45:	16	495,355	45:	87	4,345,059
31:	13	394,750	47:	48	2,308,050

Table 3 Factory Statistics: 1902, 1908 and 1920

(i) Number of Factories of Each Prefectures

	1902		1908		1920
Code of Prefectures	Number of Factories	Code of Prefectures	Number of Factories	Code of Prefectures	Number of Factories

a) Total

Code of Prefectures	Number of Factories	Code of Prefectures	Number of Factories	Code of Prefectures	Number of Factories
23:	663	23:	1,498	27:	2,688
20:	566	13:	1,404	13:	2,452
27:	507	27:	1,285	23:	2,063
21:	333	28:	1,259	28:	1,743
13:	314	26:	831	26:	1,075
18:	290	18:	711	20:	810
28:	273	11:	622	22:	801
17:	253	20:	583	18:	721
24:	191	17:	520	40:	607
33:	180	21:	482	01:	567
26:	174	22:	407	10:	545
16:	168	38:	345	34:	542
06:	158	10:	337	15:	479
15:	142	15:	317	14:	459
10:	141	24:	299	11:	450
22:	140	06:	284	24:	405
38:	119	33:	282	46:	402
03:	116	40:	270	38:	401
19:	111	34:	232	33:	384
11:	99	09:	225	17:	381
14:	98	16:	217	21:	366
36:	97	19:	207	06:	321
07:	93	39:	188	30:	314
01:	90	04:	179	12:	249
34:	79	01:	173	04:	236
08:	78	12:	168	09:	230
32:	76	14:	165	07:	212
09:	72	25:	156	39:	206
46:	59	41:	149	16:	197
40:	57	30:	135	25:	182
04:	55	07:	134	19:	181
31:	54	43:	127	37:	180
35:	54	36:	125	42:	173
37:	52	03:	121	35:	166
39:	46	31:	121	29:	165
42:	45	08:	112	43:	165
43:	44	46:	112	36:	162
12:	41	32:	102	41:	160
30:	38	37:	93	32:	141
44:	37	42:	82	05:	131
05:	34	35:	75	08:	130
25:	33	44:	73	03:	99
41:	33	29:	60	44:	98
29:	24	05:	49	31:	97
45:	22	02:	40	02:	59
02:	21	45:	32	47:	40
47:	3	47:	30	45:	39

Table 3 Continued

(i) Number of Factories of Each Prefectures

	1902		1908		1920
Code of Prefectures	Number of Factories	Code of Prefectures	Number of Factories	Code of Prefectures	Number of Factories

b) Factory with power

Code	Number	Code	Number	Code	Number
20:	496	23:	738	13:	2,090
23:	222	13:	724	27:	1,992
21:	221	27:	564	23:	1,478
13:	178	20:	537	28:	1,075
24:	150	28:	456	20:	776
27:	126	21:	276	22:	720
22:	110	22:	255	26:	553
28:	102	10:	211	01:	480
19:	93	26:	184	10:	460
14:	89	15:	168	14:	366
26:	84	24:	164	34:	336
03:	79	19:	156	15:	328
08:	70	06:	140	40:	324
06:	62	18:	133	21:	299
15:	58	01:	119	24:	297
33:	51	11:	113	11:	247
32:	44	14:	107	06:	241
38:	38	34:	103	38:	205
01:	37	38:	102	07:	190
07:	37	33:	99	19:	176
11:	35	07:	93	33:	165
31:	35	40:	93	30:	156
34:	34	30:	88	12:	147
04:	33	09:	84	09:	134
40:	33	17:	74	39:	132
18:	31	04:	73	04:	126
12:	29	03:	72	17:	126
35:	28	16:	71	29:	114
09:	26	31:	66	43:	113
10:	24	12:	65	16:	109
17:	23	08:	55	25:	104
44:	23	36:	54	08:	96
16:	21	43:	43	36:	94
25:	21	46:	39	03:	89
30:	21	25:	36	35:	89
46:	21	35:	35	18:	87
05:	18	44:	34	42:	85
36:	17	41:	32	32:	83
45:	16	42:	32	37:	82
43:	15	32:	29	41:	81
39:	13	39:	28	05:	80
29:	12	29:	27	31:	74
42:	9	37:	25	44:	69
37:	8	05:	24	46:	63
02:	7	02:	18	02:	45
41:	4	45:	13	45:	30
47:	1			47:	21

Table 3 Continued

(i) Number of Factories of Each Prefectures

	1902		1908		1920
Code of Prefectures	Number of Factories	Code of Prefectures	Number of Factories	Code of Prefectures	Number of Factories

c) Factory without power

Code	No.	Code	No.	Code	No.
23:	441	28:	803	27:	696
27:	381	23:	760	28:	668
18:	259	27:	721	18:	634
17:	230	13:	680	23:	585
28:	171	26:	647	26:	522
16:	147	18:	578	13:	362
13:	136	11:	509	46:	339
33:	129	17:	446	40:	283
10:	117	38:	243	17:	255
21:	112	21:	206	33:	219
06:	96	33:	183	34:	206
26:	90	40:	177	11:	203
15:	84	39:	160	38:	196
38:	81	22:	152	30:	158
36:	80	15:	149	15:	151
20:	70	16:	146	04:	110
11:	64	06:	144	24:	108
07:	56	09:	141	12:	102
01:	53	24:	135	37:	98
09:	46	34:	129	09:	96
34:	45	10:	126	14:	93
37:	44	25:	120	16:	88
24:	41	41:	117	42:	88
46:	38	04:	106	01:	87
03:	37	12:	103	10:	85
42:	36	43:	84	22:	81
39:	33	32:	73	06:	80
32:	32	46:	73	41:	79
22:	30	36:	71	25:	78
41:	29	37:	68	35:	77
43:	29	14:	58	39:	74
35:	26	08:	57	36:	68
40:	24	31:	55	21:	67
04:	22	01:	54	32:	58
31:	19	19:	51	43:	52
19:	18	42:	50	05:	51
30:	17	03:	49	29:	51
05:	16	30:	47	08:	34
02:	14	20:	46	20:	34
44:	14	07:	41	44:	29
12:	12	35:	40	31:	23
25:	12	44:	39	07:	22
29:	12	29:	33	47:	19
14:	9	47:	30	02:	14
08:	8	05:	25	03:	10
45:	6	02:	22	45:	9
47:	2	45:	19	19:	5

Table 3 Continued

(ii) Number of Workers at Factories

	1902		1908		1920
Code of Prefectures	Number of Workers	Code of Prefectures	Number of Workers	Code of Prefectures	Number of Workers
a) Total					
27:	58,525	27:	81,129	27:	198,654
13:	37,073	13:	74,063	13:	160,413
20:	36,645	23:	60,332	28:	139,032
23:	31,660	28:	58,124	23:	117,197
28:	29,262	20:	52,679	20:	88,255
40:	15,068	26:	23,479	14:	61,196
33:	13,534	22:	20,082	22:	46,741
24:	13,325	11:	19,952	26:	43,940
26:	12,401	24:	18,149	10:	41,132
21:	12,230	18:	16,355	40:	40,995
09:	11,522	19:	16,050	33:	36,124
15:	10,510	33:	15,582	24:	31,436
05:	10,133	21:	15,125	34:	30,165
22:	9,588	14:	13,159	38:	27,926
17:	8,767	40:	13,047	01:	25,560
18:	7,841	10:	12,745	11:	24,193
19:	7,755	38:	12,226	18:	24,024
01:	7,151	17:	12,166	21:	22,883
11:	7,079	15:	11,360	30:	22,276
42:	7,075	06:	10,976	17:	19,249
03:	6,814	34:	10,470	07:	18,201
14:	6,730	09:	10,456	15:	16,740
06:	6,653	01:	8,689	06:	16,666
16:	6,143	30:	8,086	46:	14,862
34:	5,851	04:	7,623	19:	14,205
38:	5,731	42:	7,240	43:	13,228
10:	5,484	07:	6,739	09:	12,196
07:	5,265	36:	6,493	36:	11,489
32:	5,134	16:	6,233	44:	10,481
35:	4,899	08:	5,209	35:	10,449
46:	4,240	25:	4,889	25:	10,373
04:	4,016	43:	4,793	16:	10,364
36:	3,600	46:	4,764	39:	9,795
08:	3,548	03:	4,509	29:	9,250
45:	3,435	12:	4,452	04:	8,918
30:	3,312	31:	4,261	41:	8,336
43:	3,306	39:	4,243	08:	7,984
29:	3,232	37:	3,684	37:	7,833
37:	3,187	35:	3,606	12:	7,391
12:	3,056	41:	3,430	42:	7,362
25:	2,743	29:	3,323	31:	6,439
31:	2,650	44:	3,028	03:	5,123
44:	2,184	32:	2,699	32:	4,479
39:	2,043	47:	1,889	05:	4,466
41:	1,148	05:	1,742	45:	3,235
02:	802	45:	1,377	47:	1,466
47:	299	02:	760	02:	1,448

Table 3 Continued

(ii) Number of Workers at Factories

1902		1908		1920	
Code of Prefectures	Number of Workers	Code of Prefectures	Number of Workers	Code of Prefectures	Number of Workers

b) Factories with power

Code of Prefectures	Number of Workers	Code of Prefectures	Number of Workers	Code of Prefectures	Number of Workers
27:	43,346	27:	63,039	27:	177,378
20:	33,795	13:	61,446	13:	153,054
13:	31,911	20:	51,001	28:	120,478
23:	18,523	23:	44,490	23:	102,435
28:	17,461	28:	35,608	20:	87,251
40:	13,373	22:	17,235	14:	58,894
24:	11,775	19:	15,261	22:	43,925
09:	10,217	24:	15,122	10:	39,198
33:	10,180	26:	13,145	26:	34,332
26:	10,004	33:	12,212	40:	34,145
21:	9,431	21:	11,821	24:	28,572
05:	8,867	14:	11,746	33:	24,839
22:	8,088	11:	10,586	01:	23,865
19:	7,233	10:	9,976	34:	23,209
15:	6,535	40:	9,268	21:	21,648
14:	6,254	06:	7,899	11:	20,186
42:	6,118	15:	7,860	07:	17,668
03:	5,703	09:	7,817	38:	17,458
11:	5,386	38:	7,583	06:	14,395
01:	4,702	01:	7,195	19:	14,047
32:	4,151	34:	7,176	30:	13,513
34:	3,970	30:	6,963	15:	13,405
06:	3,920	42:	6,356	43:	12,077
04:	3,327	07:	5,921	09:	10,169
45:	3,240	04:	5,497	44:	9,527
08:	3,134	18:	4,908	25:	8,757
38:	3,062	36:	4,610	36:	8,495
35:	2,973	08:	4,026	39:	7,883
07:	2,947	03:	3,588	35:	7,792
10:	2,725	46:	3,245	29:	7,460
29:	2,713	17:	3,179	08:	7,341
17:	2,295	31:	3,101	04:	7,069
43:	2,089	16:	2,987	41:	6,769
18:	2,085	43:	2,956	17:	5,796
46:	2,059	35:	2,789	31:	5,679
25:	2,027	29:	2,708	42:	5,639
31:	1,953	12:	2,485	12:	5,611
30:	1,746	25:	2,399	16:	5,376
44:	1,730	44:	2,165	03:	4,767
12:	1,568	39:	1,699	18:	4,358
16:	1,125	41:	1,498	37:	4,247
37:	961	32:	1,409	05:	3,435
39:	895	37:	1,301	32:	3,402
36:	863	05:	1,217	46:	2,839
41:	564	45:	1,085	45:	2,500
02:	201	02:	387	02:	1,110
47:	25			47:	939

Table 3 Continued

(ii) Number of Workers at Factories

	1902		1908		1920
Code of Prefectures	Number of Workers	Code of Prefectures	Number of Workers	Code of Prefectures	Number of Workers

c) Factories without power

27:	15,179	28:	22,516	27:	21,276
23:	13,137	27:	18,090	18:	19,666
28:	11,801	23:	15,842	28:	18,554
17:	6,472	13:	12,617	23:	14,762
18:	5,756	18:	11,447	17:	13,453
13:	5,162	26:	10,334	46:	12,023
16:	5,018	11:	9,366	33:	11,285
15:	3,975	17:	8,987	38:	10,468
33:	3,354	38:	4,643	26:	9,608
20:	2,850	40:	3,779	30:	8,763
21:	2,799	15:	3,500	13:	7,359
10:	2,759	33:	3,370	34:	6,956
36:	2,737	21:	3,304	40:	6,850
06:	2,733	34:	3,294	16:	4,988
38:	2,669	16:	3,246	11:	4,007
01:	2,449	06:	3,077	37:	3,586
26:	2,397	24:	3,027	15:	3,335
07:	2,318	22:	2,847	36:	2,994
37:	2,226	10:	2,769	24:	2,864
46:	2,181	09:	2,639	22:	2,816
35:	1,926	39:	2,544	35:	2,657
34:	1,881	25:	2,490	14:	2,302
40:	1,695	37:	2,383	06:	2,271
11:	1,693	04:	2,126	09:	2,027
30:	1,566	12:	1,967	10:	1,934
24:	1,550	41:	1,932	39:	1,912
22:	1,500	47:	1,889	04:	1,849
12:	1,488	36:	1,883	29:	1,790
09:	1,305	43:	1,837	12:	1,780
05:	1,266	20:	1,678	42:	1,723
43:	1,217	46:	1,519	01:	1,695
39:	1,148	01:	1,494	25:	1,616
03:	1,111	14:	1,413	41:	1,567
32:	983	32:	1,290	21:	1,235
42:	957	08:	1,183	43:	1,151
25:	716	31:	1,160	32:	1,077
31:	697	30:	1,123	05:	1,031
04:	689	03:	921	20:	1,004
02:	601	42:	884	44:	954
41:	584	44:	863	31:	760
19:	522	07:	818	45:	735
29:	519	35:	817	08:	643
14:	476	19:	789	07:	533
44:	454	29:	615	47:	527
08:	414	05:	525	03:	356
47:	274	02:	373	02:	338
45:	195	45:	292	19:	158

Table 4 Size of Enterprises by Capital and Employee: 1902, 1908 and 1920

(i) 1902

Type of Company	Capital size (ten thousand yen)	1–9	10–29	30–49	50–99	100–499	500–999	1000–1999	2000–2999	3000 over	Total
K	5 less	—	65	29	56	26	—	—	—	—	176
	5–10	—	15	12	18	18	—	—	—	—	63
	10–50	—	22	13	42	52	9	4	—	—	142
	50–100	—	3	3	2	14	12	3	—	—	37
	100–500	—	2	—	3	13	8	6	1	7	40
	500 over	—	1	—	—	3	3	—	1	2	10
	Unknown	—	5	5	10	4	—	—	—	—	24
	Total	—	113	62	131	130	32	13	2	9	492
M	5 less	1	15	10	11	5	1	—	—	—	43
	5–10	—	1	1	2	5	1	—	—	—	10
	10–50	—	3	1	3	3	1	—	—	—	11
	50–100	—	1	—	—	—	—	—	—	1	2
	100–500	—	1	—	1	1	1	—	—	1	5
	Unknown	—	—	—	1	—	—	—	—	—	1
	Total	1	21	12	18	14	4	—	—	2	72
S	5 less	—	43	26	29	24	—	—	—	—	122
	5–10	—	5	6	7	7	—	—	—	—	25
	10–50	—	3	4	4	10	—	2	—	—	23
	50–100	—	—	—	—	3	—	—	—	—	3
	100–500	—	—	—	—	—	1	—	—	—	1
	500 over	—	—	—	—	—	—	—	—	1	1
	Total	—	51	36	40	44	1	2	—	1	175

(Notes)

1) Enterprise having factories in factory directory where factories having more than ten employee are included.

2) The definition of manufacturing and non–manufacturing companies depends on the classification adopted in the company directory used.

Table 4 Continued

(ii) 1908

Type of Company	Capital size (ten thousand yen)	Employee size								
		10–29	30–49	50–99	100–499	500–999	1000–1999	2000–2999	3000 over	Total
K	5 less	79	31	35	34	—	—	—	—	179
	5–10	39	11	20	12	1	1	—	—	84
	10–50	53	24	51	54	2	—	—	—	184
	50–100	7	8	10	23	1	3	3	—	55
	100–500	10	9	12	40	12	10	1	6	100
	500 over	—	1	2	7	6	2	2	6	26
	Unknown	2	1	—	1	—	—	—	—	4
	Total	190	85	130	171	22	16	6	12	632
M	5 less	58	34	20	22	5	—	—	—	139
	5–10	7	5	4	8	—	—	—	—	24
	10–50	7	2	6	7	1	—	—	—	23
	50–100	—	1	—	4	—	—	—	—	5
	100–500	—	—	1	2	—	—	—	—	3
	500 over	—	—	—	1	—	—	—	—	1
	Total	72	42	31	44	6	—	—	—	195
S	5 less	137	42	60	43	5	1	—	—	288
	5–10	12	1	8	10	1	—	—	—	32
	10–50	4	10	7	25	1	2	—	—	49
	50–100	—	1	1	2	2	—	—	—	6
	500 over	—	—	—	—	1	—	—	1	2
	Unknown	2	1	—	—	—	—	—	—	3
	Total	155	55	76	80	10	3	—	1	380
C	5 less	1	—	—	—	—	—	—	—	1
	Total	1	—	—	—	—	—	—	—	1
		1	—	—	—	—	—	—	—	1
	Total	1	—	—	—	—	—	—	—	1

(Note) From the Factory Directory those factories matched with enterprises are controlled in order to adjust to the coverage of other years (factory having more than ten employee)

Table 4 Continued

iii) 1908*

Type of Company	Capital size (ten thousand yen)	Employee size										Total
		1–9	10–29	30–49	50–99	100–499	500–999	1000–1999	2000–2999	3000 over	Unknown	
K	5 less	49	79	31	35	34	—	—	—	—	1	229
	5–10	17	39	11	20	12	1	1	—	—	—	101
	10–50	16	53	23	51	55	2	—	—	—	—	200
	50–100	1	8	8	10	23	1	3	3	—	—	57
	100–500	4	8	10	13	40	12	10	1	6	—	104
	500 over	—	—	1	2	7	6	2	2	6	—	26
	Unknown	2	2	1	—	1	—	—	—	—	—	6
	Total	89	189	85	131	172	22	16	6	12	1	723
M	5 less	30	58	34	20	22	5	—	—	—	—	169
	5–10	4	7	5	4	8	—	—	—	—	—	28
	10–50	1	7	2	6	7	1	—	—	—	—	24
	50–100	—	—	1	—	4	—	—	—	—	—	5
	100–500	1	—	—	1	2	—	—	—	—	—	4
	500 over	—	—	—	—	1	—	—	—	—	—	1
	Total	36	72	42	31	44	6	—	—	—	—	231
S	5 less	65	138	42	60	43	5	1	—	—	—	354
	5–10	3	12	1	8	10	1	—	—	—	—	35
	10–50	2	4	10	7	25	1	2	—	—	—	51
	50–100	—	—	1	1	2	2	—	—	—	—	6
	500 over	—	—	—	—	—	1	—	—	1	—	2
	Unknown	1	2	1	—	—	—	—	—	—	—	4
	Total	71	156	55	76	80	10	3	—	1	—	452
C	5 less	—	1	—	—	—	—	—	—	—	—	1
	Total	—	1	—	—	—	—	—	—	—	—	1
		—	1	—	—	—	—	—	—	—	—	1
	Total	—	1	—	—	—	—	—	—	—	—	1

Note) Enterprise having factories in factory directory where factories having more than five employee are included.

Table 4 Continued

(iv) 1920

		Employee size										
Type of Company	Capital size (ten thousand yen)	1–9	10–29	30–49	50–99	100–499	500–999	1000–1999	2000–2999	3000 over	Unknown	Total
K	5 less	—	194	51	40	28	—	—	—	—	—	313
	5–10	2	179	55	44	32	—	—	—	—	—-	312
	10–50	—	348	235	207	191	8	1	—	—	4	994
	50–100	—	93	74	115	142	11	2	—	—	2	439
	100–500	1	61	48	92	226	46	36	8	8	3	529
	500 over	—	15	7	13	33	24	10	11	28	1	142
	Unknown	—	—	—	—	1	—	—	—	—	—	1
	Total	3	890	470	511	653	89	49	19	36	10	2,730
M	5 less	—	230	72	61	47	1	—	—	—	2	413
	5–10	—	20	13	15	12	—	2	—	—	—	62
	10–50	—	8	14	16	23	2	1	—	—	—	64
	50–100	—	2	2	2	2	2	2	—	—	—	12
	100–500	—	1	2	1	1	—	—	—	—	—	5
	Total	—	261	103	95	85	5	5	—	—	2	556
S	5 less	1	394	118	81	59	3	1	—	—	2	659
	5–10	—	40	19	21	13	2	—	—	—	—	95
	10–50	—	21	15	23	22	3	2	—	1	1	88
	50–100	—	1	1	—	3	1	—	—	—	—	6
	500 over	—	—	—	—	—	2	1	—	—	—	3
	Total	1	456	153	125	97	11	4	—	1	3	851
C	10-50	—	1	—	—	—	—	—	—	—	—	1
	Total	—	1	—	—	—	—	—	—	—	—	1

(Note) Enterprise having factories in factory directory where factories having more than ten employee are included.

Table 5 Composition of Household Members by the Kinship Relation (1920)

(Unit; 1,000 persons)

Age Class	Male Number (Thousand)				Male Permillage		
	A Ordinary household members	B Kin members	(Male with a spouse)	C Non-Kin members (servants maids etc.)	A Ordinary household members	B Kin members	C Non-Kin members (servants maids etc.)
a) Whole Japan proper							
Total	27,952	24,625	11,175	3,327	1000.0	881.0	119.0
0–4	3,800	3,691	0	109	1000.0	971.3	28.7
5–9	3,415	3,329	0	86	1000.0	974.8	25.2
10–14	3,181	2,903	0	278	1000.0	912.6	87.4
15–19	2,672	1,767	68	905	1000.0	661.3	338.7
20–24	2,216	1,411	632	805	1000.0	636.7	363.3
25–29	1,991	1,562	1,410	429	1000.0	784.5	215.5
30–34	1,899	1,717	1,677	182	1000.0	904.2	95.8
35–39	1,687	1,545	1,538	142	1000.0	915.8	84.2
40–44	1,624	1,527	1,496	97	1000.0	940.3	59.7
45–49	1,290	1,211	1,130	79	1000.0	938.8	61.2
50–54	1,134	1,076	979	58	1000.0	948.9	51.1
55–59	914	864	773	50	1000.0	945.3	54.7
60–64	839	796	659	43	1000.0	948.7	51.3
65–69	627	587	450	40	1000.0	936.2	63.8
70–74	375	358	363*	17	1000.0	954.7	45.3
75–79	203	197	n.a.	6	1000.0	970.4	29.6
80 years over	85	84	n.a.	1	1000.0	988.2	11.8
b) Tokyo area							
Total	1,245	811		434	1000.0	651.4	348.6
0–4	88	84		4	1000.0	954.5	45.5
5–9	104	100		4	1000.0	961.5	38.5
10–14	113	73		40	1000.0	646.0	354.0
15–19	187	53		134	1000.0	283.4	716.6
20–24	198	61		137	1000.0	308.1	691.9
25–29	124	65		59	1000.0	524.2	475.8
30–34	88	70		18	1000.0	795.5	204.5
35–39	99	87		12	1000.0	878.8	121.0
40–44	74	67		7	1000.0	905.4	94.6
45–49	59	54		5	1000.0	915.3	84.7
50–54	41	37		4	1000.0	902.4	97.6
55–59	23	15		8	1000.0	652.2	347.8
60–64	17	16		1	1000.0	941.2	58.8
65–69	21	20		1	1000.0	952.4	47.6
70 years over	9	9		0	1000.0	000.0	
c) Six metropolitan areas							
Total	3,008	2,111		897	1000.0	701.8	298.2
0–4	245	236		9	1000.0	963.2	36.8
5–9	264	257		7	1000.0	973.5	26.5
10–14	272	200		72	1000.0	735.3	264.7
15–19	402	135		267	1000.0	335.8	664.2
20–24	421	137		284	1000.0	325.4	674.6
25–29	321	188		133	1000.0	585.7	414.3
30–34	227	192		35	1000.0	845.8	154.2
35–39	224	196		28	1000.0	875.0	125.0
40–44	176	158		18	1000.0	897.7	102.3
45–49	146	136		10	1000.0	931.5	68.5
50–54	104	93		11	1000.0	794.2	205.8
55–59	76	67		9	1000.0	881.6	118.4
60–64	53	46		7	1000.0	867.9	132.1
65–69	48	45		3	1000.0	937.5	62.5
70 years over	29	25		4	1000.0	862.1	137.9

(Note) Male with a spouse or female with a spouse in parenthesis ( ): Number of persons with a spouse de facto.

*: Age over 70 years included here.

(Source) Teizo Toda's re-tabulation based on the permillage extracted micro data from population census data in 1920.

Table 5 Continued

Age Class	A Ordinary household members	B Kin members	(Female with a spouse)	C Non-Kin members (servants maids etc.)	A Ordinary household members	B Kin members	C Non-Kin members (servants maids etc.)
	Number (Thousand)				Permillage		

Female

Age Class	A	B		C	A	B	C
a) Whole Japan proper							
Total	27,896	25,477	11,325	2,419	1000.0	913.3	86.7
0–4	3,650	3,574	0	76	1000.0	979.2	20.8
5–9	3,421	3,331	0	90	1000.0	973.7	26.3
10–14	2,980	2,610	3	370	1000.0	875.8	124.2
15–19	2,652	1,855	447	795	1000.0	699.5	300.5
20–24	2,289	1,893	1,533	396	1000.0	827.0	172.0
25–29	1,920	1,736	1,621	144	1000.0	904.2	95.8
30–34	1,822	1,724	1,625	98	1000.0	946.2	53.8
35–39	1,723	1,660	1,535	63	1000.0	963.4	36.6
40–44	1,528	1,484	1,300	44	1000.0	971.2	28.8
45–49	1,301	1,247	1,024	54	1000.0	958.5	41.5
50–54	1,123	1,068	790	55	1000.0	951.0	49.0
55–59	962	921	608	41	1000.0	957.4	42.6
60–64	863	817	418	46	1000.0	946.7	53.3
65–69	737	694	262	43	1000.0	941.7	58.3
70–74	519	483	159*	36	1000.0	930.6	69.4
75–79	263	245	n.a.	18	1000.0	931.6	68.4
80 years over	143	133	n.a.	10	1000.0	944.1	55.9
b) Tokyo area							
Total	1,034	838		196	1000.0	810.4	189.6
0–4	99	99		0	1000.0	1000.0	
5–9	98	97		1	1000.0	989.8	10.2
10–14	94	80		14	1000.0	851.1	148.9
15–19	134	63		71	1000.0	470.1	529.9
20–24	121	68		53	1000.0	562.0	438.0
25–29	99	84		15	1000.0	848.5	151.5
30–34	89	80		9	1000.0	898.9	101.1
35–39	79	70		9	1000.0	886.1	113.9
40–44	54	52		2	1000.0	963.0	37.0
45–49	45	42		3	1000.0	933.3	66.7
50–54	38	32		6	1000.0	842.1	157.9
55–59	25	21		4	1000.0	840.0	160.0
60–64	19	16		3	1000.0	842.1	157.9
65–69	19	14		5	1000.0	736.8	263.2
70 years over	21	20		1	1000.0	955.0	45.0
c) Six metropolitan areas							
Total	2,519	2,103		416	1000.0	834.9	165.1
0–4	221	217		4	1000.0	956.0	54.0
5–9	234	226		8	1000.0	965.8	34.2
10–14	227	198		29	1000.0	872.2	127.8
15–19	299	156		143	1000.0	521.7	478.3
20–24	299	194		105	1000.0	648.8	351.2
25–29	233	196		37	1000.0	841.2	158.8
30–34	209	193		16	1000.0	923.4	76.6
35–39	167	153		14	1000.0	916.2	83.8
40–44	154	145		9	1000.0	941.6	58.4
45–49	126	117		9	1000.0	928.6	71.4
50–54	112	99		13	1000.0	883.9	116.1
55–59	80	71		9	1000.0	887.5	112.5
60–64	43	38		5	1000.0	883.7	116.3
65–69	49	42		7	1000.0	857.1	142.9
70 years over	66	58		8	1000.0	878.8	121.2

(Note) Male with a spouse or female with a spouse in parenthesis ( ): Number of persons with a spouse de facto.

*: Age over 70 years included here.

(Source) Teizo Toda's re-tabulation based on the permillage extracted micro data from population census data in 1920.